THE POLITICS
OF PROTECTION

THE POLITICS
OF PROTECTION

The Limits of Humanitarian Action

ELIZABETH G. FERRIS

BROOKINGS INSTITUTION PRESS
Washington, D.C.

Copyright © 2011
THE BROOKINGS INSTITUTION
1775 Massachusetts Avenue, N.W., Washington, DC 20036
www.brookings.edu

Library of Congress Cataloging-in-Publication data

Ferris, Elizabeth G.
The politics of protection : the limits of humanitarian action / Elizabeth G. Ferris.
   p.   cm.
   Includes bibliographical references and index.
   Summary: "Examines the evolution of the international community's understanding and
commitment to the concept of 'humanitarian protection,' focusing on the inconsistencies
inherent in responses from Rwanda to Katrina in order to demonstrate the challenges and
limitations of protecting future vulnerable populations from war and natural disasters"—
Provided by publisher.
   ISBN 978-0-8157-2137-6 (pbk. : alk. paper)
   1. Humanitarian intervention. 2. Humanitarian assistance. I. Title.
   JZ6369.F44 2011
   341.5'84—dc22   2010053914

9 8 7 6 5 4 3 2 1

Printed on acid-free paper

Typeset in Minion

Composition by Cynthia Stock
Silver Spring, Maryland

Printed by R. R. Donnelley
Harrisonburg, Virginia

To my wonderful siblings,

Mary, Bill, and Anne

Contents

Acknowledgments

As this book makes clear, many people in the humanitarian community have been writing and thinking about protection for a long time. I've been influenced by many of them, too many to name individually. I am especially indebted to my former colleagues in the crazy and chaotic world of nongovernmental organizations for their insights and to the many UN and Red Cross/Red Crescent staff with whom I've discussed various aspects of protection in various countries around the world over the past decade. Walter Kälin, the UN representative of the secretary-general on the human rights of internally displaced persons and co-director with me of the Brookings-Bern Project on Internal Displacement, has helped me to understand the relationship between legal standards and norms and the lives of civilians caught up in conflicts not of their making. I am grateful to Patrick Egloff for facilitating many interviews with key actors at the United Nations in New York and to colleagues in various international agencies for having offered substantive comments on different chapters as well as to the external reviewers of the manuscript. I also want to thank Eileen Hughes and other staff at the Brookings Institution Press for their work in finalizing the manuscript for publication.

I feel very fortunate to be at the Brookings Institution, where I have had the opportunity to think and to write—an opportunity not available to most humanitarian workers engaged in relief operations. My research efforts on this topic would not be possible without the generous support of the U.S. Agency for International Development, the Royal Danish Ministry of Foreign Affairs, the Government of Luxembourg, the Norwegian Royal Ministry of Foreign Affairs, the Swedish Ministry of Foreign Affairs, the Swiss Federal Department of Foreign Affairs, and the U.K. Department for International Development.

I have appreciated the support of my colleagues and am especially grateful to Chareen Stark for her unflagging research assistance. Her attention to detail and willingness to track down sometimes obscure sources has been invaluable. Other research assistants and interns at Brookings provided help with particular issues, including Erin Williams, Daniel Petz, Ria Bailey-Galvis, and Kim Stoltz. And as always, I thank my wonderful husband, Barry Childers, and our children, Jon and Sara, for their loving encouragement and support.

Introduction

From the beginning of my humanitarian work in 1985, I have been fascinated by the issues involved in protecting people. Others could deal with the nitty-gritty logistics of moving in relief supplies and deploying medical personnel to the world's latest hotspot, but for me, the essence of the humanitarian enterprise was protection. Protection encompassed the real life-and-death issues: taking action to stop refugees from being pushed back across borders, civilians from being massacred by vigilantes or insurgents, and women from being raped by marauding gangs and providing support to desperate people who use desperate measures to try to find safety in distant lands. Protecting vulnerable people was central to my work. It had a noble feeling about it. And although legal expertise was helpful, working on protection issues did not require much technical experience. I certainly knew nothing about the geology of drilling boreholes, but I could see that there was a relationship between the location of water sites and the safety of women. And as a political scientist, I found it easy and interesting to pick up enough international law to participate in the discussions.

In the mid-1980s, protection was largely the territory of lawyers, particularly specialists in international refugee law, international humanitarian law, and human rights law. But in the 1990s, the failure of the international community—and the humanitarians—to prevent widespread bloodshed in Somalia, Bosnia, and Rwanda forced protection advocates to rethink that approach. Urging compliance with international standards, deploying international peacekeepers, and establishing safe havens simply were not enough to protect people on the ground. In the absence of concerted political action to protect civilians, humanitarian agencies began to incorporate protection into their work, emphasizing protection in the field and incorporating protection into their programs. The burgeoning number of humanitarian actors and increased funds for humanitarian work meant that more people than ever before were not only talking about protection but also incorporating protection into their humanitarian programs.

Protection is now very much in vogue in the humanitarian world. Everyone's talking about it, everyone's "doing" it: developing policies on protection, assessing protection needs, incorporating protection into mainstream practice, developing protection indicators. Policies, manuals, guidelines, and training courses on protection abound. Scholars and practitioners alike discuss their understanding of the concept of protection at conferences organized for that purpose. Countless articles, books, studies have been devoted to the subject.

I have always been an advocate of protection, and this explosion of interest should make me happy. But instead, I find that the current focus on protection leaves me uneasy. Uncomfortable questions emerge: Can anyone "do" protection? Can humanitarian action stop violence by determined warlords? When military troops vaccinate kids, is that protection? Does monitoring the number of rapes in a community actually protect women from being raped? As the concept has been stretched to include all manner of important activities—from provision of food to curriculum development, from advocacy to monitoring, from building latrines to voter registration—has the concept of protection begun to lose its distinctive meaning? Is every humanitarian action, undertaken by any actor, protection? My unease with the expansion of the term "protection," coupled with my commitment to those whose lives have been shattered by war or natural disaster, led me to read everything I could find about protection—which, I discovered, is a full-time job. Eventually that unease led me to write this book.

This book explores the evolution of the international community's understanding of protection, with a particular emphasis on the humanitarian community. The first two chapters trace the historical development of the concept of protection through the emergence of humanitarian principles, international humanitarian law, refugee law, and international human rights law. The description of the current "architecture of protection" in chapters 3 and 4 focuses on the many actors who are involved in assisting and protecting civilians in a range of situations created by conflict. There are more humanitarian actors than ever before. At its best, the increase represents an outpouring of compassion from groups around the globe. Less positively, it signifies that when there is a vacuum in assisting and protecting people in need, other groups with less altruistic aims may step in. On a practical level, the fact that there now may be hundreds or thousands of actors in an emergency situation complicates coordination. The proliferation of humanitarian actors also raises questions about whether motivation matters when the issue is saving lives. Does it make any difference if it's the United Nations High Commissioner for Refugees or the African Union that is trying to protect people? What if it's Hezbollah or a Shiite militia in Iraq? Or Walmart or Oxfam?

Chapter 5 places the issue of protection and the differences in the understanding of protection into a larger political context. In the field of international relations, humanitarian action traditionally was seen as marginal to the great issues of war and peace. That has changed. Humanitarian issues are now front and center in security debates. At the national level, U.S. defense secretary Robert Gates has said that the fight against terrorism will not be won by troops alone: "We cannot kill or capture our way to victory." That view has been echoed in the military echelons by Admiral Michael Mullen and General Stanley McChrystal."[1] Further, the notion of protecting civilians is pivotal to counterinsurgency (COIN) guidance issued to NATO and U.S. troops in Afghanistan by two U.S. Forces–Afghanistan/International Security Assistance Force commanders: General McChrystal in 2009 and his successor, General David Petraeus, in 2010.[2] At the global level, the United Nations Security Council routinely debates the protection of civilians. The International Criminal Court issues arrest warrants for President Omar Bashir of Sudan for killing his own people. The examples could go on and on, but the issue of protecting vulnerable people, at least some vulnerable people, has moved from being soft politics to being hard politics. Politics, national interests, and, above all, concerns about national security determine which groups receive international attention, assistance, and—sometimes—protection.

What do actions taken at the global level have to do with the protection offered by humanitarian agencies on the ground? What is the relationship between efforts to improve global governance and humanitarian response? For example, in search of a more coherent response to conflict situations, the United Nations increasingly is working through integrated missions in which all UN agencies engaged in a particular country are brought together in support of a common objective and under a single leader. That means that humanitarian activities are supposed to be part and parcel of the UN's overall strategy in a particular conflict situation. But sometimes humanitarian and political objectives are at odds, as when political actors insist that refugees should return to their homes so that they can vote in a referendum while humanitarians argue that it is not yet safe to do so. What are the consequences of integrated missions for humanitarian principles and for the security of humanitarian workers?

"There are no humanitarian solutions to humanitarian problems," Sadako Ogata, former UN High Commissioner for Refugees, wrote in her memoirs.[3] What is the relationship between humanitarian action, protection, and solving the problems that create humanitarian emergencies? Protection of civilians has emerged front and center in discourse at the United Nations. By the end of the 1990s, explicit reference to the protection of civilians emerged in the UN Security Council. By adopting resolution 1296 on April 19, 2000, the Security Council placed the protection of civilians in armed conflicts at the "heart of the UN's future agenda."[4] UN Security Council resolutions increasingly affirm the importance of protection of civilians and UN peacekeeping operations now routinely mandate that their forces protect civilians. At the UN General Assembly's 2005 World Summit, held at UN Headquarters in New York, the world's leaders unanimously adopted the doctrine of the "responsibility to protect" populations from genocide, war crimes, ethnic cleansing, and crimes against humanity.[5]

Chapter 6 explores three central challenges facing humanitarian workers today: creating a "humanitarian space" or an operational environment in which humanitarian agencies can act on the basis of long-standing principles of neutrality and impartiality; the oft-lamented but never really addressed problem of transitioning from emergency relief to long-term development; and the sticky issue of accountability (is humanitarian action undertaken on behalf of donors or beneficiaries?). Chapter 6 also discusses the different interpretations of protection that humanitarian actors bring to their work, with a focus on the relationship between protection and assistance. For example, some make the case that educational programs for adolescents prevent their recruitment into insurgent groups. But can assistance become a substitute for protection, as in Bosnia, where UN convoys delivered food and medicine, keeping people alive, while humanitarian actors were powerless to prevent snipers from raining bullets on civilians in Sarajevo? Has provision of humanitarian assistance become a convenient way for governments to compensate for the lack of political action to prevent violence?

Chapter 7 looks at response to natural disasters in terms of protection. Traditionally those affected by floods, volcanoes, and earthquakes were seen as being in urgent need of relief supplies but not protection. That perception was challenged by the evaluation of the response to the 2004 Indian Ocean tsunami, in which widespread human rights abuses were apparent in both the immediate response and long-term recovery efforts. Within the international community a consensus has emerged that protecting communities affected by natural disasters is an essential task, even as the question of which international agency will be responsible for protection has become a political hot potato in humanitarian reform.

The question of who pays for protection is considered in chapter 8. On the global level, official development assistance (ODA) has increased significantly in recent years, and humanitarian assistance has increased as a percentage of overall ODA. Yet official flows of financial support are dwarfed by the impact of remittances, funds that migrants working abroad send home to their families and communities. Nongovernmental organizations (NGOs) are the main actors in the humanitarian system, responsible for spending about two-thirds of the funds raised for humanitarian response. What is the relationship between the funding of humanitarian responses and protection? And why are the UN's protection programs funded so poorly in comparison with other mainstream assistance programs, such as those for provision of food and water?

Chapter 9 identifies three interrelated challenges that are bound to impact efforts to protect civilians in the future: changes in the nature of and actors in warfare (including robots and drones); urbanization; and climate change. International humanitarian law, established to protect soldiers *hors de combat* and civilians, seems increasingly irrelevant when belligerents are terrorists, drug traffickers, and warlords motivated by greed who may never have heard of international law or even the United Nations. The majority of wars today are "civilian-based civil wars" in which "the outdoor café, the intervillage bus, the weekend marketplace [have] become battlegrounds, targeted because they are the places in which civilians live and work."[6] On a very different level, military technologies that already are available mean that military actions undertaken by developed countries increasingly will be carried out by unmanned drones and robots, raising the possibility that the *only* combat casualties will be insurgents and civilians—and probably more of the latter than the former. Few humanitarians have begun to grapple with the implications of those technologies on humanitarian action and humanitarian law.

Increasing percentages of the world's population now live in urban areas, and we are likely to see greater convergence between street gangs and insurgents, between drug traffickers and armed opposition movements. On a practical level, providing humanitarian assistance in an urban area is very different from managing a refugee camp in an isolated rural area. Although there is a lot of uncertainty about the effects of climate change, it seems certain that changing climatic conditions are increasing the severity and frequency of natural disasters. Urban populations are especially vulnerable to sudden-onset natural disasters, as evidenced by the January 2010 earthquake in Haiti. The potential impact of climate change also raises troubling questions for the international legal order. For example, what happens when small island states are submerged and no longer exist? Will the state still have a seat at the United Nations? Will anyone be obliged to give their citizens a place to live? Where will people go and who will protect them when they are forced to leave their countries because climate change has destroyed their livelihoods? Is it incumbent on the international community to protect people displaced by climate change?

Chapter 10 makes the case that current understandings of protection—and there are many—are out of synch with the international political order and the realities of conflict today. Paradigms and practices set up to protect refugees through the asylum system and in UN-managed camps do not work when most of the world's displaced people remain within the borders of their country and live, often invisibly, among urban populations. Action to protect internally displaced persons—whether through humanitarian assistance or through military action under the emerging norm of responsibility to protect—is at odds with the bedrock principle of national sovereignty. Governments of the global South increasingly view such actions as encroachment on their sovereignty and as a pretext for intervention intended to serve other, not-so-humanitarian interests. The chapter concludes by suggesting that humanitarian actors should acknowledge their limits in protecting civilians. It provides an alternative way of considering different types of protection and raises questions about the ability of the international community writ large to protect civilians in light of the coming challenges.

For twenty years I worked in the humanitarian field and grew to love the people, the institutions, and yes, even the jargon of the humanitarian world. I worked in different ways in many different crises, beginning with the 1984–85 famine in Ethiopia and on through the turbulent 1980s in crises in Central America, Indochina, and Afghanistan. The emergencies of the 1990s, beginning with the displacement of the Kurds in northern Iraq and quickly followed by crises in Somalia, Bosnia, and Rwanda, were especially troubling. I remember thinking at the time, "This isn't just about logistics or money or even politics. These are fundamental ethical questions. After the Holocaust of World War II, how can the world not act when hundreds of thousands of Rwandan Tutsis are slaughtered? How could the massacre of Srebenica happen? In Europe? In the last decade of the twentieth century? Do we all just act as if Somalia doesn't exist?" It wasn't until the 2004 tsunami that I began to see natural disasters through the perspective of protection. Before the tsunami, I had never thought about the particular protection needs of those uprooted by floods. But I came to see that the dividing line between natural disasters (some of which may not be so natural after all) and conflicts was actually quite blurry.

Through many crises on different continents, affecting people in vastly different circumstances, I have continued to believe that there is something universal in compassion, in wanting to reach out to help those who are suffering. I am touched when my eighty-three-year-old mother, having seen TV images of the Haitian earthquake in January 2010, says, "I sent a check to the Red Cross today." There is something laudable when Pakistani businessmen and civil society groups load up their cars and trucks with supplies to deliver to Pakistanis displaced from the Swat Valley by counterinsurgency campaigns. Not only do such noble actions help save lives, they also represent the best in humanity. There are some who have worked many years in humanitarian operations and have become cynical about the humanitarian enterprise. I am not one of them. But as a political scientist, I have recognized from the beginning of my engagement in humanitarian efforts that the international response to the victims of war and disaster depends more on politics than on altruism.

My hope is that this book will sharpen the understanding of what protection means in the context of humanitarian action. I certainly do not have all the answers, but I hope that by asking tough questions and providing some political analysis of the context, the book will contribute to more effective international action to protect people struggling to survive in places like the Philippines and the Democratic Republic of the Congo, Haiti and Gaza, and hundreds of other places that never make it to the front pages of Western newspapers.

THE POLITICS
OF PROTECTION

1

Humanitarian Principles and International Law

Protect: To defend or guard from danger or injury; to support or assist against hostile or inimical action; to preserve from attack, persecution, harassment, etc.; to keep safe, take care of; to extend patronage to: to shield from attack or damage.[1]

The concept of protection is an ancient one, cited liberally in the Hebrew Scriptures and later in the New Testament, the Koran, and other religious writings. The word "protect" comes from the Latin *protegere*, meaning to shield, cover, protect, defend. Over the ages in Western civilization, the term has been used in various ways: God's protection, royal protection, diplomatic protection, self-protection, protection under the law, and, more recently, equal protection, trade protection, consumer protection, social protection, environmental protection, copyright protection, and so on. "Protection" is a nice word, a noble word. It is used by historians, political scientists, anthropologists, lawyers, politicians, and even theologians with somewhat different meanings. But it always has a positive connotation.

Since the establishment of the modern international system based on nation-states, usually dated from the Treaty of Westphalia in 1648, it is a recognized responsibility of states to protect their citizens from harm, to defend them from danger, to save them from persecution—in short, to keep them safe. The ability to protect one's citizens is intrinsic to the very definition of a state. If a state cannot protect its people, it has failed as a state.[2]

But there are times when states are not able to protect all of their people and when international law—particularly international humanitarian law, human rights law, and refugee law—provides for protection by others. Most recently the 2005 World Summit adopted the doctrine of "responsibility to protect," which affirms the centrality of the state as the protector of its people but also sets out a series of measures to be taken by the international community when a state is unable or unwilling to protect its citizens.

This book focuses on the understandings and practice of protection in the international humanitarian system, but humanitarians have no monopoly on the term. Protection has become central to UN discussions—and decisions—on peacekeeping. All but one of the eleven peacekeeping missions initiated in the past decade have included the protection of civilians in their mandate.[3] Protection of civilians has become a UN-wide priority.

Protection in the Humanitarian World

The concept of protection was central to the development of international humanitarian law (IHL), the first component of the concept of protection, which initially stemmed from the need to protect soldiers who were wounded, captured, or otherwise *hors de combat*. IHL was expanded in 1949 to include measures to protect civilians, and since then the International Committee of the Red Cross (ICRC), the guardian of IHL, has tried to provide guidance on such thorny issues as distinguishing civilians from combatants and the question of the responsibility of nonstate actors to uphold IHL, including protection of civilians. ICRC also has moved to respond to new forms of warfare and has played a leadership role in the campaign to ban antipersonnel land mines. In other words, over the past 150 years or so, IHL has expanded its original remit to protect prisoners of war and wounded soldiers into a broad range of activities designed to protect civilians who are affected by but are not direct participants in conflicts.

The development of a second fundamental component of the concept of protection occurred in the aftermath of the European wars of the twentieth century, when protection of refugees emerged as a response to the plight of individuals who had fled their countries because of those wars or because of persecution. Because their governments were no longer able to protect them, it was the responsibility of host governments and the international community to do so. Just as the International Committee of the Red Cross became the guardian of international humanitarian law, the United Nations High Commissioner for Refugees (UNHCR) became the custodian of international refugee law. Still later in the twentieth century, the growing recognition that people who were displaced from their communities but remained within the borders of their countries also needed protection led to the development of international norms for protecting internally displaced persons.

A third component of the notion of protection comes from international human rights law. The Universal Declaration of Human Rights refers to "protection" ten times: "Human rights should be protected by law, "All are entitled to equal protection under the law," and so on. In fact, much of the modern human rights movement is about expanding the scope of protection: protection of the rights of racial and ethnic minorities, of children, of women, and of gay and lesbian people; protection of the cultures of indigenous people; and so on.[4] The expansion of the groups in need of protection paralleled the expansion of the understanding of human rights from its early, almost exclusive focus on the civil and political rights of individuals to its inclusion of the economic, social, and cultural rights of both individuals and communities. By the end of the 1990s, explicit reference to the protection of civilians emerged in UN Security Council resolutions.

As universal human rights broadened to include more groups, so too the concept of protection expanded in human rights discourse. Protection meant not only physical protection of people from violence and legal protection of refugees from deportation but also protection from hunger, illness, and discrimination. Similarly, one can trace the expansion of protection in the humanitarian field from protection of soldiers (*hors de combat*) to protection of refugees, to protection of children in armed conflict, to protection of internally displaced persons, to protection of women against sexual and gender-based violence, to protection of civilians.

The intersection of the concepts of protection, humanitarian response, and human rights is a close and mutually reinforcing one, although the actors in these three spheres often seem to function in their own particular "territories," with few genuinely collaborative efforts.

Protection in the Wider World

It is useful before jumping into the historical development of concepts of protection and current practices to step back for a moment to look at the big-picture developments on the international scene.

The current international order is in transition, and what the future order will be is unclear. There are new possibilities for global governance and renewed interest in multilateral efforts to address climate change, resolve conflicts, and hold war criminals accountable. On many different fronts, conceptual developments are occurring on parallel tracks, often without much cross-fertilization, but all represent a desire to do more to protect people whose governments cannot—or will not—protect them. It is almost as if there is a universal yearning for a global system that can keep people safe.

Development. The concept of economic development has expanded from the emphasis on national economic growth in the 1950s to include concerns about equitable distribution of resources; community empowerment; rule of law; environmental issues; and, most recently, human security. Human security moves away from the focus on national security to consider what causes individuals to feel secure. Although the concept remains a bit ambiguous and is interpreted in different ways, it generally refers to "freedom from threat to the core values of human beings, including physical survival" but also to community, economic, environmental, food, health, personal, and political security[5] and to health and access to education.[6] The concept of human security, it is important to recall, originated with the United Nations Development Program, but it parallels the expanded notion of protection evident in both the humanitarian and human rights worlds.

Security. Military approaches to security have broadened dramatically in recent decades, from launching interstate wars to responding to insurgencies, failed states, and terrorism. The U.S. military's current emphasis on stabilization operations recognizes that issues such as rule of law and humanitarian response are as important to security as combat operations. Security is not just about fighting and winning wars any more, it is about embracing a whole range of actions that are actually quite similar to those incorporated in the expanded notions of human security and human rights. "Winning hearts and minds" is seen as key to defeating insurgencies. In July 2008 the U.S. secretary of defense, Robert Gates, declared, "We cannot kill or capture our way to victory" in the long-term campaign against terrorism, arguing that military action should be subordinate to political and economic efforts to undermine extremism."[7]

International Accountability. The movement to bring perpetrators of war crimes and other atrocities to justice gathered momentum in the 1990s, with the establishment of international tribunals in the former Yugoslavia and Rwanda, the prosecution of war criminals by domestic courts in other countries, and the adoption of the Rome Statute in 1998, which was the basis for the establishment of the International Criminal Court. Such measures to increase accountability and establish new judicial mechanisms were not only intended to punish those guilty of war crimes, genocide, and crimes against humanity but also to deter combatants from committing mass atrocities and hence to protect civilians.

Security Council, Peacekeeping, and Responsibility to Protect. Since 1948, there have been sixty-four UN peacekeeping operations, and since the end of the cold war, the number of those operations has expanded dramatically. Today there are more than 100,000 UN peacekeeping troops, working in fifteen missions,[8] most of whom are charged not only with keeping the peace (a bit of a misnomer in many of the newer missions) but also with protecting civilians. Protection of civilians has emerged front and center in Security Council deliberations. And when the 2005 World Summit unanimously adopted the responsibility to protect doctrine, it suggested that the governments of the world were committed to ensuring that war crimes, ethnic cleansing, and genocide would be prevented through an effective international response.

The UN's Quest for Coherence. UN reform efforts over the past decade are evidence of dissatisfaction with piecemeal approaches to the world's problems and a desire to find a coherent, holistic approach. Rather than having a dozen different UN agencies (and their supporting constituencies) embark on programs to respond to particular needs in a given country, the reasoning goes, the UN could increase its impact and effectiveness through a coherent and coordinated approach. Thus the idea of integrated missions, the one-UN initiative, the capstone doctrine on UN peacekeeping, the Peacebuilding Commission, and the doctrine of responsibility to protect emerged—all recognizing that development, humanitarian response, politics, security, and peace are fundamentally linked. All of those reform initiatives represent a desire for the United Nations to become more effective, more coordinated, and more relevant in addressing the world's problems. It is almost as if, having been blocked by cold war rivalries for so long, the UN is now searching for its place in the world, and the question of the protection of civilians is central to that quest.

Different developments concerning protection are explored in greater detail in ensuing chapters, but it is important to note here the convergence that has emerged in many diverse fields toward a holistic focus on protection. As concepts, protection, human rights, and human security have much in common. They all have moved beyond a concern with physical protection of the individual to a more expansive understanding—that to protect people, uphold their rights, and provide for their security means to address their social, economic, cultural, and political needs. In their efforts to be all-inclusive, these three concepts—human rights, human security, and protection—also have expanded so much that they are ambiguous, vague, and difficult to put into operation.

Origins of the Modern International Humanitarian System

The understanding of protection in modern political discourse has been shaped by three historical strands. In the middle of the nineteenth century principles of humanitarianism and *international humanitarian law,* which was intended to protect persons affected by war and armed conflict, began to emerge. In the middle of the twentieth century, *refugee law* was developed to protect people who had left their countries because of fear of persecution and whose governments were unable or unwilling to protect them. After World War II, *international human rights law* developed as a cornerstone of the new international order. Governments were now obliged to protect their citizens during times of peace as well as during conflict, and that obligation was a matter of international law, not just a private matter between a state and its citizens. All three of these legal traditions originated in Europe in response to particular historical events, and all served the political interests of the major powers of the time. All three were codified as universal legal obligations, and they have since been accepted by the vast majority of the world's governments. Although implementation of the binding legal instruments has been (and probably always will be) uneven, the concept that people have a right to protection has become central to the international system.

While international humanitarian law regulates the protection of persons and the conduct of hostilities in armed conflict, international refugee law focuses specifically on protecting persons who have fled their countries because of persecution. International human rights law imposes standards that governments must adhere to in their treatment of persons in times of both peace and war.

Each of the three strands included binding international agreements identifying the persons to be protected, the standards of protection, and the parties responsible for providing the protection. All of them chip away at the notion of state sovereignty, the cornerstone of the international system since the Peace of Westphalia in 1648. Moreover, each strand is identified with a particular international institution: the International Committee of the Red Cross is the guardian of international humanitarian law; the United Nations High Commissioner for Refugees has a supervisory role in the 1951 United Nations Convention Relating to the Status of Refugees; the UN Commission on Human Rights, reconstituted in 2005 as the Human Rights Council, oversees various mechanisms concerned with implementation of various human rights legal instruments.

The normative framework represented in the three legal traditions has led to new political initiatives from various quarters—from calls for humanitarian intervention in the early 1990s to unanimous endorsement of the concept of responsibility to protect by the 2005 World Summit. The recognition that certain groups have particular unmet needs for protection has led to new policies, norms, and initiatives. In 1998, the representative of the secretary-general on internally displaced persons presented to the UN Commission on Human Rights the Guiding Principles on Internal Displacement, which uphold the rights of people who, although forced to flee their communities, remain within the borders of their own country. Over the past decade there has sometimes been tension between those advocating on behalf of particular groups, such as women, children, and internally displaced persons, and those arguing that singling out groups for special attention means that others are left out. The evolution of the concept of protection of civilians and the increasing emphasis on vulnerability analysis at the operational level is a response to some of the criticisms.

While it probably is true that the existing instruments for ensuring protection—the conventions and covenants, the ICRC, UNHCR, and UNICEF (United Nations Children's Fund)—could not have come into being without the support of powerful governments that saw some political advantage in creating them, it also is true that the concept of protection has become a powerful tool in defending some of the most vulnerable members of society from actions of their own governments.

This chapter traces the historical emergence of two of these three historical strands: international humanitarian law and refugee law. International human rights law is discussed in chapter 2.

Humanitarianism and International Humanitarian Law

Humanitarian principles have been part of human existence since the beginning of recorded history. In fact, anthropologists tell us that the social norm of charity was a necessity, not just a nice thing to do, for prehistoric societies.[9] The idea that it is good to protect and provide for the most vulnerable members of society—the widows and orphans, disabled and sick, foreigners and paupers—is central to all religious traditions. For example, *zakat*—which involves giving alms to the poor in part to help engender social equality—is one of the five pillars of Islam, which are obligatory acts for each Muslim.[10] Long before the development of international humanitarian law, social institutions were established in different parts of the world to care for and protect vulnerable people. Egyptian pharaohs, we are told in the Hebrew Scriptures, saved grain to feed their people during times of famine. The monasteries of Europe provided sanctuary to travelers and fed the poor.

Modern humanitarianism is generally dated to the mid-nineteenth century, when a remarkable reform movement grew up in Europe and North America, largely out of the Christian evangelical tradition of service. At that time civil society actors were challenging the institution of slavery and undertaking the reform of hospitals, mental institutions, and prisons. Nursing made its appearance as a profession with Florence Nightingale, who set off to care for British soldiers wounded during the Crimean War, and Clara Barton, who worked with the wounded and missing during the U.S. Civil War. At the height of the colonial period, thousands of missionaries and evangelists set off for distant lands, bringing the Gospel but also education and health care with them. By the end of the century, philanthropy was in full swing, with wealthy industrialists forming foundations as "private organizations with public purposes."[11]

The Industrial Revolution also was in full swing during the nineteenth century, permitting the production of new weapons that made wars more deadly, and mass conscription increased the proportion of the population at risk in war.[12] Wars between European states and the U.S. Civil War produced millions of casualties. Battlefield medical treatment was primitive, and most wounded in battle simply died. Prisoners of war were treated poorly. The U.S. Civil War produced more than 400,000 Union and Confederate prisoners, many of whom died in appalling conditions.[13] Major military powers reportedly provided more veterinarians to care for horses than doctors to care for soldiers wounded in battle.[14]

It was in the context of terrible military casualties in warfare coupled with a growing abolitionist and reformist movement that Henri Dunant, a Swiss entrepreneur, stumbled on the battlefield of Solferino in 1859, where some 40,000 Austrian and Italian troops—then at war with one another—lay wounded and dying on the battlefield. He was shocked at the carnage and enlisted women in the neighboring villages to assist the victims on both sides. Dunant returned to his native Geneva from Solferino, seized with the idea of creating an independent, neutral organization that would minister to wounded soldiers on all sides of a conflict in the name of humanity.

Dunant published *A Memory of Solferino,* a book about his experiences, and began mobilizing support for his idea of an independent humanitarian organization. Specifically, he called for the establishment of local, voluntary relief committees and the protection of the volunteers.[15] He managed to bring together representatives from sixteen nations at a conference organized by the International Committee for the Relief of the Wounded in October 1863. At the conference, the committee was transformed into the International Committee of the Red Cross, and it adopted the Red Cross emblem that is so well known today—the reverse of the emblem of the Swiss flag. A year later the Swiss government convened a diplomatic conference at which the twelve nations attending drafted and adopted the Geneva Convention for the Amelioration of the Condition of the Wounded in Armies in the Field. The Convention of 1864 became the first component of what came to be known as international humanitarian law.

At the same time that Henri Dunant was mobilizing support for voluntary relief committees, Clara Barton was serving as a nurse for the Union army during the U.S. Civil War. Shortly after the war ended, President Abraham Lincoln asked her to take charge of getting information on all the missing men in the Union army. She pursued that task diligently, tracking down the names of thousands of soldiers who had died in the war. Facing exhaustion, she traveled to Europe on her doctor's orders in 1868 to rest and regain her health, and there she was drawn into discussions with the brand-new ICRC and efforts to start national societies. When she returned from Europe, she lobbied hard for U.S. recognition of the ICRC. When the American Red Cross was founded in 1881, Barton served as its first president.

And so the Red Cross movement was born. The ICRC was established to assist soldiers wounded in war (and others who were no longer engaged in hostilities), and national Red Cross societies were created to assist civilians.[16] Clara Barton's work in tracing Union soldiers became the nucleus of a large part of the ICRC's work in tracing family members.

ICRC's mandate to aid wounded soldiers during war expanded over time to include prisoners of war, soldiers wounded or imprisoned during other types of armed conflict, and eventually civilians. ICRC's work with detainees began during World War I, when operations expanded greatly, and the ICRC was awarded the Nobel Peace Prize in 1917 for its efforts. The ICRC's role as a neutral intermediary between warring parties also gained credence during that time. After the war, ICRC and the newly formed League of Red Cross Societies responded to the mass famine in Russia, where 32 million people faced death from starvation.[17] The same crisis in Russia would prove pivotal in the development of the international refugee system.

The League of Red Cross and Red Crescent Societies—now the International Federation of Red Cross and Red Crescent Societies (IFRC)—was the umbrella group charged with coordinating the growing number of national societies. Established with only twelve national societies in 1919, the IFRC today encompasses 186 national Red Cross and Red Crescent societies with 97 million volunteers and 300,000 staff members.[18]

Over the years, the Red Cross movement expanded in scope and activities. The interwar period, during which the Russian famine and later the Spanish Civil War challenged the Red Cross to respond to widespread human need, was especially important. The interwar years also were a time of increasing tension between the ICRC and the national Red Cross/Red Crescent societies; while they were linked by a common name and history, in practice there were major differences between them. The ICRC was closely tied to the Swiss state, and from the beginning it was shaped by Swiss history, politics, and values—particularly neutrality, which has been a principle of Swiss foreign policy since the Napoleonic wars and has served to protect it from involvement in European wars. Over the decades, ICRC preserved the Swiss value of neutrality—in fact, one study found that "in the more than 140 years of the ICRC's existence, and even with the opening of the organization's archives, there is little evidence of the ICRC *intentionally* trying to favor one state or political party—with the major political exception of its deferring to the priorities of the Swiss state during the Second World War."[19]

While the ICRC clearly was (and is) a Swiss institution, the creation of the IFRC was driven by the American Red Cross. As Forsythe notes, "After all, in the First World War the Americans had deployed four times as many volunteers in the American Red Cross as the government had deployed soldiers in the U.S. expeditionary force."[20] From the beginning, the ICRC saw the League of Red Cross and Red Crescent Societies as a threat to its leadership and tried to limit its authority. In the end, ICRC managed to preserve its domain—humanitarian protection in conflict situations—leaving the less glamorous field of natural disasters to the IFRC. But relations between the two Red Cross entities were tense for much of the last half of the twentieth century. A rapprochement between the two came about in 1997 with the negotiation of the Seville Agreement, which spelled out which organization would take the lead in specific circumstances and committed the two organizations to effective collaboration in practice. While the ICRC positioned itself as a neutral intermediary and custodian of international humanitarian law, the Red Cross/Red Crescent societies, which had an official relationship with their national governments, were not immune to political pressures.

The history of the Red Cross/Red Crescent societies is fascinating, but unfortunately it is beyond the scope of this book.[21] Some of the themes that emerge from its history, however, are the same issues that confront the humanitarian movement today: expansion of mandates; tensions and turf wars between humanitarian actors; difficult political decisions over cooperating and collaborating with governments; growth in number of staff (in 1939, on the eve of World War II, the ICRC had three administrative staff members, but it quickly expanded to assist more than 30 million people during the war); and questions about accountability, staff security, and relations with partners in the international humanitarian system.

The seven organizing principles of the Red Cross/Red Crescent movement have become central to the humanitarian enterprise. Those principles include three principles that relate exclusively to the movement itself,[22] but the other four have been hallmarks of humanitarian assistance throughout the international community. In fact, when people refer to humanitarian action, they usually refer to work carried out under commitment to the principles of

—*humanity:* to prevent and alleviate human suffering, without ulterior motives

—*impartiality:* to relieve the suffering of individuals solely on the basis of their needs, with no discrimination related to nationality, race, religious beliefs, or political opinions

—*neutrality:* to refrain from taking sides in hostilities or "engage[ing] at any time in controversies of a political, racial, religious or ideological nature"

—*independence:* to maintain autonomy from governments.[23]

Those principles have formed the basis of many mission statements and codes of conduct, including, for example, the ICRC's code of conduct for the Red Cross and Red Crescent societies and for nongovernmental organizations.[24] (Chapter 6 discusses the principles and the difficulties of implementing them in the world today.)

Efforts to come up with humanitarian laws to apply during wars and conflicts have a long history. The just war tradition emerging in the twelfth to the fifteenth centuries was based on Christian religious tradition, the chivalric tradition (itself with roots in older understandings of warriorhood), Roman law, and experiences with the use of force in the service of the emerging political order.[25] The Peace of God movement, which originated in southern France in the late tenth century, represented the earliest efforts to protect persons associated with the church, peasants, and others from looting and violence by soldiers and armed groups.[26] The movement included initiatives by local clergy to convene town councils to which nobles were invited to commit themselves to common standards of behavior during warfare. Those initiatives were not always successful. However, by the thirteenth century, the principle of protecting noncombatants was firmly fixed in the canon law of the Roman Catholic Church, and subsequent development of the idea of protecting noncombatants took place within the chivalric tradition. Knights were to fight only other knights and were not use to arms against groups such as women, children, the elderly, or the ill, infirm, or mentally deficient. The tradition was clear: "only people who actually take part in war are to be treated as combatants; others, regardless of status, are non-combatants."[27] Hugo Grotius, the father of international law, emphasized the importance of protecting noncombatants in warfare—a tradition codified in military law.[28]

The Geneva Conventions of 1864 and 1906 focused on combatants who have been rendered incapable of participating in combat because of injury or illness.[29] The Hague Convention (IV) Respecting the Laws and Customs of War on Land of 1907 defines a much more extensive list of persons and property to be protected: prisoners of war (articles 4–20); occupied territory and its inhabitants (articles 42–56), including "public buildings, real estate, forests, and agricultural estates"; and "the property of municipalities, that of institutions dedicated to religion, charity and education, [and] the arts and sciences [and] historic monuments, works of art and science."[30] The convention even stipulates that "[f]amily honour and rights, the lives of persons, and private property, as well as religious convictions and practice, must be respected," in occupied territory. While there is no definition of a "noncombatant" class, there is a general understanding that civilians are not to be attacked.

International humanitarian law, also known as the law of armed conflict or law of war, is a collection of rules that protects civilians and soldiers who are no longer participating in hostilities. Its purpose is to limit and prevent human suffering in times of conflict. International humanitarian law is directed primarily at states, which have a duty to respect it and ensure that it is respected. IHL is applicable only in times of armed conflict, and it does not deal with the question of whether the use of force by states or other actors is legal. Nor does it apply in natural disasters or in situations in which states abuse their citizens. In other words, IHL accepts the reality that wars will take place and seeks to mitigate the effects of war on civilians. It is a pragmatic approach, far from pacifism, which sees war itself as evil.

In August 1949, an international conference in Geneva finalized the text of four conventions for protecting the victims of armed conflict. However, the Geneva Conventions of 1949 were not the first international treaties regulating wars. Agreements for protecting wounded soldiers had been in existence since the original Geneva Convention of 1864, and additional conventions had been signed since then, protecting prisoners of war and setting the rules for the conduct of hostilities. But the 1949 conventions provided a definitive codification of the laws of war as they were then understood, and

---

Box 1-1. *Instruments of International Humanitarian Law*

Convention for the Amelioration of the Condition of the Wounded in Armies in the Field, Geneva, August 22, 1864

Hague Convention (IV) Respecting the Laws and Customs of War on Land and Its Annex: Regulations Concerning the Laws and Customs of War on Land, October 18, 1907

Convention (I) for the Amelioration of the Condition of Wounded and Sick in Armed Forces in the Field, Geneva, August 12, 1949

Convention (II) for the Amelioration of the Condition of Wounded, Sick, and Shipwrecked Members of Armed Forces at Sea, Geneva, August 12, 1949

Convention (III) Relative to the Treatment of Prisoners of War, Geneva, August 12, 1949

Convention (IV) Relative to the Protection of Civilian Persons in Time of War, Geneva, August 12, 1949

Protocol Additional to the Geneva Conventions of August 12, 1949, and Relating to the Protection of Victims of International Armed Conflicts (Protocol I), June 8, 1977

Protocol Additional to the Geneva Conventions of August 12, 1949, and Relating to the Protection of Victims of Non-International Armed Conflicts (Protocol II), June 8, 1977

Protocol Additional to the Geneva Conventions of August 12, 1949, and Relating to the Adoption of an Additional Distinctive Emblem (Protocol III), December 8, 2005

---

they have remained the cornerstone of the law of armed conflict. According to the ICRC, they are the only international laws to have obtained universal acceptance—every country in the world is a party to them.[31]

Today, the principal instruments of international humanitarian law (box 1-1) are the four Geneva Conventions of 1949 and their three additional protocols, issued in 1977 and 2005, supplemented by other instruments, such as the 1925 Geneva Protocol banning the use of gas, the 1977 Ottawa Convention on the Prohibition of Anti-Personnel Mines, and the 1980 Convention on Certain Conventional Weapons. The Geneva Conventions apply to international armed conflicts, and they stipulate that civilians and people no longer taking part in the hostilities, such as captured or wounded soldiers, must be spared and treated humanely. In addition, article 3 of all four conventions authorizes the ICRC to offer its services in the event of noninternational armed conflicts and provides for certain minimum protections for the victims of such conflicts. That expansion from wars to armed conflicts was a major shift in terms of increasing the responsibility of the international community for developments within states. It led to a broader understanding of the responsibility of the international community for enforcing the rules for right conduct in armed conflict and to a shift toward viewing violation of the rules as a crime of war for which individuals could be prosecuted. Currently 194 states are party to the Geneva Conventions, and between 157 and 162 states are party to the protocols of 1977 and 2005.[32]

When the conventions were drafted in 1949, they were intended to apply to wars fought between the uniformed armed forces of nation-states. They were based on the European experience. Although the wars of liberation and struggles for independence in much of the global South constituted many of the conflicts in the second half of the twentieth century, they were not a reference point for the development of international humanitarian law. The two additional protocols of 1977 broadened the scope of IHL in addressing the wars that were characteristic of the postcolonial period—for example, national liberation wars and internal conflicts.

The first three of the Geneva Conventions set out a series of rules for governments on the treatment of wounded soldiers and prisoners of war. But the fourth convention contains a set of protections for civilians, both those living in occupied territories or otherwise in the hands of a party to a conflict. The two additional protocols of 1977 greatly extended the protection of civilians in international armed conflicts, particularly by forbidding attacks that could be expected to cause disproportionate harm to civilians. Subsequent specific conventions have placed limits on the weapons that combatant forces can use, such as land mines and cluster munitions.

International humanitarian law prohibits making the civilian population or individual civilians the object of attack, using starvation of civilians as a method of warfare, and launching indiscriminate attacks affecting the civilian population. Apart from the rules on the conduct of hostilities, IHL also seeks to protect civilians who find themselves in enemy hands during armed conflict by specifically prohibiting murder, torture, mutilation, rape, corporal punishment, collective punishments, taking of hostages, and denial of the right to a fair trial to civilians subject to criminal process.[33]

While the ICRC is proud of the universal acceptance of international humanitarian law by states, awareness and dissemination of the law are far from universal. A survey commissioned by the ICRC on the understanding of IHL in eight countries found that slightly less than half of the 4,000 respondents had heard of the Geneva Conventions and slightly more than half of those familiar with the conventions thought that they limit the suffering of civilians in wartime.[34] International humanitarian law and the ICRC have been criticized for making war more likely by making it more humane.[35] It is important to remember, however, that it was in the interest of the great powers of the time to create and support a neutral humanitarian institution that could serve as an intermediary between warring parties. It also was in the interests of militaries to support strong and binding laws of war. Indeed, probably the most stalwart defenders of international humanitarian law are military officers who insist that their enemy prisoners be humanely treated in accord with the Geneva Conventions—to ensure that their own soldiers will be humanely treated if captured or wounded.

Yet violations of international humanitarian law have been common over the past century—for example, by occupying powers such as the Soviet Union in Afghanistan and by military forces engaged in interstate conflicts, such as Iranian and Iraqi forces at war in the mid-1980s. Rebel groups ranging from the Khmer Rouge in Cambodia to the Mozambican National Resistance Movement (RENAMO) often have slaughtered civilians with little concern for the provisions of the international conventions. Such violations continue today, although ICRC and other mediators have found that insurgent groups often are aware, at least in general terms, of international humanitarian law—and with the establishment of the International Criminal Court and other judicial mechanisms, they are eager to avoid being charged with war crimes. While the Geneva Conventions may have seemed irrelevant to Charles Taylor's forces when they mutilated and murdered women and children in Liberia, Taylor is now facing trial on eleven counts of war crimes and crimes against humanity under the provisions of the Special Court for Sierra Leone for his actions in supporting rebel forces in Sierra Leone. At the same time, many believe that international humanitarian law has been weakened by U.S. actions to fight terrorists, particularly the use of enhanced interrogation techniques and indefinite detention of prisoners as enemy or unlawful combatants rather than as prisoners of war when international humanitarian law precludes torture.[36]

The humanitarian component of protection thus comes from efforts to limit the effects of war, to protect both soldiers who are no longer combatants and civilians. The humanitarian component includes a body of law (international humanitarian law), an international agency legally entrusted with upholding the law (the ICRC), a complex web of quasi-governmental Red Cross/Red Crescent national societies, and a set of common humanitarian principles.

While international humanitarian law applies only to situations of armed conflict, as noted above, humanitarian principles serve as the bedrock for all humanitarian action, including in natural disasters. While ICRC is the custodian of international humanitarian law, in fact most agencies, whether intergovernmental or nongovernmental, see themselves as acting in accord with those principles.

The word "humanitarian" has come not only to mean provision of life-saving assistance (in contrast, say, to long-term development assistance or to actions to promote human rights) but also to represent the values of independence, neutrality, and impartiality. And as explored in the next chapter, the term "humanitarian" has been appropriated by all manner of actors who have no commitment to—and sometimes no familiarity with—the core humanitarian principles developed more than one hundred years ago. They include, for example, actors that provide assistance to people in need but only if they are members of a particular religious group, those that provide humanitarian aid to support national foreign policy objectives, and those that distribute humanitarian assistance as a profitmaking enterprise.

Protection and ICRC

The role of the International Committee of the Red Cross in protection is unique. It is the only humanitarian actor with a mandate to take action to prevent attacks on civilians; all other humanitarian agencies focus primarily on working with the victims of such attacks.[37] In seeking to deter attacks on civilians by government forces or armed opposition, ICRC carries out behind-the-scenes negotiations with a variety of armed entities on the basis of its neutrality and impartiality. While most other humanitarian actors sometimes adopt pragmatic approaches to ensure access—for example, accepting armed escorts to protect their staff in dangerous situations—ICRC stands virtually alone in rejecting that approach in almost all situations.[38]

As part of its work in building a supportive environment for protection, ICRC also exercises a leadership role within the international community in promoting and upholding standards and guidelines for action. Following five years of consultations, the International Committee of the Red Cross adopted the following definition of protection—a definition that subsequently was accepted by the Inter-Agency Standing Committee, the body established by the UN General Assembly to coordinate humanitarian work among the world's major humanitarian actors:

> Protection is defined as all activities aimed at obtaining full respect for the rights of the individual in accordance with the letter and spirit of the relevant bodies of law, namely human rights law, international humanitarian law and refugee law.[39]

That is a broad definition: *all* activities; *full* respect for the rights of the individual. This definition, which was adopted by the Inter-Agency Standing Committee in 1999, has become the standard definition for UN agencies, the ICRC, the Red Cross/Red Crescent societies, and nongovernmental organizations.

ICRC also proposed a protection framework in which three types of activities may be considered to promote protection and may occur simultaneously:

—Responsive action: activities undertaken to respond to an abuse, aimed at stopping it, preventing its recurrence, or alleviating its immediate effects

—Remedial action: activities aimed at restoring people's dignity and adequate living conditions

—Environment-building action: activities intended to promote an environment conducive to full respect for the rights of the individual.[40]

Activities to protect people thus cover a broad range, including direct material and psychosocial assistance to victims of human rights abuses; advocacy; awareness raising; strengthening of civil society; pursuit of justice; and establishment of institutional mechanisms for response or prevention.

The humanitarian community has adopted the ICRC-promoted principle that protection means upholding all rights of the individual, not just ensuring physical security. Education is protection. The threat of indictment by the International Criminal Court is protection. Training programs on human rights is protection. The placement of latrines, the provision of reproductive health services, and livelihood projects all are protection. Handbooks have been developed, conferences organized, and policy guidelines formulated on incorporating protection into every aspect of humanitarian response.[41]

In fact, it is hard to think of any activity carried out by a humanitarian organization in the field that could not be considered protection. Building shelters, registering voters, negotiating with the government, informing the public, disabling land mines, and developing preschool curriculums—all can be considered protection activities. When asked whether the definition has become so broad as to be meaningless, ICRC staff respond that it is important to have a common "chapeau," an umbrella under which different organizations can develop their own definitions, just as ICRC has done. Without that common overarching definition, there is the risk that organizations will do very different things.[42]

To respond to the large number of humanitarian actors, ICRC also took the lead in developing minimum standards for humanitarian organizations engaged in protection to provide basic guidance about what activities can and cannot be considered protection.[43] Although the process took two years, the standards were drafted in a consultative process and, with the exception of guidance on relations between humanitarian agencies and military forces, they proved to be remarkably consensual.

Refugee Law

A second important component of protection comes from the development of the international refugee regime.[44] By the nineteenth century, an essential function of a national government was to protect its citizens when they were abroad. Citizens traveling in other countries who found themselves in trouble could appeal to their governments for help, and the government, usually through its embassy or consulate, could protect its citizens.[45] That was an important exercise of national sovereignty; in fact, there was a general understanding (though never codified in international law) that intervention in another state to protect one's own nationals constituted a legitimate use of force.[46] Thus, when Israel intervened in Uganda in 1976 to rescue nationals held hostage and when the United States intervened in Iran in 1980 to try to rescue detained Americans, both states claimed that their actions were in self-defense.[47]

People have fled their countries because of violence and persecution since the beginning of recorded history. However, it was the Russian Revolution, in 1917, and the resulting exodus of refugees that led the international community to begin to establish the norm that it was the responsibility of the international community to assist those who did not have a national government to protect them. As Gil Loescher points out, between 1 and 2 million people, mainly Russians from the Russian Empire, were uprooted as a result of "the collapse of czarist Russia, the Russian Civil War, the Russo-Polish war, and the Soviet famine of 1921."[48] Interestingly, the same crisis was an impetus for the development of the Red Cross movement. But the Russian crisis was not contained within Russia's borders. Civilians poured out of Russia as the newly established Soviet Union revoked the citizenship of many of its inhabitants. The Russians streamed into Germany and France, where they had few prospects, and the governments of those countries began to expel them from their territory. It was clearly a political problem affecting relations between European powers and a problem that violated the territorial sovereignty of states as unwanted people arrived at the borders. And so the international system began to respond in ways that it did not when the Turkish genocide of Armenians took place, when 2 million Poles migrated to Poland following the German-Polish, Austrian-Polish, and Russian-Polish partitions under the 1919 Treaty of Versailles, or when there were other mass movements of people in other parts of the world.

The first organized international effort on behalf of refugees began in 1920, when the League of Nations gave Fridtjof Nansen the task of negotiating the repatriation of Russian prisoners of war and a year later appointed him the first High Commissioner for Refugees, with responsibility for the Russian refugee problem.[49] Nansen began by working on the practical issues facing the Russian refugees, but when it came to finding long-term solutions, the refugees had few alternatives. They could not return home or settle elsewhere—many of them did not have travel documents. The Russian government had made large numbers of people stateless by taking away the citizenship of those it considered enemies of the revolution. Without citizenship, those individuals had no rights abroad and no embassy to appeal to; nonetheless, they could not appeal to the host state for protection. The resulting state of affairs "underlin[ed] the urgent importance of an *international* status for the newly unprotected."[50] "At first, the High Commissioner's staff attempted to protect them by providing consular services and diplomatic interventions with host governments that threatened their expulsion and deportation."[51] Travel documents that came to be known as "Nansen passports" in effect provided diplomatic protection to the Russian refugees, allowing them to travel outside the country where they had taken refuge. Over the thirty-year period between 1921 and 1951, the activities of successive High Commissioners for Refugees expanded, with an emphasis on resettling, finding employment for, and supporting hundreds of thousands of refugees in their efforts to become economically self-sufficient. But the commissioner's protection role was limited to providing diplomatic protection, primarily through provision of travel documents.

While the international community responded to the Russian refugees, the response to others forced to flee their countries was uneven. From the beginning, protection of and assistance to refugees was both a political and an economic issue.[52] It was relatively easy to mobilize support for work with Russian refugees because of the hostility that most members of the League of Nations felt toward the Russian revolutionary government.[53] It was more politically sensitive for states to respond to people leaving friendly countries, especially during a time of global economic depression accompanied by increasingly restrictive immigration policies. League member states therefore deliberately limited the mandate of the High Commissioner and avoided adopting any formal definition of "refugee" for fear of opening the door to movements of other groups of people. In fact, during the 1930s, European states closed their borders to Jewish "refugees" and others fleeing fascism, in part because of fears that if they allowed some to enter, many more would soon appear on their frontiers.[54] Rather than issuing a general definition of "refugee," states named specific refugee groups to be protected (Turks, Russians, Armenians, Greeks, and so forth).

In 1930, following Nansen's death, the responsibilities involved in protecting refugees were transferred to the league's secretariat, and in 1933 yet another weak refugee organization, the High Commissioner for Refugees from Germany, was created, this time with strict instructions not to get involved in political issues. But it was a difficult time, with states unwilling to accept any of the refugees as legal immigrants even when all other means of affording protection had failed. The High Commissioner for Refugees from Germany, James G. McDonald, resigned in protest, claiming that his hands were tied by his inability to confront the causes for the exodus of predominantly Jewish German refugees. Addressing the causes of the refugee problem was a political, not a humanitarian, task: "In his letter of resignation, James McDonald referred to the need to set aside state sovereignty in favor of humanitarian imperatives and to resolve the Jewish refugee problem at the level of international politics."[55] In 1938 an international conference convened at Evian, France, to deal with the Jewish refugee question, but the conference rejected Western action in spite of growing evidence of the scale of persecution in Germany. The High Commissioner was unable to protect the thousands of Jewish refugees. However, "[t]he institutions created to respond to refugee problems during the interwar period did leave one lasting and important legacy. Twenty years of organizational growth and interstate collaboration had firmly established the idea that refugees constituted victims of human rights abuses for whom the world had a special responsibility."[56]

In the period following World War II, Europe was awash in millions of displaced people, including Germans trying to return to their country, ethnic Germans driven out of neighboring countries, and people uprooted because of the war.[57] Refugee camps were set up to house the displaced persons and a UN organization, the United Nations Relief and Rehabilitation Agency (UNRRA), was created to assist them until they could be repatriated. But many of the displaced persons did not want to return, particularly to the Soviet Union or to countries under Soviet control. The mass repatriations of 1945 slowed and came to an almost complete halt by the end of 1946, leaving more than 1 million people in camps with few prospects for a solution. While UNRRA was supposed to oversee repatriation, increasing tension with the Soviet Union led some governments, particularly the U.S. government, to resist forcing refugees to return. The United States provided 70 percent of UNRRA funds, and in 1947 it decided to withhold its funds, effectively killing the agency. The United States pressed for the creation of a new organization, the International Refugee Organization (IRO), whose mission was not the repatriation of refugees but their resettlement.

> The Western bloc insisted that the mandate of the IRO be broad enough to offer protection to individuals with "valid objections" to repatriation, including objections based on "persecution, or fear, based on reasonable grounds, of persecution because of race, religion, nationality or political opinions and objections" of a political nature, judged by the organization to be valid.[58]

The criteria used by the IRO to define people in need of protection were the precursor to the definition of "refugee" included in the 1951 United Nations Convention Relating to the Status of Refugees (1951 UN refugee convention) and reflected U.S. political interests in supporting those who did not wish to return to the Soviet Union. Again, "the United States, which underwrote over two-thirds of its costs and controlled its leadership, played the key role in investing IRO's refugee protection with specific ideological content."[59] The 1951 UN convention provided the following definition of "refugee":

> [A]ny person who, owing to a well-founded fear of being persecuted for reasons of race, religion, nationality, membership of a particular social group or political opinion, is outside the country of his nationality and is unable or, owing to such fear, unwilling to avail himself of the protection of that country, or who, not having a nationality and being outside the country of his former habitual residence, is unable or, owing to such fear, is unwilling to return to it.[60]

Building on experiences with earlier groups of European refugees, the convention is based on the idea that the international community has a responsibility to people fearing persecution because they no longer enjoy the protection of their country of origin. The convention provides a set of rights for refugees, most fundamentally the right of *non-refoulement*—the right not to be forcibly repatriated to their country of origin. That definition was designed to meet the needs of individuals fleeing persecution in the post–World War II period. The 1967 Protocol Relating to the Status of Refugees removed the geographical restriction, extending the convention's provisions to all those meeting the definition of refugees laid out in the 1951 UN refugee convention.[61]

Refugee protection does not extend to persons who have committed a crime against peace, a war crime, or a crime against humanity; a serious non-political crime outside the country of refuge; or acts contrary to the purposes and principles of the United Nations. However, those who have committed such crimes, although ineligible for refugee status, do have rights under international human rights law and international humanitarian law.

Today 147 states are party to either the 1951 UN Convention Relating to the Status of Refugees or its 1967 protocol, and the UN definition of refugees has been incorporated into the laws of many countries. The 1951 UN refugee convention provided the basic definition of refugees and enumerated the rights to which they are entitled. Central to the implementation of the convention was the establishment of a UN agency to protect and assist refugees.

In contrast to the narrow definition of refugee status in the 1951 UN refugee convention, in 1969 the Organization of African Unity (OAU) developed the OAU Convention Governing the Specific Aspects of Refugee Problems in Africa that expanded the UN definition to include individuals displaced by generalized conditions of violence:

> The term "refugee" shall also apply to every person who, owing to external aggression, occupation, foreign domination, or events seriously disturbing public order in either part or the whole of his country of origin or nationality, is compelled to leave his place of habitual residence in order to seek refuge in another place outside his country of origin or nationality.

In 1984, representatives of ten Latin American governments adopted the Declaration of Cartagena, which incorporated a definition of refugee broader than that of the 1951 UN refugee convention. In addition to the criteria in that convention, the Cartagena declaration defined as refugees those "who have fled their country because their lives, safety or freedom have been threatened by generalized violence, foreign aggression, internal conflicts, massive violation of human rights or other circumstances which have

Box 1-2. *Instruments of Refugee Law*

Convention Relating to the Status of Refugees (1951)

Protocol Relating to the Status of Refugees (1967)

OAU Convention Governing the Specific Aspects of Refugee Problems in Africa (1969)

Acuerdo de Cartagena (1984)

seriously disturbed public order." Box 1-2 summarizes the basic instruments of refugee law.

The development of a regime to protect refugees was in the interests of the large powers in the post–World War II period. While civil unrest is the responsibility of the state involved, once people begin to cross borders, it becomes an international issue. A system was needed to ensure that the movement of people fleeing persecution did not become a security issue for the states to which they fled. In 1950 UNHCR was established, with a temporary mandate of three years and a budget of $300,000, to help an estimated 1 million people, mainly European civilians, displaced in the aftermath of World War II.

While UNHCR was established in the context of the cold war to suit the political interests of the major powers, there was from the beginning a tension between humanitarian principles and political interests. Paragraph 2 of the UNHCR charter states that "[t]he work of the High Commissioner shall be of an entirely non-political character and shall be humanitarian and social." Its humanitarian, nonpolitical nature was affirmed in the preamble to the 1951 UN refugee convention. In the fourth paragraph of the preamble, the contracting states "expressed the wish that all States, recognizing the *social and humanitarian nature of the problem of refugees* [emphasis added] will do everything in their power to prevent this problem from becoming a cause of tension between States."[62] Even though political actions create refugee movements, UNHCR was enjoined from political engagement, which meant that the organization's hands were tied when it came to addressing the causes that provoked the flight of refugees. At the same time, UNHCR was given a mandate to protect refugees, which often meant that it advocated with governments on their behalf. The tension between UNHCR's nonpolitical role and its mandate to protect has characterized the agency's work since its inception.[63]

REFUGEE PROTECTION AND UNHCR

Providing international protection on behalf of refugees is UNHCR's core function—a function that has been affirmed by the UN General Assembly.[64] UNHCR's Executive Committee (ExCom) assumed its functions in January 1959, and discussion of international protection has been regularly included on the agenda of one of ExCom's two annual sessions. In 1975, ExCom established a subcommittee to study in more detail some of the more technical aspects of the protection of refugees and to report its findings to ExCom. The subcommitte was replaced in 1995 with the Standing Committee on International Protection. ExCom's conclusions have served as an impressive body of soft law related to refugee protection.

During the cold war, UNHCR's protection function served the interests of Western powers. People fleeing communist regimes were deemed to be in need of international protection, and UNHCR worked to find durable solutions for them, often assisting in their resettlement in the United States and other Western democratic regimes. But when the United States and other Western powers felt constrained by working with a UN body that, after all, included the Soviet Union, they created a new organization, the Intergovernmental Committee on European Migration (ICEM) to handle logistical issues related to the resettlement of refugees. ICEM, which later became the International Organization for Migration (IOM), always existed in a sort of uneasy tension with UNHCR. But UNHCR's work also supported the foreign policy objectives of the United States and other Western nations, including their decisions regarding who deserved international protection. Refugees were seen as both a security issue and a tool to be used in the ideological war against communism. For example, with the exodus of more than 200,000 refugees following the Hungarian uprising in 1956, the General Assembly noted that solutions were to be pursued but "under due safeguards in accordance with [the High Commissioner's] responsibility . . . to provide international protection to refugees within his mandate."[65] Loescher and Milner observed that

> throughout the Cold War, refugees and the security problems they raised were addressed as part of a broader and wider set of geo-political considerations and an understanding of security based on two major assumptions: that most threats to a state's security arose from outside its borders; and that these threats were primarily if not exclusively military in nature and required a political if not military response.[66]

UNHCR responded in ways that supported the U.S. position in the cold war, partly for pragmatic reasons (the United States was, after all, the largest funder of UNHCR) but also because it coincided with the definition of refugee in the 1951 UN refugee convention. Until 1967, the definition of "refugee" was limited to Europeans, which meant that UNHCR was not involved even when there were massive movements of people from other countries, such as the displacement of an estimated 14.5 million people following the partition of India in 1947. The geographic restriction was lifted through the adoption of the 1967 Protocol Relating to the Status of Refugees, enabling UNHCR to work in many other countries, but the emphasis still was on responding to the needs of those affected by the proxy wars between the United States and the Soviet Union.

The cold war affected not only asylum but also UNHCR's protection work in developing countries. Perhaps nowhere was that more evident than in Afghanistan. When millions of Afghans fled the Soviet invasion in 1979, UNHCR launched its largest assistance program, but it bowed to pressure from Pakistan and the United States to make assistance to the refugees contingent on their support of U.S. and Pakistani political interests. Refugees had to be registered to be protected and to receive assistance; however, to register, they needed to demonstrate membership in one of seven approved Afghan political parties.[67]

After the end of the cold war, UNHCR was able to exercise more independence, but it had to struggle to get the attention—and the support—of the United States to protect and assist refugees who were not of U.S. strategic interest. That difficulty was coupled with a growing asylum crisis as people fleeing conflicts increasingly sought protection in developed countries, and UNHCR's protection role frequently put it at odds with the U.S. government.

While governments in the global North accepted UNHCR's work in countries of the South, things began to change when increasing numbers of asylum seekers began to arrive on their doorsteps. Germany, for example, experienced an increase in the number of asylum seekers from 9,627 in 1975 to 110,000 in 1985 and 350,000 in 1989.[68] Similar increases were experienced in other developed countries. Improved transportation and communication, coupled with deteriorating conditions in the neighboring countries to which refugees initially fled, seem to have been the major reasons for the increased flow.

Governments of developed countries have enacted increasingly restrictive policies over the past two decades to make it more difficult for asylum seekers to reach their territories or, if they do, to receive asylum. Accelerated refugee determination procedures, visa requirements, fines against airlines transporting asylum seekers without proper documentation, and use of detention of asylum seekers served to reduce both the number of asylum seekers arriving in Northern countries and the number actually granted refugee status. Other initiatives to deal with the asylum crisis in the North included support for regional solutions and the development of the concepts of subsidiary and complementary protection, which were intended to prevent people from being sent back to places where their lives might be in danger without giving them refugee status. In the United Kingdom, for example, asylum seekers whose claim for refugee status was denied might be allowed to remain in the country temporarily on humanitarian grounds.

For governments of countries hosting refugees (two-thirds of which were in developing countries), there were other protection challenges, including cross-border attacks, militarized refugee camps, friction between refugees and host communities, and violence within refugee communities, and in some cases governments closed their borders to refugees or imposed other limitations on protection.[69]

During the 1990s a whole host of questions were raised about protection of refugees and about UNHCR's role—or the role of any humanitarian agency—in protecting people in situations in which the political will to address the causes of insecurity was lacking. From the failure of UN safe areas in Bosnia to the lack of action to prevent genocide in Rwanda and the global shrugging of shoulders over Somalia, protection of refugees took second place to strategic concerns. In 1992, the UN High Commissioner for Refugees, Sadako Ogata, began to report regularly to the Security Council on the potentially destabilizing effects of the refugee and displacement crisis. UNHCR engaged in new ways of providing protection, including temporary protection, cross-border delivery of assistance, preventive protection (working in countries of origin so that would-be refugees could be assisted and protected without having to leave the country), and working with military resources to deliver assistance. According to Gil Loescher,

> [f]or the world's most powerful states, the provision of humanitarian assistance was financially and politically a relatively low risk option because it satisfied the demands of the media and public opinion for some kind of action to alleviate human suffering. But it was also used repeatedly by governments as an excuse for refusing to take more decisive forms of political and military intervention.[70]

By the turn of the twenty-first century, protection of refugees was in danger, in large part because of increasing restrictions on asylum by the liberal democratic governments that had been the bedrock of the refugee protection regime. If wealthy countries were arguing that they could not afford to accept more refugees, why should governments of much poorer countries adopt more generous policies? The refugee regime had been characterized by the consensus that refugees had a special claim on the international community and that it was the responsibility of the international community to provide protection and assistance to refugees—not just the responsibility of the governments of the countries in which they happened to arrive. But by the mid-1990s, European governments were devoting considerable energy to discussions of which government was responsible for examining asylum requests for would-be refugees who had traveled through several European countries. Governments began to apply the UN definition of refugees in a more restrictive way, and increasingly questions were raised about the suitability of the definition in an age in which most refugees are displaced by war and violence rather than by individual persecution and travel to developed countries in search of protection. Many Iraqis and Iranians fleeing the Iran-Iraq war, for example, had a hard time proving that they were singled out for persecution.

Traditionally, people fleeing for political reasons followed traditional paths of economic migration. So in the 1980s, large numbers of Central Americans seeking protection from the consequences of the region's conflicts followed well-established migration routes through Mexico into the United States. But the line between economic and political motivations for flight became increasingly blurred. Some Central Americans fled because they had been specifically targeted by guerrilla groups or death squads, but many more fled because the conflicts had disrupted markets, transportation, and livelihoods. When they fled to neighboring countries, they generally were accepted as refugees on prima facie grounds, but when they sought protection in the United States, they entered the asylum system, which required individual determination of refugee status. UNHCR's efforts to protect asylum seekers increasingly brought it into conflict with the governments of the developed liberal democracies that were the main funders of its operations.

Even as UNHCR's protection role was becoming more difficult, the agency was under strong pressure from donor countries to become more active in emergency response generally.[71] According to Loescher, the biggest shift at UNHCR in recent years has been from its focus on protection to its focus on emergency assistance: Writing in 2008, he asserted that "UNHCR is not primarily concerned with preserving asylum or protecting refugees. Rather, its chief focus is humanitarian action."[72] While the needs of refugees and others affected by conflict certainly merited increased humanitarian response, there also was an element of political interest. If refugees could be adequately cared for and protected in their regions of origin, they would be less likely to seek protection further afield—particularly in Europe, North America, and Australia.

In 2000, the UNHCR launched a three-year process of global consultations on protection, struggling to regain donor governments' support for the 1951 UN refugee convention and for refugee protection.[73] Generally, the consultations were intended to reaffirm states' commitment to the convention, to resolve interpretive inconsistencies, and to devise new tools and approaches to situations not fully covered under the convention. The process, which included two years of focused expert meetings, resulted in two documents: the 2001 Declaration of States Parties to the 1951 Convention and the Agenda for Protection, which the UN General Assembly endorsed in 2002.

At the same time, the mandate of UNHCR was expanding. In some cases, UNHCR began to work more extensively with people who were displaced within their own country. Working with internally displaced persons (IDPs) brought the agency into different sorts of relationships with governments of affected countries. Unlike providing assistance to host governments to support their protection of refugees arriving from neighboring countries, working with IDPs meant that UNHCR had to become involved in what were essentially domestic political concerns. Because of donor pressure—and the fact that the vast majority of the world's refugees had no prospect of being able to return to their homes in the foreseeable future—the agency needed to demonstrate its commitment to finding long-term solutions for refugees. The 1990s therefore were heralded as the decade of repatriation. UNHCR's engagement in countries of origin was key to ramping up repatriation, but inevitably its engagement involved the agency in more political issues.[74]

While UNHCR's mandate includes both protection and assistance, protection clearly was the agency's raison d'être. Others could deliver relief, but UNHCR ensured that refugees would be protected. The Director of International Protection was the second-most important person in the organization, and a certain mystique grew up around UNHCR's protection role. Loescher reports that changes in the organization in the past decade seemed to indicate a relative downgrading of UNHCR's protection work, perhaps because many of the protection issues confronted by UNHCR in the 1990s involved asylum practices in wealthy countries that were the main funders of UNHCR. The decline in UNHCR's protection work has been of much concern to refugee advocates. For example, in 2003 NGOs argued against reductions in or stoppages of food rations by agencies including UNHCR and WFP, because such actions "effectively play a role in the forcible return of displaced persons" to unsafe conditions, such as in the case of Burundian refugees in Tanzania and Afghan IDPs.[75]

In the past several years, UNHCR has moved to expand its operations in several areas, by becoming more actively engaged in situations of internal displacement, by addressing at least some migration issues through the so-called asylum/migration nexus, and most recently by indicating a willingness to address displacement resulting from natural disasters and long-term climate change.[76] As the number of refugees in the world declines, there is growing attention to other categories of people forced to move, a tendency resisted by some donors and some within the organization who fear that it will lead to a decline in UNHCR's ability to protect refugees. Internal debates within both UNHCR's secretariat and its governing body have been heated, with some asking how UNHCR can expand its work to encompass more groups when its protection and assistance programs for refugees still have many shortcomings.

UNHCR's standing in the international community has in large measure depended on its commitment to refugee protection; for example, its ability to persuade governments to allow refugees to remain in their territory has depended on the agency's moral authority as well as its persuasive powers. Guy Goodwin-Gill observes that

> [f]or UNHCR, the politics of protection derives, as a matter of institutional principle, from the responsibility entrusted to it by the General Assembly. Protection must be humanitarian and "non-political" but it is also about individual rights and solutions. The art for UNHCR is not to allow solutions or assistance to have priority over protection. For if it cannot provide protection, it will be judged a failure and accountable, and not merely excused because it tried hard in difficult political circumstances.[77]

The centrality of UNHCR's work in protection is echoed in current discussions of peacekeeping operations in which there is growing consensus that the success of the operations will be judged by how well they protect civilians. Refugee protection then was important not only for the institutional development and perhaps even survival of UNHCR; it also was an essential component in the way that the international community has thought about protection of groups besides refugees. Refugees were to be protected because they crossed international borders, creating an international issue. Over the decades, refugees also were perceived to be a security issue, although the number of refugees involved in military actions, sometimes called "refugee warriors," was always a minority of the world's refugee population.

It is interesting to note that the international refugee regime was created in response to the collapse of the Russian empire in 1917 and underwent major changes (some would say collapsed) with the fall of the Berlin wall in 1989. In other words, the refugee regime was bookended by events occurring in Russia. The events of 1989 were responsible for fundamental changes in the nature of refugee protection and in UNHCR's role in that system.

Before looking at the third component of protection—the international human rights system, discussed in chapter 2—it is useful to digress a bit and look at a relatively recent group of people claiming a need for protection—internally displaced persons.

Internally Displaced Persons

Most people who are displaced by either conflict or natural disaster remain within the borders of their own country; they are internally displaced persons. Those displaced by conflict and violence are estimated to number about 27 million, with another 36 million displaced by sudden-onset natural disasters.[78] In comparison, there are about 15 million recognized refugees in the world, about 4.8 million of whom are Palestinian refugees registered with the *United Nations Relief and Works Agency* for Palestine Refugees in the Near East (UNRWA); the remaining 10 million fall under the mandate of the UN High Commissioner for Refugees.[79]

While the history of the international community's engagement with refugees dates back to the 1920s, the recognition that large numbers of people are displaced within the borders of their countries dates back only twenty years or so. In the early 1990s, a small group of human rights advocates began pressing the UN Human Rights Commission to take up the issue of IDPs, and in 1992 they succeeded in having a resolution passed creating the position of Representative of the Secretary-General (RSG) on Internally Displaced Persons.[80] Over the course of the next six years, Francis Deng, the first RSG, worked to compile existing international law applicable to IDPs and to formulate guiding principles to address the gaps in international standards. Within the course of a decade, the issue of IDPs was firmly on the international agenda. Roberta Cohen and Francis Deng explain the reasons for recognizing the IDP issue were of international concern. First, the numbers of IDPs were increasing. A report by Sadako Ogata, then UN High Commissioner for Refugees, estimated that some 10,000 people a day were displaced in 1993 and 1994, including both refugees and IDPs.[81] As tools for estimating the number of internally displaced improved, the number of IDPs was found to surpass that of refugees. But beyond the numbers, governments were concerned with preventing would-be refugees from reaching their territories; they wanted to address the needs of IDPs so that IDPs would not have to leave their countries. Dubernet goes so far as to suggest that protection of IDPs was a deliberate device to "contain" potential refugee flows.[82] Improvements in communications, the end of the cold war, and the growing recognition that consolidation of peace requires supporting displaced people through reintegration programs or finding other solutions to their displacement often were factors in decisions to give more attention to IDPs.[83]

There is no legally binding instrument upholding the rights of internally displaced persons specifically, as there is for refugees. However, international humanitarian law stipulates that civilians cannot be displaced in international armed conflicts, although the provisions are less straightforward for internal armed conflicts. However, according to Lavoyer, "as victims of armed conflicts or disturbances, internally displaced persons unquestionably come under the mandate of the ICRC. They consequently enjoy the general protection and assistance it affords to the civilian population."[84] But while international humanitarian law, international human rights law, and, by analogy, refugee law, are applicable to IDPs, the legal provisions for IDPs certainly do not have the visibility accorded to those for other groups protected by those international instruments.

The Guiding Principles on Internal Displacement were developed to address that gap. Presented to the UN in 1998, those principles reflect and are consistent with existing international human rights law and international humanitarian law and restate in greater detail existing guarantees that apply to IDPs in particular. However, the guiding principles are not an international convention or treaty or a legally binding instrument. There are occasional calls to develop an international convention on IDPs, but doing so has been resisted as a time-consuming process with uncertain prospects for success. However, once ratified by fifteen states of the African Union, the African Union Convention for the Protection and Assistance of Internally Displaced Persons in Africa, which is based on the guiding principles, will enter into force as a legally binding instrument. The Kampala Convention, as it is known, was adopted by African heads of state and government at a special summit in Kampala, Uganda, on October 22–23, 2009. It will be the first legally binding instrument related to preventing mass displacements and addressing the vulnerabilities and needs of those who have been displaced. IDPs are defined in the UN Guiding Principles on Internal Displacement as

> [p]ersons or groups of persons who have been forced or obliged to flee or to leave their homes or places of habitual residence, in particular as a result of or in order to avoid the effects of armed conflict, situations of generalized violence, violations of human rights or natural or human-made disasters, and who have not crossed an internationally recognized State border.[85]

The definition of an IDP is quite different from the definition of a refugee; it refers specifically to persons or groups of persons, unlike the definition of refugee, which focuses exclusively on the individual. Moreover, the accepted causes of displacement are broader, including natural or human-made disasters as well as the effects of armed conflict. For example, a person fleeing Port-au-Prince, Haiti, because of the devastation of the January 2010 earthquake is an IDP if he or she moves elsewhere within the country, but if the same individual, fleeing the same earthquake-caused devastation, goes to another country, he or she is not a refugee under the 1951 UN refugee convention. Similarly, while a person forced to leave his or her community because of a large-scale development project, such as dam construction, is an IDP under the definition in the guiding principles, that person would not be a refugee under the 1951 convention if he or she crossed an international border.

Responsibility for protecting and assisting IDPs lies with national authorities, which is obviously problematic in cases in which national authorities have contributed to the displacement. IDPs—although they far outnumber refugees—have a descriptive rather than a legal definition, have no binding international convention, and have no dedicated UN agency charged with their protection and assistance. Furthermore, because international recognition of the particular needs of IDPs dates back only ten or twenty years, there is much less academic scholarship, jurisprudence, and international awareness concerning IDPs than there is concerning refugees.

Humanitarian reform processes initiated in 2005 were intended in large measure to address the lack of an institution with dedicated responsibility for IDPs and the inadequacy of informal collaborative mechanisms to designate lead agencies on an ad hoc basis. Currently UNHCR has been given responsibility under the cluster system for protection of IDPs displaced by conflict, for emergency shelter, and for camp management. But the system is still in a state of transition, and the extent to which the needs of IDPs will be met remains uncertain.

While UNHCR has a mandate to protect and assist refugees, the primary responsibility for protecting IDPs lies with national authorities, even though national authorities often have created or contributed to the displacement in the first place. On a practical level, that means that while UNHCR generally counts on good relations with governments of host countries, such relationships often are more difficult in the case of IDPs.

THE PALESTINIANS

As a result of the Arab-Israeli war of 1948–49, some 700,000 Palestinians fled their country. By July 1948, the ICRC was providing protection and assistance to those affected by the war.[86] In November 1948, the UN General Assembly established the UN Relief for Palestine Refugees (UNRPR) to take care of the immediate needs of the refugees;[87] a month later, the UN created the UN Conciliation Commission for Palestine (UNCCP) to protect the rights of the refugees and to negotiate durable solutions to their situation. UNRPR contracted with the ICRC, American Friends Service Committee (AFSC), and the League of Red Cross Societies (LRCS) to provide humanitarian assistance.[88] However, a year later, as legal scholar Lex Takkenberg notes, two key factors led the UN General Assembly to create another entity charged with assisting the Palestinian refugees:

> The draft came in response to the announcement that the nongovernmental agencies providing relief to the more than 700,000 Palestinians, who had become refugees as a result of the 1948–9 Arab–Israeli War, would be unable to continue the aid operation beyond the autumn of 1949. In addition, during the second half of 1949, the United States, as chair of the UNCCP, began seeking alternatives to repatriation as the solution to the plight of the refugees.[89]

So one year after establishing the UNRPR, the General Assembly established the agency that would replace it, the United Nations Relief and Works Agency for Palestine Refugees in the Near East (UNRWA). UNRWA began its operations in 1950 as a temporary agency with a three-year mandate. UNRWA was set up to provide assistance to Palestinian refugees—primarily by creating jobs and supporting their local integration—but not to resettle them or to seek a political solution to the conflict that had forced them from their communities.

Unlike that of UNHCR, UNRWA's mandate extended only to the provision of assistance to the refugees, not to protection. Not only was a separate UN agency established for the Palestinian refugees, but around the same time, as Takkenberg points out, the UNHCR Statute excluded Palestinian refugees receiving assistance from UNRWA.[90] Takkenberg concludes that the "fact that UNRWA was only intended to provide assistance and that, as a consequence of this provision, the Palestinians would lack international protection, was not considered. It was also not considered what 'level' of assistance would be sufficient to exclude the Palestinians from the jurisdiction of UNHCR."[91]

In addition, in 1951, when the UN refugee convention was drafted, it was decided to exclude Palestinian refugees who were assisted by UNRWA from the convention. According to Takkenberg, analysis of the *travaux préparatoires* of the 1951 convention reveals that Arab states, who favored the exclusion clause, were concerned that if included under UNHCR's mandate, the issues specific to Palestinian refugees would become lost among those of myriad refugee populations.[92] Unlike that of UNCCP, UNRWA's mandate was nonpolitical and not explicitly oriented toward "protection" of Palestine refugees. Indeed, protection was viewed as separate from assistance and was not to be included in UNRWA's mandate.

Thus, a separate system emerged in the international community's response to Palestinians, one that did not emphasize protection. According to UN General Assembly Resolution 393 of December 2, 1950, the agency's role was geared toward the integration of Palestine refugees in the countries to which they had fled or subsequently had been resettled pending repatriation to Palestine. The agency also sought to prepare the refugees "for the time when international assistance is no longer available, and for the realization of conditions of peace and stability in the area."[93]

Some Palestinians were allowed to integrate into host countries, but most stayed in camps in the region, in accordance with the desires of Arab governments that opposed both resettlement and assimilation, which would have made it difficult for them to contest the legitimacy of the newly established Jewish state or to construct a Palestinian state in the future. Arab states insisted that Palestinians be excluded from resettlement programs. In this respect, in the early 1950s UNRWA served a useful purpose by providing "stability in a strategically important region by materially assisting the refugees and by preserving the internal security of the Arab states as a bulwark against communist subversion."[94]

It is the state's responsibility to protect those within its boundaries, but when the Israeli military seized control of the West Bank and the Gaza Strip during the 1967 war, those areas became "occupied territory." Under international humanitarian law, the responsibility to protect the population lies with the occupying power—in this case, the Israeli state. International protection was to be provided by ICRC, while UNRWA's role as initially conceived—in contrast to UNCHR's role with refugees—was not to protect Palestinian refugees (particularly not vis-à-vis the Israeli authorities) but to provide basic assistance. While that assistance was extended for humanitarian reasons, it also was intended to prevent the Palestinians from becoming a destabilizing force in the region. The reasoning seemed to be that UNRWA would feed them, educate them, and provide health care but avoid taking steps that would threaten the status quo. It is to UNRWA's credit that it has been able to expand its protection role over the past six decades, as evidenced, for example, in the deployment of staff with particular responsibilities for protection.

As decades passed and UNRWA continued serving an ever-expanding refugee population, the agency evolved to include protection more explicitly in its programming. The outbreak of the intifada in December 1987 transformed the nature of Palestinian resistance to continued Israeli rule in the occupied Palestinian territory. Frustrated by the inability—or unwillingness—of Arab governments to successfully take up their cause and impatient with the leadership of their own organizations, Palestinians, particularly young Palestinians, took on a more confrontational role.

The intifada also brought about further changes in the role of UNRWA. Over the years, UNRWA earned the respect of the Palestinians for its humanitarian work and the commitment of its staff, but there also was some ambivalence. UNRWA is seen by most refugees as a strong advocate on their behalf. But there are some who are more critical of UNRWA's role, seeing the agency as one "selected by the international community to perpetuate the status of the Palestinians as refugees."[95] In response to the protests and violence of the intifada, Israel closed the schools, sometimes for long periods of time. UNRWA estimates that about half of the teaching time for the first two years of the intifada was lost because of school closures and strikes. The violence strained UNRWA's capacity, although it began providing health care to nonregistered inhabitants of the occupied Palestinian territory. But the agency—like all humanitarian actors—was unable to prevent the violence. Under international humanitarian law, ICRC is charged primarily with overseeing the protection of civilians under occupation. But in the case of the occupied territory, ICRC depended on the cooperation of the Israeli authorities. At times, they were willing to let ICRC play that role; at other times, they prevented it from performing even minimal services.

In 1988, as casualties and abuses mounted, the UN secretary-general asked UNRWA to increase its international staff "to improve the general assistance provided to the refugee population."[96] In response, UNRWA hired "refugee affairs officers" to monitor the human rights situation in the occupied territory and to report on violations. There is some evidence that their presence served to deter violence in some cases.[97]

There are differing interpretations of the extent to which UNRWA has been involved in protection, even in the absence of an explicit protection mandate. Of course, within the meaning of the Inter-Agency Standing Committee's definition of protection—aimed at obtaining full respect for economic and social rights—UNRWA clearly is involved in protection.[98] Lex Takkenberg, a legal scholar and longtime UNRWA employee, maintains that UNRWA has been engaged in protection activities since its inception. He points to UNRWA's early emergency assistance and works projects, noting that "although officially committed to resolution 194, UNRWA's initial attempts towards initiating massive public work projects were tantamount to advocating local integration as an alternative solution to the refugee problem."[99] Given those two forms of assistance and UNRWA's role in facilitating Palestinians' labor migration, mainly to the Persian Gulf, and its longstanding education, health, and relief programs, Takkenberg notes:

> From this perspective it may be argued that UNRWA has been providing international protection to the "Palestine refugees" under its care from the very moment of its establishment. However, in the absence of an explicit protection mandate similar to that of UNHCR, the more traditional aspects of international protection, often referred to as legal and political protection, were for a long time not expressly addressed by the agency.[100]

While UNRWA's efforts to protect Palestinian refugees have expanded over time—including the creation of new staff positions such as refugee affairs officers and later operation support officers and a senior policy protection adviser[101]—other actors, such as the ICRC and the UN's Office for the Coordination of Humanitarian Affairs, have carried out important protection functions. In 2009, for example, ICRC's annual report notes that it "repeatedly sought compliance by Israel with its obligations under

IHL towards the Palestinian population living under its occupation, as well as respect for civilians by Palestinian authorities and armed groups." The report goes on to state that over the course of the year, ICRC made more than 1,650 oral and written representations to the Israeli authorities regarding the adverse impact of Israeli policies and practices on the civilian population. ICRC has shared confidential reports with authorities on the treatment and living conditions of detainees and, in 2009, on the conduct of hostilities during military operations in Gaza. In addition, ICRC's assistance policies in the occupied territory include support to thirty hospitals and provision of food and essential household items to individuals as well as water, shelter, agricultural, veterinary, and microeconomic initiatives. ICRC has made a major commitment to the occupied territory; in fact its operations there are its second largest in the world, after those in Darfur.[102]

UNRWA has had a more difficult row to hoe than UNHCR has had in protecting Palestinian refugees. A UNRWA paper found that "[t]he success of the UNHCR in offering real and substantial refugee protection, outside of the context of asylum, has almost always been contingent on active UN Security Council intervention or consent of the parties to the conflict."[103] Although Palestinian issues have been the objects of numerous Security Council resolutions, the Security Council has not championed and enhanced the protection role of UNRWA, nor has the occupying power, the Israeli government.

The tension between protection and assistance is vividly illustrated by Israel's attack on Gaza in late December 2008. The surprise Israeli military operation, code-named Operation Cast Lead, had the stated goal of ending rocket attacks into Israel by armed groups in Gaza, including those affiliated with Hamas. The attack by Israeli armed forces included the repeated firing of white phosphorus munitions over densely populated areas of Gaza.[104] Over the course of twenty-two days, aerial and land attacks killed 1,400 Palestinians, including women and 340 children, and wounded 5,000 others.[105] The attacks constituted an "unprecedented destruction of civilian infrastructure across the Gaza Strip, including hospitals, schools, mosques, civilian homes, police stations, and United Nations compounds," according to Al-Haq, an NGO affiliated with the UN and the International Commission of Jurists based in Ramallah, in the West Bank, which had field workers in Gaza during the operation.[106] In the course of the campaign, the Israeli military shelled well-marked UNRWA installations, including schools and its headquarters in Gaza City, which were shelled with at least three high-explosive and white phosphorus munitions. At the height of the crisis, UNRWA schools and other UNRWA installations provided shelter—and protection—for up to 50,000 people.[107] Israeli spokespersons justified the attacks as a response to firing by militants from those locations, but international observers and UNRWA denied that claim.[108]

When Secretary-General Ban Ki-moon visited the Gaza Strip and condemned the attacks on UN installations, "fire and plumes of smoke were still clearly visible, smoldering behind him, as he spoke in front of the UNRWA compound."[109] The secretary-general said that he was "appalled" by what he saw and said that two days prior he had received apologies from top Israeli officials for the UN attacks and assurances that they would not happen again. Ban said, "I strongly demand a thorough investigation into these incidents, and the punishment of those who are responsible for these appalling acts." Later in 2009, a UN Human Rights Council fact-finding mission conducted an investigation. Led by Richard Goldstone, a former judge of the Constitutional Court of South Africa and former prosecutor of the International Criminal Tribunals for the former Yugoslavia and Rwanda, the mission conducted a three-month investigation into the actions of the Israeli military and Palestinian armed groups during Operation Cast Lead. The mission, which presented its findings in a report in September 2009 to the council, found that serious violations of international human rights and humanitarian law were committed by Israel and that Israel committed actions amounting to war crimes and possibly crimes against humanity.[110] The mission also found that Palestinian armed groups had committed war crimes as well as possible crimes against humanity.[111] The mission recommended that the Security Council establish a body of independent experts to report to it on the progress of the Israeli and Palestinian investigations and prosecutions and called for the Security Council to refer the matter to the International Criminal Court prosecutor if the experts did not find that there was progress within six months.[112]

UNRWA has followed a protection strategy similar to that employed by many NGOs and international organizations: protection by presence, protection by monitoring, and protection by negotiation or advocacy.[113] As seen in the concluding chapter of this volume, those strategies have strengthened the resilience of communities and have mitigated some of the effects of the occupation. But when the bombs fell in Gaza in January 2009, UNRWA was not able to protect Palestinians; that responsibility ultimately lay with the Israeli state. As in other conflict situations, the role of humanitarian actors in protecting civilians from overwhelming military force is limited.

International humanitarian law mandates that civilians be protected in situations of armed conflict by all parties to the conflict, including governments and nonstate actors. But when those responsible for protecting civilians are unwilling or unable to do so, humanitarian actors often try to step into the breach, doing what they can to keep people physically safe and to ensure that their basic human rights are upheld. Humanitarian actors have been courageous and creative in coming up with measures to protect people when bullets are flying, bombs are falling, and land mines are maiming civilians going about their daily lives. And in many cases, they make the convincing case that the situation would have been much worse for civilians if it had not been for their actions. That is undoubtedly true, in situations ranging from Darfur to Gaza to land mine–affected areas of Angola. However, such efforts cannot keep people safe in the absence of will and cooperation from the parties to the conflict, a fact that humanitarian actors recognize. Consequently, they have devoted substantial energy over the years to trying to build an environment conducive to protection, by encouraging armed parties to respect international humanitarian law, and by engaging in public advocacy. It is not an indictment of the shortcomings or lack of commitment by humanitarian actors to point out that their efforts are often not very effective in keeping people safe. That responsibility lies elsewhere.

2 | *Human Rights and Protection*

Today the issue of protecting people, at least among humanitarians, is framed largely in the language of human rights. In fact, many use the term "protection" as shorthand for "protecting a person's basic human rights." After briefly describing the origins of understandings of human rights, this chapter looks at the relationship between human rights and protection and the burgeoning number of human rights instruments. While modern human rights law usually is dated to the 1948 adoption by the United Nations General Assembly of the Universal Declaration of Human Rights—which predates the UN Convention Relating to the Status of Refugees, adopted in 1951—humanitarian actors often have kept at a distance from human rights law. Defending human rights often means taking sides in a dispute, which conflicts with the humanitarian principles of neutrality and impartiality.

International Human Rights Law

The idea of universal human rights is of fairly recent origin. While there are many documents that are precursors of the modern human rights movement, such as the Magna Carta (1215), the English Bill of Rights (1689), the French Declaration on the Rights of Man and Citizen (1789), and the United States Constitution and Bill of Rights (1791), they often excluded women and people of certain social, racial, religious, economic, and political groups. The movement to abolish slavery in the mid-nineteenth century was an important precedent, as was the establishment of the International Labor Organization (ILO) in 1919, which was devoted to protecting the rights of workers, including their health and safety. But in general, while the concept of individual rights was well-known in Western countries, international law and relations between states were not generally concerned with such rights, which traditionally involved the relation of the citizen to the national state. The individual was not regarded as a subject of international law, and consequently his rights were not regarded as a matter of international concern, for international law regulated the relations of states, and international tribunals arbitrated or adjudicated cases between them.[1]

The idea of economic and social rights emerged in terms of workers' rights, and the concept of the right of self-determination emerged in the early 1900s.

The precursors of international human rights law focused primarily on protection of religious minorities, for good reason: if they were not protected, they would become a source of conflict and interstate war. Thus the Treaty of Westphalia (1648), which brought an end to the Thirty Years' War, established equality of rights for both Roman Catholics and Protestants in Germany. While the roots of the war were complex, one significant cause was conflict between Protestants and Catholics in the Holy Roman Empire—a conflict less about religion itself than about the political interests of those championing a particular religion. In order to prevent future conflicts over religion, peace treaties began to include protection of religious minorities. A number of Catholic governments insisted on including provisions protecting the rights of Catholic subjects of Protestant princes,[2] and in 1774, in a treaty with Turkey, Russia was allowed to protect Christians in the Ottoman Empire. The Congress of Vienna of 1815, which followed the Napoleonic wars, provided for the free exercise of religion and for the equality of the Christian religions in Germany, and it included "probably . . . the first provision . . . in an international treaty and instrument aiming at the improvement of the status of Jews."[3] The Treaty of Berlin (1878), which ratified the independence of Montenegro, Serbia, and Romania from Turkey, guaranteed religious freedom and equality—again protecting minorities in order to prevent religious differences and discrimination based on religion from becoming a source of renewed conflict.

Thus there was early recognition that peace agreements needed to protect minorities, particularly religious minorities, because protection of minority rights was essential to peace and stability between nations. In fact, the freedom and nondiscrimination clauses of the Treaty of Berlin were the predecessor not only of efforts to protect minority rights in the aftermath of World War I but also of the human rights provisions of the United Nations Charter.[4]

Following World War I, the Covenant of the League of Nations did not mention human rights and fundamental freedoms. It was concerned primarily with maintaining security and resolving disputes, and in that context, it was concerned about the protection of minorities in Central Europe, a focus that reflected the traditional idea that the rights of the citizen are a matter for the concerned state, not for the international community.[5] In particular, a number of treaties and declarations on the protection of minorities were established with the League of Nations as guarantor, providing for the "full and complete protection of life and liberty to all inhabitants without distinction of birth, nationality, language, race or religion and provid[ing] other guarantees."[6] Essentially they were bilateral treaties in which the rights of minorities were upheld, particularly with newly established sovereign states. Thus in June 1919, Poland was required to sign the "Little Treaty of Versailles," which protected national and ethnic minorities in its territory, before Polish independence was recognized and before Poland was allowed to sign the Treaty of Versailles. Often the provisions affording protection to minorities were imposed as a condition for admission to the League of Nations. In other words, while the League of Nations, the expression of global governance of its era, did not include a statement on human rights, it did recognize the importance of recognizing minority rights in maintaining international peace and security. Therefore there was an implicit recognition that human rights were not exclusively a domestic matter but an issue of legitimate international concern.

World War II marked a turning point in the development of international human rights law, through which the world's governments strove to ensure that the horrifying genocide of Jews and others under Hitler's Third Reich would never be repeated. President Franklin D. Roosevelt's Four Freedoms, set forth in his message to the U.S. Congress in January 1941, emphasized freedom of speech and expression, freedom of worship, freedom from want, and freedom from fear. The concept of human rights was further spelled out by Roosevelt in a speech to Congress in January 1944: the right to jobs, adequate medical care, and good education—rights that would later be recognized as economic, social, and cultural rights.

After World War II, the ideas of human rights became intertwined with the development of the United Nations. Member states of the United Nations pledged to promote respect for the human rights of all, and the UN established the Commission on Human Rights, which, although proposed by the U.S. government, was largely an initiative of NGOs.[7] The commission was charged with the task of drafting a document spelling out the meaning of the

---

Box 2-1. *Conventions on Human Rights in General and for Specific Groups*

Universal Declaration of Human Rights (1948)

Convention on the Prevention and Punishment of the Crime of Genocide (1948)

Convention against Torture and Other Cruel, Inhuman, or Degrading Treatment or Punishment (1984)

Convention Relating to the Status of Stateless Persons (1954)

Convention on the Reduction of Statelessness (1961)

International Covenant on Civil and Political Rights (1966)

International Covenant on Economic, Social, and Cultural Rights (1966)

International Convention on the Elimination of All Forms of Racial Discrimination (1965)

Convention on the Elimination of All Forms of Discrimination against Women (1979)

Convention on the Rights of the Child (1989)

Convention on the Rights of All Migrant Workers and Members of Their Families (1990)

Convention on the Rights of Persons with Disabilities (2006)

---

fundamental rights and freedoms proclaimed in the UN Charter. Guided by Eleanor Roosevelt's leadership, the process captured the world's attention.

International human rights law affirms that all human beings have certain basic human rights, regardless of their legal status, and that each person has inherent dignity and worth. The first human rights instrument developed by the United Nations was the Universal Declaration of Human Rights. It sets out basic rights to be protected, including the right to life, liberty, and security of persons; freedom from torture or cruel, inhuman, or degrading treatment or punishment; and the right to a fair trial, to seek and enjoy asylum, to an adequate standard of living, to education, to work, and so forth. Since then, in addition to the central human rights conventions upholding the full gamut of rights for all human beings, many other instruments have been adopted (to varying degrees) on specific rights for specific groups (see box 2-1).

Human rights law is applicable in all circumstances, including armed conflict. However, in emergencies, states party to certain treaties may exceptionally and temporarily suspend (derogate) their obligations on certain civil and political rights. Others can never be derogated. For example, the International Covenant on Civil and Political Rights (1966) provides that the following may never be derogated: the right to life; the prohibition of torture or cruel, inhuman, or degrading treatment or punishment; the prohibition of slavery and servitude; and freedom of thought, conscience, and religion.

As discussed, protection of minority rights and religious rights was one of the earliest manifestations of the international community's interest in human rights, perhaps because it was directly linked to peace and security. Wars had begun because a government oppressed members of a minority with links to a neighboring country, and in order to prevent such conflicts, guarantees were needed to protect the rights of such minorities.

During the long years of the cold war, human rights became a highly politicized issue. While the early resolutions, which had a general focus on human rights, were adopted by the General Assembly by unanimous or nearly unanimous vote, as the substantive issues became more specific, more opposition developed—between the Soviet bloc and the West and between developed and developing countries.[8] Human rights and protection issues remain highly politicized today. While the UN system can and does act to protect human rights in countries such as Timor Leste and Kosovo, it remains paralyzed in other areas in which there have been egregious human rights violations, such as Chechnya, Tibet, and Guantánamo—areas in which major powers have obvious political interests.

The International Human Rights Architecture

The UN Commission on Human Rights (CHR) was established on December 10, 1946, at the first session of the Economic and Social Council. As Paul Lauren points out, political interests were at work from the very beginning.[9] The tension between international human rights and respect for national sovereignty, inherent in the UN Charter itself, played out in discussions on the structure and mandate of the commission.[10] One of the commission's first tasks was to draft what was to become the Universal Declaration of Human Rights. While that declaration has become the cornerstone of the international human rights system, the original idea was to develop not just a set of principles, but a binding convention on human rights with mechanisms for implementation and enforcement. But the political interests of both the Soviet Union and the United States prevented the declaration from becoming a binding convention.

Over the years, the CHR was responsible for setting standards and drafting important human rights instruments such as the International Convention on the Elimination of All Forms of Racial Discrimination (1965), the International Covenant on Civil and Political Rights (1966), and the International Covenant on Economic, Social, and Cultural Rights (1966). "Never before in history had human rights been so clearly articulated and incorporated into legal instruments, and most of these created specific mechanisms composed of experts rather than government representatives designed to monitor and implement the actual treaty provisions."[11]

Through its confidential "1503 procedure," the CHR could investigate individual complaints against governments. It organized fact-finding missions, established working groups on both country-specific and thematic issues such as arbitrary detention; and named special rapporteurs or independent experts to investigate a wide range of human rights issues. The commission organized global conferences, beginning with the World Conference on Human Rights in 1993, and widely disseminated information on human rights. It was an opportunity for hundreds of NGOs to provide information on human rights issues, and its annual six-week session became a forum and a global network for human rights activists. The commission included thirty special procedures on thematic and country situations, and its Subcommission on the Promotion and Protection of Human Rights (formerly the Subcommission on the Prevention of Discrimination and Protection of Minorities) was made up of twenty-six independent experts.

The Commission on Human Rights was a highly politicized body, influenced by cold war and North-South tensions.[12] NGOs accused the commission of having double standards, of routinely criticizing some governments for human rights abuses while largely ignoring abuses when major powers were responsible. The five permanent members of the Security Council were virtually guaranteed seats on the CHR. Moreover, the single annual six-week session provided insufficient time to address the gamut of human rights issues arising around the globe. Following the terrorist attacks of 9/11, governments in many regions began to justify hard-line policies as antiterrorism measures. Most of all, there was concern that the commission was becoming dominated by states that abused human rights rather than those that upheld human rights. In 2002, for example, the United States unexpectedly failed to win a seat on the commission, and a year later the Libyan ambassador was elected to chair the commission.

Growing criticism of the CHR was reflected in *A More Secure World,* a report by the UN secretary-general's High-Level Panel on Threats, Challenges, and Change, which identified the commission as an institutional weakness of the United Nations, suffering from a legitimacy deficit and in need of remedy: [13]

> We are concerned that in recent years States have sought membership of the Commission not to strengthen human rights but to protect themselves against criticism or to criticize others. The Commission cannot be credible if it is seen to be maintaining double standards in addressing human rights concerns. [14]

Even the UN secretary-general referred to the commission's "credibility deficit": "We have reached a point at which the Commission's declining credibility has cast a shadow on the reputation of the United Nations system. Unless we re-make our human rights machinery, we may be unable to renew public confidence in the United Nations itself." [15]

A number of specific recommendations were made by the high-level panel, the most important being that member states should consider upgrading the Commission on Human Rights to a "Human Rights Council" that would no longer be a subsidiary of the Economic and Social Council but a charter body standing alongside it and reporting to the Security Council. A few months later, in March 2005, a UN report included a call by the secretary-general urging heads of state to agree to replace the CHR with a smaller standing Human Rights Council, which would be a principal organ of the United Nations or a subsidiary body of the General Assembly whose members would be elected directly by the General Assembly by a two-thirds majority of members present and voting. [16] In the intense political discussions preceding the World Summit, the recommendation that the Human Rights Council report to the Security Council was dropped in favor of making the council accountable to the General Assembly.

On October 24, 2005, the World Summit agreed to create a Human Rights Council; [17] that agreement was followed in March 2006 by a General Assembly resolution establishing the council. [18] The outgoing commission held its final session in Geneva three months later, followed within days by the first meeting of the Human Rights Council. The language establishing the council was aspirational: It was established to promote universal respect for the protection of all human rights and fundamental freedoms for all. It was to address violations of human rights, including gross and systematic violations, and to make recommendations thereon as well as to promote inclusion of human rights principles throughout the United Nations system. It was to be guided by the principles of universality, impartiality, objectivity, and nonselectivity and to encourage constructive international dialogue and cooperation in order to enhance the promotion and protection of all human rights—civil, political, economic, social, and cultural rights, including the right to development.

One innovation was the agreement to undertake a universal periodic review (UPR), based on objective and reliable information, of the fulfillment by each member state of its human rights obligations and commitments in a manner that ensures universal protection of human rights among its citizens.[19] The UPR is a peer review mechanism through which states issue recommendations to one another based on the information contained in three reports: a state's own assessment of its human rights record; the compilation document of the Office of the High Commissioner for Human Rights, which synthesizes all UN human rights information on the state; and a summary of stakeholder submissions. It ensures equal treatment of all states, and states can accept or reject the recommendations. While the state-issued recommendations have been soft, every state has shown up for its review session, and NGOs have contributed to the process. In addition, the council was asked to promote the prevention of human rights violations through dialogue and cooperation and to respond promptly to human rights emergencies.

The Human Rights Council has continued to use special procedures to focus attention on particular human rights issues. Currently there are thirty-one thematic and eight country special representatives and special rapporteurs who communicate by sending letters of allegation and urgent appeals, conduct country visits and in some cases conduct follow-up visits, and develop new normative principles.[20] In that regard, the work of the UN Representative of the Secretary-General on the Human Rights of Internally Displaced Persons can be highlighted for developing the Guiding Principles on Internal Displacement. A number of special procedures are relevant to the rights of civilians in armed conflict and natural disasters, including those concerned with adequate housing; arbitrary detention; the right to education; the right to food; and violence against women, including its causes and consequences. Virtually all of the countries with special representatives have experienced or are experiencing major conflicts (for example, Afghanistan, Cyprus, Haiti, Iraq, Timor-Leste, Western Sahara, Liberia, and the Democratic Republic of the Congo).

The Human Rights Council consists of representatives of forty-seven member states, elected by the General Assembly on the basis of geographical distribution, and the General Assembly can suspend, by a two-thirds majority of the members present and voting, the membership on the council of a council member that commits gross and systematic violations of human rights.

The record of the Human Rights Council is mixed. The provision for equitable geographical distribution has meant that African and Asian members now have a comfortable majority on the council (at least twenty-six of forty-seven votes), and they are using it set the council's agenda. The fact that countries such as Angola, Bangladesh, China, Pakistan, Thailand, and Uganda are members of the council raises questions about its commitment to the aspirational human rights spelled out in its founding documents. The council sits for ten weeks a year, and it is relatively easy to convene special sessions; only a third of its members are required to make the request. The resolution establishing the council provided for review of its functioning after five years, a task to be completed in 2011.

The mandate of the Office of the High Commissioner for Human Rights (OHCHR), created in 1993, is

> to promote and protect the enjoyment and full realization, by all people, of all rights established in the Charter of the United Nations and in international human rights laws and treaties. The mandate includes preventing human rights violations, securing respect for all human rights, promoting international cooperation to protect human rights, coordinating related activities throughout the United Nations, and strengthening and streamlining the United Nations system in the field of human rights. In addition to its mandated responsibilities, the Office leads efforts to integrate a human rights approach within all work carried out by United Nations agencies.[21]

Other human rights institutions that have addressed a number of rights issues are national human rights institutions (NHRIs). Since the UN General Assembly adopted the so-called Paris Principles in 1993—minimum standards concerning national human rights institutions—many countries have worked with the UN to establish or strengthen such bodies. Currently there are more than 100 NHRIs, with varying relationships with their governments, whose mandates may include commenting on existing or draft laws; monitoring domestic human rights and acting on complaints or petitions from individuals or groups; advising on compliance with international standards; cooperating with regional and international bodies; and educating and informing the public about human rights.[22] In his 2002 report, Secretary-General Kofi Annan placed a priority on the development by the UN of the capacity of NHRIs:

Building strong human rights institutions at the country level is what in the long run will ensure that human rights are protected and advanced in a sustained manner. The emplacement or enhancement of a national protection system in each country, reflecting international human rights norms, should therefore be a principal objective of the Organisation. These activities are especially important in countries emerging from conflict.[23]

As national-level organizations, NHRIs are well placed to monitor and advise on human rights issues emerging from conflicts, but in practice only a few NHRIs have done so. NHRIs have rarely taken the lead in considering the human rights implications of communities affected by conflict, and many are institutionally weak and are viewed as being too close to their governments.

One of the obstacles for both OHCHR and NHRIs to becoming more engaged in addressing the human rights of people affected by conflict is the dominant role played by the humanitarian actors, especially the International Committee of the Red Cross (ICRC) and the UN High Commissioner for Refugees (UNHCR). When resources are scarce and staff are stretched thin, it is hard for human rights organizations to decide to devote additional resources to human rights violations, which are understood to be the mandate of other organizations.

Over the years international human rights law has expanded to address the situations of specific groups, as indicated in table 2-1.

The Convention on Genocide

In 1946, the United Nations passed a resolution calling for a new convention on genocide. After a drafting process that took two years, the Convention on the Prevention and Punishment of the Crime of Genocide was passed by the General Assembly in December 1948, and it came into force in January 1951. The convention defines "genocide" as

> any of the following acts committed with intent to destroy, in whole or in part, a national, ethnical, racial or religious group, as such: Killing members of the group; Causing serious bodily or mental harm to members of the group; Deliberately inflicting on the group conditions of life calculated to bring about its physical destruction in whole or in part; Imposing measures intended to prevent births within the group; Forcibly transferring children of the group to another group.[24]

Table 2-1. *Normative Framework for the Protection of Specific Groups*

Group to be protected	Relevant international normative framework (year)	Competent international body
Wounded or sick combatants; hospital and ambulance staff	Convention for the Amelioration of the Condition of the Wounded in Armies in the Field (1864)	ICRC
Wounded, sick, and shipwrecked members of armed forces; prisoners of war and detainees; civilians; staff of relief operations; staff of civil defense agencies	Geneva Conventions (I, II, III, IV) (1949) and additional protocols (1977)[a]	ICRC
Palestine refugees	Resolution 302 (IV) (1949)	UNRWA
Stateless	Convention Relating to the Status of Stateless Persons (1954); Convention on the Reduction of Statelessness (1961)	UNHCR
Refugees	Convention Relating to the Status of Refugees (1951) and its protocol (1967)	UNHCR
Women	Convention on the Elimination of All Forms of Discrimination against Women (1979)	Committee on the Elimination of Discrimination against Women
Children	Convention on the Rights of the Child (1989); optional protocols (2000)[b]	Committee on the Rights of the Child
Migrant workers	Convention on the Rights of All Migrant Workers and Members of Their Families (1990)	Committee on Migrant Workers
Elderly	UN Principles for Older Persons (Resolution 46/91, 1991)[c]	None
Internally displaced persons	Guiding Principles on Internal Displacement (1998)	OHCHR
Persons with disabilities	Convention on the Rights of Persons with Disabilities (2006)	Committee on the Rights of Persons with Disabilities
Indigenous people	Declaration on the Rights of Indigenous Peoples (2007)	UN Permanent Forum of Indigenous Peoples[d]

a. Convention (I) for the Amelioration of the Condition of the Wounded and Sick in Armed Forces in the Field, Geneva, 12 August 1949; Convention (II) for the Amelioration of the Condition of Wounded, Sick, and Shipwrecked Members of Armed Forces at Sea, Geneva,

Table 2-1 (*continued*)

12 August 1949; Convention (III) Relative to the Treatment of Prisoners of War, Geneva, 12 August 1949; Convention (IV) Relative to the Protection of Civilian Persons in Time of War, Geneva, 12 August 1949; Protocol Additional to the Geneva Conventions of 12 August 1949 and Relating to the Protection of Victims of International Armed Conflicts (Protocol I), 8 June 1977; Protocol Additional to the Geneva Conventions of 12 August 1949 and Relating to the Protection of Victims of Non-International Armed Conflicts (Protocol II), 8 June 1977; Protocol Additional to the Geneva Conventions of 12 August 1949 and Relating to the Adoption of an Additional Distinctive Emblem (Protocol III), 8 December 2005.

    b. Optional Protocol on the Involvement of Children in Armed Conflict; Optional Protocol on the Sale of Children, Child Prostitution, and Child Pornography.

    c. Adopted in pursuance of the Vienna International Plan of Action on Aging, the first international instrument on aging, which was endorsed by UNGA Resolution 37/51 (1982). The Fourth Geneva Convention also contains two articles relating specifically to protection of the elderly.

    d. The forum was established by UN Economic and Social Council (ECOSOC) resolution 2000/22 on July 28, 2000.

The convention declares genocide itself, incitement to commit genocide, and attempts to commit or complicity in committing genocide to be a crime under international law. All signatories are bound to take measures to prevent and punish any acts of genocide committed within their jurisdiction by enacting appropriate national legislation and providing penalties for violators. Individuals are to be held responsible for such acts whether they were committed in their official capacities or as private individuals. Crimes of genocide are to be tried before the courts of the territory where the crime took place or by an international criminal court (which, at the time, was far from being established). Unlike other international human rights conventions, the genocide convention does not have a monitoring body or a committee charged with overseeing its implementation.

The genocide convention has seldom been used. In 1998, a Rwandan mayor was the first person convicted of genocide by the International Criminal Tribunal for Rwanda, but even then some questioned whether the massacres in Rwanda constituted genocide. The definition of genocide is fundamentally based on the intent of the perpetrators, and there are questions about what level of violence is needed for crimes to constitute genocide. The convention refers to acts intended to destroy a group "in whole or in part." There also are questions about the relationship of genocide to ethnic cleansing, a term that entered the international vocabulary as a result of the conflicts in the former Yugoslavia in the mid-1990s. Schabas notes that while ethnic cleansing seeks to rid a territory of an ethnic group by terror, rape, and murder "in order to convince those inhabitants to leave," genocide seeks to "destroy the group, closing the borders to ensure that none escape."[25]

There have been very few prosecutions under the convention. The provision that crimes are to be tried in the territories where they occurred means that it is unlikely that governments that are responsible for such crimes will ensure that they are effectively prosecuted. There is a better chance that they will be prosecuted when the government is no longer in power (as in Nazi Germany, Rwanda, and the former Yugoslavia).

The genocide convention was intended not only to punish those committing genocide but also to prevent it from occurring in the first place. In that respect, the convention has not been successful. Then UN Secretary-General Boutros Boutros-Ghali said that the UN Security Council was hesitant to call the massacres were taking place in Rwanda genocide "out of fear that if the council agreed that genocide was taking place, it would have no alternative but to intervene militarily."[26]

On September 9, 2004, U.S. Secretary of State Colin Powell testified before the Senate Foreign Relations Committee on Darfur. Investigations by U.S. officials, he said, had found "a pattern of atrocities: killings, rapes, burning of villages committed by *Jinjaweed* and government forces against non-Arab villagers [were] a co-ordinated effort, not just random violence." He then stated that "the evidence leads us to the conclusion, the United States to the conclusion that genocide has occurred and may still be occurring in Darfur." He went on to say,

> [S]o let us not be too preoccupied with this designation. The people are in desperate need and we must help them. Call it civil war, call it ethnic cleansing, call it genocide, call it "none of the above." The reality is the same. There are people in Darfur who desperately need the help of the international community.

But he did not suggest that the U.S. military intervene in Dafur in response to the genocide; instead he emphasized that it was up to the African Union to intervene.[27]

Rights of Stateless Persons

States are responsible for protecting their citizens. But what happens to people who have no nationality or who are unable to access the rights due to citizens—for example, the many Russians whose citizenship was revoked by their government during the Russian Revolution? The phenomenon of statelessness has been recognized as an issue for decades, and yet it has been largely marginal to the major debates on protection. Although statelessness often has been an "invisible" problem, in recent years there have been encouraging developments.

UNHCR estimates that 12 million people in the world are stateless, meaning without nationality or citizenship, in both developed and developing countries.[28] Without documentation as citizens of their country, they face discrimination and myriad difficulties in exercising their basic rights, such as establishing a legal residence, accessing basic services, voting, obtaining formal employment, and purchasing property.

While some are *de jure* stateless, meaning that they are not recognized as nationals according to the legislation of any state, most are *de facto* stateless, meaning that they have a formal nationality but cannot enjoy their basic human rights. Often the line between the two is blurred. De jure stateless persons are covered under the 1954 Convention Relating to the Status of Stateless Persons and customary international law, while de facto stateless persons are not covered by the convention.[29]

Statelessness occurs in a number of ways. In some cases, citizenship is simply revoked by the government, and at times revocation is accompanied by forced removal, as in Bhutan, Côte d'Ivoire, and Germany from 1933 to 1945. In other cases, lack of opportunity to register births and marriages, high registration fees, or cumbersome procedures make it difficult to access citizenship, as in Croatia, Ecuador, and Fiji. In still other cases, ill-defined nationality laws following conflict, defederation, state succession, or state restoration take citizenship away, as in Bosnia and Hercegovina, Croatia, Ethiopia, and Eritrea. Sometimes provisions in nationality laws are intentionally or unintentionally interpreted to discriminate between groups, and sometimes groups are removed from the census or gender-biased legislation prevents women from transmitting nationality, as in Bangladesh, the Dominican Republic, or Georgia.[30]

Statelessness is self-perpetuating. Without a nationality, parents have difficulty registering the births of their children and passing their citizenship on to them. Lack of documentation makes it difficult to marry, own property, access the labor market, enter into contracts, open bank accounts, start a business, or enter or leave a country. Stateless people face discrimination, heightened risk of trafficking and sexual and gender-based violence, and limited or no access to education and health care.[31]

UNHCR is the agency charged by the General Assembly with addressing statelessness, including the identification, prevention, and reduction of the phenomenon as well as the international protection of stateless persons.[32] The General Assembly has endorsed the UNHCR Executive Committee's conclusion on statelessness, which called on states to prevent statelessness, to take measures to end the phenomenon where it already exists, and to protect stateless persons. The conclusion also called on UNHCR to play a more active role in identifying and responding to statelessness.[33] UNHCR provides technical assistance to states to introduce legislation to prevent and reduce the prevalence of statelessness. Planning and budgetary limitations within UNHCR as well as competing priorities, such as large-scale return operations, have until recently limited the agency's response. However, UNHCR has responded to internal demands for greater capacity to address statelessness, namely by including the statelessness program in its 2010–11 budget as one of its four "pillars," or areas of work, in its results-based management framework, and in its planning software.[34]

Only a handful of states are party to the 1954 Convention Relating to the Status of Stateless Persons and the 1961 Convention on the Reduction of Statelessness: sixty-five states are party to the former and thirty-seven to the latter.[35] However, a number of instruments, which have large numbers of signatories, are relevant to the protection of the human rights of stateless persons in that they prohibit nationality-based discrimination, such as the Universal Declaration of Human Rights and the International Convention on the Elimination of All Forms of Racial Discrimination.

Women's Rights

Early champions of women's rights date back to the late eighteenth century, when Mary Wollstonecraft wrote *A Vindication of the Rights of Woman* and Olympe de Gouges penned the *Declaration of the Rights of Woman and the Female Citizen*. In 1946 the Commission on the Status of Women was established to promote the advancement of women throughout the world, and it focused on legal measures to protect the human rights of women. The 1948 Universal Declaration of Human Rights affirms the equal rights of men and women. Over the years a number of conventions have addressed specific aspects of women's rights,[36] and in 1979 the General Assembly adopted the landmark Convention on the Elimination of All Forms of Discrimination against Women (CEDAW), which is sometimes referred to as the universal declaration of women's rights. CEDAW enumerates a range of rights of women, including the right to education, health, and political participation and also the right to decide on the number of children that they will have and the right to shared parenting. The Committee on Elimination of Discrimination against Women has adopted twenty-six general recommendations on issues ranging from reporting guidelines to women migrant workers.

In 1993, at the Vienna Conference on Human Rights, the international community officially recognized violence against women as a human rights violation, and in the same year the General Assembly adopted the Declaration on the Elimination of Violence against Women. A year later, the Commission on Human Rights adopted a resolution for "integrating the rights of women into the human rights mechanisms of the United Nations and [eliminating] violence against women," appointing a special rapporteur on violence against women.[37] In 2004, the Commission on Human Rights established a special rapporteur on trafficking in persons, especially women and children.

Over the years, the United Nations has passed many resolutions regarding women, and it convened global conferences on women in 1974, 1980, 1985, and 1995. UN Security Council resolution 1325, on women, peace, and security, focused particular attention on the role of women in preventing and resolving conflicts and called on all actors involved in negotiating and implementing peace agreements to consider gender issues, including by addressing the special needs of women and girls during repatriation and in postconflict reconstruction. The resolution also called on all parties to armed conflict to take special measures to protect women and girls from gender-based violence.[38]

A particular theme in recent years has been the focus on sexual and gender-based violence, manifested in UN resolutions; in the adoption by individual humanitarian and development agencies of statements, guidelines, and principles on sexual abuse and exploitation; and in the development of new laws and policies at the national level. In 2006, for example, a law was passed in Liberia that, for the first time, made rape a crime.[39] In 1998 the International Tribunal for Rwanda made history by finding rape to be a crime of genocide and a war crime.

Rights of Children

Before World War I, there was little interest in the issue of child protection. Children were part of the private sphere, and they were to be protected by their families; they were not an issue of international concern. What really marks the entry of the child on the international stage was the Declaration on the Rights of the Child, written in 1923 by Eglantyne Jebb, founder of the Save the Children Fund in England, and adopted by the General Assembly of the League of Nations in 1924.[40] Consisting of only five principles, the declaration established the concept of the rights of the child and drew a link between child welfare and children's rights.[41] Reflecting the experiences of World War II, in 1948, the Geneva Declaration on the Rights of the

Child included as its first statement "The child must be protected beyond and above all considerations of race, nationality or creed."[42]

In 1959, the General Assembly adopted the Declaration of the Rights of the Child[43] and in 1989 adopted the Convention on the Rights of the Child. The convention noted that "the need to extend particular care to the child" was recognized in instruments such as the Universal Declaration of Human Rights, the International Covenant on Civil and Political Rights (in particular in articles 23 and 24), and the International Covenant on Economic, Social, and Cultural Rights (in particular in article 10) as well as in the statutes and relevant instruments of specialized agencies and international organizations concerned with the welfare of children.[44]

It was the Convention on the Rights of the Child that became the gold standard for defining the protection of children. The convention, which has been ratified by 194 governments (the only hold-outs being Somalia and the United States, although both have signed the convention), enumerates various rights of all children, including

—freedom from violence, abuse, hazardous employment, exploitation, abduction, and sale

—adequate nutrition

—free compulsory primary education

—adequate health care

—equal treatment regardless of gender, race, or cultural background

—the right to express opinions and freedom of thought in matters affecting them

—safe exposure and access to leisure, play, culture, and art.[45]

The principles of nondiscrimination, participation, and the "best interests of the child" are the foundation of the convention, which states that "[i]n all actions concerning children, whether undertaken by public or private social welfare institutions, courts of law, administrative authorities or legislative bodies, the best interests of the child shall be a primary consideration."[46] That principle has been incorporated into the work of many UN agencies and NGOs. For example, UNHCR uses the best interests of the child in determining the best temporary care arrangements and durable solutions for refugee children who are unaccompanied or separated from their parents.

In 2000, the Convention on the Rights of the Child was expanded by the adoption of two optional protocols: on the involvement of children in armed conflict and on the sale of children, child prostitution, and child pornography.[47] The Committee on the Rights of the Child, based in Switzerland and composed of independent experts, is the formal convention monitoring body; it receives reports from individual countries and makes recommenda-tions about how governments can improve the lives of children.[48]

Among UN agencies, the United Nations Children's Fund (UNICEF) has been at the forefront in embracing a rights-based approach to child welfare and grounds its work on both the Convention on the Rights of the Child and the Convention on the Elimination of All Forms of Discrimination against Women. According to UNICEF's mission statement, "UNICEF is mandated by the General Assembly to advocate for the protection of children's rights, to help meet their basic needs and to expand their opportunities to reach their full potential."[49] Accordingly, the main themes of UNICEF's work are young child survival and development, basic education and gender equal-ity, child protection, HIV/AIDS, policy advocacy, partnerships for children's rights, and humanitarian assistance. The agency's income for 2009 was $3.25 billion, the majority coming from UN member states.[50]

UNICEF defines child protection as "preventing and responding to vio-lence, exploitation and abuse against children—including commercial sex-ual exploitation, trafficking, child labour and harmful traditional practices, such as female genital mutilation/cutting and child marriage."[51] In that defi-nition, child protection does *not* include ensuring that children have access to education, medical care, or even adequate food and water, although that is a central part of UNICEF's rights-based programming. The child protection architecture includes not only the Convention on the Rights of the Child, UNICEF, and a number of international NGOs focusing on children but also a series of General Assembly resolutions and a special representative on chil-dren. Notably, in 1996, a former president of Mozambique, Graça Machel, presented a report on children and armed conflict. As she later explained,

> [w]hen my report was published in 1996 there was a strong, but little acknowledged perception that children were at best marginal to the "real" security issues of the "real" world. Now the UN Security Coun-cil regularly discusses children and armed conflict and the long-term protection of children is seen as a cornerstone of peace and security.[52]

The report was groundbreaking. In the same resolution that welcomed the report, the General Assembly also established the mandate for the Special Representative of the Secretary-General for Children and Armed Conflict.[53]

Rights of the Elderly

While child protection and women's rights have a long history of inter-national action, much less attention has been paid to the particular needs and rights of elderly persons. In fact, there is no binding international treaty upholding their rights, although the principle of nondiscrimination enshrined in many human rights instruments is widely interpreted as prohibiting discrimination on the basis of age. The *Convention on the Rights of Persons with Disabilities* specifically addresses age, noting the difficult conditions faced by persons with disabilities who are subject to multiple or aggravated forms of discrimination, including, among others, discrimination based on age. And yet globally, one in ten individuals is now sixty years or older, a percentage expected to increase to one in three by 2150. However, there are striking regional differences: while one in five Europeans is sixty years old or older, only one in twenty Africans is.[54] Perhaps reflecting the reality that the countries of North America and Europe face the progressive aging of their populations, there is increasing awareness of both the specific needs of the elderly and violations of their rights. Several regional human rights instruments explicitly mention older persons as a group in need of special protection, and there have been various efforts at the UN to raise the visibility of the issue of the elderly.[55]

Rights of Migrant Workers

More than 190 million people live outside their country of origin, either permanently or temporarily, including migrant workers and their families, refugees, asylum seekers, and immigrants. In fact, one in every thirty-five people is an international migrant.[56] While international protection is well developed for refugees and even asylum seekers, other migrants do not benefit from such protection, in part because their migration is assumed to be voluntary. However, standards for protecting migrant workers were initially developed by the International Labor Organization, and in 1990, the International Convention on the Protection of the Rights of All Migrant Workers and Members of Their Families (ICRMW) was opened for signature. ICRMW came into force thirteen years later, when twenty governments ratified the convention, and its implementation is monitored by the Committee on Migrant Workers (CMW). Notably, no government that receives large numbers of migrant workers has yet signed the convention. Nonetheless, human rights provisions applying to migrants can be found in binding international legal instruments, such as the International Convention on the Elimination of All Forms of Racial Discrimination.[57] Another legal instrument for the protection of migrants' rights is the Protocol against the Smuggling of Migrants by Land, Sea, and Air, which supplements the UN

Convention against Transnational Organized Crime, which was opened for signature in November 2000 and has yet to come into force.[58]

Further buttressing the rights of migrants, the position of UN special rapporteur on the human rights of migrants was created in 1999 by the Commission on Human Rights to monitor the rights of migrants in all countries, whether or not the state has ratified the convention.[59]

However, protection of migrant workers—especially undocumented migrants—is much less developed in international human rights law than the protection of refugees. Many observers note that the inclusion of undocumented migrants in the 1990 treaty on the rights of migrant workers is one of the reasons that it has failed to garner widespread acceptance, particularly among countries hosting large numbers of such migrants. The right to determine requirements for entry into national territory is one of the hallmarks of sovereignty, and governments have been reluctant to accept restrictions on that right.

International Humanitarian Law, Refugee Law, and Human Rights Law: Drawing the Connections

The three distinct legal strands of protection—international humanitarian law, refugee law, and human rights law—are clearly interconnected. Human rights law is the broadest in scope, applying in peacetime and war; to refugees, internally displaced persons, and those who have never been displaced; to civilians and belligerents. International humanitarian law, which predates both refugee and human rights law, seeks to limit the means and methods of warfare and to protect all those who do not (or who no longer) participate in hostilities. ICRC views the provisions for war-related needs articulated in humanitarian law as complementing the protections provided by human rights law.[60] It is important to note that human rights law is intended to limit abuses by governments while international humanitarian law is binding on armed groups as well as governments.

The drafters of the 1951 Convention Relating to the Status of Refugees took as their departure point the principles contained in the Universal Declaration of Human Rights, and the General Assembly adopted a number of resolutions strengthening the protection and rights component of UNHCR's work with refugees. The idea, according to Jane McAdam, was that the refugee convention would develop in tandem with human rights law.[61] She notes that in 1947, the Commission on Human Rights adopted a resolution that "early consideration be given by the United Nations to the legal status of persons who do not enjoy the protection of any Government, in particular the acquisition of nationality, as regards their legal status and social protection and their documentation."[62] In later years, the Human Rights Commission adopted resolutions regarding mass exoduses, and it was the first UN body to recognize the need for a normative framework to address the needs of internally displaced persons for protection and assistance.

Over the years, there have been efforts to bring human rights and refugee law instruments closer together. The UN High Commissioner for Refugees has addressed the Human Rights Commission and the Human Rights Council, and the High Commissioner for Human Rights has similarly addressed UNHCR's Executive Committee. The Human Rights Commission adopted a number of resolutions relating to the mass exodus of displaced persons and took the lead in addressing internal displacement when UNHCR was unable to do so. The UNHCR Executive Committee has affirmed the importance of working with UN human rights mechanisms, such as special rapporteurs, human rights field missions, and the Human Rights Council itself.[63] But there are reasons that humanitarian organizations such as UNHCR, ICRC, and many NGOs keep a certain distance from human rights issues generally and from the highly politicized environment of the Human Rights Commission. Humanitarian organizations are aware that their continued operations may be threatened if they are perceived as taking sides in conflicts or political controversies.[64]

States and academic and other institutions have been reluctant to view human rights law, refugee law, and humanitarian law as branches of an interconnected, holistic regime. The mandates of the protection organizations—ICRC, UNHCR, UNICEF, and OHCHR—all assign particular responsibilities to the institutions, making coordination difficult in practice. And yet there are clear links among them. Individuals, for example, who do not meet the criteria of refugees according to the 1951 UN refugee convention can be offered complementary protection by governments on human rights grounds (as well as compassionate grounds). Some refugee advocates have used the Convention against Torture and other Cruel, Inhuman, or Degrading Treatment or Punishment (1984) to prevent deportation of rejected asylum seekers. International humanitarian law contains provisions prohibiting the forced displacement of civilian populations during conflicts.

Both refugee law and international humanitarian law have been shaped by the development of international conventions on child protection and protection of women. On the operational level, organizations such as UNHCR have developed extensive resources, guidelines, and training materials focusing on both women and children. Humanitarian organizations increasingly are adopting rights-based approaches to their work. And in all three areas of international law, there has been a tendency to expand the scope of coverage of the relevant normative instruments. Thus international humanitarian law moved beyond protection of soldiers *hors de combat* to protection of civilians. Protection of refugees expanded beyond the geographic region of Europe to encompass the whole world and to include new groups of concern, such as returnees and those displaced within the borders of their country. And over the past fifty years, human rights law has broadened to include new groups, from children to indigenous persons to persons with disabilities—a trend that has influenced the way that humanitarian actors carry out their work.

These three branches of international law come together in their understanding of protection as an issue of basic human rights. Humanitarian and human rights actors have a broader view of what it means to protect people—they include the full gamut of political, economic, social, and cultural rights. In contrast, when military and peacekeeping forces refer to protection of civilians, they usually mean physical security and safety. But as the following chapters point out, different actors play different roles in protecting people in conflicts and natural disasters.

3

Protection and Humanitarian Assistance: Communities and Governments

While the concept of protection has a firm foundation in different strands of international law, the way that people are protected depends on the actors who are protecting them and their interpretation of what protection entails. Although everyone recognizes that it is the fundamental responsibility of national governments to protect those living within their boundaries, if governments were able to consistently carry out this essential function, there would be no need for humanitarian assistance or for the UN Security Council to grapple with what it means to protect civilians. But the reality is that governments often are unable to protect their people.

Communities' self-protection measures are the first line of defense from civil conflict. When armed groups enter a village, for example, and government troops or police are unable to protect the civilian population, communities respond in time-honored ways—by fighting back, hiding, fleeing, or trying to negotiate with the armed groups. A vast and complex international system of humanitarian response has developed to assist and protect communities when neither they nor their governments are able to provide sufficient protection. But it is important to remember that when international agencies leave—as they often do when the situation becomes too dangerous for them to carry out their work—communities are left on their own. That reality is recognized by all the major international actors, even though much—and perhaps most—of their work focuses on strengthening their own ability to intervene instead of supporting local communities' self-protection mechanisms. The Inter-Agency Standing Committee (IASC) asserts that "practical protection is provided first of all by and through the local community,"[1] and a recent paper on protection observes that "[i]n reality, locals are typically the first and last providers of their own protection."[2]

Former UN Secretary-General Kofi Annan, in presenting his 2001 report on protection of civilians, concluded that local actors are "the basic source of protection, especially when all other layers of protection fail . . . [F]unding and training [them] is thus an important investment."[3]

While chapter 4 looks at UN agencies and nongovernmental organizations and their approaches to protection, this chapter looks at protection from the perspective of affected communities, their governments, nonstate actors, donor governments, and military forces.

Affected People and Communities

The authors of a well-researched multicountry study on protection in practice conclude that "[m]ost people survive and do so without assistance from external parties."[4] It is well-known—though not often publicized by international agencies—that most of the lives saved in the aftermath of an earthquake or a cyclone are due to the efforts of local actors. The draft revision of the Sphere Humanitarian Charter 2010 acknowledges that "[i]t is firstly through their own efforts, and through the support of community and local institutions, that the basic needs of people affected by disaster or armed conflict are met."[5]

As Casey Barrs explains, when governments cannot protect their people, individuals and communities change their habits—they move, they hide, they rely on informal networks to get information, to protect assets, and to find alternative livelihoods. They may deliberately strip themselves of economic assets in order to avoid attack, seek to accommodate armed groups or political leaders, or pay off would-be aggressors. They may join insurgent groups or flee their communities or countries.[6] They also use a range of tactics for economic survival. Barrs notes that local communities "place such importance on economic survival that they often knowingly accept trade-offs in physical safety."[7] Such tactics might include subsistence agriculture, foraging, diversifying livelihood strategies, hiding or liquidating assets, and paying bribes or protection money. Families often rely on social networks to obtain liquid funds, either through loans or contributions from family connections.

In fact, when aid agencies, donors, and investors withdraw due to imminent crises, diaspora groups often increase their contributions to individuals at risk.[8] Schmeidl and others report that in Kandahar, Afghanistan, extended families often help the displaced, enabling men to seek jobs elsewhere while women and children remain under the protection of a male relative. Some of the coping strategies reflect the desperation of vulnerable people. Also in Kandahar, "the arranged marriages of underage girls, especially to less attractive suitors, are also an indication of a certain level of desperation and vulnerability."[9] While the international community often takes pride in the volume of funding transferred from Western countries to those experiencing a disaster, the amount of funding sent to people in crises through private remittances actually dwarfs all international assistance.[10]

In southwest Colombia, local communities have organized for the past decade to protect their rights, even as they have been attacked and displaced. That region of Colombia, including the departments of Cauca and Nariño, historically has been beset by land disputes between groups of settlers (mostly mestizo) and indigenous groups that have defended and reclaimed their land. In the last decade, conflicts pitting indigenous and Afro-Colombian groups against new biofuel and palm projects as well as coca growers have increased. The indigenous and Afro-Colombian groups are targeted by armed groups that seek to displace them so that they can pursue their licit or illicit economic ventures. In response to the attacks and to their internal displacement, the Afro-Colombian communities from Cauca and Nariño have formed resistance organizations such as COCOCAUCA (Coordination of Community Councils and Grass-Roots Organizations of the Black Population of the Caucan Pacific). These groups advocate neutrality toward the armed actors, seek dialogue with them, and promote the development of mechanisms for ascertaining accountability for past crimes (such as truth and reconciliation commissions) in order to obtain justice and in some cases reparations. Despite the challenges—including the adverse political climate, intensification of armed conflict, and, in some cases, persecution by the armed groups—the community organizations in the region have been able to unite their communities in efforts to reclaim or hold on to their land. The national and international visibility that they have attained has permitted them to continue working in the midst of increasingly adverse political conditions. In fact, the indigenous communities have been more successful in resisting displacement than nonindigenous communities.[11]

In another example, a protection strategy followed by internally displaced persons (IDPs) in Kandahar, Afghanistan, was to seek protection from local strongmen and power brokers. In return for political support, the strongmen delivered protection for the displaced, including land and access to cross-border trade. But as a coping strategy, patronage is not always reliable. When the power brokers turn to other interests, their protection of the IDPs may end, leaving the displaced grasping for alternatives.[12]

Barrs notes that most international actors devise protection strategies that are quite independent of those developed by the communities at risk. He suggests that international agencies emphasize community preparedness in the areas of physical safety and life-critical sustenance and services—and that they do so before violence forces communities to leave. That could include, for example, encouraging communities to develop safe exit routes and temporary accommodations in safer areas and ensuring access to accurate information. He also offers suggestions of ways in which international actors can continue their operations in dangerous environments by helping prepare local staff or partners for low-profile service delivery (with practical suggestions on downplaying identity, downsizing infrastructure, dispersing staff and supplies, and delegating work to others).[13]

Barrs is one of the few writers advocating that international actors complement their current approaches to protection by proactively helping locals brace themselves for violence. But there are ethical issues in such an approach that Barrs does not directly address. In Bosnia, for example, humanitarian agencies agonized over the question of whether to help people escape and thus save their lives, even though by doing so they would be contributing to ethnic cleansing. Is it more ethical to encourage or teach communities to hide, to strip themselves of their assets, or to bargain with the aggressors? Or even to give them guns to defend themselves? In places like Somalia and Afghanistan, people can protect themselves in the short term by paying tribute to individual warlords or abandoning their assets to them, but doing so, of course, fuels the conflict.

While few humanitarian agencies have followed Barrs's advice on how to protect civilians through community-based approaches, there is a growing movement within the humanitarian community to consult with beneficiaries in the design and implementation of programs, including protection programs. In fact, accountability to beneficiaries is one of the innovations in the humanitarian world. For example, the Humanitarian Accountability Partnership International (HAPI) and the peer review process within the Steering Committee for Humanitarian Response (SCHR) are efforts to make humanitarian efforts accountable to the people that they are intended to serve.[14] But a study carried out by the Brookings-Bern Project on Internal Displacement found that consulting with beneficiaries is not an easy process.[15] In the immediate aftermath of an emergency, people may be so traumatized that they are not ready to participate in decisionmaking. It is usually difficult for international agencies to identify the interlocutors or spokespersons for communities that they seek to assist, particularly when people are dispersed within host communities. When people are organized, leadership of refugee and IDP communities often excludes women. Should international agencies make efforts to identify alternative leadership, even when it is contrary to local norms? Sometimes consulting with beneficiaries puts them at risk, and in recent years, leaders of Colombia's IDP communities have been targeted for assassination, especially when they raise issues of land ownership.[16] But efforts to increase the accountability of humanitarian agencies to beneficiaries and to involve them in program design and implementation are based on the recognition that protection must be rooted in local communities.

For local communities, protection means first and foremost ensuring the personal security of people at risk. But protection also has a broader meaning, evident in community concern with protecting livelihoods and economic assets. Some Iraqis protected themselves from sectarian violence in 2006 and 2007 by leaving their country in search of safety in neighboring countries, but many Iraqis regularly return to Iraq in order to check on or sell property, receive pension payments, or engage in other economic activities necessary to support their families.[17] The International Committee of the Red Cross (ICRC) has documented similar ways that affected communities ensure their economic survival, including through sale of food aid in camps.[18] When governments are unable to protect them, individuals and communities develop innovative and often courageous ways of doing so—even or perhaps especially in the absence of international humanitarian actors.

Governments of Affected Countries

That it is the responsibility of national governments to protect their people is a principle enshrined in international law and affirmed by the United Nations. For example, in 1991 the UN General Assembly affirmed the following:

> Each State has the responsibility first and foremost to take care of victims of natural disasters and other emergencies occurring on its territory. Hence, the affected State has the primary role in the initiation, organization, coordination, and implementation of humanitarian assistance within its territory.
>
> The magnitude and duration of many emergencies may be beyond the response capacity of many affected countries. International cooperation to address emergency situations and to strengthen the response

capacity of affected countries is thus of great importance. Such cooperation should be provided in accordance with international and national
laws. Intergovernmental and non-governmental organizations working
impartially and with strict humanitarian motives should continue to
make a significant contribution in supplementing national efforts.

States whose populations are in need of humanitarian assistance are
called upon to facilitate the work of these organizations in implementing humanitarian assistance, in particular the supply of food, medi-
cines, shelter and health care, for which access to victims is essential.[19]

Many governments do a good job of ensuring that their citizens and others living within their territories are assisted and protected when calamity
occurs. Even when governments are overwhelmed by the magnitude of a
disaster—whether a natural disaster or a conflict—they usually play a major
role in humanitarian response. From a state perspective, a government may
perceive international involvement as an opportunity to deliver services that
it cannot deliver; it may tolerate international engagement, recognizing that
it cannot shut the door; or it may have an attitude of outright hostility.[20] Its
response is related to what Ashraf Ghani and Clare Lockhart refer to as the
"sovereignty gap"—a disjunction between the state's capacity to govern by
law and its capacity to provide for the needs of the people in practice.[21]

Being able to deliver services to its population is crucial to the legitimacy
and authority of the state—particularly during conflicts and in postconflict
situations. In fact, Britain's Department for International Development
(DFID) defines fragile states as "those where the government cannot or will
not deliver core functions to the majority of its people, including the poor."[22]
As Robert Zoellick, president of the World Bank Group, said,

> Legitimacy must be achieved through performance. It needs to be
> earned by delivering basic services, especially visible ones. Clean up the
> garbage. Build institutional capacity by doing things: supplying clean
> water; sanitation; simple roads to connect territories that may have
> been cut off from one another; electricity for some part of the day;
> basic preventative health care such as immunization.[23]

Zoellick goes on to say that to improve the legitimacy of the government,
it matters who provides the services: "They should be undertaken by the
government and local people as soon as feasible."[24]

But relations between the humanitarian community and governments
of countries experiencing humanitarian emergencies often are difficult,

particularly in conflict situations. When a government feels threatened by insurgents, it needs to be seen as being capable of delivering services to its people, and sometimes the government believes that the humanitarian agencies that ostensibly have come to help are sympathetic to the insurgents or have other agendas. Thus relations between the Sri Lankan government and the international humanitarian community often have been tense. While the humanitarians believe that they are trying to protect the rights of an ethnic minority that has suffered as a result of war, the Sri Lankan government often has accused them of supporting terrorists.[25]

From the perspective of humanitarian actors, national governments often are obstacles to the international humanitarian community's response. Sometimes humanitarian organizations argue that their principles of neutrality and independence mean that they need to keep a distance from governments—an argument that may hold up when the governments themselves are responsible for the conflict but one that often conveniently justifies freedom of action on the part of the international actor. In comparison with development agencies, which are more likely to work with states, humanitarian agencies tend to avoid working with national governments, often perceiving them as part of the problem. That stems in part from the nature of the work. In order to be sustainable, development projects need to be carried out and owned by governments. But humanitarian actors are not as concerned about the sustainability of their work, which, after all, is intended to be an emergency, short-term fix. In practice, there are many examples of cases in which international actors did not work closely with the state, with negative results. For example, in northern Kenya a U.S. military unit built schools for the population but did not coordinate their efforts with local authorities, which meant that there were no teachers to staff the schools.[26]

As Paul Harvey points out, governments have four principal roles to play in emergencies: they are responsible for identifying a crisis and inviting international assistance; for providing assistance and protection themselves; for monitoring and coordinating external assistance; and for establishing regulatory and legal frameworks to govern assistance.[27] But there is tremendous variation in the capacity of governments of countries experiencing conflict and natural disasters to carry out those roles. Sometimes governments are reluctant to admit that there are widespread humanitarian needs, as in Iraq, where the fact that by 2007 15 percent of its population was displaced was evidence that stability was far from being restored. The scale of the crisis may be such that the normal mechanisms for assisting citizens in need simply cannot cope. And in the task of monitoring and coordinating foreign assistance, national mechanisms often are overwhelmed by the sheer number of international actors responding to an emergency. Hundreds of organizations arrived in Haiti following the devastating January 2010 earthquake—many of whom had no experience or interest in being coordinated. That fact, coupled with an already weak government, led other actors to take the lead in fulfilling the government's responsibility for coordinating assistance. Similarly, governments vary in terms of their capacity to establish regulatory and legal frameworks to govern assistance.

Governments have a responsibility to ensure that international organizations entering their countries—even with the best of intentions—do so in support of the government and in compliance with its laws and policies. Sometimes that is frustrating for humanitarian actors eager to get on with the business of saving lives. Government agencies can be very slow to process visas, expedite the logistical planning required for the import of relief goods, and provide necessary certification for medical personnel.[28] In the case of Cyclone Nargis, the Burmese government initially refused the many offers of assistance that it received from international actors, which was widely interpreted as its desire to cover up the scale of the disaster and its own inadequate response. Indeed, French foreign minister Bernard Kouchner and others suggested that the refusal to expedite the delivery of relief supplies was grounds for implementation of the responsibility to protect doctrine.[29] While it is likely that the Burmese government's rejection of assistance was politically motivated, in other cases there may be legitimate concerns about the effects of humanitarian assistance. The arrival of large numbers of relief workers from hundreds of different organizations can be a nightmare for governments worried about assisting their people and about the political, economic, and social consequences of vast quantities of relief. Even the demands of hundreds of organizations for visas can overwhelm the bureaucratic process. Even the powerful U.S. government was unable to even acknowledge, much less respond to, the many offers of international assistance that it received in the days following Hurricane Katrina.[30] The fact is that receiving international assistance is labor intensive for governments. Robert Zoellick points out that the average developing country hosts 260 visits from donors each year. For example, Cambodia has twenty-two different donors in the health sector that provide support for more than 100 separate projects.[31]

Even when humanitarian actors are allowed to provide assistance, there are concerns about the impact of their actions on the host state. While a principle of international humanitarian assistance is to support governments in their efforts to protect and assist people or to complement their work, sometimes—as ICRC points out in its statement of professional standards for protection work—substitution for a state authority may be necessary.[32] But substitution is a double-edged sword. It may provide needed assistance when governments are unable to do so, but it also can let governments off the hook for carrying out their responsibilities to their own population. The government of Sudan, for example, has to devote fewer resources to caring for its Darfuri population because of the infusion of $1.5 billion a year that it receives from the international humanitarian community. Harvey notes that "[a]id agencies and donors currently bypass and marginalize governments partly because of a lack of trust in the ability of states to deliver effective and accountable relief."[33]

By creating parallel structures, NGOs and international organizations can undermine state authority. Sometimes they act without sufficient consultation and end up providing scant tangible benefit, as in the many cases in which schools were built by international actors but host governments did not have funds to pay teachers to keep them going. Some refer to Haiti as the "Republic of NGOs" because of the disparity in resources controlled by NGOs and those controlled by the government.[34] The concerns that host governments have about being overwhelmed by humanitarian agencies are real, particularly in large-scale disasters and particularly when media pressure inspires the establishment of many new organizations to respond to an emergency.

The various guidelines and manuals produced by international actors recognize the importance of working with governments. For example, the *Handbook for the Protection of Internally Displaced Persons,* produced by the Global Protection Cluster Working Group, has a chapter that recognizes the role of national actors and suggests ways to support the efforts of governments to carry out their duties, such as by collecting data on the number of IDPs, and to exercise their responsibilities to adopt laws and policies regarding internal displacement.[35]

As discussed in the next chapter, humanitarian reform has brought into being a set of coordination mechanisms. Clusters of international and national agencies and NGOs, coordinated by designated cluster lead agencies, are now the standard mechanism for responding to large-scale emergencies. The Inter-Agency Standing Committee's "Operational Guidance for Cluster Lead Agencies on Working with National Authorities" emphasizes that clusters are set up "to support and/or complement wherever possible the efforts of national authorities in key sectors of preparedness and response."[36] Specifically, "the Resident or Humanitarian Coordinator and

Cluster Lead Agencies are responsible for consulting national authorities on existing coordination mechanisms, in order to determine how best to support and/or complement national efforts and to identify and address any gaps in response." The resident or humanitarian coordinator and cluster lead agencies may have to take the lead role in coordinating the response, but they still must support national authorities, even when the authorities are not able to access part of their territory.

Clusters are expected to organize themselves whenever possible in a way that supports and strengthens national structures and does not create parallel structures that may undermine or weaken existing government structures. One way to do that is to set up clusters so that they mirror existing structures or ministries in order to support government humanitarian programs. One country in which that has happened is the Philippines, where the standard set of clusters was adapted in order to mirror national ministries. The Ethiopian context is characterized by strong government leadership; while clusters exist, they work to support separate preexisting government-led structures (sectoral task forces). The implementation of clusters has been uneven in practice because of confusion about leadership and the relationship of the clusters to sectoral task forces. The government co-leads the clusters.[37] Generally, coordination with national authorities is easier in sectors such as health and education because the clusters parallel the line ministries of health and education. In other sectors, such as early recovery and protection, a number of different ministries and government agencies need to be consulted in order to ensure effective coordination.

While national governments are essential actors in humanitarian response, they are not monolithic. Differences between central government structures and local authorities are common. For example, in Colombia, although the national legislative framework for responding to those displaced by conflict is strong, at the municipal level, mayors often lack the resources to carry out their responsibilities to the displaced.[38] Local military forces, particularly in areas of conflict, are important interlocutors and often act independently of national military authorities. Agreements negotiated at the national level may not mean much when humanitarians encounter roadblocks manned by local military forces—and much less when manned by paramilitaries.

It is the primary responsibility of governments to protect all individuals within their jurisdiction. While sometimes they lack the will or capacity to do so, sometimes what they lack is the will to protect *some* of their citizens— those of different clans, ethnic or religious groups, or political loyalties. For example, a mayor in El Salvador explained that aid was slow in reaching his village, which had been damaged by mudslides, because he did not belong to the political party that currently ran the government.[39]

There are few studies on how governments understand protection, but one intriguing study looked at differences between military and police understandings of protection in France. The study concluded that while the French military sees protection as linked to defense of territory and borders, the gendarmes (police) see protection not in terms of protecting national territory but in terms of protecting the population. Therefore gendarmes see everything that they do, from investigating crimes to policing traffic, as supporting the protection of the population.[40] While military forces tended to conceptualize protection in terms of national security, the study found that police forces had a more inclusive understanding of protection, as community well-being.

Nonstate Armed Groups

The presence of nonstate actors or armed groups is characteristic of internal conflicts, and it affects the provision of both relief and protection to vulnerable groups. The UN defines nonstate armed groups as groups

> that have the potential to employ arms in the use of force to achieve political, ideological or economic objectives; are not within the formal military structures of States, State-alliances or intergovernmental organizations; and are not under the control of the State(s) in which they operate.[41]

For the purpose of distinguishing between combatants and civilians, the ICRC has stated that

> [i]n non-international armed conflict, organized armed groups constitute the armed forces of a nonstate party to the conflict and consist only of individuals whose continuous function it is to take a direct part in hostilities ("continuous combat function").[42]

Often, given its mandate and the nature of the conflict, ICRC has exclusive access to areas of a country under the control of nonstate actors. For other humanitarian actors, such areas are considered "no-go" areas.

Nonstate actors (NSAs) come in many varieties, from warlords launching sporadic attacks on villages to groups exercising quasi-governmental functions over a defined territory to paramilitary forces that are closely tied to and controlled by state military forces. NSAs that are a party to the conflict are bound by obligations under international humanitarian law, including the obligation to protect civilians. In practice, there are diverging attitudes toward protection of civilians by nonstate actors. In southern Sudan before the 2005 peace agreement was signed, the Sudan People's Liberation Movement/Army (SPLM/SPLA) administered the southern part of the country, establishing ministries and institutions that largely functioned like those of a state. That also was the case in Eritrea and Tigray in the long years leading up to the independence of Eritrea. In such circumstances, it often is possible for humanitarian actors to negotiate with nonstate actors to secure the provision of assistance. The relief provided by humanitarian agencies serves the interests of the NSA by assisting its people; in fact, the provision of such relief may allow the NSA to use resources to support its war effort that, in the absence of relief, it would have to use to support its people. Thus, negotiations between UNICEF, the government of Sudan, and the SPLM enabled life-saving assistance to reach people in need through Operation Lifeline Sudan (OLS). Officially launched in April 1989, OLS was jointly negotiated by the government of Sudan, the SPLA, and the United Nations Children's Fund (UNICEF). But when a coup d'état occurred in June 1989, the cease-fire along the relief routes was suspended. While OLS continued to allow assistance to enter areas under both rebel and government control, it did so on an ad hoc basis, and the government of Sudan came to play the dominant role. Most observers make the case that the OLS negotiations contributed to a climate in which peace negotiations became possible.[43]

There always have been nonstate actors that not only are uninterested in protecting civilians but also seek to displace them in order to gain control of a territory. Many nonstate armed groups are led by warlords that are more interested in economic gain or embroiled in personal vendettas than they are concerned about protecting civilians or in upholding international humanitarian law. As Hugo Slim points out in *Killing Civilians*, nonstate actors have many different motivations.[44]

While humanitarian actors may need to work with NSAs to secure access to affected populations, there are costs in doing so. By negotiating with armed groups, humanitarian agencies may increase the legitimacy of such groups, incur security risks to their own operations, and enable relief supplies to be used, directly or indirectly, to support the conflict.[45] For example, in the early 1990s, relief workers wanting to provide assistance in Somalia had to pay armed escorts because the situation was too dangerous to allow unarmed civilians to deliver relief. And yet the money used to pay for protection of humanitarian workers was used to purchase weapons that fueled the conflict.

It has been recognized for some time that international assistance is not neutral and that relief goods are economic assets that can be used to strengthen armed actors. There are winners—usually only a few, especially armed groups that are enriched by territorial conquest, theft, and taxation. And there are losers—usually large numbers of civilians. Mary Anderson's classic book, *Do No Harm*, spelled out in some detail the ways in which relief can exacerbate conflicts. In particular, she summarizes five predictable ways in which that happens:

—Aid resources often are stolen by combatants and used to support armies and buy weapons.

—Aid affects markets by reinforcing either the war economy or the peace economy.

—The distributional impacts of aid affect intergroup relationships, either feeding tensions or reinforcing connections.

—Aid substitutes for local resources required to meet civilian needs, freeing them to support conflict.

—Aid legitimizes people and their actions or agendas, supporting the pursuit of either war or peace.[46]

For example, inequitable distribution of aid—or even the perception that certain groups are being favored over others—can intensify conflict between different ethnic groups. Often that happens because relief workers are simply unaware of ethnic or social divisions within a community. They may not even know that the local staff that they hire come from one particular ethnic or religious group or caste or that they are favoring one group over another.[47]

International Nonstate Actors

Discussions of the international humanitarian system rarely dwell on the primary actors in humanitarian response: host country governments, nonstate armed groups, and affected communities themselves. Nor do they focus on the multitude of local civil society actors that mobilize to provide assistance and frequently protection. They usually mention the importance of those actors in passing and then quickly move on to discussing the international players. For example, a recent assessment of the humanitarian enterprise by the Active Learning Network for Accountability and Performance (ALNAP) acknowledges the key roles of local actors but then moves right into discussion of the international players.[48]

International humanitarian action is a growth industry. During the 1970s and 1980s, humanitarian assistance represented less than 3 percent of all Official Development Assistance (ODA), but since 1999 has taken 10 percent of the total.[49] And not only is more funding being devoted to humanitarian response, but humanitarian issues have moved to the center of the political agenda. For decades, humanitarian issues were seen as marginal to the great issues of war and peace, but there is growing recognition that the way humanitarian issues are addressed can make either peace or war more likely. As will be discussed in the next chapter, this awareness has led to a number of reform efforts within the UN system—and indeed by donor governments through "whole of government" approaches—in which humanitarian assistance is to be used in pursuit of broader political objectives.

In fact, humanitarian assistance has become the preferred method of dealing with political situations in which civilians are being slaughtered. One scholar analyzed the ways that the international community can respond to major humanitarian crises, including military responses, coercive measures (such as sanctions), and humanitarian relief. Not surprisingly, he found that humanitarian relief was the most common response.[50] In cases in which the international community does not want to commit peacekeepers or take hard action—for example, by applying sanctions—humanitarian relief is a relatively low-cost response. Bosnia probably was the conflict in which it first became apparent that humanitarian assistance was being used as a substitute for political action to address the causes of conflict—if you cannot stop the violators from wreaking havoc on the civilian population, at least you can make sure that people receive basic assistance. The phrase "the well-fed dead" was coined by renowned American disaster specialist Fred Cuny in reference to the UN response in the Balkans, where the UN provided food assistance to the people yet ultimately did not protect them from being massacred.[51]

But while humanitarian issues have moved from the sidelines to the center of Security Council deliberations, not all humanitarian issues are front and center—only those that are important to the powerful countries of the world. Conflicts in the Central African Republic or the Solomon Islands or brush fires in Paraguay do not receive much attention from international actors, who rarely rush in teams of personnel to respond to such situations. Even humanitarian crises that are high on the international agenda do not stay there for long. Liberia, Bosnia, Sierra Leone, Georgia, Timor Leste—the landscape is littered with abandoned humanitarian orphans.

Today there is much more interest in humanitarian issues than ever before. More books have been written, conferences organized, academic papers presented, journals launched. Governments are spending more money than ever on humanitarian assistance. The UN system is devoting far more energy to reforming the humanitarian system than ever before. Field workers are spending a lot of time trying to develop coordination mechanisms, even when it means taking time away from working with beneficiaries. As one field worker said recently, "There are 400 international humanitarian workers in Afghanistan. Because of security they spend most of their time in Kabul. Actually they spend most of their time sitting in their compounds, sending emails to each other."[52]

Humanitarian action is big business. It is a tool of foreign policy of donor governments. It is the bread and butter of the estimated 210,000 staff working in humanitarian response—a figure that has increased at an average annual rate of 6 percent over the past decade.[53] At the same time, it represents a compassionate outpouring of support from ordinary people in every corner of the globe. Humanitarian assistance is full of contradictions—contradictions in motives, experiences, and impact.

Donor Governments

Donor governments—a small group of Western governments that provide more than 90 percent of the funds required for the international humanitarian system—are the drivers of humanitarian action. That funding is provided in different ways: donors both provide direct funding to the governments of affected countries and channel support to affected populations through UN agencies, Red Cross/Crescent agencies, and international and local NGOs that deliver the bulk of relief assistance on the ground. They have staff positioned around the world to monitor humanitarian operations.

While other governments, such as China and Russia, and other groupings, such as the Group of 77, wield influence at the United Nations when other forms of protecting civilians are considered, the donor governments wield power in humanitarian operations because they control the purse strings. Although "most donor behavior is rational from a donor point of view," as Carolyn McAskie notes, "the sum total of all donor behaviors doesn't produce a rational whole."[54]

In some cases humanitarian assistance is explicitly intended to further the interests of a particular donor government. Most dramatically, in the case of Iraq, U.S. Agency for International Development administrator Andrew Natsios made it very clear to U.S. NGOs receiving government funding to support humanitarian work there that their work was to support U.S. government objectives:

> If you even mention your own organization once when you're in the villages, I will tear up your contract and fire you. . . . You are an arm of the U.S. government right now, because we need to show the people of Iraq an improvement in their standard of living in the next year or two. And I have to have it clearly associated with the U.S. government.[55]

More often, governments require NGOs to identify or brand the assistance that they deliver as coming from the donor government or agency. That donor governments see humanitarian assistance as a tool of foreign policy and a way of furthering their own political interests is not a new development. Speaking in the mid-1960s of humanitarian assistance, Dean Acheson said:

> The overriding guide must be achievement of a major goal of policy—in this case, creating an environment in which free societies may flourish and undeveloped nations who want to work on their development may find the means to do so. . . . The criteria should be hard-headed in the extreme. Decisions are not helped by considering them in terms of sharing, brotherly love, the Golden Rule, or inducting our citizens into the Kingdom of heaven.[56]

While there is general recognition that foreign policy objectives are a major consideration in allocating the far larger amounts of development assistance (witness flows to Egypt and Israel from the United States, for example), there has sometimes been an assumption that humanitarian assistance is more immune to political pressure and is motivated primarily by human need. But the few studies on humanitarian assistance do not support that assumption. Using a sample of 2,337 cases of disaster assistance between 1964 and 1995, Drury and colleagues tested the role of political influence in U.S. overseas disaster assistance. They concluded that "foreign policy and domestic factors not only influence disaster assistance and allocations but that they are the overriding determinant."[57]

Another study found that "disproportionate spending is likely to flow to emergencies that are closer to donor countries than to those that are farther away." So Australia was a big responder in Timor Leste, the United States and Canada to Hurricane Mitch, and Europe in the Balkans.[58] Response consists not only of funds but also political energy and support for solutions under the aegis of the United Nations. Thus Australia sent troops to Timor Leste to lead the UN peacekeeping operations, while NATO airstrikes were ultimately responsible for driving the Serbs to the negotiation table, where they eventually signed the Dayton peace agreement, which ended the conflict in Bosnia.

Geography, of course, is just one of many factors that drive donors' responses to particular emergencies. Domestic constituencies are important in driving foreign aid, but surprisingly they have not been a major factor in determining response to mass atrocities. There was no grassroots movement demanding action in the face of the Rwandan genocide, the ongoing war in the Democratic Republic of the Congo, the final offensive of the Sri Lankan government against the Tamil Tigers, or the conflict in Somalia. In several cases, however, such as the response to the massive displacement of Iraqi Kurds in 1991 and to the conflict in Bosnia in the 1990s, transnational advocacy networks have played important roles. In Darfur, grassroots organizing led to the powerful Save Darfur alliance, which has been vocal in raising the issue of human rights violations in Darfur and successful in generating huge amounts of humanitarian assistance, although it has been less successful in bringing about an end to the violence, which has killed and displaced so many people. Response to emergencies can serve a public diplomacy or public relations purpose. The U.S. response to Muslim countries affected by the Indian Ocean tsunami and to the Pakistan earthquake resulted in at least temporary increases in positive perceptions of the United States in some Muslim populations.[59] Smillie and Minear report that while egregiously disproportionate responses are not new, they

> are the reasons that multilateral humanitarian institutions and the Red Cross movement were created: to provide an anchor against the prevailing political winds and to reduce the influence on humanitarian action of unilateralism and of bilateral political agendas. Today, however, the foreign policy interests of donor countries exercise growing influence on the humanitarian behavior of UN agencies and NGOs, skewing their efforts and muting the advocacy on behalf of victims.[60]

Sometimes those interests are expressed directly in meetings between donors and multilateral bodies, but they also operate via a sort of "self-censorship" on the part of the international agencies, as when an agency does not suggest a particular course of action because it knows that it will be opposed by a major donor.

At least some donor governments are increasingly emphasizing protection in their approaches to and their funding of emergency situations, including funding channeled through NGOs. For example, protection is one of the ten sectors funded by the Office of U.S. Foreign Disaster Assistance (OFDA):

> Protection activities assist internally displaced persons and other vulnerable populations in reducing or managing risks associated with violence, abuse, harassment, and exploitation. OFDA strongly encourages implementing partners to mainstream protection considerations into the design, implementation, and evaluation of assistance programs wherever possible and appropriate. Since 2005, USAID has funded protection of vulnerable populations as a stand-alone humanitarian sector.[61]

According to Cohen and Calabia, the USAID/OFDA *Field Operations Guide* had earlier excluded "protection" from USAID responsibilities and funding. But Cohen and Calabia note that the 2004 policy

> breaks ground in addressing the "protection" needs of the beneficiaries, pointing out that "material assistance alone often cannot ensure the well-being of IDPs." It speaks of enhancing "the safety" of IDPs from "violence, abuse, exploitation, and harassment," calls for the inclusion of "practical protection measures" in humanitarian assistance and development strategies, and notes that relief and development assistance are often jeopardized by conflict, unchecked human rights violations and the physical endangerment of IDPs.[62]

In terms of funding protection, OFDA reports that in FY2009 it provided "more than $30 million to 25 UN agencies and non-governmental organizations (NGOs) for stand-alone protection activities in 14 countries, addressing child protection, gender-based violence, psychosocial support services, and protection coordination and advocacy." In the first six months of FY2010, OFDA provided some $13.5 million for protection work in eleven countries.[63]

In contrast to USAID, the United Kingdom's Department for International Development does not refer as clearly to protection in its programming. The country plans for its top two recipients of humanitarian aid, Sudan and the Democratic Republic of the Congo, do not mention protection. However, references to protection are scattered throughout its descriptions of programs, as when it refers to its "Protection of basic services programme" for small grants for welfare, education, health, agriculture, water and sanitation, and government and civil society. It labels its HIV/AIDS work for women and girls who were sexually assaulted during the Rwandan genocide as "Protecting the most vulnerable."[64] DFID also has "social protection" programs that provide cash or both cash and food for the poorest of the poor affected by economic crises in, for example, Bangladesh, Pakistan, Mozambique, Ghana, and Ethiopia.[65] As DFID's 2000 white paper explains, the government of the United Kingdom holds that investing in the poor and in social protection is critical to advancing economic development: "The UK government believes that good social policy goes together with good economic policy: investment in social services and social protection is an essential investment in economic development."[66]

Switzerland and the United Kingdom have developed major programs in support of "protection of civilians" and, like other donors, have funded NGOs to carry out protection work on the ground in many situations. Like other international actors, they have very different, almost ad hoc understandings of what protection entails in practice. The government of Sweden is far more straightforward. In Sweden's 2004–05 policy on humanitarian aid, protection is one of the two pillars of humanitarian assistance, the other being "material aid." In its policy, Sweden defines protection as including "measures designed to ensure respect for the rights of people in need, in particular the right to physical safety and dignity." The policy goes on to state:

> Related measures include calling attention to the obligations of armed groups, registration of the status of refugees or internally displaced persons and education about rights and obligations under international law. In many cases, individual humanitarian actions comprise both material aid and protection, since material aid protects the rights of vulnerable person and protective measures improve the individual's chances of receiving material aid. The crucial criterion for humanitarian action is the individual's need of material aid or protection, or both.[67]

Canada's Department of Foreign Affairs and International Trade (DFAIT) includes the Stabilization and Reconstruction Task Force (START), created in 2005, which is involved in "civilian protection," among other activities, under the rubric of "enhancing reconstruction and stabilization" in fragile states through its Global Peace and Security Fund, which has a $146 million budget for fiscal year 2010–11.[68] The humanitarian affairs pillar of START includes activities for the "human rights and protection of civilians," which includes "legal and physical protection of civilians." DFAIT notes on its website that Canada has played a key role in strengthening protection in the international system, including at the UN Security Council vis-à-vis resolutions on protection and through the International Criminal Court, and it notes its "historical role" in the protection of children in armed conflict.[69]

In addition to the Western donors, there are new "nontraditional" donor governments, particularly in China and central European states. Chinese foreign assistance is a bit mysterious, as the government does not produce official data and some Chinese aid seems to resemble ODA while other aspects of it seem like foreign investment.[70] China began reporting to the Financial Tracking Service of the Office for the Coordinator of Humanitarian Affairs in 2007, but it is not consistent in doing so.[71] According to research by New York University in 2007–08,

> which is largely based upon news reports of Chinese foreign economic activity, PRC foreign assistance and government-supported economic projects in Africa, Latin America, and Southeast Asia grew from less than $1 billion in 2002 to $27.5 billion in 2006 and $25 billion in 2007. Aid and related investment to Africa showed the most significant increase. These totals, however, should be interpreted with caution. Some aggregate values may be inflated: Some PRC loans or aid pledges may not have been fulfilled and some aid pledges that include multiple projects or that span several years may have been counted more than once. Some PRC investment activities may more closely resemble FDI [foreign direct investment] than aid. In other ways, totals may be undervalued, such as when economic projects or data have not been reported or when the values of Chinese materials and labor have not been included.[72]

Good Humanitarian Donorship Initiative

At a time when donors were pressuring NGOs to increase their accountability, the donor governments themselves were criticized for lack of accountability. In June 2003, representatives of donor governments, multilateral institutions, the UN, the Red Cross/Red Crescent agencies, and NGOs met in Stockholm to discuss the disarray of humanitarian funding that had been found in studies previously commissioned under the rubric of the Humanitarian Financing Initiative. The conference resulted in the creation of the Good Humanitarian Donorship Initiative and agreement on a set of principles, including

—the need to allocate funds based on needs

—the critical importance of international humanitarian, refugee, and human rights law

—the necessity of preserving the principles of humanity, impartiality, and independence of humanitarian aid

—the importance of using civilian channels of assistance whenever possible.

Several years later, a Spanish NGO, Development Assistance Research Associates (DARA) launched the Humanitarian Response Index to measure and evaluate how well donor governments are living up to their own principles.[73] The index, which is published annually, ranks governments against their commitments using nearly sixty indicators. Perhaps not surprisingly, the top-ranked states in the index have been Norway and Sweden—countries that rank near the top of most assessments of official development assistance.

Military Forces

It is important to recognize that the donors are far from monolithic. For example, there are differences between foreign ministries and specialized aid agencies. In the case of the U.S. government, some twenty-eight different departments and agencies are involved in overseas assistance, ranging from the Department of Agriculture to the Federal Emergency Management Agency (FEMA). In spite of various foreign assistance reform efforts and interagency processes, coordination often is lacking.[74] Moreover, military actors are becoming increasingly important in delivery of humanitarian assistance. In the United States, the military's share of overall foreign aid (not just emergency aid) increased from 5 to 22 percent between 1998 and 2005.[75]

Military forces globally are becoming more engaged in protecting civilians, whether coalition forces fighting in places such as Afghanistan or UN peacekeeping forces in places where protection of civilians has become an accepted (though not unambiguous) part of UN peace operations. Sadako Ogata reports that in the 1990s, the UN High Commissioner for Refugees (UNHCR) began to work more intensively with military forces, which led the agency to change both the way that it viewed the military and its perception of itself. And in Bosnia and later in Kosovo, NATO forces took the lead not only in bombing and military campaigns, but also in the efforts to build and maintain refugee camps in neighboring countries.[76]

The terrorist attacks of 9/11 and the resulting global war on terror propelled military engagement in work traditionally considered humanitarian. Strategically, involvement with humanitarian work was a way of "showing the world, and particularly Muslim populations, that operations in the 'War on Terror' are not uncaring of innocent civilians in conflict zones."[77] Indeed, President George W. Bush nearly doubled official development assistance (ODA) between 2001 and 2006, from $12.6 billion to $23 billion—most of it destined to support the fight against terrorism in Iraq, Afghanistan, and other "frontline states."[78] But that increase in assistance was accompanied by a trend in which Western governments increasingly view their militaries as "the most secure vehicle through which to channel and target aid."[79] Some have suggested that the increasing emphasis on humanitarian assistance may also be a useful recruitment tool for military forces. A Steering Committee for Humanitarian Response position paper refers to television commercials produced by defense ministries in the United Kingdom and the Netherlands, for example, that "reinforc[e] the public's understanding that military are humanitarian workers in uniform."[80]

While the involvement of European military forces has been evident in the Balkans, Afghanistan, and other areas, the militarization of assistance has been most dramatic in the United States. As Brigety remarked in 2008, "No other ministry of defense within the donor community approaches the share of national ODA earmarked by the Pentagon."[81] This discussion therefore focuses largely on the U.S. military's engagement with protection.

It should be noted that while humanitarian agencies draw clear distinctions between humanitarian and development assistance, the military uses the terms interchangeably.[82] According to the U.S. *Civil Affairs Operations* field manual, foreign humanitarian assistance programs are "conducted to relieve or reduce the results of natural or man-made disasters or other endemic conditions such as pain, disease, hunger or privation that might present a serious threat to life or that can result in great damage to or loss of property."[83] The funding mechanisms are called humanitarian and civic assistance (HCA) and humanitarian assistance (HA). HCA is limited to activities that promote the security interests of the United States and the host country, and those activities must contribute to the operational readiness of U.S. military forces and must be carried out by U.S. military forces; HA faces fewer restrictions. HA is intended to be "used for the purpose of providing transportation of humanitarian relief and for other humanitarian purposes worldwide and can be implemented by local contractors."[84]

The military's increasing engagement in humanitarian assistance stems from several factors:

the realization on the part of the military that counterinsurgency campaigns require increased attention to civilian protection and well-being; the decreasing capacity of traditional U.S. development agencies, particularly USAID; and the search for a new military role relevant in the post–cold war era. The U.S. counterinsurgency manual states that counterinsurgency (COIN) "is an extremely complex form of warfare. At its core, COIN is a struggle for the population's support. The protection, welfare, and support of the people are vital to success. Gaining and maintaining that support is a formidable challenge."[85] The manual later acknowledges the difficult but important task of protecting noncombatants in the midst of counterinsurgency operations.[86] Finally, in the context of civil-military operations (CMO), the manual says

> The military's role is to provide protection, identify needs, facilitate CMO, and use improvements in social conditions as leverage to build networks and mobilize the populace. . . . There is no such thing as impartial humanitarian assistance or CMO in COIN. Whenever someone is helped, someone else is hurt, not least the insurgents. So civil and humanitarian assistance personnel often become targets. Protecting them is a matter not only of providing a close-in defense, but also of creating a secure environment by co-opting local beneficiaries of aid and their leaders.[87]

The U.S. military tends to see protection as the physical defense of particular "individuals, communities and installations."[88] Paul Williams, writing about civilian protection for the National Defense University, suggests adapting ICRC's "egg model" to an "onion model" of protection, in which physical protection from imminent violence is at the center, surrounded by three layers: provision of basic necessities, enjoyment of human rights, and maintenance of an environment conducive to protection and human rights. He argues that while people can survive without the outer three layers, physical protection is essential to all the layers. He goes on to outline four military strategies for protecting civilians, two of which focus on physical protection (deterrence of violence through military presence or threat and defense of vulnerable civilians in fixed locations) and two of which focus on halting the actions of perpetrators (compellence, or disruption of the means and capabilities of perpetrators; and offense, or military attack and defeat of perpetrators).[89]

Protection of civilians thus has become part of the military's understanding of counterinsurgency operations. But as Victoria Holt argued in 2006, "military actors have worked with other agencies—humanitarian, human rights, developmental and political—in the field, but they do not share a joint understanding of what civilian protection means or what it requires."[90] For the military, the reason for protecting civilians is not based on humanitarian principles of humanity, neutrality, and impartiality, but because it is an important element in attaining military objectives.

The increasing involvement of the military in areas that traditionally have been the purview of civilian humanitarian and development actors has been widely noted. As George Will explains, this "civilianization" of the military is evident in General Petraeus's interest in such issues as electricity output, chlorine supplies at water-treatment plants, and even chicken embryo imports.[91] This is perhaps an inevitable consequence of the military's engagement in the complex task of nation building. "Counterinsurgency," Will sums up, "is not primarily about holding real estate. Rather, it is about protecting, and improving the well-being of, the population."

Clearly one of the reasons for the military's increasing involvement in humanitarian assistance is the lack of civilian capacity. USAID reduced its foreign and civil service staff from a high of about 12,000 personnel during the Vietnam War to about 2,000 today, while the U.S. Information Agency (USIA) saw its 1996 global staff of 8,000 decimated.[92] With more than half of its staff now contractors rather than foreign or civil service officers, USAID channels more than half of its budget through NGOs. Even as he recognizes the key role played by civilian assistance, Robert Gates, the U.S. secretary of defense, laments the decline of civilian capacity at the State Department and USAID:

> In the campaign against terrorist networks and other extremists, we know that direct military force will continue to have a role. But over the long term, we cannot kill or capture our way to victory. What the Pentagon calls "kinetic" operations should be subordinate to measures to promote participation in government, economic programs to spur development, and efforts to address the grievances that often lie at the heart of insurgencies and among the discontented from which the terrorists recruit. . . . It has become clear that America's civilian institutions of diplomacy and development have been chronically undermanned and underfunded for far too long—relative to what we spend

on the military, and more important, relative to the responsibilities and challenges our nation has around the world.[93]

Certainly some in the military feel that their increased involvement in humanitarian assistance is meeting a need that civilian agencies should but cannot provide because they lack the capacity to do so.[94] Binnendijk and Cronin trace how the Department of Defense reluctantly began to take on these new responsibilities in the aftermath of the U.S. invasion of Iraq, when the lack of civilian planning for the postconflict operations was apparent to all. In 2004, the National Defense University published *Transforming for Stabilization and Reconstruction Operations,* which identified a "gap" between the end of military operations and the start of stabilization activities necessary to consolidate the peace and called on the military to adapt and develop skills to fill the gap. While the State Department created a new office, the Coordinator for Reconstruction and Stabilization (S/CRS), which in turn drafted the new National Security Presidential Directive 44, naming the State Department as the lead agency, the office remained "underfunded, understaffed, and unappreciated within the State Department. Whereas the Department of Defense (DOD) had dedicated tens of thousands of military personnel to these operations, S/CRS had a staff of fewer than 100, most of them detailees."[95] As a result of the gap and the inability of civilian agencies to meet the need for humanitarian assistance, "inevitably and necessarily, DOD was forced to fill the overall gap with military resources and personnel and with private contractors."[96] However, the military still needs civilian agencies to ensure that a successful military mission is followed by development programs, including support for governance and rule of law, which are necessary to prevent renewed conflict.[97]

There is resistance to moving in this direction from some military personnel who have the very strong feeling that militaries are meant simply *to fight.*[98] Or, as Defense Secretary Gates says, "the United States military should never be mistaken for the Peace Corps with guns."[99] Nonetheless, as noted by Charles MacCormack:

> Traditionally, the military provided security and corporations assisted relief efforts by improving war-torn infrastructure (for example, dredging harbors and fixing oil wells.) Today, however, these roles are sometimes reversed. Private corporations and civilian contractors now provide security, while the armed forces are deployed to help repair schools, immunize infants, and provide nutrition.[100]

There also are concerns about the cost of using troops to carry out work normally performed by civilian agencies. The average cost of keeping a U.S. soldier on the ground in Afghanistan in 2006 was $215,000 a year (a figure that has increased since then) while the average cost of an aid worker was less than a tenth of that amount, largely because most aid workers are Afghans, not expatriates.[101] In addition, there are questions about how effective hearts-and-minds strategies are in these programs. Andrew Wilder found after two years of research in Afghanistan that "far from winning hearts and minds, current aid efforts are more likely to be losing them"[102] due to complaints about the poor quality or inappropriate nature of the assistance, to perceptions that other groups are getting more, and mostly to the perception of massive corruption. A study by Larry Minear found that "many soldiers seem largely unaware of the downsides of military civic action, including the extent to which such activities complicate the work of humanitarian organizations and draw local communities more deeply into the conflict."[103] And there are concerns with the ability of the military to actually carry out humanitarian assistance well. As Robert Egnell of the Swedish National Defence College says, just as you would not expect a civilian to do very well as an amateur soldier, so you would not expect a soldier to perform especially well as a relief worker.[104]

The re-orientation of the U.S. military toward greater engagement in humanitarian work is manifested in different ways. The establishment of a new U.S. military command structure for Africa with an explicitly humanitarian role (U.S. Africa Command, or AFRICOM) has triggered debate within Africa and the broader international community about U.S. military interest in the region.[105] The Commander's Emergency Response Program (CERP) is a Department of Defense project that allows commanders in the field to approve up to $25,000 to respond to urgent needs in their area of operation. Where provincial reconstruction teams (PRTs) exist, commanders are expected to coordinate their assistance with them. In Afghanistan, the CERP most often funds water and sanitation projects though it also has funded expenses such as those for cars and Viagra. The *Washington Post* reported that as of mid-2008, almost $3 billion had been spent in Iraq through CERP funds.[106]

PRTs have been one of the most visible efforts to combine military and civilian assets in responding to humanitarian needs in support of broader political and military objectives. The teams were created first in Afghanistan in 2002 and then in Iraq in 2005 in recognition both of the difficult security environment in which civilian agencies had to work and the key role of assistance in supporting U.S./coalition military objectives. Although PRTs in both countries work on the three tasks of governance, reconstruction, and security, they have different organizational models. The PRTs in Iraq have a balance between civilian and military staff while the twenty-five U.S.-run PRTs in Afghanistan comprise military personnel almost entirely. In addition, in Afghanistan, PRTs are under the control of the International Security Assistance Force (ISAF); indeed, in addition to the twenty-five U.S.-led PRTs, there are thirteen others led by other coalition partners in various parts of the country. PRTs have been criticized for being too improvisational; for lacking agreed-on objectives, training programs for staff, and defined roles for civilian and military staff; and for having inadequate mechanisms for follow-up and implementation.[107]

Military forces have doctrines on civil-military cooperation (CIMIC)— for example, the NATO CIMIC doctrine (AJP-9), the NATO policy on CIMIC (MC 411/1), the U.S. joint doctrine for civil-military operations, and the British "Joint Doctrine Publication 3-90 on Civil-Military Cooperation." In all of the doctrines, "[r]esponding to the needs of the population becomes a constituent part of a strategy to defeat the enemy."[108] There also have been many initiatives to clarify and strengthen relations between military and civilian actors in emergency response.[109]

As the SCHR position paper states, most CIMIC doctrines are problematic for humanitarian actors because they subordinate humanitarian and development assistance to political and military goals and often assume a "common goal" uniting political, military, and humanitarian actors.[110] While there seems to be some movement in Europe to separate humanitarian work from other objectives in order to preserve humanitarian space, that is not the case in the United States.[111] From the military perspective, coordination with the NGO community is more difficult because there "is a lack of predictable, dependable control arrangements at the operational level across the UN family of organizations and among NGOs."[112]

The Important Role of Communities and Governments

While there are dozens of books and hundreds of studies examining the protection roles of UNHCR and nongovernmental organizations, there is a paucity of research on the ways in which communities protect themselves. In fact, only a handful of studies have examined the protection strategies used in places such as Myanmar, Democratic Republic of Congo, and Darfur.[113]

Some of those studies suggest that the concept of protection itself is understood differently by communities living in conflict situations. For example, displacement can be an effective self-protection strategy for individuals and communities when they are confronted with imminent violence. The study by independent Burma and Southeast Asia analyst Ashley South on self-protection strategies in Burma concludes: "Years of public advocacy campaigns have had limited positive impact on the lives of the victims of abuse" while behind-the-scenes negotiations with power holders can sometimes provide protection to those at risk.[114] Paying off power holders is another protection strategy that is at odds with the definition of protection used by most humanitarians, which includes all activities intended to protect an individual's human rights. Most international humanitarian organizations would not advocate either displacement or bribery as a protection strategy. But if humanitarians are to be more effective in protecting people and in supporting communities' efforts at self-protection, they need first to understand how people protect themselves when international actors are not present.

Governments are responsible for protecting their citizens. In many of the world's hotspots, governments deliberately do not protect their people and international actors have little choice but to step in when possible and do what they can. Sometimes, however, the problem is not a lack of political will but of government capacity, as in the case of post-earthquake Haiti. In such cases, international actors have a responsibility to work to build the capacity of national and local authorities as part of their emergency response. Yet often it is simply easier to bypass governments and get on with the job of providing assistance. Building capacity takes time and can be seen as slowing down the process of aid delivery. But when it comes to protection, working with national and local authorities on issues such as community policing, human rights training, and policy development can pay off over the long term. Similarly, ICRC and mediators working with nonstate actors have found that they often can and do understand basic principles of international humanitarian law.

Donor governments are the funders and drivers of the international humanitarian system. They were in the forefront of efforts to create the current system of multilateral institutions, and they provide the funds for almost all of the operations of UN agencies, other international organizations (like ICRC and the International Organization for Migration), and international NGOs. They are, of course, not just donors but also politically powerful countries with interests in maintaining international peace and security. These governments—which, with the exception of Japan, are all Western democracies—have also been in the forefront of efforts to create and uphold international law, human rights, and humanitarian values. Even as there is increasing recognition that the global power structure is changing as a result of the influence of the emerging powers—sometimes known as BRIC (Brazil, Russia, India, and China)—there are few signs that those countries are seeking to play a more active role in the international humanitarian system. Nor have the oil-rich countries been especially generous in contributing to relief efforts, likely because they have other priorities, because the humanitarian enterprise is perceived as a Western undertaking, and because they do not think that the system is of direct benefit to them. Neither the BRIC countries nor the Gulf states have required international humanitarian assistance. These countries also are uneasy with the concept of protection, evidenced by the fact that some have been the most outspoken opponents of the concept of responsibility to protect and have sought to limit UN action on protection of civilians. The traditional donor countries therefore continue to play the dominant role in maintaining the international humanitarian system and its increasing focus on protection.

4

The UN and NGOs in Humanitarian Operations

When people think of international response to conflicts and disasters, they usually think of UN agencies and international NGOs rushing to the scene. They also may think of government officials committing large sums of money for disaster relief. But in fact, as discussed in the previous chapter, it is national governments that are responsible for protecting people within their borders and communities often take measures to protect themselves. But the most visible part of the international humanitarian system is indeed the vast array of UN agencies and nongovernmental organizations.

The UN System

Traditionally the international humanitarian system has centered around the United Nations, which continues to play the leadership role in humanitarian response. The roles played by the panoply of UN agencies are varied—and as some have noted, contradictory. An external evaluation report published by the Office for the Coordination of Humanitarian Affairs identified four principal roles that the UN plays in emergency response: a normative role in advocating humanitarian standards and principles; a leadership role; a coordination role; and a service delivery role. The authors of the study argue that the UN system has to choose between its role as a service provider and its role as the true standard-bearer, noting that a conflict of interest arises when the UN acts as purveyor of norms and standards while seeking resources to sustain its own operations.[1]

As discussed in chapters 1 and 2, three UN agencies have explicit protection mandates: the UN High Commissioner for Refugees (UNHCR), to protect refugees; UN Children's Fund (UNICEF), to protect children and women; and the Office of the High Commissioner for Human Rights (OHCHR), to promote and protect human rights, to take action to prevent human rights violations, and to work with states to realize all aspects of human rights. OHCHR's mandate is the broadest of the three, but its operational capacity is very limited. In addition, the International Committee of the Red Cross (ICRC), although not, of course, a UN agency, is explicitly mandated to protect civilians during conflict and to work with all parties in an armed conflict to protect persons affected thereby and to implement international humanitarian law.

But because protection is defined by humanitarian agencies as involving "all activities aimed at obtaining full respect for the rights of the individual in accordance with the letter and the spirit of the relevant bodies of law (i.e. human rights, humanitarian law and refugee law)," the cast of UN characters working on protection is much broader (see table 4-1). The World Food Program (WFP) and the Food and Agriculture Organization (FAO) are mandated to help governments with their responsibility to provide food security; the International Labor Organization (ILO) is tasked with supporting efforts regarding employment standards; and the World Health Organization (WHO) is mandated to promote the right to health. The UN Fund for Population (UNFPA) is an international development agency that promotes the right of every woman, man, and child to enjoy a life of health and equal opportunity.[2]

That is a formidable list of agencies, and they mobilize substantial resources. Although humanitarian response is only one part of the overall activities of many of the agencies, such as the World Health Organization and the UN Development Program (UNDP), they all try to respond when there are large-scale emergencies, albeit at different phases. Thus UNDP is more likely to be involved in postconflict situations while the International Federation of Red Cross and Red Crescent Societies (IFRC) often is at the forefront of response to natural disasters. Each of the actors has a different mandate, governance structure, and funding mechanism, making coordination difficult. Each also has an institutional interest in being seen to be active, particularly in high-profile emergency situations. That concern with visibility (which also is evident in the work of nongovernmental organizations) can lead to competition and turf battles between agencies eager to demonstrate their relevance and competence to donors.

In December 1991, the General Assembly adopted resolution 46/182, designed to strengthen the UN's response to emergencies. The resolution created the position of emergency relief coordinator (ERC) and the Inter-Agency Standing Committee (IASC), intended to provide a forum for international agencies working in humanitarian assistance. Soon after, the secretary-general established the Department of Humanitarian Affairs (DHA) and assigned the ERC the title of under secretary-general for humanitarian affairs, with offices in New York and Geneva, to provide institutional support. Resolution 46/182 also created the consolidated appeals process (CAP) and the Central Emergency Revolving Fund (CERF). As part of a reform effort, DHA was reorganized in 1998 into the Office for the Coordination of Humanitarian Affairs (OCHA) and its mandate was expanded to include coordination of humanitarian response, humanitarian advocacy, and policy development. Though OCHA is a UN agency, its coordination work also extends to NGOs, ICRC, and others. OCHA has about 1,900 staff members in New York, in Geneva, and in the field, and it had a budget of about $237.7 million in 2009. As shown in box 4-1, eighteen UN agencies and representatives of the World Bank, International Organization for Migration, ICRC, IFRC, and the NGO community are members or standing invitees of the IASC.

While IASC is the closest thing to a coordination policy mechanism in the international system and OCHA is expected to provide coordination on the ground, everyone active in the humanitarian world recognizes that coordination is a problem, both between agencies' headquarters and between headquarters and staff in the field. There are several reasons for this persistent difficulty, most notably the autonomy of UN agencies, other international organizations, and NGOs.[3] Organizations such as WFP and WHO are intergovernmental legal entities independent of the UN General Assembly. Even UNHCR, UNICEF, and UNRWA have their own constituencies and governance structures outside the General Assembly. "They accept no hierarchical commands from the GA [General Assembly] or ECOSOC. In fact, what passes for instructions to them—in the form of requests from the GA—is negotiated with their officials or actually derived from these officials."[4]

Each agency jealously guards its independence, often using its mandate to justify its inability to work collaboratively. Coordination becomes even more difficult when NGOs, military actors, and others are added to the mix. With respect to civil-military relations in humanitarian assistance, the Steering Committee on Humanitarian Response (SCHR) distinguishes between coordination and cooperation, explaining that

> *Coordination* [emphasis in original] is a process to avoid duplication, ensure the best use of available resources and ensure the safety of the recipient population and humanitarian staff in the theatre of operations of armed actors, whilst retaining independent operational decision-making. *Cooperation* involves a degree of joint planning, joint implementation and/or alignment of goals, objectives or strategies.[5]

Table 4-1. *International Agencies*

International agency	Headquarters	Most recent annual budget	Number of staff	Main focus	Source
UNHCR	Geneva	$3.1 billion (2010)	6,880	Protecting rights and well-being of all refugees; working with stateless people, asylum seekers, returnees, and refugees	www.unhcr.org
UNICEF	New York	$3.3 billion (total income 2009)	6,379	Realizing the rights of every child	www.unicef.org
UNRWA	Gaza; Amman	$1.23 billion (2010–11)	Nearly 30,000	Providing basic services, emergency services, and microfinance to Palestinian refugees	www.unrwa.org
WHO	Geneva	$4.2 billion (2008–09)	5,552	Promoting health issues: standards, advocacy, research	www.who.int
OHCHR	Geneva	$115.3 million in regular budget funding plus $119.9 million in voluntary contributions (2008)	850+ (April 2007)	Ensuring protection, realization, and implementation of all human rights for all people	www.ohchr.org
FAO	Rome	$929.8 million (2008–09)	3,535	Defeating hunger in developed and developing countries	www.fao.org
WFP	Rome	$6.7 billion (2009)	4,132	Providing food aid in emergencies; rebuilding communities	www.wfp.org
OCHA	New York	$237.7 million (2009)	1,900	Alleviating human suffering in disasters and emergencies	http://ochaonline.un.org/

	Location	Budget	Staff	Mission	Website
UNFPA	New York	$259.8 million gross (2008–09)	1,529	Promoting the right of every human being to enjoy a life of health and equal opportunity	www.unfpa.org
UNIFEM	New York	$39.8 million (2010–11)	1,119	Advancing women's rights and achieving gender equality	www.unifem.org; www.womensenews.org
ICRC	Geneva	Initial appeal for 2010: $1 billion	11,000 approximately	Protecting and assisting vulnerable people affected by armed conflict and other situations of violence	www.icrc.org
IFRC	Geneva	$222 million (2010); $204 million (2011)	97 million volunteers in 186 national societies, which employ around 300,000 people	Protecting and assisting vulnerable people	www.ifrc.org
IOM	Geneva	$40 million (2009)	7,000+	Promoting humane and orderly management of migration	www.iom.int
UNDP	New York	$828.3 million (2010–11)	5,916	Promoting poverty reduction, crisis management, good governance, environmental protection, energy resource management, and response to HIV/AIDS	www.undp.org

Sources: All information from organizations' websites or annual reports.

Box 4-1. *IASC Members and Standing Invitees*

American Council for Voluntary International Action (InterAction)

Food and Agricultural Organization (FAO)

International Committee of the Red Cross (ICRC)

International Council of Voluntary Actions (ICVA)

International Federation of Red Cross and Red Crescent Societies (IFRC)

International Organization for Migration (IOM)

Office of the High Commissioner for Human Rights (OHCHR)

Office of the Special Rapporteur on the Human Rights of Internally Displaced Persons

Steering Committee for Humanitarian Response (SCHR)

United Nations Children's Fund (UNICEF)

United Nations Development Program (UNDP)

United Nations High Commissioner for Refugees (UNHCR)

United Nations Human Settlement Program (UN HABITAT)

United Nations Population Fund (UNFPA)

United Nations Office for the Coordination of Humanitarian Affairs (OCHA)

World Food Program (WFP)

World Health Organization (WHO)

World Bank

The international humanitarian system is far from even discussing cooperation. One obvious area in which collaborative efforts would be useful is needs assessment. Currently, when there is an emergency, each UN agency, international NGO, and Red Cross society carries out its own assessment of the situation. Each typically sends in its teams with its agency-specific questionnaire to assess needs, and the resulting assessment then serves as a basis for program planning. Everyone recognizes that carrying out good assessments is essential for the development of appropriate programs. But the fact that each agency carries out its own assessment makes it difficult to develop joint programs later down the road. And since many of the assessments cover the same issues—such as basic health conditions and food supplies—local officials and affected communities end up giving essentially the same information to a parade of visitors, including UN agencies, donor governments, NGOs, and in some cases military units. While there are interagency assessments from time to time, they are still the exception. And when there is a joint assessment, some participants still carry out their own additional assessment. The IASC began to tackle the question of joint assessments in 2010.[6]

In terms of protection, the IASC—and more recently the Protection Cluster Working Group—adopted the definition of protection developed by the ICRC in 1999:[7]

> [A]ll activities aimed at obtaining full respect for the rights of the individual in accordance with the letter and the spirit of the relevant bodies of law (i.e. human rights, humanitarian law and refugee law). Human rights and humanitarian actors shall conduct these activities impartially and not on the basis of race, national or ethnic origin, language or gender.[8]

But UN agencies continue to define protection in different ways, in accord with their own mandates. As Bo Viktor Nyland, UNICEF's senior adviser on child protection in emergencies, recently admitted, the organization's definition of protection "varies a lot. UNICEF's [2008] child protection strategy states [that it] is 'preventing and responding to violence, exploitation and abuse to ensure children's rights to survival, development and well-being,' but UNICEF also signs up to a broader, rights-based inter-agency definition of protection through the protection cluster."[9] UNHCR defines international protection as

> All actions aimed at ensuring the equal access to and enjoyment of the rights of women, men, girls and boys of concern to UNHCR, in accordance with the relevant bodies of law (including international humanitarian, human rights and refugee law).[10]

Although organizations define protection in different ways, they all are concerned about incorporating protection into their humanitarian work on the ground. OCHA has provided guidance on integrating protection into multisectoral assistance programs, explaining that a variety of actions can be taken to protect people, which can be divided into two groups: those that are stand-alone protection activities that have protection as their primary or sole objective; and mainstreamed or integrated activities that incorporate protection into sectoral programming—for example, into water or food programs. OCHA suggests that in order to incorporate protection into sectoral work, four factors are essential: participation of affected communities; non-discrimination; capacity building; and an ethos that enjoins organizations to "do no harm" or to avoid doing harm.[11]

The guidance note goes on to list specific actions that can be taken in each of the identified sectors. The actions represent the range of activities associated with the maximalist definition of protection. Some clearly are intended to protect the safety of affected communities—for example, "escort girls to and from school, if necessary, in order to protect them from sexual violence that can occur en route to and from school." Others would seem to fall equally into the category of good programming—for example, "establish protocols for referral of pre-natal care and ensure that all pregnant and nursing women are fully and directly informed of these services"; "provide jerry cans or other water collection containers of a size and shape that children, women and older persons can carry safely"; "when possible procure goods/ inputs locally to ensure support of existing resources and local productive networks"; "consult with women to determine the role that they wish to play in [food] distribution systems and networks"; "ensure that [agricultural] services are provided free of charge"; "ensure staff represents all different groups present in affected population (including older men and women)."

All of those instructions can, of course, be related to protection in the sense of physical security. If agricultural services are not provided free of charge, then people who do not receive the services can resort to violence against those who do or turn to crime or prostitution. If staffing is not diverse, it is more difficult for agency staff to be aware of the protection needs of specific groups. But the agencies represented in IASC and OCHA have definitely taken the expansive view of protection as encompassing "all activities aimed at obtaining full respect for the rights of the individual" rather than as having a particular relationship to the physical security of groups.

International NGOs

International NGOs (INGOs) have long been recognized for the role that they play in the international humanitarian system. Then UN Secretary-General Boutros Boutros-Ghali stated that "NGOs were more important in Somalia than the agencies of the United Nations. When the agencies of the United Nations were afraid of the situation, the NGOs were already on the ground."[12]

All of the major international NGOs—from CARE International to Oxfam—first started out by providing assistance in times of war. Almost all of them have moved into long-term development work, the major exception being Médecins sans Frontières (Doctors without Borders). The large international NGOs are major players in the humanitarian arena; less than a dozen of them deliver 90 percent of the funds mobilized by the NGO community.[13] Not only do these NGOs mobilize large sums of money, they also have a global reach, operating in many countries. The five largest international NGOs (CARE, Oxfam, Médecins sans Frontières, World Vision, and Save the Children) are all "families" themselves, with affiliates in different countries. The large international NGOs have developed high professional standards, and they have been the moving force behind efforts to increase NGO accountability, including accountability to beneficiaries. They have the expertise and the human resources to carry out research and to play a leadership role in the development of policies. They have the ability to generate front-page stories in Western newspapers; in fact, media coverage of humanitarian situations usually depends on NGO support.[14]

The growth of the NGO sector in humanitarian response is well known. In 1970, public sector funding of NGOs was only 1.5 percent of overall NGO budgets; by the mid-1990s, it had increased to 40 percent and was increasing.[15] "With governments everywhere privatizing just about everything in sight, the share of those aid flows that are funnelled through private NGOs has nearly tripled from 4.6 percent in 1995 to 13 percent in 2004."[16]

The large international NGOs have multiple accountabilities, including to their own governing bodies, to donors, and to coalitions of which they are members. Thus Oxfam-GB is a member of the British Disasters Emergency Committee as well as the Steering Committee on Humanitarian Response, the International Council of Voluntary Agencies (ICVA), and Voice. It participates in country-level coordination mechanisms in countries where it is operational and in many global coalitions on specific issues.

As international NGOs grow and become more professional, they run the risk of becoming increasingly similar to UN agencies. As the head of one UN agency said in the July 2007 meeting of the Global Humanitarian Platform, "I'm worried when I hear the NGOs speak—they sound just like us. Please don't become like us. We need you to remain NGOs." In fact, the large international NGOs probably have more in common with UN agencies than they do with national NGOs based in the global South.

INGOs have enjoyed a positive reputation over the years. While sometimes portrayed as "naive do-gooders," they generally have been seen as more flexible, self-sacrificing, and creative than their more bureaucratic counterparts in governments or UN agencies. But in the last decade or so, that image has begun to change. Rather than being seen as the compassionate critics of the system, INGOs are increasingly depicted as part and parcel of that system and as contributing to the chaos and the negative impacts of the relief industry. As INGOs channel increasing proportions of emergency assistance—which itself is increasing—the financial interests are becoming large scale. Minear and Smillie explain that most governments split allocations for humanitarian response to conflict-related emergencies three ways: one-third goes to UN agencies, another third to Red Cross/Red Crescent affiliates, and another third to NGOs, primarily international NGOs. However, NGOs also are major implementers of UN programs, receiving between a third and half of what major UN agencies spend, and they raise about 10 percent of total humanitarian donations from private donors. Thus NGOs, primarily INGOs, program half or more of the relief assistance in any given emergency.[17]

That assistance is big business, and INGOs are competing with new actors, such as for-profit contractors, as well as existing intergovernmental agencies and local NGOs for market share. When funding depends on visibility and branding, coordinating diverse actors obviously becomes more difficult. Moreover, the sheer economic impact of NGO activity can distort local economies; particularly hard-hit are local NGOs (and local government officials) who lose staff and sometimes areas of work to INGOs that can pay higher salaries.

Although NGOs stress their independence even when working with government funds, they frequently are under pressure to support the foreign policy objectives of the donor government. In that respect, U.S. NGOs accepting U.S. funding for Iraq and Afghanistan have come under especially intense pressure.

INGOs also have been criticized for weakening the role of the state. By providing aid, they relieve governments of the responsibility for providing for the welfare of their populations.[18] Others have noted that when national governments are unable to provide services, "NGOs provide services quickly and flexibly. At the same time, they help to create a de facto decentralization of authority that can complicate the design of national sectoral strategies and can frustrate the attempts of post-conflict state leaders to consolidate their power."[19] INGOs also have been criticized for prolonging conflicts, in part by providing resources that can be used for fueling conflicts, although a recent study by Goodhand finds that this criticism is overblown.[20] At times the criticism of INGOs is especially strident, as when they are charged with ignoring the sovereignty of the countries in which they work:

> Every NGO has its own agenda that is not necessarily identical to all domestic interests of the people and states that are the target of the organizations' activities. Those organizations are not the angels who we have seen on television. . . . [W]e also have our own national NGOs to seek their help and they know better about what we need or suffer from.[21]

A Rwandan journalist claimed that "NGOs are financed and directed by the various imperialist agencies, the imperialist governments and the comprador regimes . . . and seek to demobilize the masses by diverting them from the path of struggle and co-opting the best elements into the establishment and reformism."[22]

Human Rights NGOs and Humanitarian NGOs

At the global level, NGOs have played an important role in raising awareness of human rights violations, which have led to humanitarian emergencies in dozens of different situations. Indeed, NGOs are an essential part of the international human rights machinery. Human rights organizations such as Amnesty International, Human Rights Watch, and Refugees International have provided credible analyses and information about both the causes and the consequences of conflicts. Gil Loescher makes the case that "[u]ntil the capacity of the UN human rights regime is fully developed, nongovernmental organizations (NGOs), especially human rights NGOs, will have to assume a larger share of responsibility for ensuring the protection of forcibly displaced people."[23]

While human rights NGOs carry out investigations, denounce human rights violations, and offer policy alternatives, they do not engage in the day-to-day operations involved in providing humanitarian assistance on the ground. In contrast, humanitarian NGOs, which often are well placed to observe human rights violations, generally refrain from speaking out on human rights issues, particularly when the government of the affected country is implicated and doing so may threaten their continued access. As one representative of a humanitarian NGO working in Darfur said in 2008, "whenever the Save Darfur Coalition launches a new campaign, we feel it on the ground. They may be right in trying to address the causes of the conflict, but it's our people that get beaten up."[24] In the past, humanitarian NGOs often tried to distance themselves from their counterparts working on human rights for precisely such reasons.

However, the distance between humanitarian and human rights organizations may be diminishing. Many NGOs (and UN agencies too, for that matter) have adopted a rights-based approach to both their humanitarian and development work. Under a rights-based approach, which is "a conceptual framework for the process of human development that is normatively based on international human rights standards and operationally directed to promoting and protecting human rights,"[25] human rights are the means, the end, the mechanism of evaluation, and the central focus of sustainable human development.

This approach starts from the ethical position that all people are entitled to a certain standard of material and spiritual well-being. Accordingly, people are engaged as holders of claims to rights rather than as beneficiaries of charity and aid; they are considered active participants in rather than objects of development. Governments, intergovernmental organizations, and NGOs are therefore seen as duty bearers that must ensure that the human rights of claim holders are met and not abused.[26] Adopting a rights-based approach has meant that humanitarian and development NGOs have become more familiar with international human rights law and have developed closer relations with human rights actors. For some NGOs, it also has meant a fundamental change in their relationship with beneficiaries, who are no longer seen in terms of their needs but rather as individuals and communities seeking to claim their basic human rights.

Over the past twenty years, there has been increasing recognition of the important role that NGOs play in providing protection to refugees and of the links between protection and assistance. *Protecting Refugees: A Field Guide for NGOs*, a joint UNHCR-NGO publication, was an early effort to provide resources to NGOs, whose programs often offer protection to refugees.[27] Taking a rights-based approach to assistance requires all aspects of NGO planning to adopt a deliberate focus on protection.

National NGOs

National NGOs (NNGOs), those that work in one country only, often are the first responders when disaster strikes. In fact, they usually are the ones that deliver food and pull most of the survivors from the rubble while UN agencies and the international NGOs are either getting to the scene or getting supplies and staff to their national affiliates. While international NGOs may decide to withdraw from a given country—for example, when their priorities change—national NGOs are there for the long haul. National NGOs vary tremendously in size and capacity; while some have only a handful of staff, others employ hundreds of people and have high professional standards.

The number of NNGOs is growing dramatically. For example, a political scientist at Obafemi Awolowo University reports that the number of NNGOs in Nigeria increased from seven in 1940 to forty-one in 1980 and 224 in 1995.[28] Current estimates report 10,000 national and local NGOs in Iraq, of which more than 9,000 are linked to particular individuals, political parties, business interests, or militias.[29]

UNHCR carries out much of its work through both international and national NGOs. In 2007, UNHCR had 550 agreements with 424 national NGOs, for a total of $89.4 million in funding, and it had 417 agreements with 151 international NGOs, for a total of $138 million. While UNHCR has far more national NGO partners, much more funding goes to international NGOs. Working with national NGOs is a challenge for UNHCR; as one UNHCR staff member said, "It's as much work to develop and monitor an agreement for $10,000 with a national NGO as for an agreement for $1 million with an international NGO. And our monitoring capacity is limited."[30]

National NGOs are recognized as playing a significant role in the international humanitarian system, and there have been attempts over the years to include them in important humanitarian initiatives, such as UNHCR's Partnership in Action (PARINAC) process. Several national NGOs participated in Global Humanitarian Platform (GHP) meetings from 2006 to 2008, but there were far fewer of them than of international NGOs. One African NGO participant in the 2007 GHP meeting recounted that at a meeting in his country to talk about the principles of partnership, there were twenty-seven UN representatives, twenty-six international NGO representatives, three representatives from the Red Cross, and only one from a national NGO.

NNGOs generally are assumed to be close to the poor, encouraging popular participation; to be flexible, innovative, sustainable, and cost-effective; and to have committed staff.[31] Their weaknesses are their limited financial and management expertise, limited institutional capacity, low level of self-sustainability, isolation and lack of coordination, ability to conduct only small-scale interventions, and limited understanding of the broader social or economic context.[32] The late Fred Cuny captured a typical view of the comparative advantages of national and international NGOs when he wrote:

> International NGOs will continue to bear the brunt of operations [to reach the victims of conflict]. While many new local NGOs will spring up and some of the existing ones may expand and become more

professional, most will find it difficult to work in conflicts because their governments can pressure their staffs to comply with government policies. . . . International NGOs, supported by donors, can better stand up to repressive governments.[33]

One author argues that because of the pressure that NNGOs often face from their governments, "most national NGOs have de facto been transformed into QUANGOs [quasi-autonomous NGOs]."[34] In other words, rather than representing independent nongovernmental action, NNGOs may become another expression of their government's policies. Yet such pressures also affect international NGOs. In Sri Lanka, for example, the scope of action for both NNGOs and INGOs is limited by the political climate. And "international and especially local agencies noted that 'you can't be outspoken on protection.' 'It is not possible to use the P-word' (protection) openly."[35] Dawit Zawde, president of Africa Humanitarian Action, reported that

> international NGOs dominate the humanitarian arena, ostensibly because they have experience, competence and wider coverage. Yet as the security environment changes and calls to involve local actors increase, the need for local capacity cannot be overemphasised. . . . Strong indigenous organizations are essential for effective humanitarian response in Africa. Empowerment of African NGOs is, therefore, a critical goal, especially given the new vision of Africa's regeneration, in which Africa takes the lead in defining its problems and finding solutions.[36]

That theme was picked up at a meeting of 300 African aid workers who called on Northern donors to channel not less than 25 percent of their contributions to humanitarian work in Africa directly through African NGOs.[37]

On the other hand, there is growing recognition that protection is "provided first of all by and through the local community, through a complex social network including family, clan, village, or tribe."[38] While local NGOs can be politicized and become part of ethnic or sectarian conflicts, international agencies are beginning to recognize that taking a longer-term commitment to particular communities enables them to understand better the threats that they face, their vulnerabilities, and their own capacity to build approaches that are relevant to the local context.[39] O'Callaghan and Pantuliano found in the case of Darfur that "throughout the field research for this study, national staff proved considerably more aware of key protection issues related to land and new power structures in the camps; expatriate personnel would rarely refer to these problems unless prompted."[40] At a 2001 workshop on practical protection organized by the Institute for the Study of International Migration at Georgetown University and the American Red Cross, participants concluded that

> establishing strategic partnerships is among the most effective means by which NGOs can broaden their protection roles in the field, gain access to target populations and increase the resources available for more explicit protection activities . . . [F]or most of the international NGOs at the workshop, local NGOs offer a way of reaching vulnerable population groups and assessing their protection needs.[41]

The relationship between national and international NGOs—in spite of the rhetoric of NGO solidarity—clearly reveals that power dynamics are at play. The larger international NGOs have greater financial resources and sometimes subcontract with national NGOs to carry out certain projects. But international NGOs also are increasing their presence in Southern countries. The number of international NGO field offices rose 31 percent to 39,729 between 1993 and 2003, and the number has surely increased since then.[42] Some major donors now require the field presence of an international NGO as a condition for funding. National NGOs complain that in some cases, the international NGOs are displacing them from work that they have carried out for many years. They also report that they often lose their best staff to international NGOs that offer salaries that national NGOs cannot afford to pay. While there are many cases in which relations between international and national NGOs are based on mutual respect and complementarity, it also is clear that their relationship is usually an unequal one. While NNGOs often call for increased support by INGOs for NNGOs' capacity-building initiatives,[43] the main purpose of INGOs is not to increase the capacity of local NGOs but to deliver needed services. Local agencies want strong and genuine partnerships that go beyond funding relationships.

In research carried out by the Brookings-Bern Project on Internal Displacement, NNGOs in four countries were interviewed about their views on a number of issues. The NNGOs' responses to the question "What does protection of IDPs mean?" covered a wide range. Less than half of respondents drew a direct relationship between protection and human rights, but even when they did not use that terminology, their responses indicated a holistic understanding of protection. Protection includes a range of activities from humanitarian assistance to people in need to access to land to legal rights.

It was interesting to note that NNGOs that have been working with internally displaced persons for many years, as in Georgia, were more likely to see protection in terms of legal rights, although that may reflect the particular Georgian context.[44]

A subset of NNGOs facing particular challenges in the post-9/11 world are Muslim NGOs, which have received relatively little attention from the academic community although they are estimated to represent around 20 percent of the world's humanitarian NGOs and to contribute about $3 billion in assistance every year. Karin von Hippel argues that Islamic charities may do a better job of providing services than Western agencies because they are more closely aligned with local needs and may work in a more discreet fashion, operating in accordance with Islamic law, "which stipulates that aid should be given in a way that does not humiliate the recipient."[45] She goes on to note that boundaries between the political and social worlds often are blurred, as evidenced in the work of the Muslim Brotherhood and Hezbollah, which carry out widespread charitable activities. For example, of the approximately 5,000 registered NGOs and associations in Egypt, 20 percent are estimated to have connections with the Muslim Brotherhood. In the 1992 Cairo earthquake, the organization provided medical and financial resources to victims, even donating $1,000 to every newly homeless person in Cairo—the government response, in contrast, was much slower. Hezbollah, considered a terrorist organization by both the United States and the European Union, has an annual budget of $190 million (much of which comes from Iran) and has supported schools, hospitals, and agricultural centers. Jihad-al-Bina, an NGO set up by Hezbollah to run development programs, was first on the scene in the 2006 Israel-Lebanon conflict, assessing damage, providing health services, and compensating people for the loss of their homes, long before the government was able to respond.[46]

In addition to the coordination agencies used by the United Nations (IASC and OCHA), there are coordination mechanisms within the NGO world. On the global level there is the International Council of Voluntary Agencies (ICVA), which brings together more than seventy-five international and national NGOs from the global North and South.[47] ICVA has had its ups and downs. In the late 1990s, its executive committee decided to disband the coalition because of serious financial difficulties, but it was resuscitated in 2000 with a new, exclusive focus on humanitarian action. One of the problems with the original formulation of ICVA was that it encompassed a wide range of issues, including development and the environment as well as humanitarian issues.

The Steering Committee for Humanitarian Response was formed in 1972 as a different sort of inter-NGO coordination mechanism. This committee brought together the CEOs of some of the largest nongovernmental bodies to talk informally about a range of issues. Made up of CARE, Caritas Internationalis, IFRC, ICRC, Lutheran World Federation, Oxfam, Save the Children, World Council of Churches/ACT, and World Vision, the coalition provides a forum for discussing some of the burning issues of the day. SCHR was largely responsible for developing the widely used Red Cross/Crescent NGO code of conduct.[48]

On the national level, InterAction in the United States is a robust coalition of 165 agencies working in a wide range of fields, while VOICE brings together 100 European humanitarian NGOs to work on issues of common concern, focused in particular on the European Union. There are a host of national-level NGO coordination mechanisms in the field, ranging from the Consortium for Humanitarian Action in Sri Lanka to the NGO Coordination Committee in Iraq. Sometimes the mechanisms serve as a useful forum for national and international NGOs to sort out their relationships and share information.

NGOs and Protection

A decade ago, Cohen and Deng identified the following four types of protection that NGOs can provide to IDPs and other vulnerable groups:
   —protection that results from having a presence and providing assistance
   —protection deriving from community-building efforts
   —protection that results from advocacy work
   —direct interventions to protect the physical safety of vulnerable groups.[49]
A long-standing mantra in the NGO world has been that international agencies protect people by being physically present.[50] When international staff can serve as witnesses, for example, authorities are less likely to abuse civilians and armed attacks on refugee camps are less likely to occur. Canadian aid worker and researcher Greg Hansen called on international NGOs to reestablish their physical presence in Iraq, arguing that while relief could be distributed by intermediaries and local staff, an international presence provided protection.[51] But there have been few studies to evaluate the extent to which their presence protects civilians on the ground. In reviewing field-based protection in Darfur, Sorcha O'Callaghan and Sara Pantuliano found that protection by presence has limits and can in fact create a false sense of security among communities that feel that the international community has made a commitment to protect them by sending in protection officers.[52]

A great deal of attention in the NGO world has focused on the ways in which assistance can be used to protect people, with distinctions often made between protection mainstreaming and stand-alone protection programming. Organizations such as Oxfam and World Vision, for example, have emphasized the importance of protection mainstreaming—looking at all assistance activities through the lens of protection and of incorporating protection into every aspect of operations. That means that decisions about how to distribute food or where to place water pumps should be based not only on obvious technical factors but also with a view to how those decisions affect the safety of communities. Specialist or stand-alone protection programming consists of activities designed to meet specific protection objectives—for example, monitoring human rights violations, registering displaced persons, or developing programs to respond to victims of sexual and gender-based violence. Some organizations both mainstream protection into all assistance activities and have specific protection programs to meet the needs of specific groups.[53]

While most international NGOs now have either developed protection policies, strategies, or programs or tried to mainstream protection into their assistance programs, there have been few efforts to identify the extent to which those initiatives have resulted in better protection for beneficiaries. While there is anecdotal evidence that some initiatives reduce the risk to vulnerable groups (such as provision of fuel-efficient stoves to women in Darfur so that they do not have to walk so far or so often outside the camps to search for firewood), measuring impact is especially difficult in the case of protection. Occasionally NGO staff admit that in spite of their increased emphasis on protection, there are limits to what they can achieve. For example, Bill Forbes of World Vision provides a more limited conception of what protection means in practice: "World Vision is committed to doing everything possible to ensure that our activities do not put children at risk. . . . We do not promise that children in our target communities will be safe. We do not take on the responsibility for security, other than ensuring all efforts to not put people at risk of harm through participation in activities."[54]

While there often are discussions in NGO forums on best practices for protecting people, there has been very little questioning of whether NGOs should be trying to incorporate protection into their ongoing work or even of what protection means. In 2006, Robbie Thomson, a former staff member of IFRC, wrote an opinion piece in which he noted the rapid growth in concern with protection and observed that the humanitarian response in Darfur was unique in the large number of protection officers deployed—seventy-five according to the UN Mission in Sudan (UNMIS), not counting ICRC and UNHCR staff.[55] But Thomson questioned whether the presence of so many protection personnel was having a positive impact on protection of the population. He noted the difficulty in recruiting experienced protection staff, which forced NGOs to employ recent human rights law graduates who had little or no field experience. "The impact of such hiring is illustrated by the fact that quite junior protection officers in Darfur were to be found writing criticisms of the mandate of peacekeepers while ignoring (or not noticing) the fact that women waiting for a food distribution were often left for many hours in the sun with no shelter or water." Thomson also was critical of the rights-based approach, noting that there was a tendency for some agencies to reduce their assistance to devote more resources to advocacy efforts. "While it's far more intellectually stimulating," he wrote, "to address the Security Council than dig a latrine," such advocacy efforts may not improve the protection of populations on the ground.

More recently Marc DuBois, director of Médecins sans Frontières–United Kingdom, has written several articles on protection work by humanitarian actors, calling it a "fig leaf" that does not address the fact that the violence is perpetrated by others. "Suddenly, rape, murder, pillage and general mayhem are a failure of aid-givers, and are addressed *in the first* instance through protection activities aimed at bridging the [protection] gap rather than directly stopping the crimes."[56] He argues that physical protection of civilians is not the job of humanitarian actors and that the protection work of NGOs may actually undermine the rights of people, impede the neutrality of humanitarian actors, and increase the risk of losing access to people in need of assistance.[57]

The Media

While the media are not usually seen as protection actors, media coverage of an emergency can trigger the mobilization of resources and involvement of donor governments. It was a BBC broadcast in 1985 that led to a generous outpouring of support in response to the famine in Ethiopia; without that broadcast, it is unlikely that the world community would have known of the crisis or responded with such generosity. But in order for media coverage to generate action, certain conditions must be met, as enumerated by Rony Brauman, co-founder of Médecins sans Frontières : First, there must be photographs available because pictures, not words or analysis, capture the world's attention. Second, the crisis must be isolated because the world cannot respond to more than one humanitarian crisis at a time. So while a given crisis may receive considerable attention, if another crisis of a similar magnitude occurs, both will suffer from a lack of media coverage. Third, there must be a mediator, a guarantor who certifies that the conflict is authentic. Brauman notes that the Somali crisis of the early 1990s went unnoticed until visits by high-ranking Western government officials authenticated the suffering: "Once the victims have been identified as *bona fide* by acknowledged mediators, they can become the object of our compassion."[58] Finally, there must be an acceptable victim—which means that the victim must always be innocent and blameless.

Brauman contrasts the media attention paid to the rescue of "innocent" ice-trapped whales off the Canadian coast in 1988 with the general indifference to a famine that killed tens of thousands of Sudanese. Others have noted the intense media interest in the effect of the Rwandan genocide on native gorillas and in pets left homeless by Hurricane Katrina.[59] Often, people are seen as innocent victims only when the perpetrator of their suffering has been labeled a tyrant by Western governments. Gassing Iraqi Kurds in the largest-scale chemical weapons attack since World War II did not make Saddam Hussein a tyrant; attacking Kuwait did.[60]

The media generally depict a given emergency as what Hammock and Charny refer to as a morality play, complete with suffering masses, the expatriate relief worker as angel, and the military hero. And Michael Ignatieff writes, "We cannot have misery without aid workers. They conjure away the horror by suggesting that help is at hand."[61] But the morality play leaves out analysis of the root causes, ignores local capacity, and puts the relief worker— rather than the affected community—in the center of the story.[62] Both the media and humanitarian organizations are notorious for oversimplifying crises, and both have strong interests in keeping the message simple.[63] Relief organizations want to persuade people to give money and thus have an interest in sensationalizing the story, as do the media.[64]

On any given day, hundreds of crises are occurring, and yet the media are selective. Often the extent to which the media cover a given emergency depends on issues such as access to affected communities. In the early 1990s, there was much greater coverage of war and famine in Somalia than in Sudan, in part because Somalia was easier to get to. When a news agency had only one reporter in a regional office, it was simply easier to go to Somalia for a day than to take at least three days to go to Sudan. Moreover, the UN provided free transport for journalists to travel to Somalia while journalists traveling to Sudan not only had to make their own travel arrangements but also faced difficulties in getting visas to enter the country.[65]

The changing nature of the news industry means that there are fewer foreign offices and increased competition between news outlets and non-traditional media. One journalist complained that "Iraq is draining every-one's resources. It is so expensive to keep an office in Iraq that it limits the resources that are available to cover other conflicts."[66]

The role of traditional media is changing. Local media working in con-flict zones often have to work under the direct control of local authorities or under threats from insurgent groups while the number of foreign offices of traditional international media is shrinking. In this context, the increased use of social media is changing the access of local communities and NGOs to the broader public. "We don't live in a world anymore where simply getting BBC to give you 5 minutes of air time is going to create a tipping point or make a difference—we need to create a momentum, a buzz."[67] One advocacy group using social media, the Save Darfur campaign, increased the number of donors on their list from 200,000 to 1.2 million in the course of a year.[68]

Social media create a network in which every user has the ability to pro-duce and consume content rather than being confined to listening to broad-cast media monologues; blogs, wikis, Facebook, Twitter, and Flickr are some of the most visible examples. Individuals have been using social media for the past decade, but now businesses, the U.S. military, and governments have joined them.[69] In the aftermath of the January 2010 earthquake in Haiti, social media played an important role in enhancing technical search and res-cue operations, expanding volunteerism opportunities, enabling efficient systems for donations, and increasing the coverage of Haiti in the media.[70] Social networking sites Facebook and Twitter enabled people to find their missing relatives. Open-source mapping software was used by a variety of organizations to locate people buried in rubble as well as to map the loca-tions of relief centers and medical clinics. The U.S. Department of Home-land Security created the Haiti Social Media Disaster Monitoring Initiative to track social media websites as a basis for reporting to U.S. government agen-cies working in Haiti.[71] Volunteers in other countries were able to directly contribute to the relief effort by developing computer programs, includ-ing collaborative mapping initiatives and sites for tracing missing relatives, modeling a new way for volunteers to engage in disaster relief.[72] A Red Cross mobile phone campaign raised more than $21 million in $10 donations in one month; in 2009 mobile donations to all charitable organizations totaled about $4 million.[73] The mainstream media also relied on social media to update their news coverage, which was especially important after the media reporters had returned to their home countries.

The new technologies offer possibilities for new forms of protection, as in the examples from Haiti of people being reunited with family members and rescue teams being directed to particular dwellings to search for people buried in the rubble. But they also create new dangers. The International Committee of the Red Cross has a long history of providing tracing services to reunite families, and it has built many safeguards into the process. But when an individual posts a photograph of an unaccompanied child on Facebook or on Google's search page and asks "Does anyone know this child?" the child's safety can be put at risk.

Most observers argue that raising awareness of an emergency situation can increase protection by mobilizing international response and donor commitment. But sometimes there can be high levels of awareness of a particular situation without corresponding action that results in protection on the ground. In Darfur, increased media coverage of the desperate situation of displaced persons led to an outpouring of humanitarian assistance that perhaps indirectly provided protection but that did not, in the short term at least, lead to a decrease in the killing.

New Actors: Philanthropic Capitalists, Celebrities, and Private Security Companies

Several relatively new actors also have arrived on the scene: philanthropic capitalists, celebrities, corporate donors, and private security companies. (See chapter 8 for a discussion of the financing of protection and the role of new donors).

Philanthropic Capitalists

Philanthropic capitalists (and corporate donors) not only contribute funds, they also help set the international agenda and they may actually deliver humanitarian assistance. Ted Turner gave $1 billion to the United Nations in 1997, while the Soros Foundation and the Open Society Institute donate half a billion a year. The Jimmy Carter Center in Atlanta undertakes a range of programs and is involved in peacemaking in many countries. But it was the $25 billion endowment of the Bill and Melinda Gates Foundation in 2000, now the largest private foundation in the world, that demonstrated the power of corporate wealth to change the game. In 2006 foundation trustee and U.S.

businessman Warren Buffet pledged the bulk of his estimated $31 billion fortune to the Gates Foundation, to be paid in annual installments. While the foundation has developed innovative ways of working, particularly in the health field, it has the potential—due to the sheer scale of its resources—to have an impact on the entire international humanitarian system.

Celebrities

The advent of the celebrity activist enlisted in the service of humanitarian causes also is an interesting development. Although not a new phenomenon—Danny Kaye was the first "ambassador-at-large" working to support UNICEF in the 1950s—celebrity activists have brought increased attention to international humanitarian crises. Celebrities embark on such causes for a variety of reasons, but public relations usually is one motivating factor. "Charitable work rounds out and humanizes your image," comments one publicist.[74] Writing about Mia Farrow's involvement in Darfur, Alex de Waal notes that "a celebrity playing a humanitarian role, such as Farrow does, acts as a bridge between a (Western) audience and a faraway tragedy. She is a focus for empathy, an emotional interpreter."[75] UN agencies working in humanitarian issues all have celebrities associated with them, which helps to raise awareness—and funding for their work.

Corporate Donors

Corporate donors usually are seen in terms of the funds they raise, but they also are developing partnerships with UN agencies and with NGOs such as Oxfam, Care, and the Save the Children Fund. For example, immediately after the Haiti earthquake, global telecommunications companies such as T-Mobile, AT&T, and Sprint as well as phone manufacturers and distributors Sony Ericsson, Motorola, Samsung, and LG provided critical telecommunications equipment to Trilogy International Partners and its Haitian wireless company, Voilà. Because Voilà was then able to provide tens of thousands of phones to relief agencies, the equipment helped expedite the emergency response.[76] The UN has encouraged such collaboration through its Global Compact, a corporate responsibility initiative with nearly 9,000 private sector and other participants that pledge to uphold ten key principles related to human rights, the environment, anticorruption efforts, and labor standards.[77] In fact, its principal recommendation to NGOs is to recognize that markets are central to their future. Wal-Mart contributed $170 million in local community and nonprofit funding, $27 million of which was associated with international operations. But humanitarian agencies often are uneasy with corporate actors working as humanitarians, recognizing that their motivations are different from those of traditional humanitarians. Stephen Hopgood asks: "If Walmart offers supplies that save 100,000 people but does so in order to make a profit by appealing to middle-income consumers, should it be turned down?"[78] He goes on to say, "One strong argument against Walmart is that it will abandon humanitarian work when the profits dry up, having in the meantime displaced local capacity and NGOs."[79] As noted in chapter 8, the funds raised by corporate donors in support of humanitarian response account for just a small percentage of those contributed by traditional government donors, and most corporate funding is directed toward sudden-onset, high-visibility natural disasters rather than to conflict situations.

Private Security Companies

Since the 1990s, private security companies (PSCs) have become increasingly important actors in humanitarian operations. That growth has been attributed to both supply and demand side factors. On the supply side, the number of individuals in national armed forces fell by over 5 million worldwide between 1988 and 1994, and, as Spearin points out, a smaller military means fewer opportunities for promotion and thus contributes to the decisions of military personnel to leave the military.[80] For many former military personnel, security-related work in the private sector offers lucrative possibilities—remuneration rates are up to four times the compensation offered in the public sphere.[81]

On the demand side, the war in Iraq created an unprecedented opportunity for PSCs. Since 9/11 there has been large-scale growth in private security contracts and private firms have assumed increasing responsibilities. For example, Aegis's contract in Iraq, for $300–400 million, included running a "hearts and minds" campaign among the Iraqis.[82] The use of private security companies in the theaters of war in Iraq and Afghanistan—by the U.S. military and other parties—is striking. By mid-2009, some 18,000 armed security contractors were being used in Iraq and Afghanistan (13,000 in Iraq and 5,000 in Afghanistan). As of March 2010, the Department of Defense (DOD) employed some 11,000 armed private security contractors in Iraq and more than 16,000 in Afghanistan—a marked increase reflecting the U.S. military surge there.

These private security contractors account for only a fraction of the total number of DOD contractors (6-12 percent) and even less of Department of State contractors, although security and other contractors actually

outnumber the troops in Afghanistan.[83] In Iraq, most of the security contractors are third-country nationals, and in Afghanistan, the overwhelming
majority are Afghan. Although prohibited from engaging in combat operations, PSCs are supposed to perform many of the functions necessary to
support military operations in those countries. Defense acquisition specialist
Moshe Schwartz notes, "According to government officials, both DOD and
the Department of State would be unable to execute their missions in Iraq
and Afghanistan without the support of private security contractors."[84] The
heavy reliance on contractors by the U.S. government is due in large part to
the fact that they can be hired and fired quickly and therefore cost less than
longer-term government personnel. They also can provide critical skills lacking in government staff, and they are considered a practical solution for freeing up combat troops.[85] But it is not just the Department of Defense that uses
private security companies. When other U.S. government agencies, private
companies, and other governments are included, the number of private security contractors is estimated at 30,000 in Iraq and 70,000 in Afghanistan.[86]

Currently PSCs look to humanitarianism as a future market opportunity.
As the United States reduces its troops in Iraq and possibilities of large-scale
private sector contracts in the country decrease, security companies are
looking elsewhere for new business, and involvement in humanitarian operations allows for commercial diversification.[87] In 2005, at the height of PSC
involvement in Iraq, $60 billion was directed toward security, governance,
and reconstruction projects, of which 10 to 36 percent was for provision of
security. But with funding reduced in Iraq, a buyers' market is emerging. By
diversifying into humanitarian assistance, PSCs hope to respond to changing
market conditions.[88]

While private security companies have a long history of involvement in
demining operations, they increasingly are becoming multiservice agencies.
Presently the use of private security companies in humanitarian operations
is primarily to provide security for humanitarian work carried out in an
increasingly dangerous environment. Donor governments have been willing
to pay large amounts of money to support security for their staff and implementing partners. The United Kingdom's Department for International
Development, for example, reports that the security cost for a staff member
in Afghanistan was about £100,000 a year, compared with £3,600 a year for a
staff member working in Nepal.[89]

The security services offered by PSCs include not only armed escorts but
also threat and context assessments, security audits, policy development for
risk control and evacuation, security training, and the provision of security

management and guards for both convoys and compounds.[90] A 2008 study found that contracting out certain security functions has become increasingly common among humanitarian actors worldwide but that the use of armed escorts by commercial firms is very much the exception.[91] They also found that local private security providers are more likely to be used than international ones. "Interestingly, however, in some of the most insecure contexts, such as Darfur, Sudan and Iraq, humanitarian agencies have used private security in only very limited ways if at all, relying more on the tactic of withdrawing, suspending operations and remotely managing their programmes to deal with security threats."

Although the number of providers in the private security industry has increased dramatically, their efforts to engage with humanitarian agencies have declined in recent years, though the private security companies are still interested. But there is a lack of policy and guidance within the humanitarian community on when and how to engage with private security companies; in fact, it is rarely discussed at the interagency level.[92] Humanitarian agencies have been reluctant to talk about their use of private firms to provide security for their staff, in part because using security firms is seen as being at odds with their humanitarian image. Some humanitarian organizations, notably ICRC, pride themselves on never hiring firms to provide security for their staff, relying instead on their knowledge of and acceptance by local populations.

So far, the United Nations has shied away from using private security companies, perhaps because they are viewed as uncomfortably similar to mercenaries. That means that while PSCs are used to protect the staff of humanitarian agencies, they are not used to protect communities at risk of armed violence, which is the purview of UN peacekeeping operations. Alexander Van Taulleken reported that Executive Outcomes, a private security company,

> performed a retrospective analysis of whether it would have had the capacity to intervene in Rwanda in 1994. They estimated the cost to provide protected safe havens from the genocide to be $600,000 a day, a total of $150 million. The UN operation cost over $300 million and was deemed to be a complete failure.

He then asked whether it would be possible to imagine a consortium of NGOs spending the $150 million asked by a company like Executive Outcomes. Would it be possible to think of them funding preemptive attacks on groups that threaten security or human rights?[93] Given the constraints on the international community's ability to protect populations at risk, that is perhaps not such a far-fetched notion, although it raises a different—and mind-boggling—set of issues related to responsibility, accountability, and complex practical matters.

Humanitarian Reform

Humanitarian reform was launched in 2005 by Jan Egeland, then the emergency relief coordinator, to address the widely recognized gap in the international response to the need of internally displaced persons for protection and assistance, but within a few months the effort had become a system-wide reform initiative.

Until the summer of 2005, the UN's response to IDPs was organized through what was called the "collaborative approach." That model, adopted by the IASC in 1999, was based on the recognition that no single UN agency had an international mandate to respond to IDPs. Instead it was left to the most senior UN official in each country, the resident and/or humanitarian coordinator, to coordinate the activities of the various UN agencies and to raise the plight of the IDPs with the national government. Responsibility for IDPs was to be determined on an ad hoc basis in a collaborative manner between UN agencies operating in the area.

The failures of the collaborative approach have been well-documented.[94] Few UN resident coordinators (RCs) or humanitarian coordinators (HCs) had an understanding of their responsibilities for IDPs or enough experience to coordinate response operations.[95] Furthermore, there is an inherent tension between RCs, who are responsible for coordinating UN agency operations in a given country and thus depend on good relationships with the government, and HCs, who usually work with IDPs when strong advocacy is needed with the government to ensure that IDPs are protected in the midst of internal conflict.[96] For each new IDP situation, the collaborative approach left wide open the question of which agency would take responsibility for what tasks. An agency's willingness to assume responsibility for an undertaking often depended on the availability of funding, a reality that meant that there was considerable competition to be named lead agency in some—particularly high-visibility or politically important—IDP situations and virtually no interest in being responsible for others. Such cherry-picking meant that there was little certainty that IDPs would receive anything resembling a consistent response. It also meant that the protection of IDPs— one of the most daunting challenges of all—sometimes fell in the hands of the least-equipped agency.[97] And occasionally there were cases in which an agency would assume leadership responsibility for IDPs in a given country but simply cease operations when the funding ran out, leaving IDPs even more vulnerable.

Several contextual factors came together in the 2004–05 period that made humanitarian reform possible: the growing realization that the collaborative approach to IDPs was not working; a dynamic emergency relief coordinator in the person of Jan Egeland; a high-visibility crisis in Darfur to which the international response had been slow and inadequate; and various other UN reform initiatives detailed in the next chapter. NGOs and UN agencies alike were advocating taking a more proactive and deliberate approach to IDPs rather than leaving them to the vagaries of the collaborative approach. Jan Egeland brought heightened visibility to humanitarian crises through outspoken advocacy initiatives and careful use of the media.

The international community's response to Darfur was especially troubling. Although the conflict intensified in 2003, the international response was slow and often ineffective. Both UN agencies and NGOs were slow to start operations and, by and large, did not deploy the seasoned humanitarian workers needed to work in such a difficult environment. At the same time, there were a number of international initiatives in related areas—the "One UN" movement, the report of the high-level panel on system-wide coherence, the development of integrated missions, and the Good Humanitarian Donorship initiative—indicating that other parts of the international community were in the mood for change.

Finally, there were changes in the humanitarian agencies themselves that contributed to a hospitable climate for humanitarian reform. António Guterres was appointed UN High Commissioner for Refugees, and his willingness to consider taking on more responsibility for IDPs was in marked contrast to the approach of his predecessors, who were much more cautious about assuming additional responsibilities without assurance of additional funding. The World Health Organization embarked on an ambitious process of decentralization. Under the leadership of Jan Egeland, OCHA sought to play a more proactive role in coordinating humanitarian response—a proposal that had been vociferously opposed by previous high commissioners for refugees. The creation of a senior network on internal displacement under the leadership of Dennis McNamara, followed by the establishment of the Internal Displacement Division (IDD) within OCHA, gave more visibility to and provided more expertise on IDPs within the international humanitarian community.

In February 2005, an independent review of the humanitarian system was commissioned. By June, the review, which included thirty-six specific recommendations, was circulated.[98] Among other things, the review found a serious need for collaboration among the three international humanitarian networks (UN; ICRC and Red Cross/Red Crescent national societies; and NGOs) and highlighted particular weaknesses in protection:

> As a sector, protection requires special and urgent attention. Specific examples of this are the many instances of gender-violence in Darfur. A complicating element is that the different perceptions of roles and responsibilities often confuse discussion on the issues. The NGO and the UN communities approach issues on the ground in distinctly different ways. The NGOs generally focus on a lack of ability to provide "protection" in a loosely defined manner. Whereas the UN system, while acknowledging weakness in the actual provision of protection, tends to regard the subject in terms of far more defined institutional roles.[99]

Humanitarian reform initially focused on three issues: improved humanitarian leadership (particularly the strengthening of humanitarian coordinators), more predictable and accountable response through the new "cluster" approach, and faster, more predictable funding through reform of the Central Emergency Response Fund. The review focused primarily on intergovernmental agencies, a fact lamented by the NGO community. Subsequently, a fourth initiative, the Global Humanitarian Platform, was initiated in 2006 to bring about a closer partnership between the UN, NGOs, and ICRC and the Red Cross/Red Crescent national societies.

The Cluster Approach

In 2005, the cluster approach was endorsed by the IASC "to address gaps in the humanitarian response to large-scale IDP situations beyond the scope of any one agency and ensure a more predictable, harmonized approach.[100] The cluster approach began with eight clusters and later expanded to eleven (see box 4-2). Originally, the cluster approach was intended to fill perceived gaps in assistance (particularly concerning IDPs), but it has come to be much broader, encompassing system-wide reform. Hence, no sectors were established for food, education, agriculture, or refugees because WFP, UNICEF, FAO, and UNHCR were assumed to be responsible for those areas.[101] But there were fears that if there was not a cluster on an issue, it would be ignored and receive less funding. Thus the NGOs lobbied for creation of an education cluster, and currently there are efforts to name a cluster on food security.

The cluster system was the most visible of the changes brought about by humanitarian reform, and the agencies participating in the clusters as well

Box 4-2. *Clusters and Lead Agencies*

Shelter (UNHCR)

Health (WHO)

Nutrition (UNICEF)

Water, sanitation, hygiene (UNICEF)

Education (UNICEF, Save the Children)

Agriculture (FAO)

Early recovery (UNDP)

Camp management (UNHCR and IOM)

Telecommunications (OCHA)

Protection in conflict situations (UNHCR)

Logistics (WFP)

as the IASC and its working group devoted considerable energy to setting up the system, devising terms of reference and work plans. There were questions about when and how and which clusters were to be activated when an emergency occurred. Official guidance was developed, specifying that

> the number and configuration of clusters will depend in each case on the specifics of the humanitarian emergency in question and the response capacities of the national and international actors involved. If necessary, the names of individual clusters may be adapted to the context to allow for better integration with government coordination structures and for a smooth transition once the emergency phase is over. If there are significant objections to using the terminology of "clusters," Humanitarian Country Teams should agree on an alternative; the principal concern should be to apply the principles embedded in the cluster approach, rather than to be rigid about the terminology.[102]

THE PROTECTION CLUSTER

The Protection Cluster Working Group adopted the IASC definition of protection ("all activities aimed at ensuring full respect for the rights of the individual in accordance with the letter and the spirit of the relevant bodies of law (i.e. human rights, humanitarian law and refugee law)").[103] In 2009, it issued a concept paper on protection mainstreaming that stated that

[i]n a nutshell, the position of this document is that *protection main-streaming* refers to the *minimum* requirements for all humanitarian actors to ensure that a protection lens is incorporated into their doctrine and practice: revolving around the principles of '*do no harm*'; *equality; participation and empowerment; and accountability.*

The paper defines protection integration as designing humanitarian assistance to fulfill objectives considered proper to protection activities; it goes beyond protection mainstreaming to include the need for humanitarian actors to integrate the necessary protection doctrine and knowledge in their structures and to abide by recognized standards of protection work. That means that the humanitarian actor seeking to empower women to prevent domestic violence through an income generation project will need experience in and knowledge of women's rights. The document concludes that "therefore, *protection mainstreaming* is a requirement for all humanitarian actors, while *protection integration* and the implementation of *standalone protection activities* are not."[104]

While UNHCR was willing to assume the leadership role in the protection cluster in cases of conflict, it was reluctant to take on that responsibility in natural disasters, and a somewhat cumbersome process evolved in which UNHCR, UNICEF, and OHCHR were to consult with each other on natural disasters and then decide which of the agencies would take the lead. There were hopes that UNICEF would assume that responsibility, but in 2008, UNICEF decided not to take on the task and the system reverted to the ad hoc negotiation system. Following the January 2010 earthquake in Haiti, OHCHR assumed leadership of the protection cluster although, as a nonoperational agency, its ability to provide necessary leadership was limited.

As of March 2010, there were a total of thirty protection clusters, of which eight were established to respond to natural disasters and twenty-two to respond to complex emergencies. Of the thirty clusters, twenty-one were led by UNHCR, five by UNICEF, and one by OHCHR. Two clusters had been deactivated (Georgia and Samoa), and seven were "in transition" as humanitarian activities were being phased out due to political changes in countries such as Uganda and Burundi.[105]

CLUSTERS: MAKING A DIFFERENCE?

From the beginning, the emergency relief coordinator gave priority to the introduction of clusters, which were intended to be the interagency planning framework for new and ongoing emergencies. Clusters were expected to provide the necessary coordination between different international and national actors and to improve accountability and the speed of response. The cluster leads were not expected to carry out all operations in their respective sectors but to provide a forum for ensuring that the necessary work got done. And importantly, cluster leads at the country level were required to be providers of last resort.[106] One of the confusing aspects of the cluster system was the relationship between global clusters and clusters organized on the national level. In November 2006 the *IASC Guidance Note on Using the Cluster Approach to Strengthen Humanitarian Response* was published, and generic terms of reference were developed for cluster coordinators at the country level.[107] Those documents spelled out the fact that global cluster leads are accountable to the ERC for ensuring technical capacity and system-wide preparedness. At the country level, cluster lead agencies are accountable to the humanitarian coordinator. As early as 2007—two years after the cluster system was introduced—the Humanitarian Policy Group (HPG) found that

> the lack of a consistent, clear conceptualisation of the cluster approach is not just a product of poor communication, but stems from deep-seated inconsistencies and lack of consensus between member states, UN agencies and non-UN humanitarian actors about the role of cluster leads, and the relationship between them, affected states and non-UN humanitarian actors.[108]

In 2007, the first phase of the cluster evaluation process found that participation in the clusters by NGOs—particularly national NGOs—was weak.[109] At the global level, Save the Children was the only global NGO co-lead, sharing responsibility for the education cluster with UNICEF as provider of last resort. Only rarely have national NGOs assumed leadership positions at the national level.

The cluster system was intended to improve accountability and predictability. With designated lead agencies, who was to be responsible for acting in a given situation would be clear, and as provider of last resort, cluster leads would increase accountability. A review of the engagement of NGOs in humanitarian reform found that NGOs often were unaware of the clusters and that in some cases their initial attempts to participate were not appreciated: "Where NGOs do engage with clusters, they often feel overwhelmed by meetings, they do not feel respected as equal partners and they do not see reform grounded in accountability to crisis-affected communities."[110] And the establishment of clusters has meant an increase in the number of meetings, raising particular concerns about local NGOs, which often are alienated by the sheer quantity of meetings and the fact that they usually are conducted in English.

> Cluster members frequently complain that meetings are not effective or efficient; and discussions tend to [be] more information-sharing than strategic. There are a number of reasons cited by participants, including lack of the "right" people in the room, frequent turnover of cluster coordinators, inadequate links with staff outside the capital, lack of coordination between different clusters and poor meeting management. Information management systems often pose obstacles for certain cluster members either because of language issues (meetings are usually in English), or are based on UN/donor systems unfamiliar to local organizations, or rely on good internet activity. INGO staff often claim they lack the necessary staff or time to attend all the meetings that are related to their activities, but the strain on national NGOs is even more, including constraints due to language issues. Most decision-making takes place in the capital and, as the cyclone Nargis IA-RTE example showed, cluster coordinators rarely go to the field.[111]

Humanitarian Leadership

Formally, humanitarian coordinators are accountable to the emergency relief coordinator, but double- or triple-hatting (the resident coordinator is responsible to UNDP; the deputy special representative of the secretary-general is responsible to the special representative of the secretary-general) can increase the reporting difficulties and confusion of the humanitarian coordinators. In 2006, the IASC principals endorsed an action plan to strengthen the humanitarian coordinator system to improve the appointment process for HCs, strengthen their accountability to the humanitarian community, and provide better training and ongoing support for them.[112]

A study by six NGOs and ICVA found that in four of the five countries studied, there was a lack of strong and qualified humanitarian leadership. There were cases in which HCs sidelined humanitarian issues because they were subsumed under other agendas. And unfortunately, many HCs do not understand humanitarian action or the role of NGOs.[113]

Global Humanitarian Platform

The early lack of consultation and engagement of NGOs in the cluster system led to resistance to reform on their part. NGOs were offended because they were barely consulted during OCHA's Humanitarian Response Review.[114] As a result of an NGO initiative, Jan Egeland agreed to create a Global Humanitarian Platform, to be based on three equal pillars: the UN system; the NGO system; and ICRC and the Red Cross/Red Crescent national societies.[115]

In July 2007, leaders of UN agencies, INGO consortia, national NGOs, and ICRC and the Red Cross/Red Crescent national societies came together to endorse the principles of partnership, which were intended to form the basis of relationships within and between the three humanitarian families.[116] They agreed to base their partnership on the principles of equality, transparency, a results-oriented approach, responsibility, and complementarity. In succeeding years, the principles of partnership were discussed in regional consultations and the global meeting of the platform incorporated more national NGOs.

The jury is still out as to whether these efforts to reform the humanitarian system are resulting in more efficient delivery of assistance or higher standards of protection. As the review of NGO engagement with the humanitarian reform process indicated, there was "no hard evidence that UN-centered humanitarian reforms have improved the provision of humanitarian response thus far. . . . The ultimate test for humanitarian reform will be the extent to which it improves the lot of crisis-affected people, rather than whether it streamlines the international humanitarian system."[117]

Evolving Understandings of Protection and Assistance

While ICRC was established to protect certain categories of combatants and civilians during armed conflict and UNHCR was created to protect refugees, much of the work of other UN agencies and NGOs originally was intended to provide material assistance to people in need. But over the course of the last two decades, the sharp distinction between protection and assistance has broken down as aid workers have come to see that the way that assistance is provided can affect the protection of people. For example, the way camps are laid out can affect the physical safety of inhabitants. When material assistance is inadequate in refugee camps or urban centers, people may turn to petty crime or prostitution. Women who are able to provide for their families are less likely to engage in prostitution. The differences in defining protection make it difficult to assess the results of all this protection work. When protection is defined as "all activities aimed at obtaining full respect for the rights of the individual in accordance with the letter and the spirit of the relevant bodies of law (i.e. human rights, humanitarian law and refugee law),"[118] then measures of school enrollment or infant mortality can be used as indicators of protection. But when protection is seen in terms of physical security or safety, different indicators are needed, such as the number of attacks or sexual assaults taking place. Thus far, there has been little systematic work to develop protection indicators for humanitarian action—at least beyond the reporting of the activities undertaken by humanitarian agencies.

5

Global Governance

While every epoch has its humanitarian catastrophes, three crises that occurred in the 1990s—in Somalia, Bosnia, and Rwanda—constituted a particular assault on humanitarian principles and on the UN system as a whole.[1] While the world had rushed massive relief to the victims of the 1984–85 famine in Ethiopia and had reacted with horror to reports of genocide in Cambodia, and while hundreds of thousands of Vietnamese had been resettled following that country's war, the events of the 1990s represented a turning point in humanitarian principles and in UN engagement in protecting people in danger. While some of the earlier crises had been larger in scale—some 1.5 million people, 20 percent of the population, were killed in the Cambodian genocide between 1975 and 1979, for example—there was an expectation in the post–cold war era that the international community could prevent future bloodbaths. In Somalia, no less than four peacekeeping operations failed to bring even a modicum of stability to the country. The war in Bosnia, where peacekeepers were helpless to prevent the massacre of thousands at Srebenica, demonstrated that European countries were not immune to widespread carnage. And peacekeepers were unable to stop the genocide in Rwanda. Television coverage of the tragedies beamed the deaths into homes of millions of people. Never again could the world say "If we'd only known" or "If the UN had only been able to act." In all three cases, the UN was present and failed to protect people. In all three cases, humanitarian actors were compromised. These three cases marked the end of "humanitarian innocence," if such a thing had ever existed. They also ushered in new reform processes at the UN, even as they revealed the limits of humanitarian protection.

These three crises also marked the end of the dream that the post–cold war era would usher in an era of peace and stability. When the Berlin wall was breached there was a hope that the world had fundamentally changed for the better. The UN would be able to assume a new activist role, unhindered by the continual threats of a Soviet veto. Without proxy wars being fought in support of cold war alliances and without a continual flow of weapons from one side or another, regional conflicts could well simply disappear. There was a moment, marked by the euphoria of a reunited Germany, when it seemed that a new world order—a major peace dividend—was possible.

That optimism ended in Somalia. In 1991, Somali president Major General Mohamed Siad Barre was overthrown, ushering in what was to become a decades-long civil war. A new government, under the leadership of the United Somali Congress, was formed, but it was unable to bring about an end to the violence. Gangs of armed men terrorized the inhabitants of Mogadishu. Social norms and values degenerated as hospitals were attacked, children were killed, and everything of value was stolen. Rather than ideology or economics, the conflict seemed to be based on intra- and inter-clan rivalry. The ICRC and a few NGOs continued to provide very limited assistance, but they were hampered by a lack of partners and, above, all by widespread insecurity, making it dangerous to distribute aid. Fully laden ships turned back from Mogadishu because they could not unload.

By early 1992, it was estimated that between one-quarter and one-third of all Somali children under the age of five already had died.[2] The UN sent a few missions to the country, but a cease-fire proved elusive. After months of torturous negotiations, the UN and Red Cross began importing significant amounts of food in 1992, but they had to hire small armies of mercenaries to protect the relief. By mid-1992, ICRC was devoting half of its entire worldwide emergency budget for its relief operations in Somalia.[3] In April 1992, the UN Security Council agreed to establish a UN Operation in Somalia (UNOSOM I) and dispatched fifty UN observers to promote a political settlement. In August, the Security Council approved the deployment of an additional 3,000 troops, but the widespread violence prevented them from playing an active role. Operation Provide Relief, which lasted from September 1992 until February 1993, focused on improving the logistics of relief delivery. By late 1992, 1.5 million people faced imminent starvation; almost 5 million were totally dependent on food aid. In resolution 794, the Security Council determined that the "magnitude of the human tragedy caused by the conflict in Somalia constituted a threat to international peace and security." With televised images of starving Somalis filling television screens at the UN and over a million refugees seeking safety outside of the country, in

December 1992 the UN Security Council accepted the U.S. offer of military troops to establish a "secure environment for humanitarian relief operations" in Somalia. The United Task Force (UNITAF), also known as Operation Restore Hope, mobilized some 38,000 troops, led by U.S. forces. The operation was able to restore a modicum of order, and in 1993 it was replaced by UN troops (UNOSOM II), but in October 1993, strongman Mohammad Farad Adid attacked the peacekeepers, killing thirty Pakistani troops. In October 1993, eighteen U.S. troops—and 300 civilians—were killed in the fighting, and U.S. troops withdrew. UNOSOM II remained in the country, increasingly beleaguered and circumscribed, until 1995.[4]

Somalia was a shock to the international community. Humanitarians wrestled with the ethical issues of hiring security guards—typically teenagers with guns—to provide protection for relief operations. Such protection was essential if relief operations were to be carried out, but paying these youth meant that humanitarian agencies were in fact paying warlords who could use the money to buy more weapons to prolong the war. And paying for protection went against the grain of humanitarian organizations. Humanitarians were there to do good, to help the people, and there was an assumption that that should be recognized and respected. Somalia also was a case in which peacekeeping and humanitarian assistance were intertwined from the beginning—UN peacekeepers were deployed not to keep peace between warring factions (there was no peace agreement, in fact) but to protect delivery of humanitarian relief. As Taylor Seyboldt points out in his excellent study, as long as the peacekeepers confined their work to providing security for humanitarian operations, they were all right.[5] But when they began to take sides, they were targeted by the armed groups, with the result that they became ineffective and were forced to leave. The United Nations lost face, and future U.S. support for UN peacekeeping efforts would be limited.

While there had been earlier heart-rending images of starvation in Africa—notably in the 1984–85 famine in Ethiopia—the Somalia crisis demanded an international response. But the international community could not figure out how to respond. Humanitarian relief was urgently needed, but to provide such relief, compromises had to be made that contributed to the conflict by providing money for weapons. Security was needed to provide assistance, but UN troops were no longer seen as neutral. Since the early 1990s, the carnage has continued, with occasional lulls and foreign intervention by the Ethiopians. But by and large the international community has failed to protect or assist Somali civilians in Somalia. Somali refugees have been protected and assisted in neighboring Kenya and some have been resettled in other countries, but in mid-2010, displacement and death continued in Somalia, and the international community has been unable to stop the violence.

Then there was Bosnia, a conflict occurring in Europe. The Bosnian conflict was a direct result of the breakup of the former Yugoslavia. A quick war between Slovenian and Yugoslav federal armed forces resulted in Slovenian national independence in 1991, but conflict continued in Croatia and from 1992 in Bosnia. The former Yugoslavia had been an ethnically diverse country—as one observer noted, they were "all minorities"—and battles for political power and independence became a conflict over territory. Forcible displacement of minorities—or ethnic cleansing—was not just incidental to war efforts, it was the principal objective of the conflicting parties. The conflict in Bosnia was between three groups: Serbs, Bosniaks, and Croats. In April 1992, the UN Protection Force for Yugoslavia (UNPROFOR) was created with a mandate "to create the conditions of peace and security required for the negotiation of an overall settlement of the Yugoslav crisis." With a force of 30,000 troops, UNPROFOR was one of the largest peacekeeping operations of its time, but it was unable to create those conditions. Its mandate was expanded to include assisting the humanitarian airlift during the siege of Sarajevo, escorting humanitarian relief convoys, and protecting Bosnian civilians in designated "safe areas."

The displacement of large numbers of people led to fears in Europe of a large refugee outflow and therefore to demands that people be assisted internally. Therefore UNHCR, which had occasionally worked with IDPs in other situations, became the principal relief agency in the country. Most of those that it served were IDPs, not refugees. Protection of humanitarian operations became the central thrust of UNPROFOR's activities. Although the UN established protected areas, they failed to protect civilians, most dramatically in the case of Srebenica, where Dutch peacekeepers stood by while men were separated from their families and taken away to be shot, in part because of the limited mandate of UNPROFOR and the lack of NATO air support. There were ethical issues facing humanitarians as well—did humanitarian agencies help people escape and thus contribute to ethnic cleansing or did they stand by and watch people be killed? In spite of many peace envoys and negotiations, the Serbs ultimately were brought to the negotiating table only by three weeks of NATO airstrikes in Operation Deliberate Force. The Dayton Peace Agreement of 1995 brought an end to the conflict, but even now, fifteen years later, there are still over 100,000 internally displaced people in Bosnia.[6]

Bosnia had a profound impact on both the United Nations and the humanitarian community. The UN, in spite of support from its members and the deployment of large numbers of peacekeepers, was unable to protect civilians. It was unable to stop ethnic cleansing or the massacre of people in so-called safe areas.

Finally there was Rwanda. Although Hutu-Tutsi violence had a long history in Rwanda—it had driven hundreds of thousands of Tutsi refugees to neighboring Uganda in the 1950s—the UN's involvement was limited to relatively small-scale peacekeeping missions. In 1993, UN Security Council resolution 872 created the UN Assistance Mission to Rwanda (UNAMIR) to monitor a peace agreement signed earlier that year. But the situation deteriorated, and after the death of President Hayarimana on April 6, 1994, hardline Hutu militants seized power and began a vicious national campaign of genocide. Even as reports began to mount of hundreds of thousands of people being slaughtered and Lieutenant General Roméo Dallaire, the UNAMIR commander, asked for reinforcements, the UN not only refused to increase the number of UN troops but actually reduced it. The Rwandan Patriotic Army (RPA), organized in exile, mounted an attack on Rwanda, eventually reaching the capital city of Kigali in July. In the following weeks, over a million refugees, mainly Hutu, fled to neighboring Zaire and Tanzania. When the killing had begun in April, almost all the humanitarian agencies left the country. ICRC remained and managed to provide small-scale assistance and to save some lives during the crisis, but its actions were woefully inadequate to stop the carnage.

However, the humanitarian community did swing into full gear in responding to the refugees. The refugees, concentrated around Goma, were sick, hungry, and thirsty. Some 50,000 people died in a cholera outbreak in just a month.[7] UNHCR, together with over 100 NGOs, set up camps and began large-scale relief programs with the help of a military airlift. Perhaps motivated by guilt at having failed to prevent the genocide, the international community provided enormous amounts of humanitarian assistance. It was a massive humanitarian response, but the armed groups began re-arming and using the refugee camps to mount attacks against Rwanda. It took some time for the humanitarian agencies to realize that rather than helping innocent victims, much of their aid was assisting the *génocidaires* and enabling them to reorganize and carry out further military attacks. The Rwandan experience also raised questions about the meaning of impartiality in both humanitarian and peacekeeping operations. For example, UNAMIR asked on several occasions to take preemptive action that might have mitigated some of the violence, but its requests were denied because doing so would move the peacekeepers away from impartiality into an active role in the conflict.

Rwanda—coming as it did after Somalia and in the midst of the Bosnia crisis—led to profound soul-searching within both the United Nations and the humanitarian community. For the UN, the genocide was evidence of the failure of the international community to take action to prevent mass atrocities—even in a case in which there was little doubt about what was going on. Drawing parallels between the efforts of the international community in Somalia, Bosnia, and Rwanda, Taylor Seyboldt noted that

> governments once again chose to treat the humanitarian symptoms of a political crisis rather than address the deeper causes of the suffering. The UN military force was severely undercut by member states that did not want to face the costs and risks which aggressive action would have required.[8]

For the international community, the genocide led directly to efforts to improve accountability, reaffirm humanitarian principles, and strengthen transitional justice. For example, the IFRC/NGO code of conduct, which had been drafted before the genocide, was quickly completed and a process, known as Sphere, was begun to incorporate a rights-based approach to humanitarian response through development of a humanitarian charter and minimum standards for disaster response.

The crises of the 1990s set the stage for humanitarian actors to become more engaged in protection. If neither the UN nor powerful governments could protect people, at least humanitarian agencies could take some actions. At the same time, they propelled the broader international system to look seriously at protection. This chapter looks at some of the ways that the UN system as a whole—not just the humanitarians—has tried to deal with protection. Somalia, Bosnia, and Rwanda were humanitarian crises to be sure—and humanitarian agencies were on the front lines in all three cases—but they were fundamentally political failures of the international community and particularly of the United Nations.

UN Reform

The possibilities opened up by the end of the cold war, coupled with the UN's failures in Somalia, Bosnia, and Rwanda, directly contributed to the emergence of new reform efforts, beginning with peace operations, that in turn led to an often-expressed demand for greater coherence in UN operations. UN reform efforts over the past decade show dissatisfaction with piecemeal approaches to the world's problems and a yearning for a coherent, holistic approach. Rather than having a dozen different UN agencies embark on programs to respond to particular needs and constituencies, the UN could increase its impact and effectiveness through a coherent, coordinated approach. Thus proposals for integrated missions, the one-UN initiative, the capstone doctrine on UN peacekeeping, the Peacebuilding Commission, and the doctrine of responsibility to protect emerged. All recognized that development and humanitarian response are fundamentally linked to peace. At the same time, efforts to increase accountability and to end impunity gathered steam. The movement to bring perpetrators to justice gained momentum in the 1990s, with international tribunals established in the former Yugoslavia and Rwanda, with domestic courts seeking to prosecute war criminals in other countries, and eventually with the establishment of the International Criminal Court in 2002, when the 1998 Rome Statute came into effect.[9]

Each of the reform initiatives, summarized in table 5-1, was concerned, to some degree, with increasing international protection. Rather than taking a chronological approach, this chapter begins with peacekeeping; it then discusses some of the efforts to increase coherence and protect civilians and concludes with the responsibility to protect doctrine. But it is important to note that all of the efforts were mutually reinforcing. Efforts to strengthen peacekeeping, for example, directly impacted integrated missions.

The Brahimi Report

Since its inception, peacekeeping has been central to the work, the credibility, and the legitimacy of the United Nations. In the words of one UN staff member, "The UN can run good humanitarian or development programs, but is judged by how well it keeps the peace."[10] The 1990s had been disastrous for UN peacekeeping operations. The UN's failure to prevent the 1994 genocide in Rwanda and its failure to prevent massacres in Srebenica led to a great deal of soul-searching. It also led major powers to turn to non-UN military operations in the Balkans. In fact, it was bombing by NATO forces that led the Serbs to capitulate and paved the way for the Dayton peace agreement in 1995. Reflecting the lack of confidence in UN peacekeeping operations, two UN-sanctioned but independently organized initiatives sought to protect delivery of humanitarian assistance in Somalia, while in Rwanda, the French military created a safe area under the rubric of Operation Turquoise. Although the UN peacekeeping apparatus was largely sidelined for several years following the Rwandan genocide, by 1999 there were new possibilities for UN action in Kosovo, East Timor, and the Democratic Republic of the

Table 5-1. *Summary of UN Reform Initiatives, 1999–2008*

UN Reform Initiative (report)	Date	Focus
Report of the Secretary-General on the Protection of Civilians in Armed Conflict (S/2009/277)	1999	Protection of civilians
Report of the Panel on United Nations Peace Operations (Brahimi report) (A/55/305–S/2000/809)	2000	UN peacekeeping
The Responsibility to Protect: Report of the International Commission on Intervention and State Sovereignty	2001	Responsibility to protect
We the Peoples: Civil Society, the United Nations, and Global Governance: Report of the Panel of Eminent Persons on United Nations–Civil Society Relations (Cardoso report) (A/58/81)	2004	UN relations with non-government organiza-tions and civil society
A More Secure World: Our Shared Responsibility: Report of the Secretary-General's High-Level Panel on Threats, Challenges, and Change	2004	Threats to international peace and security
In Larger Freedom: Towards Development, Security and Human Rights for All: Report of the Secretary-General	2005	Economic and social rights
Report on Integrated Missions: Practical Perspec-tives and Recommendations: Independent Study for the Expanded UN Executive Committee on Humanitarian Affairs (ECHA) Core Group (Integrated missions report)	2005	Unity of UN action at the country level
2005 World Summit Outcome Document (A/RES/60/1)	2005	Human Rights Council; responsibility to protect
Delivering as One: Report of the High-Level Panel on United Nations System-Wide Coherence in the Areas of Development, Humanitarian Assistance, and the Environment	2006	Development, humanitar-ian assistance, and the environment
United Nations Peacekeeping Operations: Principles and Guidelines (Capstone doctrine)	2008	Peacekeeping operational and doctrinal issues

Congo. The UN also took over the responsibilities of the Economic Commu-nity of West African States Monitoring Group (ECOMOG) in Sierra Leone by establishing the United Nations Mission in Sierra Leone. Yet as Willliam Durch points out, in 1999 the elements of the UN Secretariat responsible for peacekeeping were underfunded, understaffed, unprepared to run a country (and were politically constrained from preparing to do so even if they had possessed the requisite expertise), and not up to dealing with ruthless, diamond smuggling gangs who passed for treaty signatories, such as Sierra Leone's Revolutionary United Front.[11]

It was in that context that the UN decided to undertake a review of UN peacekeeping operations. A ten-person panel, chaired by former Algerian foreign minister and UN envoy Lakhdar Brahimi, was established to present a clear set of specific, concrete, and practical recommendations to improve UN peacekeeping and security activities. Its report provided a blunt assessment of the weaknesses of UN peacekeeping operations, finding problems every step of the way: overly ambitious mandates, deployment of inadequately trained and equipped forces, a cumbersome bureaucracy, and little coordination between agencies. The panel concluded that decisionmaking was far too slow and that there was an absence of the political will needed to make peacekeeping forces more effective. The Brahimi report, issued in August 2000, made a total of fifty-seven recommendations on doctrine, strategy, and decisionmaking; UN capacities; headquarters structure for planning and supporting peacekeeping operations; information technologies; and the commitment of member states. The Brahimi report stressed the need for the political will of member states to support the UN politically, financially, and operationally to enable it to be a credible force for peace.[12]

Protection of civilians figured prominently in the panel's findings. It said, for example, that United Nations peacekeepers—troops or police—who witness violence against civilians should be presumed to be authorized to stop it, within their means, to support basic United Nations principles. Moreover, it insisted that operations that had been given a broad and explicit mandate for civilian protection be given the resources needed to carry out that mandate.[13] But the report stopped short of calling for a blanket mandate to protect civilians, noting that

> there are hundreds of thousands of civilians in current United Nations mission areas who are exposed to potential risk of violence, and United Nations forces currently deployed could not protect more than a small fraction of them even if directed to do so. Promising to extend such protection establishes a very high threshold of expectation. The potentially large mismatch between desired objectives and resources available to meet it raises the prospect of continuing disappointment with United Nations follow-through in this area. If an operation is given a

mandate to protect civilians, therefore, it also must be given the specific resources needed to carry out that mandate.[14]

The recommendations of the Brahimi report were endorsed by UN Secretary-General Kofi Annan and by the Security Council,[15] and the secretariat made progress in acting on many of the recommendations.[16]

The implications for humanitarian actors, however, went beyond references to protection of civilians. Traditional humanitarian understandings of impartiality differed from the Brahimi report's definition of impartiality of peace operations, which requires

> adherence to the principles of the [UN] Charter: where one party to a peace agreement clearly and incontrovertibly is violating its terms, continued equal treatment of all parties . . . can in the best case result in ineffectiveness and in the worst may amount to complicity with evil.[17]

Peacekeepers are not neutral; rather, they are deployed on the basis of mandates agreed by Security Council members to take explicitly political action against parties to a conflict—arresting war criminals in the Balkans, for instance.

However, for humanitarians, impartiality means something quite different: the delivery of assistance on the basis of need alone. As a report at the time by the Humanitarian Policy Group (HPG) argued, "There is a risk that too close a relationship between the peacekeeping mission and the humanitarian operation implicates humanitarians in political action."[18] While the HPG report drew connections between threats to humanitarians as a result of too close an alignment with peacekeepers, the Brahimi report suggested that humanitarian action could support peacekeeping missions. It recommended combining quick-impact projects and disarmament, demobilization, and reintegration programs into complex peace operations. Both types of activities were largely implemented in the years following the report. But quick-impact projects—intended to demonstrate the benefits of UN peacekeeping to local populations—brought peacekeeping into the territory of humanitarian assistance and began to raise questions about whether humanitarian principles would take second place to political considerations in deploying and managing peacekeeping missions.

One of the recommendations in the Brahimi report was that integrated mission task forces (IMTFs) should be the standard vehicle for mission-specific planning and support. The idea was that various UN agencies and departments should work together in planning peacekeeping operations before deployment—a theme that was picked up in different contexts by a number of other reform initiatives and one that raised even more questions about the space for humanitarian actors.

The Brahimi report thus led to changes in peacekeeping operations, with more emphasis on protection of civilians; made the initial case for an integrated approach to UN operations, in which humanitarian assistance is viewed as part of the overall UN peacekeeping and political approach to a given situation; and emphasized the central role of political will in determining UN operations in the field.

Integrated Missions

The idea for integrated missions first appeared on the UN reform agenda in the 1997 Programme for Reform report of the secretary-general,[19] which called for more integrated and effective UN action both at headquarters and at the country level. Secretary-General Kofi Annan declared that systemwide integration would be one of his key objectives, particularly with respect to peacekeeping activities, to ensure "that humanitarian strategies as well as longer-term development aims are fully integrated into the overall peace-keeping effort."[20] The drive for integration, which, as mentioned, was given greater impetus by the Brahimi report in 2000, grew out of the conviction that the failures of the 1990s were at least partially the result of independent operations by different UN entities. If the UN could act more coherently, the argument went, at least in highly complex situations, it would have a better chance of success.

Efforts to increase integration began with increasing the authority and responsibilities of the special representative of the secretary-general (SRSG) and "multi-hatting" deputy special representatives of the secretary-general (DSRSGs), making them the nominal heads of UN country teams and humanitarian coordinators (and in some cases, resident representatives of the UN Development Program).[21] The SRSG, the senior UN representative in a country, reports to the secretary-general through the under secretary-general for peacekeeping operations. Up to that point, the humanitarian coordinator had remained outside peacekeeping mission structures, and there was concern that integration would mean the subordination of humanitarian activities to political pressures. In his 2006 *Note of Guidance on Integrated Missions*, the UN secretary-general tried to address that concern by noting that the SRSG will uphold humanitarian principles in the implementation of the mission's mandate.[22]

An independent study, *Report on Integrated Missions: Practical Perspectives and Recommendations,* was prepared for the UN Expanded Executive Committee on Humanitarian Affairs (ECHA) Core Group.[23] The report defines an integrated mission as "an instrument with which the UN seeks to help countries in the transition from war to lasting peace, or address a similarly complex situation that requires a system-wide UN response, through subsuming various actors and approaches within an overall political-strategic crisis management framework." According to the report, an integrated mission should entail a clearly defined purpose for UN engagement, a structure to ensure integrated action and communication, and "a process whereby the wider United Nations system is mobilised and collaborates [in support of] the integrated mission."[24]

The report went on to explain that UN integrated missions incorporate three separate undertakings, each of which includes different actors, priorities, and objectives: first is to restore stability, law, and order; second is to protect civilians, and third is to establish a foundation for long-term recovery, development, and democratic governance.[25] While peacekeepers see integrated missions in terms of supporting peace agreements, development actors look at the situation from a longer-term perspective, and humanitarian actors try to provide assistance on the basis of humanitarian principles of impartiality and neutrality—principles not easily reconciled with broader political objectives.[26]

The role of the Office for the Coordination of Humanitarian Affairs (OCHA) in integrated missions is ambiguous. OCHA, with its remit of coordinating humanitarian activities in a particular country, reports to the emergency relief coordinator (ERC), although sometimes the OCHA country director is also expected to report to the SRSG. The independent report suggests that OCHA should be staffed by representatives of UN agencies but should not be part of the overall mission structure. There also are tensions between the objectives of human rights officers and the overall objectives of the mission, although the report recommended that human rights advisers should report directly to the SRSG, a position upheld in the secretary-general's guidance note of 2006.[27] Negotiating humanitarian access also calls into question the nature of integrated missions. While humanitarian organizations may need to negotiate with nonstate actors to get humanitarian relief in, the fact that they are "asking for favors" can impact larger peace negotiations.[28] These issues, and particularly the role of OCHA in countries with integrated missions, came to the fore in 2008 in Afghanistan, where humanitarian actors called for an independent OCHA outside the UN Assistance Mission in Afghanistan (UNAMA) structure, arguing that OCHA was best placed to carry out the humanitarian diplomacy needed to ensure access for humanitarian work. An independent OCHA office eventually was established—although the deterioration of the security situation in the country resulted in decreased access by humanitarian agencies.

Humanitarians' nervousness at the prospect of integrated missions stemmed from experiences in which political and military considerations had taken precedence over the needs of humanitarian agencies. For example, in Somalia in 1992, the SRSG was reported to have told the World Food Program that food to feed almost 250,000 IDPs could not be offloaded "in order to teach their leaders (the warlords) a lesson."[29] In Liberia in the early 1990s, Economic Community of West African States Monitoring Group bombardments during Operation Octopus hindered humanitarian work, thereby increasing the need for aid and putting humanitarians themselves at risk.[30] In addition, the decision to allow ECOMOG to halt cross-border aid from Côte d'Ivoire proved deleterious to humanitarian work because it caused a split between the UN, which supported the decision on political grounds, and the NGOs, which opposed it.[31] And in 2004, after fourteen years of civil war in Liberia, the SRSG had encouraged IDPs and refugees to return to ill-prepared home areas so that they could vote in mission-supported elections.[32]

The secretary-general's 2006 *Note of Guidance on Integrated Missions* attempted to bring some clarity to the integration agenda. The note reaffirms integration as "the guiding principle for the design and implementation of complex UN operations in post-conflict situations" and puts forth two basic criteria for integrated missions: they must be based on a strategic plan and they must contain a "shared understanding" of priorities, programmatic interventions, and basic sequencing.[33]

The reaction of humanitarian actors to integrated missions was largely negative. There was a widespread view throughout the community that humanitarian principles of neutrality and impartiality would be irrevocably undermined by integrated missions and that humanitarian principles would be sacrificed to political expediency. But their concerns lost out to the desire for more coherence in UN operations. In fact, humanitarian organizations found ways of maintaining a high degree of autonomy within integrated structures and in some cases came to find some advantages to the missions. Harmer, for example, notes that some UN agencies, such as UNICEF and UNHCR, and aid organizations, such as Oxfam, "have recognized that integration can provide an opportunity to influence the course of political and military strategies so that they take account of humanitarian principles and are not detrimental to humanitarian outcomes."[34]

The ICRC perspective on integrated missions notes the risk for humanitarian action in its integration into "a political and military strategy to defeat the enemy. In other words, [in] the subordination of humanitarian activities to political goals, using aid as a tool for local or foreign policy."[35] Integration risks the security of humanitarian staff and engenders skepticism about the accountability of humanitarian actors. However, ICRC went on to accept that the integrated approach is here to stay and made some suggestions for recognizing the particular complementarities of specific actors and for developing coordination structures that serve the needs of all actors.

Our Shared Responsibility

The High-Level Panel on Threats, Challenges, and Change (HLP), chaired by former Thai prime minister Anand Panyarachun, was established to examine the institutional weaknesses in the current UN responses to international peace and security threats. The goal of the panel was to assess what policies and institutions need to be strengthened to enable the UN to provide collective security in the twenty-first century.[36] The panel reviewed a wide range of threats to collective security, such as economic and social threats, including poverty, infectious disease, and environmental degradation; interstate conflict; internal conflict, including civil war, genocide, and other large-scale atrocities; nuclear, radiological, chemical, and biological weapons; terrorism; and transnational organized crime.[37]

The HLP came up with over 100 recommendations, ranging from recommendations to reform the Security Council, establish a Peacebuilding Commission, and restore the credibility and effectiveness of the Commission on Human Rights to more traditional recommendations on nuclear proliferation and the role of peacekeepers. Notably, the panel made major contributions to the developing concept of the responsibility to protect.

The recommendations were intended to strengthen the international community's ability to protect populations at risk—whether to prevent the recurrence of future conflicts through sustained attention to peacebuilding or to increase the ability of the Security Council to respond to security threats emanating from complex emergencies. As part and parcel of protecting civilians, the panel urged full respect for the Geneva Conventions and other treaties related to protection of civilians, the Rome Statute, and the 1951 Convention Relating to the Status of Refugees. The panel also called on all actors to follow the secretary-general's ten-point platform for protecting civilians in armed conflict, with particular emphasis on improving access to affected communities by humanitarian actors.

The panel noted the lack of capacity and will of the Security Council to respond to "particularly egregious violations" such as the militarization of refugee camps and called on the council to fully implement resolution 1265 (1999) on the protection of civilians. The panel also placed emphasis on protecting women from "sexual violence as a weapon of conflict" and the related need for peacekeeping operations (PKOs) to have explicit mandates and adequate resources to address that issue. Noting Security Council resolution 1325 (2000) on women, peace, and security, the panel called on the Security Council, UN agencies, and member states to fully implement the recommendations in the resolution's associated Independent Experts' Assessment. As humanitarian activities to protect civilians depend on funding, the panel also called on donors to "fully and equitably" fund protection and assistance programs.[38]

The report of the High-Level Panel served to identify the future reform agenda of the United Nations, and many of the measures identified—from reforming the UN's Human Rights Commission to establishing a Peace-building Commission—were implemented in the years that followed.

Delivering as One

The Secretary-General's High-Level Panel on United Nations System-wide Coherence in the areas of Development, Humanitarian Assistance, and the Environment was intended to improve coherence within the UN structure at the country, regional, and headquarters levels. The assumption was that if the UN were more unified, it would be better equipped to work with and meet the needs of countries working toward their Millennium Development Goals and other agreed-on development goals.[39] The resulting reform—labeled "Delivering as One United Nations (DAO)" or "One UN"—called for one UN office at the country level, with one leader (a resident coordinator), one program, and one budget. The panel designated the United Nations Development Program (UNDP) as the lead agency, with responsibility for coordinating all UN-related development activity at the country level, and called for five pilot "one country programs" to be established by 2007. The panel also called for consolidating the three existing gender institutions—the Office of the Special Advisor on Gender Issues and the Advancement of Women, Division for the Advancement of Women, and UN Development Fund for Women (UNIFEM)—into a single gender-equality and women's empowerment program. Finally, the panel called for designating the UN

High Commissioner for Human Rights (UNHCHR) as the lead on protection efforts, working in coordination with and through governments, relevant institutions, civil society, and individuals. An external evaluation of the Delivering as One initiative began in late 2010 and is scheduled for completion in 2011.[40]

In 2006, eight countries—Albania, Cape Verde, Mozambique, Pakistan, Rwanda, Tanzania, Uruguay, and Viet Nam—volunteered to serve as pilot countries for the one country programs. In accordance with UN General Assembly resolution 62/208, an independent evaluation was conducted in each country to assess the relevance, effectiveness, efficiency, and sustainability of the Delivering as One programs. In June 2009, two years after implementation of the programs, the coordination officers in the eight countries published a joint report examining the lessons learned with respect to challenges in programming, budgeting, governance, operations, procurement, communication, and other areas. The authors recommended that their report be used in conjunction with guidance notes on developing "one program" for implementing the Delivering as One initiative in other countries.

As of March 2010, country-led evaluations were ongoing in seven of the eight pilot countries, which have been meeting to exchange lessons learned; they met in Kigali in October 2009 and again in Hanoi in June 2010.[41] At the Kigali meeting, the eight pilot countries "were unequivocal in their agreement that 'there is no going back.'"[42] In her assessment of the pilot projects in June 2010, Helen Clark, chair of the UN Development Group, noted that the success of the initiative was due in large measure to the fact that it had engaged the national governments in question and that as a result, the UN country offices had become more responsive to and aligned with national development priorities and processes. The one-budget framework had helped the UN to sharpen its strategic focus and respond more flexibly to national development needs. Clark noted that the "one Leader is central to the success of this reform, particularly the enhanced role of the UN Resident Co-ordinator and a strengthened UN Country team," and that efficiency gains were made from the pooling of common services.[43]

Peacebuilding Commission

The High-Level Panel on Threats, Challenges, and Change called for the creation of a Peacebuilding Commission (PBC) as a way to prevent the recurrence of conflict after a peace agreement is in place, which occurs in more than half of all conflicts within five years of an agreement.[44] Momentum built with the release of Secretary-General Kofi Annan's report, *In Larger Freedom*, which noted a "gaping hole" in the UN's efforts to assist countries recovering from conflict.

The establishment of the Peacebuilding Commission turned out to be a hot political issue on several levels. In particular, there was political opposition to giving the commission an early-warning function. While the high-level panel wanted the commission to report to the Security Council, there was opposition to that proposal in the General Assembly; a compromise therefore was agreed on, in which the commission is subsidiary to both the General Assembly and the Security Council and an advisory body to the Economic and Social Council (ECOSOC).[45] Interestingly, while Western states tend to see peacebuilding as a political and security issue associated with the Security Council, governments of developing countries tend to see peacebuilding in terms of economic and social issues and thus more closely tied to ECOSOC and the General Assembly. The PBC was established in 2005, and, after considerable negotiation, representatives of four groups—including the Security Council, ECOSOC, financial contributors to UN peacekeeping operations, and troop-contributing countries—took their seats along with representatives elected by the General Assembly.

The Peacebuilding Commission's mandate is to marshal resources for, advise on, support, and coordinate the development of integrated strategies for postconflict peacebuilding and recovery. With members from the major UN charter bodies (Security Council, General Assembly, and ECOSOC), the Peacebuilding Commission reflects a broad and representative UN constituency, and the inclusion of all major actors with a stake in the success of peacebuilding gives the commission significant legitimacy. Despite its lack of direct operational capacity, the commission is tasked with making recommendations and providing information to improve the coordination of all relevant actors within and outside the UN. Shortly after it began its work, the Peacebuilding Commission also faced criticism: for having a limited country focus, for being led by the agenda of national authorities, and for having quickly become politicized.[46]

Justice and Accountability

One of the major advances in human rights in recent decades has been the movement to end the impunity of those responsible for committing mass atrocities against civilians and to develop institutions and procedures to ensure that they are held accountable. The first international criminal tribunals, the Nuremberg and Tokyo Tribunals (1945 and 1946, respectively), were a watershed in international criminal justice, as they held individuals, not states, accountable for crimes against peace, war crimes, and crimes against humanity committed during the Second World War. Until the early 1990s, accountability was solely the responsibility of national legal institutions and extradition was a central tool in its enforcement. After the close of the Nuremberg trials, some other Nazi leaders were located and extradited for trial, including Rudolph Hoess, commandant of Auschwitz, who was tried and executed in Poland in 1947, and the "architect of the Holocaust," Lieutenant Colonel Adolph Eichmann, who was tried and executed in Jerusalem in 1962.

Three models of international criminal justice have emerged since the 1990s: ad hoc tribunals establish by the Security Council (International Criminal Tribunals for the former Yugoslavia and for Rwanda); hybrid courts, such as the Special Panels for Serious Crimes in East Timor and the Special Court for Sierra Leone; and a permanent treaty-based jurisdiction (International Criminal Court). Other attempts to implement transitional justice have been the result of actions by postconflict governments, such as the establishment of the Truth and Reconciliation Commission of South Africa. And increasingly, development and humanitarian actors are addressing justice issues through work to establish the rule of law in societies emerging from conflict.

Transitional justice refers to a set of measures that can be implemented to redress the legacies of massive human rights abuses that occur during armed conflict and under authoritarian regimes. They include, for example, criminal prosecution, reparation programs, truth commissions, and justice-sensitive security sector reform—measures that seek to ensure recognition for victims, to foster civil trust, and to promote possibilities for peace, reconciliation, and democracy.[47]

In May 1993, the first of the ad hoc tribunals was established to address crimes in the former Yugoslavia. It was given jurisdiction over genocide, crimes against humanity, and war crimes. Eighteen months later, the Rwanda tribunal was created with essentially the same mandate, although there were more charges of genocide than in the former Yugoslavia. The Rome Diplomatic Conference of June-July 1998 went much further, establishing the International Criminal Court (ICC). The ICC's jurisdiction is limited to genocide, crimes against humanity, and war crimes committed after June 30, 2002, if they are not investigated or prosecuted at the national level. A case can be initiated in three ways: a state party or the Security Council acting under chapter VII can refer a situation to the court; the prosecutor may initiate an investigation; and the Security Council can refer a case—and also can ask for a deferral period of twelve months. Eight cases involving four countries have been brought before the court since it was established. The prosecutor has initiated an investigation following three referrals from state parties to the Rome Statute—Uganda, the Democratic Republic of the Congo, and the Central African Republic. The prosecutor also opened an investigation when the UN Security Council referred the situation in Darfur, Sudan—a nonstate party. In addition, an investigation into the situation in Kenya was authorized in March 2010 following the November 2009 decision of the presidency of the ICC to assign the situation in Kenya, a state party, to the court.[48]

The international community turned to UN-national ("hybrid") tribunals for so-called "justice on the cheap" to prosecute mass atrocities after becoming disillusioned with the exorbitant costs involved in the ad hoc tribunals for Yugoslavia (ICTY) and Rwanda (ICTR), which by 2000 represented over 10 percent of the UN's regular budget. "ICTY and ICTR grew into sprawling institutions, employing thousands, requiring budgets of over $100 million and threatening to operate for 15 years."[49] Since 1998, several hybrid UN-national tribunals have been created, including the Special Court for Sierra Leone (SCSL), the Special Panels for Serious Crimes (SPSC) in East Timor, and the Extraordinary Chambers in the Courts of Cambodia.[50] For its part, the SPSC was unable to mete out justice to high-level officials with command responsibility. By the time the United Nations closed the SPSC in 2005—before investigations could be concluded to bring more charges forward—the SPSC had tried 101 of the 440 defendants charged with the most serious crimes; eighty-seven were tried to a verdict, thirteen had their cases withdrawn or dismissed, and one was found mentally incompetent to stand trial.

Due to lack of cooperation by Indonesian authorities, most of those tried were low-level perpetrators. The majority of the 339 remaining defendants were located outside the country, and the court, which could not conduct trials in absentia, lacked an extradition agreement with Indonesia.[51] In addition, lack of funding and resources constrained the court considerably. Lack of political will also was reflected in the refusal of East Timorese authorities to forward the arrest warrant for former General Wiranto, the commander of Indonesian troops in East Timor in 1999, to INTERPOL, likely because East Timor did not want to tarnish its relations with Indonesia. Justice efforts were further mired when the even the UN distanced itself from the indictment of Wiranto, insisting that East Timor and not the UN had indicted him because the Serious Crimes Unit (which had in fact received backing from the UN) was part of the Timorese Office of Public Prosecution, not part of the UN.[52]

Trials in the Special Court for Sierra Leone, which combines international and domestic law, opened in 1994. By February 2009, convictions of eight pro-government and rebel leaders had been obtained by the court for war crimes and crimes against humanity, including the first-ever convictions for "forced marriage" and conscription of child soldiers by three former leaders of the Revolutionary United Front (RUF), known to be one of the most brutal rebel movements.[53] Former Liberian president and warlord Charles Taylor, accused of fueling the bloody civil war in Sierra Leone, was arrested and transferred to the SCSL in 2006. That action was of great symbolic importance, but the UN decided in 2007 to transfer his trial to the Hague to avoid instability in the region. His trial resumed in June 2007, and a trial judgment is due in mid-2011, with an appeal to be resolved by early 2012.[54]

Unlike the international criminal tribunals for Yugoslavia and Rwanda, the International Criminal Court was not established through a Security Council resolution; hence, the statute binds only those that are party to it, not every member state. In fact, to date, only two permanent Security Council members have ratified the statute: France and the United Kingdom. Russia has signed and indicated that it will eventually become party to the agreement, while China has neither signed nor ratified the treaty. The United States is in the strange position of having signed and then retracted its signature. State parties are obligated to cooperate fully with the ICC, but the statute lacks any mechanism to respond to noncooperation.[55]

The relationship between justice, peace, and humanitarian assistance is complex. At the most basic level, by holding individuals accountable for atrocities committed during war, justice initiatives seek to prevent atrocities from occurring in the first place. If warlords know that they will face trial and imprisonment, the argument goes, they will be less likely to commit atrocities. Some, however, have pointed to the fact that in such situations, warlords may be more likely to kill their victims than leave them wounded or displaced in order to prevent evidence from being used against them in a future trial. Negotiations over amnesties have assumed greater importance in light of the emergence of prosecutions for war crimes. In some cases, the issuing of indictments by the ICC has affected the peace process. Such was the case in Uganda, where two years of peace talks collapsed after the ICC issued arrest warrants for rebel leader Joseph Kony and four of his top commanders. Kony refused to sign the final peace agreement in Juba, Sudan, conditioning his signature on the dropping of the warrants by the ICC.

For humanitarian organizations, the relationship is similarly complex. On the most basic level, humanitarian organizations depend on government permission to carry out their operations, and they constantly struggle with how to deal with human rights abuses. The most striking example was the action of the Omar al-Bashir government of Sudan to expel sixteen organizations (thirteen international and three national) in March 2009, accusing them of collaborating with the ICC by providing evidence leading to indictments against the Sudanese head of state. The fear of being suspected of collaborating with international justice mechanisms has led most operational humanitarian agencies to maintain a careful distance from them, even though it is undoubtedly the case that many staff of humanitarian organizations would personally like to see perpetrators of atrocities brought to justice.

But increasingly humanitarian actors also are engaging with broader justice issues, even in the early days of an emergency. A recent policy paper states that "[c]rimes and abuses, such as theft, rape and domestic violence, are widespread in camps and other settings . . . they cannot wait for long-term justice sector reform."[56] Access to justice is seen as part of the reestablishment of the rule of law, which, in turn, is central to efforts to recover after war. UNDP has defined access to justice as "the ability of people to seek and obtain a remedy through formal or informal institutions of justice, and in conformity with human rights standards."[57] Although humanitarian actors have long worked to provide legal assistance to refugees, asylum seekers, and others affected by conflict—for example, through the Norwegian Refugee Council's information, counseling, and legal assistance (ICLA) initiatives—increasing their engagement with justice issues can change their relationship with the governments of the countries in which they operate.

Protection of Civilians and the Responsibility to Protect Doctrine

Efforts at UN reform have increased the possibilities for effective and coherent UN engagement in a range of conflict situations. We turn now to discussion of two issues—protection of civilians and the responsibility to protect doctrine—that emerged within a few years of each other to try to delineate the international community's responsibility to victims of conflict. The 2008 Capstone Doctrine on peacekeeping missions emphasized the importance of protection of civilians as a concept and linked its effective implementation to the robust use of force.[58]

Protection of Civilians

Since the subject entered UN discourse in 1999, protection of civilians has become central to debates within the Security Council and has become a new mandate of peacekeeping operations. Much of the conceptual work on protection of civilians, which is intended to be a UN-wide endeavor, has been carried out by the Office for the Coordination of Humanitarian Affairs. Governments and nongovernmental organizations also have developed policies and programs on protection of civilians. Discussion of protection also has served as an entrée to discussions of humanitarian issues, particularly access and security.

In addition to the reform efforts already mentioned, a number of landmark UN reports set the stage for the development of the concept of protection of civilians within the United Nations, including the 1996 Graça Machel report on the impact of conflict on children; the Department of Peacekeeping Operations' "Comprehensive Report on Lessons Learned from the UN Operation in Somalia (UNOSOM), 1992–1995"; the 1999 secretary-general's report on the fall of Srebrenica; and the 1999 report of the independent inquiry commission on the Rwandan genocide (Carlsson report).[59]

Rather than assigning blame for the failures in Somalia, Bosnia, and Rwanda to a particular UN department, these reports concluded that the international system itself was responsible. For example, the Carlsson report argued that the failure to halt the Rwandan genocide went beyond UNAMIR—that it was a failure of the UN system as a whole. The fall of Srebenica revealed the overall inadequacy and lack of political will of the international community vis-à-vis civilian protection in Bosnia.

Two reports by UN Secretary-General Kofi Annan in 1998 moved the concept of civilian protection to center stage. In his report on Africa, Annan identified protecting civilians in situations of conflict as a "humanitarian imperative."[60] That was followed in January 1999 by a briefing on humanitarian activities of the Security Council by the under secretary-general for humanitarian affairs, Sergio Vieira de Mello, in which protection of civilians was a major theme[61] and a month later by the council's adoption of presidential statement 1999/6, which expressed "willingness to respond, in accordance with the Charter of the United Nations, to situations in which civilians, as such, have been targeted or humanitarian assistance to civilians has been deliberately obstructed." That statement, which asked the secretary-general to provide recommendations for the council's future work in protecting civilians, led to a landmark report by the secretary-general on September 8, 1999, in which he provided some forty recommendations. The Security Council took up many of the recommendations in two resolutions, resolution 1265 (1999) and resolution 1296 (2000), which stressed the need to ensure compliance with international humanitarian law; address impunity;

improve access for and safety of humanitarian personnel; and tackle the problem of conventional armaments. But the council shied away from some of the secretary-general's more demanding recommendations, notably those to establish council working groups on volatile situations and to develop standby arrangements to ensure that UN peacekeeping troops would be available in the event that they were needed to protect civilians.[62] Resolution 1296 emphasized the need to proceed on a case-by-case basis, taking into account particular circumstances, indicating a cautious approach that limited the council's thematic and norm-setting role in civilian protection.[63]

In March 2001, the secretary-general presented his second report on protection of civilians, noting that only a few of his recommendations had been taken up and suggesting additional recommendations, notably those to engage with armed parties to ensure safe access for humanitarian workers, to support the development of clear criteria for separating armed elements from displaced populations, and to investigate links between illicit trade in natural resources and the conduct of war. There was strong support for three of the suggested initiatives: compiling the provisions in resolutions 1265 and 1296 into a roadmap indicating the responsibilities of various UN organs; creating an *aide-mémoire* to assist the council in its consideration of country-specific situations, particularly peacekeeping mandates; and improving coordination between the UN's Department of Peacekeeping Operations (DPKO) and OCHA.

On March 15, 2002, the Security Council adopted the *aide-mémoire*, which was presented to the council in the secretary-general's third report on protection in November 2002, but there was no formal council reaction. Momentum on protection of civilians seemed to be slowing down—perhaps a victim of the September 11 attacks, increasing concern with terrorism, and the fallout from the U.S.-led invasion of Iraq. In 2003, emergency relief coordinator Jan Egeland proposed ten action points drawn from the roadmap, ranging from the special needs of displaced persons to impunity to humanitarian access.[64] Egeland's list of recommendations was an ambitious call to action, but the council agreed, in presidential statement 2003/27, only to update the *aide-mémoire* and to note "with interest" the issues requiring action suggested by Egeland, which included safety of humanitarian personnel; humanitarian access; particular needs of internally displaced persons, children, and women; shortcomings in the approach to disarmament, demobilization, reintegration, and rehabilitation; the proliferation of small arms and light weapons; impunity; measures to promote the responsibility of armed groups and nonstate actors; and the needs of vulnerable populations in "forgotten emergencies."[65]

In 2005, pressure built as a result of the deteriorating humanitarian situations in Sudan, Colombia, Democratic Republic of the Congo (DRC), Iraq, Somalia, and Northern Uganda, leading to another resolution on protection of civilians, resolution 1674. At the same time that the Security Council was increasingly using the term "protection of civilians," it also used thematic approaches to recognize the need to protect specific groups, particularly women and children. Resolution 1325 (2000) on women, peace, and security represented the first time that women were linked to the peace and security agenda; more recently, resolution 1920 (2008) on women, peace, and security, focuses particularly on sexual and gender-based violence. While there have been many resolutions on children in armed conflict, resolution 1612 (2005) created a monitoring and reporting mechanism (MRM) to monitor six specific types of abuse of children and established a council working group to issue conclusions and recommendations.[66]

Since 2004, more than half of the council's meetings have focused on country situations in which protection of civilians has been a major concern. In assessing Security Council engagement with protection of civilians, a security council report found that the council had become more active in speaking out when civilians were threatened and there had been better and more reporting on specific country situations, such as those in DRC, Uganda, and Kenya, but that the council had been hesitant to discuss issues arising in places where major powers were involved, such as Iraq, Afghanistan, and Georgia. The report noted the absence of political will to engage on issues such as Somalia and Timor-Leste and stated that while the council had become much more active in calling for improved physical security in the field for civilians and humanitarian actors and in including protection of civilians in the mandates of UN peacekeeping operations, implementation continued to be marked by practical difficulties and inconsistent interpretations of protection mandates.[67]

In addition, the report noted, there were inconsistencies in the way that the secretary-general reported on protection of civilians, and the council had been less effective at prevention, tending not to engage until a full-scale conflict emerged. In fact, since Macedonia in the early 1990s, the Security Council had not authorized preventive deployments. The council sometimes had been divided on protection issues, and there were always problems with implementation—for example, arms embargoes in Somalia and Darfur were consistently violated and UNAMID in Darfur suffered from a serious lack of resources. And in a number of other crises, such as those in Colombia and Sri Lanka, the council had not become involved in protection issues, except with regard to the impact of the crisis on children.[68]

In 2009, ten years after the concept of protection of civilians appeared on the UN scene, the Security Council held two open debates on protection of civilians, updated the *aide-mémoire* on protection of civilians, adopted a new resolution, and decided to create a new tool—an informal council expert group on protection. The new expert group, convened by the United Kingdom, meets in connection with mandate renewals for UN missions that have an existing protection dimension. Also in January 2009, the Security Council held a private meeting on respect for international humanitarian law, addressing this key element of protection of civilians for the first time.[69]

In November 2009, the Security Council unanimously adopted a new resolution on protection of civilians (resolution 1894). The council recognized the need to consider protection early in the formulation of peacekeeping mandates and to provide comprehensive guidance on carrying out protection mandates. Many speakers in the general debate called for bolstering the protection of civilians in the mandates of UN peacekeeping operations, although the representative of China and others stressed that protection mandates should be decided on a case-by-case basis and the Russian representative stressed that it is the responsibility of states to protect civilians. Like other resolutions, this one calls for increased respect for international humanitarian law, condemns attacks on civilians, notes that deliberate targeting of civilians may constitute a threat to international peace and security, affirms its strong opposition to impunity, stresses the importance of humanitarian access to civilians affected by armed conflict, and "stresses the importance for all, within the framework of humanitarian assistance, of upholding and respecting the humanitarian principles of humanity, neutrality, impartiality and independence." The resolution further reaffirms the practice of including protection of civilians in mandates of peacekeeping operations, asks the secretary-general to develop an operational concept for the protection of civilians, and expresses its desire for indicators of progress regarding the protection of civilians to develop benchmarks for peacekeeping mandates. Finally, the resolution asked the secretary-general to report again on the protection of civilians in armed conflict by November 2010. On November 22, 2010, the Security Council received a new report by the secretary-general and adopted a statement expressing deep regret at continuing civilian casualties and demanding that all parties respect international humanitarian law protecting civilians. The council also adopted an updated *aide-mémoire* on protection of civilians and urged that it be used on a more consistent basis.[70]

The increasing politicization of Security Council engagement with protection of civilians is evident, paralleling discussions of the responsibility to protect concept. Governments that are involved in a conflict and their allies "have been increasingly resistant to Council involvement in protection activities, perhaps feeling that this will limit their options."[71] The Security Council's report on engagement of the council with protection of civilians suggests that a major problem for council engagement lies in council dynamics: the council has demonstrated a persistent inability to act effectively in some of the worst situations for civilians because of the tension between the political interests of its members and their protection commitments.[72] Some countries support the council's involvement in protection; others (China, Russia, and the Non-Aligned Movement [NAM]) emphasize that protection responsibilities are first and foremost the responsibility of national governments and that international involvement, including council action, must respect territorial integrity. They take a similar position on the role of national authorities in ensuring accountability and justice. Another key dynamic within the Security Council is the tension between protection of civilians and efforts by some countries to give priority to counterterrorism measures even when they may result in civilian casualties.[73]

While the Security Council has been active for the past decade in hearing reports and discussing protection of civilians, its major efforts have been directed at incorporating protection of civilians into mandates for peacekeeping operations. In the November 2009 Security Council debate, Ann Taylor, the U.K. minister for international defense and security, said that "protecting civilians is an important measure of the credibility of peacekeeping operations [that] goes to the very heart of what people admire and respect about the United Nations in action."[74]

PROTECTION OF CIVILIANS AND PEACEKEEPING OPERATIONS

As of August 2009, there were fifteen peacekeeping operations with a total of 83,000 uniformed personnel, almost 12,000 police, and 23,000 civilian staff.[75] Only one of the peacekeeping missions established since 1999 (Ethiopia-Eritrea) does not have a protection-related element in its mandate. Even for those in which the United Nations does not have the lead in terms of military capability, such as Kosovo, Timor-Leste, and Chad/Central African Republic, the Security Council authorized multinational deployments with protection mandates. Paralleling the council's discussions on protection of civilians in 1999, the mandates given to peacekeeping forces in Sierra Leone (UNAMSIL) and Timor-Leste (INTERFET and UNTAET) were the first to include a provision allowing the use of force, if necessary, to protect civilians. That began the trend in which UN peacekeeping operations were asked to protect civilians.[76]

In resolution 1270 of October 1999 on Sierra Leone, the council, operating under chapter VII, decided that in discharging its mandate, UNAMSIL "may take the necessary action to ensure the security and freedom of movement of its personnel and, within its capabilities and areas of deployment, to afford protection to civilians under imminent threat of physical violence."[77] But although the mission's protection mandate increased expectations among the civilian population, UNAMSIL's lack of resources and the safety concerns of some troop contributors meant that it was unable to fulfill its mandate. In mid-2000 the rebel Revolutionary United Front carried out a major offensive in which it kidnapped 500 UNAMSIL troops. That was a huge humiliation for the UN forces and resulted in a loss of credibility for the peacekeeping operation.[78] Protection of civilians within the mandates of PKOs did not get off to a strong start.

Nonetheless, protection of civilians has become central to mandates of UN peacekeeping operations although there is a lack of consensus or understanding on what kinds of activities fall under protection of civilians.[79] Victoria Holt argues that while military actors have worked with other agencies in the field, they "do not share a joint understanding of what civilian protection means, or what it requires." The concepts developed by humanitarian and human rights actors on protection simply do not align with the way that peacekeepers see their mission.[80] And Holt argues that protection is usually one task among others within a mission with broader goals. Neither national militaries nor regional bodies, such as the African Union (AU) and NATO, have developed doctrines addressing civilian protection as an active concept.

In addition to mandates to protect civilians, other objectives of a UN mission usually include tasks that have direct consequences for civilian protection, such as increasing security, combating militias, fostering security sector reform, improving the rule of law, and working on disarmament, demobilization, and reintegration. But while peacekeeping operations are charged with protecting civilians, there is little consistency in terms of what that means on the ground and there are limitations in the mandates themselves.[81] The mandates of peacekeeping operations typically have caveats regarding the way in which protection of civilians is handled. The most typical caveats are to protect civilians within its "areas of deployment"; to protect civilians "within its capabilities"; and to protect civilians "without prejudice to the responsibility of" the host country.[82]

At the operational level, there are questions about what it means to protect civilians while they are under imminent threat, while taking into account the host government's responsibilities, or while acting within a PKO's capabilities or areas of deployment. And protection activities have synergies with other mission activities, such as generally deterring or countering violence or extending state authority.[83] So a variety of different activities—from simple patrolling or securing UN premises—often are seen as protecting civilians.[84]

How do peacekeepers protect civilians? Holt and Smith argue that there are five broad strategic options for halting widespread attacks on civilians. First is protection by presence, which also is often used by NGOs in their efforts to protect people. Often the assumption is made that the presence of peace operations will deter attacks on civilians, but they caution that "providing an international or regional military presence is insufficient, however, if there is no accompanying plan to respond in case presence alone falters, as seen by the failures in Rwanda, Bosnia and the DRC." A second strategic option is static protection (defensive), in which military forces protect civilians at risk in a defined safe area—for example, a church or refugee camp. But the authors recall the example of Srebenica, where Bosniak factions began attacks within the so-called safe haven to provoke a confrontation with Serb forces outside the safe area. They caution that either safe areas must be demilitarized and the belligerents agree on their protected status or they must be fully defended by a credible military deterrent.[85] A third option is to disrupt the ability of the perpetrators to act, for example, through roadblocks, checkpoints, or raids on arms caches.[86] A fourth option is to coerce or compel perpetrators to halt attacks, which involves the escalation of force, as in NATO's bombing campaign to coerce Serbian president Milosevic into pulling his military out of Kosovo. Finally, a fifth strategic option to achieve the mission's primary objective of halting attacks and protecting civilians is to militarily defeat the perpetrators. The fifth option is generally beyond the mandate and capacity of UN-led forces.[87]

But in practice, only the UN Organization Stabilization Mission in the DRC (MONUC) currently engages in offensive operations against militias and includes a physical protection dimension. The United Nations Interim Force in Lebanon (UNFIL) has limited ability to fulfill its protection role—the mission operates under strict constraints and functions as essentially a monitoring and verification mission. Similarly, the United Nations Missions in Sudan (UNMIS) had a strong mandate to "protect civilians under imminent threat," explicitly authorized under chapter VII, but in practice it is a monitoring and verification operation. Although it has been criticized for not providing civilian protection, it was not equipped for robust protection. Growth in UN policing activities has added another layer of difficulties—virtually all operations since 1999 have sizable police contingents, reflecting the fact that much of the need for civilian protection arises from the lack of rule of law and generalized lawlessness.[88] But there is no guidance for police forces as to what protection means.

Holt and Smith also underline the need for guidance on protection of civilians to be codified in doctrine of peace support operations[89]—an issue picked up by the Security Council in its 2009 resolution when it recognized

> the need for comprehensive operational guidance on peacekeeping missions' tasks and responsibilities in the implementation of protection of civilians mandates and request[ed] the Secretary-General to develop in close consultation with Member States, including troop and police contributing countries and other relevant actors, an operational concept for the protection of civilians and to report back on progress made.[90]

There have been a number of efforts to assess peacekeeping operations in terms of protection of civilians. In March 2009, the Special Committee on Peacekeeping Operations for the first time addressed protection of civilians in its report. The Department of Peacekeeping Operations and the Department of Field Support launched an internal review of peacekeeping under the name "New Horizon," presented in July 2009, that identified protection of civilians as one of three cross-cutting peacekeeping tasks that present particular challenges (the other two were robust operations and peacebuilding). In late 2008, DPKO and OCHA commissioned an independent study on implementation of protection mandates in peacekeeping operations, which was released in November 2009.[91]

The DPKO-OCHA study, based on many interviews with peacekeeping staff in headquarters and in four field operations, identifies a number of differences in the definition of the concept of protection of civilians, in the way that missions are planned and executed, and in the extent to which protection of civilians is deemed feasible:

> Strikingly, despite ten years of statements by the Council, adoption of three iterations of the *Aide Mémoire* and a number of mission-specific and thematic resolutions, no Council document offers an operational

definition of what protection of civilians means for peacekeeping missions; nor has the Council tasked the Secretariat, which may be the most appropriate organ to develop such guidance, to do so.[92]

In their interviews, the authors of the OCHA-DPKO study found a wide variation in interpretations of what protection of civilians means to peacekeepers. They summarize those views in three groups: those following the Inter-Agency Standing Committee (IASC) consensus that protection is a broad concept encompassing international humanitarian and human rights law; those focusing more on physical protection; and those that define protection of civilians as the inherent goal of peacekeeping and therefore redundant as an additional mandated task.[93] The authors conclude that

> UN peacekeeping strategies to protect civilians cannot be developed independently from strategies to support peace agreements, assist in organizing elections, monitor and advocate for human rights, support humanitarian access, enhance effective governance, rebuild the rule of law or the myriad other peacebuilding tasks UN missions undertake.[94]

The authors note also that humanitarian actors and peacekeepers have different interpretations of which of PKOs' many activities constitute protection. OCHA considers activities such as ensuring humanitarian assistance, protecting human rights, providing law enforcement, and maintaining security and neutrality in refugee camps as "protection," but DPKO staff consistently treated these activities as part of other categories, such as ensuring the rule of law; demobilization, disarmament and reintegration (DDR); accountability; or peace building.[95]

The authors note that recent efforts by UNMIS to develop a conceptual framework for protection of civilians (POC) offer a possible way forward. That framework, although still in draft form, is far and away the most complete effort to specify what protection of civilians means for peacekeepers on the ground. It defines POC in terms of the broad IASC definition: "a concept that encompasses all activities aimed at obtaining full respect for the rights of the individual in accordance with the letter and spirit of the relevant bodies of law (i.e. human rights law, international humanitarian law and refugee law)." But the framework carves out a narrower meaning by stating that

> [t]he full gamut of POC is very wide. UNMIS is taking a layered approach to developing an UNMIS-specific POC strategy. Three layers of protection will be covered in the strategy: protection of civilians under imminent threat of physical violence; protection of civilians

with regard to securing access to humanitarian and relief activities; and the longer-term aspect of protection in the context of human rights and conflict prevention and management. . . . Sexual, gender or child violence will not be treated separately in this concept as they are all forms of physical violence.[96]

Increasingly UN peacekeeping operations have been mandated to undertake law enforcement and monitoring of international humanitarian law as well as to protect civilians. However, Security Council involvement in justice issues and violations of international humanitarian law seems to have decreased since the 1990s. The momentum that informed the establishment of tribunals in the former Yugoslavia, Rwanda, and Sierra Leone seems to have waned, with the major exception of the referral of crimes committed in Darfur to the ICC in 2005. China, Russia, and some African and Asian members have a strong aversion to the council's use of such tribunals. The Security Council has largely abandoned recourse to full-scale economic sanctions, using targeted sanctions instead, which have proven to be unevenly implemented and thus ineffective in protecting civilians.[97]

Similarly, there is some concern that the Security Council is focusing too much on peacekeeping operations and neglecting other aspects of protection of civilians. As one humanitarian organization representative noted, while the secretary-general proposed a ten-point toolkit, the Security Council is overemphasizing one of them.[98] And as evidenced in press coverage of difficulties in the DRC, in at least some cases peacekeeping operations can become a part of the conflict, further complicating efforts to protect civilians.

The UN Organization Stabilization Mission in the DRC was dispatched to the Democratic Republic of the Congo in 2000 to monitor the implementation of a cease-fire agreement and, among other tasks, to protect civilians under imminent threat. It was a daunting task, given the vast size of the country and the complexity of the conflict. Over the past decade, the UN Security Council has revised, strengthened, and extended its mandate, and currently some 20,000 military and police forces are present in the country—the largest peacekeeping mission in the world. At a cost of $1 billion per year, MONUC represents nearly one-quarter of the entire UN peacekeeping budget. But in 2004, allegations surfaced that MONUC personnel were involved in widespread sexual abuse of women and girls.[99] In 2009, MONUC was widely criticized for its decision to participate in joint military operations with the Congolese army in which the armed forces reportedly killed many civilians deliberately.[100] While the UN has taken some measures to address those issues, MONUC's experiences are indicative of both the difficulties of implementing a mandate to protect civilians in an extraordinarily difficult situation and the possibility that international forces themselves can become caught up in the violence that they were intended to prevent.

Even within the United Nations and its governing bodies, there are fundamental differences in interpreting what protection means. Holt, Taylor, and Kelley find discrepancies in the way that the Security Council has used protection of civilians, noting that it has implicitly used the terms of protection in a variety of ways, ranging from a broad normative concept to the narrower concept of "physical" protection offered by a peacekeeping mission's military and police personnel.[101] Some have noted that protection of civilians has come to be identified with specific groups—women, children, the displaced—rather than an overarching concept. Several UN and NGO staff have observed that much more progress has been made on protection of children than on protection of civilians, in part because of its more specific focus and in part because data collection and monitoring mechanisms for child protection have been put in place. There continues to be a gap between DPKO and humanitarian understandings of protection, and although the joint study identified a number of concrete recommendations to overcome that gap, it is uncertain whether there is sufficient political will to take the actions needed to do so.

Finally, there is deep concern that the political backlash against the responsibility to protect doctrine (R2P) could have a negative impact on Security Council deliberations on protection of civilians. "These are two completely different approaches," one UN representative explained. "We've got to keep them completely separate or else we're back to square one."[102]

While this discussion has focused on the Security Council's approach to protection of civilians, it has been incorporated into the work of at least some UN agencies. In particular, OCHA has been at the forefront of supporting Security Council deliberations through its *aide mémoire* and in developing the policy framework for the culture of protection, including through regional and country-specific workshops on POC and production of supporting resources.[103]

Protection of civilians in armed conflict has been central to the work of the International Committee of the Red Cross, long before the Security Council took up the issue. Since overseeing the process that culminated in the 1999 definition of protection (later adopted by the Inter-Agency Standing Committee), ICRC has moved to further refine that definition for its own use. According to ICRC, the intention was to come up with a general definition of protection under which all humanitarian actors could develop their own specific definitions.[104]

> For the ICRC, protection, in the broadest sense, aims to ensure that authorities and other actors respect their obligations and the rights of individuals in order to preserve the lives, security, physical and moral integrity and dignity of those affected by armed conflicts and/or other situations of violence. Protection includes efforts that strive to prevent or put a stop to actual or potential violations of international humanitarian law (IHL) and other relevant bodies of law or norms that protect human beings. Above all, protection aims to eradicate the causes of violations, or the circumstances that lead to them, by addressing mainly those responsible for the violations and those who may have influence over them. This definition of protection also includes activities that seek to reinforce the security of individuals and indirectly to reduce the threats they face and their exposure to risks, particularly those arising from armed conflict and other situations of violence.[105]

In comparison with other civilian actors, ICRC's emphasis on preventing violence, including by negotiating with armed groups, is unique. Other humanitarian actors, such as UNHCR, often are involved in humanitarian diplomacy, through which they seek to facilitate humanitarian access and expedite delivery of humanitarian assistance. But, unlike ICRC, they are rarely involved in negotiations with armed actors to stop military operations targeting civilians. ICRC has spelled out the ways that it designs and implements protection activities, including activities aimed at reducing or eliminating violence.[106]

As the guardian of international humanitarian law, ICRC is a leader in the international community on protection issues, as witnessed by its convening a series of consultations to come up with a definition of protection and more recently to develop minimum standards for protection. The process of developing minimum standards was an open-ended one. ICRC did not begin with a preconceived notion of what the standards would be and even wondered if it would be possible to reach agreement among diverse actors. The two-year process resulted in a consensus document. According to involved ICRC staff, the only area in which it was not possible to reach consensus was relations with the military.[107] Development of the standards was motivated in large part by the reality that many actors, coming from very different backgrounds and using different conceptual frameworks, are now involved in protection. The standards were intended to provide at least a basic common ground.[108]

PROTECTION OF CIVILIANS AND OTHER ACTORS

As noted in chapter 4, human rights NGOs have always focused on protection issues, monitoring and documenting human rights abuses during conflicts, and humanitarian NGOs have increasingly incorporated protection into their programmatic work. In some cases, they have mainstreamed protection into all assistance programs, seeking to minimize threats against civilians. Or they have developed stand-alone programs to enhance protection of civilians, such as programs to distribute fuel-efficient stoves to minimize the threats to women when they are collecting firewood. But NGOs have by and large been able to prevent attacks on civilians by negotiating with governments and armed opposition groups. And in at least some cases, NGOs look to peacekeeping operations to provide security for their operations.[109]

When it comes to protection of civilians, however, there is a gap between the UN and NGO approaches. NGOs certainly have paid close attention to Security Council discussions, where much of the impetus has come from, lobbying for stronger language and watching the discussions of specific PKO mandates closely. But for NGOs not in New York, the discussions seem far from reality:

> Protection of civilians? That's just the diplomats talking in New York. That doesn't have anything to do with our protection work on the ground. We don't pay much attention to those discussions.[110]

The NGOs that have developed policies on protection of civilians—which tend to be the large international organizations—have done so with little reference to discussions in the Security Council. One exception was Oxfam International, which in 2003 published "an agenda for action to protect civilians in neglected conflicts."[111] Interestingly, the Oxfam agenda does not start with the IASC definition of protection. Rather, it states that "humanitarian protection is concerned with preventing or mitigating the most damaging effects, direct or indirect, of war on civilians. It relates mainly to the way in which armed conflict is conducted and to the way in which people, including refugees and displaced people, are treated." It goes on to state:

> Oxfam believes that a coherent approach to the protection of civilians should mean that people have a right to live free from: violence or the threat of violence (including but not limited to: murder, torture, rape, wounding, abuse and abduction); coercion (including forced displacement, forced return, forced prostitution, or forced recruitment); and deprivation (including denial of access to humanitarian assistance, the

destruction of shelter, property, or livestock, and the prevention of the means to earn a living).[112]

Oxfam's description of protection of civilians thus focuses on physical violence, rather than the broader array of elements in the IASC definition, which seeks to protect all human rights. Oxfam's agenda for action is not addressed primarily to Oxfam itself. It includes recommendations to governments and warring parties to plan their military tactics to safeguard civilians; to the Security Council to use more tools to protect civilians in neglected crises; to donor governments to give aid based on need rather than political priorities; to governments to recognize the independent, impartial, and civilian character of humanitarian aid; and to humanitarian agencies to consistently strive for quality, accountability, and efficiency in their actions to protect and assist civilians.[113]

Several donor governments have made protection of civilians a fundamental objective of their humanitarian action programs. For example, Switzerland, using the IASC definition of protection, developed a strategy on civilian protection that cites four reasons for focusing on protection of civilians: Switzerland's constitutional duty to contribute to the relief of populations in need and to promote respect for human rights, democracy, and peaceful coexistence; the fact that promotion and defense of international law is one of the central pillars of Swiss foreign policy; its unique position as depositary and high contracting party to the Geneva Conventions and their additional protocols; and the fact that its parliament has provided the necessary instruments and resources in a number of policy areas, including protection of civilians.[114]

The overall objective of the strategy is, not surprisingly, to strengthen the protection of civilians in armed conflict. Toward that end, the Swiss Federal Department of Foreign Affairs (FDFA) chose three strategic objectives: ensuring that the normative framework regarding the protection of civilians in armed conflict is adequate, known, and respected by all parties involved; that the operational response regarding the protection of civilians in armed conflict is effective; and that the FDFA possesses the necessary competencies and skills to protect civilians in armed conflict.[115] Switzerland, building on its tradition of emphasizing international law, emphasizes the normative framework. Within the operational response, three issues are highlighted: respect for humanitarian principles of humanity, neutrality, independence, and impartiality by all relevant operational actors; guarantee of humanitarian access as well as the safety and security of all relevant operational actors;

and assistance to civilians in armed conflicts, which takes into account the rights and specific needs of the vulnerable groups, in particular women, children, refugees, and displaced persons.

A second example of the way in which a donor government has addressed the issue is the United Kingdom's strategy on protecting civilians in armed conflict.[116] The strategy begins with three reasons that protection of civilians matters: it is a moral imperative; it is a legal obligation; and protecting civilians can contribute toward managing and reducing the direct impact of conflict. The U.K. strategy, like the Swiss strategy, uses the IASC definition of protection. The policy notes that the confused and messy nature of conflict today means that "separating the 'people' from the conflict is often impossible and their protection relies on a comprehensive approach to conflict resolution which this strategy is designed to support."[117]

The strategy outlines four policy areas. The area of political engagement includes U.K. bilateral political action with other governments on protection; strengthening international political action on protection (particularly through the Security Council); strengthening international, regional, and national human rights and humanitarian law monitoring; supporting transitional justice initiatives; and strengthening international justice mechanisms. The second area, peace support operations, includes working for better and more consistent language on protection in the mandates of peace support operations; better reporting on protection issues by peace operations; better execution of protection tasks within a peace operation; and increased protection capacity of troop and police contributing nations. The third area, humanitarian action, includes improving humanitarian access; strengthening the work of humanitarian agencies with an international protection mandate; strengthening the leadership and coordination of humanitarian protection; and strengthening the work of humanitarian agencies that do not have an express protection mandate. The fourth policy area, state capacity, includes building the capacity of states to protect civilian populations; improving the international community's response to security and justice issues; and strengthening national capacities for human rights monitoring.

Both the Swiss and U.K. strategies start from the broad IASC definition of protection, and both ground their strategies in international law, although the Swiss emphasize national specificities more and the British include both moral and pragmatic reasons in their rationale for focusing on protection of civilians. While both emphasize the importance of international legal norms, the Swiss seem more focused on disseminating and promoting international law while the British devote more attention to monitoring and reporting.

The British focus quite a bit of attention on both regional mechanisms and the Security Council, which are not mentioned in the Swiss strategy. In contrast, one of the three central objectives of the Swiss strategy is to increase Switzerland's own capacity to work on protection issues.

Evolution of the Principle of Responsibility to Protect

The emergence of the concept of "responsibility to protect" grew out of outrage at atrocities such as the Holocaust and the massacres in Cambodia. Support for the concept grew during the 1990s, which witnessed further atrocities, such as those in Rwanda, Srebrenica, Kosovo, northern Iraq, Haiti, Sierra Leone, and Timor-Leste. The debate quickly became one between advocates of humanitarian intervention, which entailed the right to intervene militarily, and those with a Westphalian view of sovereignty, who ardently rejected the concept.[118]

The principles of sovereignty and nonintervention are central to the current international order. In 1965, for example, the UN General Assembly adopted resolution 2131, which states:

> No State has the right to intervene, directly or indirectly, for any reason whatever, in the internal or external affairs of any other State. Consequently, armed intervention and all other forces of interference or attempted threats against the personality of the State or against its political, economic, or cultural elements are condemned.[119]

In practice, there have been many cases in which states have intervened in the affairs of others. As noted in chapter 1, the right of a state to intervene in support of its nationals has a long history. More recently, however, there have been cases in which intervention has been used in support of non-nationals. For example, in 1979 Vietnam invaded Cambodia to put an end to the genocide as well as to advance its own foreign policy goals. That action was widely condemned as interfering in the life of an independent state—although it did serve to stop the genocide under the Khmer Rouge. In contrast, a year earlier, the government of Tanzania invaded Uganda to overthrow the brutal regime of Idi Amin and was praised for its actions.

The crises of the early 1990s, particularly in Somalia, led to increased advocacy for the international community to respond to prevent suffering. In 1991 UN secretary-general Javier Pérez de Cuéllar wrote:

> It is now increasingly felt that the principle of non-interference within the essential domestic jurisdiction of states cannot be regarded as a

protective barrier behind which human rights can be massively or systematically violated with impunity. The fact that in diverse situations the United Nations has not been able to prevent atrocities cannot be accepted as an argument, legal or moral, against the necessary corrective action, especially when peace is also threatened.[120]

Humanitarian and political actors alike called for enhancement of the capacity of the United Nations to take action, including military action, to bring an end to atrocities and to the suffering of civilians. But from the beginning of global discussions, the issue of humanitarian intervention was a North-South issue. The states that advocated humanitarian intervention were primarily developed countries that knew that it would not be *their* sovereignty that was overridden by the United Nations. "Most Southern or developing states knew very well that it was their jurisdiction that would be penetrated, their authority that would be superseded."[121]

The work of Frances Deng and Roberta Cohen on "sovereignty as responsibility" for the protection of IDPs is lauded by proponents of R2P and serves as a rebuttal to its noninterventionist critics.[122] By affirming both the sovereignty and the responsibility of states to protect their people, the discourse moved away from the contentious term "intervention."[123] Political leaders presented the issue in humanitarian terms, as evidenced by U.S. president Bill Clinton's remarks to NATO troops in Macedonia in 1999:

> We can say to the people of the world, whether you live in Africa, or Central Europe, or any other place, if somebody comes after innocent civilians and tries to kill them en masse because of their race, their ethnic background, or their religion, and it's within our power to stop it, we will stop it.[124]

In April 2000, Kofi Annan challenged the Millennium Summit by stating that

> [h]umanitarian intervention is a sensitive issue, fraught with political difficulty and not susceptible to easy answers. But surely no legal principle—not even sovereignty—can ever shield crimes against humanity. Where such crimes occur and peaceful attempts to halt them have been exhausted, the Security Council has a moral duty to act on behalf of the international community. The fact that we cannot protect people everywhere is no reason for doing nothing when we can. Armed intervention must always remain the option of last resort, but in the face of mass murder it is an option that cannot be relinquished.[125]

Later that year, the Canadian government and major foundations announced to the General Assembly the establishment of the International Commission on Intervention and State Sovereignty (ICISS). The ICISS was not a UN body; it was set up by the Canadian government to reflect and make recommendations on the contentious issue of humanitarian intervention. In fact, the name of the commission was changed from "Commission on Humanitarian Intervention" to its current title to placate critics of humanitarian intervention.

Over the next several months, the ICISS met five times and hosted a series of eleven roundtables and national consultations in both the global South and North.[126] The commission succeeded in turning the debate from one on the right to intervene to one on responsible sovereignty.[127] It finished its work in August 2001, but delayed publishing the report until December given the events of September 11, 2001. The report, *The Responsibility to Protect*, affirmed that states are responsible for the protection of their populations from serious harm but that when a state is unwilling or unable to do so, the international community has a duty to act.[128] In other words, the principle of nonintervention yields to the international community's responsibility to protect populations at risk.

As formulated by the ICISS, the responsibility to protect doctrine includes the responsibility to prevent, react, and rebuild. It spells out the basic principles of military intervention as follows: The "just clause" principle holds that intervention can be justified in the event of large-scale loss of life or ethnic cleansing, whether or not there is genocidal intent. In order to be legitimate, the intention of the intervention should be to halt or avert human suffering. The intervention should be a last resort after nonmilitary options have been exhausted, and it must be of proportional means, must have a reasonable prospect of successfully ending the suffering, and must not be more harmful than inaction. Furthermore, the action must be taken by the UN Security Council, the most appropriate body to authorize military intervention for human protection purposes. The report also calls on the permanent five members of the council to agree not to apply their veto power unless vital state interests are involved. Finally, the ICISS recommends that operational principles be developed with clear objectives, a common military approach, acceptance of limitations, rules of engagement that are in line with the operational principles, and adequate coordination mechanisms.[129]

In his detailed account of deliberations on the concept of R2P, Alex Bellamy notes that opposition to the concept was apparent from the time that the report was issued and maintains that it is surprising that the concept even survived in the lead-up to the 2005 World Summit.[130] The strong opposition of the Non-Aligned Movement and the U.S. invasion of Iraq (justified by some U.S. officials on humanitarian grounds) threatened to derail the concept completely. Bellamy attributes its survival to four factors: intense public advocacy by the Canadian government and the ICISS Commission; the strong support of the UN secretary-general and the support of the High-Level Panel on Threats, Challenges, and Change; growing U.S. willingness to engage in R2P discussions; and the adoption by the African Union of principles similar to those of the responsibility to protect doctrine.[131]

The African Union, established in 2002, moved away from the emphasis placed on noninterference by the Organization of African Unity (OAU) to a much more robust understanding of its role in taking action to prevent the abuse of human rights by states.[132] Article 4(h) of the AU's Constitutive Act gave the union the right to intervene in the affairs of its member states in the case of genocide, war crimes, or crimes against humanity. However, the AU has never authorized the use of military force without the consent of state authorities.

ICISS identified three components of the responsibility to protect concept: the responsibility to prevent, to react, and to rebuild. However, most of the attention has focused on the responsibility to react, particularly with regard to the use of military force in situations in which the government of the country does not consent to it. Some critics have argued that ICISS spent much more time deliberating on the responsibility to react than on either prevention or rebuilding and that the prevention and rebuilding components were added to make the responsibility to react component more palatable to its opponents.[133]

In April 2004 (which marked the tenth anniversary of the Rwanda crisis), Kofi Annan created the Office of the Special Adviser on the Prevention of Genocide to collect information, to serve as an early warning mechanism to the secretary-general, and through him, to make recommendations to the Security Council on actions to be taken to prevent genocide. In 2004, it was a part-time office with only two staff members, but in December 2007 the position was made full-time and elevated to the level of under secretary-general and "mass atrocities" was added to its title. Long-time IDP advocate and respected Sudanese diplomat Francis Deng was named to the post. But it was a highly politicized position, and the phrase "and mass atrocities" was dropped from the title, in part because of fears that it would be more likely to lead to intervention. So the office was to remain focused exclusively on genocide, but the mandate continued to be politically sensitive—no state wanted to be seen as nearing genocide.

In 2005, responsibility to protect was adopted at the World Summit as a blueprint for action; however, it is important to note that further action by the Security Council and General Assembly is needed to translate it into reality.[134] Nonetheless, the World Summit was hailed by proponents of the concept as a key milestone, although there was resistance by some states to the outcome document.[135] Divisions and negotiations to reach consensus resulted in "the limiting of R2P's scope to four crimes as opposed to ICISS's additional criteria of 'serious harm' [as well as the omission of] criteria for the use of force and references to the responsibility to rebuild."[136] The final outcome document also failed to include a code of conduct on the use of the veto by the five permanent Security Council members on implementing R2P, which had been advocated by ICISS. But there was not much discussion of how R2P would be used by the international community in the immediate aftermath of the World Summit. Rather more emphasis was placed on creating the Peacebuilding Commission and the Human Rights Council than on R2P.

Since its adoption by the World Summit in 2005, R2P has been widely endorsed in the Security Council and in the General Assembly and yet opposition to its implementation has grown. The U.S.-led invasion of Iraq in 2003 led many to see R2P as confirmation of the West's intention to ride roughshod over smaller countries. Opposition has come from various quarters, beginning with countries that are cynically self-interested and do not want any restrictions on their internal behavior. In addition there are academics who have a strong aversion to imperialism and "who remain instinctively unwilling to concede in principle that external intervention—and in particular military intervention—could ever wholly avoid having that character."[137] There also are what Gareth Evans calls "unhelpful friends" who see R2P exclusively in military terms or those who seek to broaden it as a panacea for all ills, such as climate change and HIV/AIDS. Finally, U.S. officials who have portrayed the U.S. invasion of Iraq as a form of humanitarian intervention have definitely hurt the concept.

In April 2006 the Security Council unanimously adopted resolution 1674, on the protection of civilians in armed conflict, in which it reaffirmed the World Summit conclusions relating to the responsibility to protect. The Security Council officially references the responsibility to protect for the first time in this resolution, and it did so again in resolution 1706, on Darfur, in August 2006. The resistance to R2P was evident in December 2007, when Secretary-General Ban Ki-moon announced his intention to appoint Edward Luck as special adviser on the responsibility to protect. Eventually

Ban Ki-moon removed "responsibility to protect" from the title due to opposition to the term; Luck is now simply "special adviser."[138]

Following the 2006 discussions on Darfur, the concept of responsibility to protect was not debated in the General Assembly until 2009. In his opening statement at the debate in the General Assembly in July 2009, Luck listed some of the main criticisms of R2P and defended the concept.[139] Although the UN General Assembly eventually reached consensus through the adoption of a resolution that recalled the 2005 World Summit Outcome Document, especially paragraphs 138 and 139 thereof, in which the General Assembly stated that it would "continue its consideration of the responsibility to protect," the concept met with strong opposition from many states.[140]

In January 2009, Secretary-General Ban Ki-moon released the first comprehensive document from the UN Secretariat on R2P and suggested a three-pillar approach for advancing the R2P agenda by focusing on the protection responsibilities of the state; international assistance and capacity building; and timely and decisive response to prevent and halt genocide, war crimes, ethnic cleansing, and crimes against humanity. The first pillar addresses the fundamental responsibility of the state to prevent atrocities. The second pillar focuses on the need for the international community to support the state in the exercise of its responsibility by providing necessary financial and technical assistance. The third pillar is "the responsibility of Member States to respond collectively in a timely and decisive manner when a State is manifestly failing to provide such protection" through diplomacy, regional initiatives, and coercive measures. This approach stresses the need for such activities to respect the provisions of the UN Charter.[141]

In November 2009, during the eighth debate on protection of civilians in the Security Council, member states renewed their commitment to R2P in resolution 1894, which came on the heels of the General Assembly's adoption by consensus in September 2009 of a resolution entitled "The Responsibility to Protect." In 2010 a conference organized by the Stanley Foundation came up with a list of actions that can be taken in the near term to move the debate on the responsibility to protect forward, including developing early warning and assessment capacity; improving the UN capacity for emergency response, including by taking timely decisions and action; merging the offices working on genocide prevention and the responsibility to protect; making R2P operational throughout the UN system by engaging, among others, the Human Rights Council and the Peacebuilding Commission; and encouraging and improving UN regional and subregional interaction and communication.[142]

Cases in which the international community has mobilized to advocate for implementing R2P include that of Burma. In response to human rights violations by the junta against ethnic minorities, sixty British members of parliament and, in a separate instance, a group organized by Norwegian members of parliament urged the UN to apply R2P in the case of Burma.[143] Following Cyclone Nargis in May 2008 and the Burmese government's restriction of access to affected areas of the country, there was heated debate about whether R2P should be implemented in the case of this large-scale natural disaster. French foreign minister Bernard Kouchner argued that the widespread suffering and death resulting from the Burmese government's denial of international humanitarian access constituted crimes against humanity, which were intended to be addressed by R2P. Kouchner noted, "We are seeing at the United Nations whether we can implement the Responsibility to Protect, given that food, boats and relief teams are there, and obtain a United Nations' resolution which authorizes the delivery [of aid] and imposes this on the Burmese government."[144] Others argued that state neglect of its population and obstruction of aid delivery do not fall under the four crimes for which R2P is to be invoked and that invoking it in this case would weaken its applicability elsewhere.[145]

As Gareth Evans noted, there are problems in stretching the concept of R2P to such situations.[146] R2P was intended to respond to four specific categories of crimes—genocide, war crimes, ethnic cleansing, and crimes against humanity—through three modes of action: the responsibility of individual states to protect their people from such crimes, the responsibility of other states to assist them to do so, and the responsibility of states to take appropriate collective action, including as necessary forcible action under chapter VII of the Charter, when a state is "manifestly failing" to fulfill its own responsibility. As Evans explains, even if the Myanmar government had not eventually relented and allowed international assistance, it would be difficult to prove that its actions constitute crimes against humanity because it is difficult to prove intentionality. Military intervention was not intended to be used in cases of incompetence. He concludes that "*any* widening of the application of R2P terminology, expressly or by implication, beyond its core business of addressing mass atrocity crimes is dangerous from the perspective of undermining R2P's utility as a rallying cry."[147] On the other hand, Roberta Cohen argued that "saying that R2P should apply does not necessarily mean that military intervention should have been undertaken but rather that the Security Council should have met to consider what steps to take and should have used the R2P umbrella to galvanize political and humanitarian action."[148]

The international community's response to election violence in Kenya in early 2008 is held up by R2P advocates as the only successful instance of the application of R2P to date. While tensions remain in Kenya, mediation efforts (and not military intervention) led by Kofi Annan were critical in halting further violence and displacement there at that time. While advocates of R2P see Annan's efforts as a successful case of its implementation, others note that it was not a straightforward success. Indeed, Roberta Cohen argues that while application of R2P was successful in stopping the violence, it did not prevent it, nor did it address the long-term needs of the people displaced by the violence. Prior to international involvement, 1,500 people were killed and some 600,000 uprooted.[149] Whatever success R2P is said to have had in the case of Kenya, it is interesting to note that the secretary-general and Francis Deng used the phrase "responsibility to protect" in the initial stages of the violence but that mediators intentionally refrained from employing the term during negotiations, essentially to avoid a political quagmire.[150] Nonetheless, Annan has said that his efforts in Kenya owed something to the existence of R2P as a moral instrument.[151] The engagement of the international community in mediation efforts in Kenya is seen by many as having generated new interest in R2P.[152]

The case of Burundi, on the other hand, is what International Crisis Group vice president Don Steinberg calls the "unwritten story of where genocide prevention actually works." The international community, he insists, responded exactly right:

> They sent in a preventive force from South Africa. They convened an international donors' conference to support peace-building efforts. They sent in mediators to work on the conflict. They sent relief to key players who might be tempted to take another route. They looked at strengthening the rule of law. And thirteen years later, we haven't seen that genocide.[153]

Samantha Power argues that in order for R2P to have a chance of meaningful implementation, three things need to happen: R2P must be linked to national interest; the resurgence of sovereignty as a deterrent has to be overcome; and what she calls the "Iraq syndrome" (in which the United States justified its military intervention in Iraq in humanitarian terms) has to be dealt with. The rise of China, Russia, and Venezuela as major powers has given confidence to developing countries to stand up to the West. The Group of 77 (which now includes 133 of the UN's 192 members) is increasingly vocal in its opposition to R2P, and Power argues that more, not less pushback on R2P can be expected. Given the fact that the Iraq syndrome weakened U.S. credibility and legitimacy, she concludes that the United States cannot take the lead on discussions about R2P.[154]

Efforts to justify the Iraq intervention as a humanitarian intervention fail. Kenneth Roth says:

> In sum, the invasion of Iraq fails the test for a humanitarian intervention. Most important, the killing in Iraq at the time was not of the dire and exceptional nature that would justify military action. In addition, intervention was not the last reasonable option to stop Iraqi atrocities. It was not motivated primarily by humanitarian concerns. It was not conducted in a way that maximized compliance with international humanitarian law. It was not approved by the Security Council. And while, at the time it was launched, it was reasonable to believe that the Iraqi people would be better off, it was not designed or carried out with the needs of Iraqis foremost in mind.[155]

Growing Opposition to R2P

Many of the critics of R2P hold that the concept is "intervention" or "humanitarian intervention" repackaged as a Trojan horse in the neat phrase "responsibility to protect." These critics hold that R2P is used selectively as a tool of intervention or even imperialism by the strong against the weak to advance their own interests. UN special adviser Edward Luck identified these and two other main criticisms of R2P at the July 2009 General Assembly debate on the responsibility to protect when he noted

> [t]he twisted notion that sovereignty and responsibility are somehow incompatible when, as the Secretary-General has often underscored, they are mutually reinforcing principles and his plan aims to strengthen, not weaken, state capacity [and] the tired canard that RtoP offers new legal norms or would alter the Charter basis for Security Council decisions, when it is a political, not legal, concept based on well-established international law and the provisions of the UN Charter.[156]

Protection of Civilians and Responsibility to Protect

Over the course of the past decade, UN reform efforts have sought to strengthen the ability of the international system to prevent and respond to atrocities such as those that occurred in the 1990s. Through integrated missions, revitalization of peacekeeping operations, and the "one UN" initiative, multilateral institutions were directed to adopt a comprehensive approach to complex conflict situations. Humanitarian assistance was to be included as one component of a unified UN approach. While humanitarian actors reacted with alarm at the potential compromise or subordination of humanitarian principles to the political objectives of integrated missions, there has been remarkably little discussion of potential tensions between integrated missions and the growing humanitarian engagement in protection—and development, for that matter. One can imagine, for example, that efforts by humanitarian agencies to engage Afghan communities in addressing protection threats could complicate efforts by the SRSG to build strong relationships with the government and strengthen the security sector.

Protection of civilians and responsibility to protect initiatives have different institutional "homes," have developed different constituencies, and have developed along almost parallel tracks.[157] Protection of civilians has been a main feature of the secretary-general's statements, has been a focus of Security Council resolutions, has been incorporated into mandates of peacekeeping operations, and, on the humanitarian side, has been "appropriated" by OCHA. A few donor governments—notably the United Kingdom and Switzerland—and a few NGOs have embraced the notion of protection of civilians. But so far, the concept has failed to be translated into concrete action to protect people on the ground. While Security Council resolutions have certainly called attention to the problem that civilians are dying in large numbers and have included protection of civilians in peacekeeping mandates, more is needed. It is good to remind states and nonstate actors of the importance of respecting international humanitarian law and permitting access by humanitarian actors, but such reminders are insufficient in the context of today's wars. The recommendations to develop a doctrine for peacekeeping operations on what a mandate to protect civilians means have been repeated in many forums. Such a doctrine should be developed, tested, refined, and implemented. It simply is not fair to peacekeepers, troop-contributing countries, DPKO, or, especially, affected communities that there is still lack of clarity about this essential part of the mandate—eleven years after the first peacekeeping operation was asked to protect civilians as part of its mandate.

The conceptual clashes between the Office for the Coordination of Humanitarian Affairs and the Department of Peacekeeping Operations over protection of civilians (in spite of the solid, jointly commissioned study released in November 2009) are an unfortunate reflection of the fact that the UN is far from achieving its objective of coherence. The two units have different histories and different mandates. DPKO's mandate is to plan, prepare, manage, and direct peacekeeping operations. As has been noted, there is an urgent need for DPKO to provide further guidance on what protection of civilians means to its peacekeeping operations. OCHA's mandate is quite different in that it has three core functions: coordination of humanitarian response; policy development and coordination; and advocacy, including through briefings to the Security Council. OCHA's *aide mémoire* was intended to support the Security Council's engagement in protection of civilians, in part by reminding it of actions that it has previously taken. But if OCHA is to take the lead within the humanitarian community on protection of civilians, further work is needed, either by OCHA or within the global protection cluster.

There is a need to reflect on what protection of civilians means in practice and to identify—and publicize—good practices. Any strategy to protect civilians should begin with support for communities to protect themselves and with engagement with concerned national and local authorities. Additional analysis is needed to reconceptualize protection of civilians beyond protection of children, women, and displaced persons. These three groups have obvious protection needs, but the concept of protection of civilians should be more than an agglomeration of specific groups. And in order to support coordination of action on the ground, a short statement of what protection of civilians means could be drafted and widely circulated among actors involved in humanitarian response.

Within the humanitarian community and the broader constituency concerned with protection of civilians, there is fear of being associated too closely with R2P. In spite of the volumes that have been written to explain that R2P includes a range of potential actions, when governments or agencies refer to R2P they almost always mean nonconsensual military intervention in developing countries experiencing conflict. It may simply be that too much opposition has built up against the concept and it should be permitted to quietly slip away.

But if R2P is to move forward, it has to become a global rather than a North-South issue and it has to be used in more ways than military intervention. When initiatives are undertaken to prevent atrocities—as in Kenya in early 2008—they should be identified as R2P. At present there is a bit of a dilemma: diplomats and UN staff are reluctant to identify their efforts as part of R2P for fear of being associated with military intervention, but as long as they do not use the term to refer to broader preventive actions, it will continue to be used as a code word for military intervention.

The Universal Periodic Review mechanism of the Human Rights Council, which will regularly assess human rights in all 192 UN member states, represents an innovative way of "universalizing" human rights issues. If R2P is to become a global concept, rather than a contentious North-South issue, similar creativity is needed to make it clear that R2P has universal application. Finally, it might be helpful to put greater emphasis on the role of national governments—which is, after all, the bedrock of the international system—in R2P. It would be helpful, for example, to have a substantive research project focusing on cases in which governments are exercising responsible sovereignty. Governments are not perfect, of course, and each positive example could undoubtedly be countered with more critical ones. But there is insufficient public acknowledgment of the ways that governments are exercising their sovereignty responsibly or of the positive steps that they undertake in very difficult circumstances—for example, government programs to protect the displaced, to counter sexual and gender-based violence, or to develop social protection or livelihoods. By most accounts the Chinese government responded admirably to the 2009 Szechuan earthquake, the Colombian government has been exemplary in developing national legislation to uphold the rights of IDPs, the Rwandan government managed the extraordinarily difficult task of reconciliation extraordinarily well, and the government of Syria has provided protection to Iraqi refugees. There are shortcomings in all those cases, and it is certainly easier to criticize governments than to analyze the factors that have enabled them to take positive measures to protect civilians. But as the bedrock of the international order is national sovereignty, R2P can be effective only if it focuses on ways of enhancing the will and capacity of governments to exercise their sovereignty responsibly.

6 | *Humanitarian Dilemmas*

Humanitarian work has long been complicated, political, danger-ous, and difficult. There was no golden era of humanitarian endeavor when refugee camps were calm, access to affected populations was easy, and all assistance was strictly nonpolitical. During the 1980s, for example, conflicts in Central America created large-scale displacement; while many NGOs protested the forced relocations and military incursions into refugee camps, others saw the camps as havens for guerrilla forces. Many other areas were simply out of reach for most humanitarian actors—such as Afghanistan dur-ing the Soviet occupation and Cambodia during the Khmer Rouge regime. During the cold war, response to humanitarian crises was routinely used to support foreign policy objectives. For example, in 1982 Eugene Douglas, the U.S. coordinator for refugee affairs, wrote that U.S. refugee policy

> must counter Soviet expansion and limit Soviet options everywhere our real interests are threatened. It must seek to wean away client states from Soviet domination and to unmask the ideologies of Marxism-Leninism before they gain power wherever that is threatened.[1]

Humanitarian workers had to understand complex political dynamics in order to implement straightforward relief programs in places like the Thai-Cambodian border, and it was not unusual for refugee camps to be attacked by factions seeking to assert their control over them. Humanitarian workers in the field often had difficulty communicating with their headquarters, liv-ing conditions were difficult, and relief workers occasionally were killed in crossfire or by land mines.

But as difficult as the conditions were, there was general acceptance of the humanitarian imperative and respect for those seeking to provide assistance.

While governments sometimes denied access to humanitarian agencies seeking to work with particular populations, humanitarian actors were largely respected as neutral and nonpartisan organizations (although they were sometimes seen as naïve.)

The situation has changed. In many parts of the world, humanitarian workers are now targeted *because* of their humanitarian work. Access to populations is impeded not only by recalcitrant governments but also by nonstate actors and by the restrictive security protocols of humanitarian agencies themselves. "Humanitarian space" is the term usually used to denote the operating environment in which humanitarian work can be carried out— and that space is restricted because of lack of security, because of difficulties in accessing affected populations, and, perhaps most fundamentally, because perceptions of humanitarian work have changed. On one hand, there has been a certain mission creep within humanitarianism as it has evolved from providing impartial life-saving assistance to suffering people to addressing broader social change initiatives. At the same time, the perception is growing that humanitarian efforts are being carried out to support specific Western political, economic, or religious agendas rather than universal humanitarian principles. Many humanitarian workers trace their current problems to efforts by Western governments not only to channel humanitarian aid through NGOs, but to use NGOs and UN agencies to support their political objectives. The fact that military and civilian aid workers are operating side by side has blurred the lines between military and humanitarian operations. In Macedonia in 1999, NATO carried out air strikes against Serbia at night while soldiers from NATO member countries worked to build camps for Kosovar refugees during the day. Certainly the refugees drew the connections between the military's kinetic and humanitarian work—but they also tended to see the civilian humanitarian workers as part of the same military effort.

The proliferation of humanitarian actors has undoubtedly influenced such perceptions. While experienced relief workers with a long history in a particular country have developed long-term relationships with local actors and are sensitive to cultural mores, there are many stories of newly formed NGOs making cultural blunders that have implications for the humanitarian community in general. While NGOs and UN agencies are acutely conscious of the differences between their organizations, affected populations, governments, and nonstate actors often perceive them as the same. At the same time, competition between humanitarian agencies—fundamentally competition for funding—can also lead agencies to take risks by venturing into areas where no one else dares to go.

This chapter begins by exploring some of the dilemmas around "humanitarian space," including security and perceptions, and then looks at two additional dilemmas facing humanitarian work today: the gap between the phasing out of humanitarian work and the beginning of development assistance and the issue of accountability. The chapter concludes with an assessment of how these dilemmas have shaped the international community's focus on protection.

Humanitarian Space

Humanitarian space is usually defined in terms of freedom—freedom to access people in need, to evaluate needs, to distribute aid independently and impartially, and to monitor impact. The phrase "humanitarian space" was first used in reference to Central America in the early 1990s,[2] but it came into widespread use when Rony Brauman, then president of Médecins sans Frontières (MSF) defined it as a "space of humanitarian action where we are free to evaluate needs, free to monitor the distribution and use of relief goods, and free to have a dialogue with the people."[3] Given its widespread usage, it is interesting to note that the "we" in the phrase seems to refer almost exclusively to international actors rather than to affected communities.

The Inter-Agency Standing Committee took up the issue of humanitarian space in 2007, setting up a working group to analyze changes in humanitarian space and its effect on humanitarian work. The concept of humanitarian space, the working group concluded, refers to both a safe physical location and an operating environment conducive to effective humanitarian action.[4] Interestingly, the concept of humanitarian space seems to be applied only in situations of conflict. Humanitarian agencies may not have physical access to people affected by an earthquake because the roads have been blocked, but the assumption is that they are otherwise free to provide humanitarian assistance. However, when disasters occur in areas of conflict, the question of access can be especially complicated because governments typically try to limit travel by humanitarian agencies to those areas.

UNHCR explicitly ties the concept of humanitarian space to protection, defining it as

> a social, political and security environment which allows access to protection, including assistance, for populations of concern to UNHCR, facilitates the exercise of UNHCR's non-political and humanitarian protection mandate, and within which the prospect of achieving solutions to displacement is optimized.[5]

In other words, humanitarian space is not just about humanitarian agencies being able to assist people affected by conflict but also about those agencies being able to protect them. As the paper goes on to note, protection activities usually are more political and more likely to generate opposition than assistance: "Experience in certain operations has demonstrated that protection-related activities, especially as they relate to internally displaced persons (IDPs) are often less acceptable to governments than purely assistance-driven programmes."[6]

Humanitarian space can be limited by a number of factors. Most obviously, the conflict itself can prevent humanitarians from accessing people in need. The breakdown of law and order that accompanies most conflicts can lead to higher levels of criminality and to impunity when attacks against humanitarian workers occur. Moreover, relief supplies are economic assets that parties to a conflict often try to control. Humanitarian space also can be limited by the government of an affected country when it believes that the humanitarian agency is not acting in the country's best interest—either because it is allied with a donor government or party to the conflict or because its programs conflict with the government's priorities. For example, during its military offensive against the Tamil Tigers in May 2009, the government of Sri Lanka severely curtailed humanitarian access to civilians trapped behind conflict lines. Humanitarian space can be limited by governments and non-state actors that fear that humanitarian workers will witness serious human rights violations and provide evidence to the International Criminal Court. Armed groups can restrict humanitarian space because humanitarian actors are perceived as partial to the government or occupying power or because the groups oppose humanitarian efforts to empower local communities. Humanitarian space also can be limited by the blurring of the distinction between military and humanitarian organizations. For example, in Iraq, the United States has used private contractors to provide assistance traditionally handled by the government, the United Nations, and NGOs, such as water supplies and education. In some cases, humanitarian actors are closely aligned with the military, which contributes to the blurring of this distinction. Again, in Iraq UN humanitarian agencies are almost entirely dependent on multinational forces for security, presence, and mobility. Finally, humanitarian space can be limited by the culturally insensitive behavior of some humanitarian workers or by perceptions that humanitarians are squandering resources or that they are promoting specific social, cultural, or religious agendas.[7]

Apart from the conflict itself, perceptions are the main factor limiting humanitarian space—perceptions by the population, by governments, and by armed elements that humanitarians are not who they say they are: impartial providers of assistance to people in need. Some such perceptions come from the presence of political groups or militias that also provide assistance, but some stem from the growing involvement of humanitarian workers with protection. Protection work—even when undertaken for humanitarian reasons, with no link to a political agenda—is always political. To use an example from a different area of work, to set the broken arm of a woman who has been beaten by her husband is a humanitarian act. To try to protect the woman by providing a safe space for her to live, by going to court to get an injunction against her husband, or by physically coming between her and her husband is a different order of interaction—one that is inherently more dangerous for the person trying to protect the woman.

When humanitarian principles and humanitarian space intersect, impunity is an especially tricky issue. As UNHCR spelled out in its paper on humanitarian space,

> UNHCR clearly has a strong interest, underpinned by its protection mandate, in advocating for impunity to be addressed, including through national and (where appropriate) international criminal prosecutions. At the same time, if UNHCR is perceived as facilitating such processes, this may have serious implications for its continued presence and activities. This requires a complex balancing of the imperative of tackling impunity against a potential reduction in humanitarian space.[8]

When sixteen NGOs were expelled from Darfur in March 2009 by the Sudanese government, the reason given was that they were collecting evidence of human rights abuses to give to the International Criminal Court. The involved NGOs denied that they had done that, and some observers pointed out that the government had targeted precisely those NGOs that had been most active in protection activities.[9] Calling for justice is consistent with international humanitarian law; the dilemma is that if humanitarian agencies provide evidence in the pursuit of justice, their neutrality is compromised.

The concern with seeking justice and ending impunity also is related to security. When aid workers are attacked, humanitarian agencies want justice; specifically, they want the attackers to be punished (which rarely occurs). But it becomes difficult when humanitarian agencies can call for justice when their workers are killed but are prevented from providing evidence against forces attacking the civilians that they are trying to help.

The concept of humanitarian space usually is presented as a given—a contextual factor that sets the limits to international humanitarian work.

Dorothea Hilhorst and Maliana Serrano suggest the alternative phrase "humanitarian arena," in which "multiple actors seek and negotiate considerations and delivery of aid while furthering their interests and shaping conditions of aid."[10] That broadens the concept beyond international actors to include local NGOs, nonstate actors, and local and national governments. Humanitarian space is not just given, it is an operating environment that is negotiated and that changes.

Security of Humanitarian Workers

All humanitarian actors face difficult decisions about how to balance their responsibility to protect their own staff with their mission to assist and protect vulnerable people. Many humanitarian actors believe that in order for international agencies to protect people, they need to be physically present among them. While international law and norms clearly prohibit attacks on humanitarian actors, the gap between the standards and their implementation is large.

International law addresses the issue of security of humanitarian workers. In particular, the Convention on the Safety of UN and Associated Personnel, adopted in 1995, is a key legal instrument that provides for the security and the environment needed by United Nations and associated personnel to do their work.[11] The convention, which entered into force in 1999, addresses general rights and duties of both states party to the convention and UN and associated personnel and the individual criminal responsibility of perpetrators of attacks against such personnel. In 2005, an optional protocol was adopted by the General Assembly, making the convention easier to apply.[12]

International humanitarian law defines the obligations of states to provide for or ensure access to humanitarian assistance in armed conflicts in article 18 (2) of Protocol II (relating to victims of non-international armed conflicts) of the Convention Relative to the Protection of Civilian Persons in Time of War (the Fourth Geneva Convention, 1949). The UN's Guiding Principles on Internal Displacement state that

> international humanitarian organizations and other appropriate actors have the right to offer their services in support of the internally displaced. Such an offer shall not be regarded as an unfriendly act or interference in a State's internal affairs and shall be considered in good faith. Consent thereto shall not be arbitrarily withheld, particularly when authorities concerned are unable or unwilling to provide the required humanitarian assistance.[13]

Under international law victims of conflict have a right to international protection and assistance when national authorities are unwilling or unable to provide such assistance. Humanitarian access, which is an essential ancillary right to protection and assistance, should not be considered a concession granted to humanitarian organizations.[14]

On several occasions, the UN Security Council has taken up the issue of attacks on humanitarian workers, most notably in resolution 1502 in 2003, which was adopted in the aftermath of the August 2003 attack on UN headquarters in Baghdad. Among other provisions, the resolution includes the following:

> *Requests* the Secretary-General to address in all his country-specific situation reports, the issue of the safety and security of humanitarian personnel and United Nations and its associated personnel, including specific acts of violence against such personnel, remedial actions taken to prevent similar incidents and actions taken to identify and hold accountable those who commit such acts, and to explore and propose additional ways and means to enhance the safety and security of such personnel.[15]

Three years later, the United Nations again took up the issue of attacks on humanitarian workers, adopting resolution 1674, in which the Security Council

> *Condemns* all attacks deliberately targeting United Nations and associated personnel involved in humanitarian missions, as well as other humanitarian personnel, *urges* States on whose territory such attacks occur to prosecute or extradite those responsible, and *welcomes* in this regard the adoption on 8 December 2005 by the General Assembly of the Optional Protocol to the Convention on the Safety of United Nations and Associated Personnel.[16]

This resolution reflects the fact that working for a humanitarian organization is becoming increasingly dangerous. Not only are more aid workers getting killed, they are getting killed *because* they are aid workers. The first sign that the era of immunity from attack had ended for humanitarians occurred in 1996, when six ICRC delegates in Chechnya were deliberately and brutally murdered by masked gunmen while they slept in a hospital residence. In Stoddard, Harmer, and DiDomenico (2009), the only recent comprehensive study of the security of humanitarian workers, the authors note that international aid work has the fifth highest job-related death rate among U.S. civilian occupations and is the only one for which the cause of death is predominantly intentional violence. Between 1997 and 2005, nearly as many aid workers were killed in intentional violence as were international peacekeeping troops.[17]

In 2008, the number of deaths of aid workers exceeded that of UN peacekeeping troops.[18] In addition, the study found that nearly 80 percent of aid worker victims were national staff and that the number of national staff victims more than doubled between 1997 and 2005 while the rate for internationals remained stable or declined. In other words, not only is humanitarian work risky for everyone, it also is becoming increasingly dangerous for national staff of INGOs and UN agencies. While risks to international aid workers may not have greatly increased on an aggregate level, the perception of insecurity and victimization by aid workers themselves has certainly grown.[19]

There also is a double standard in media coverage of attacks, kidnappings, and killings of humanitarian workers. More attention is given to cases in which international staff are attacked than to cases in which victims are local staff of international agencies—and even less attention is given to victims who are on the staff of national NGOs. While international organizations often assume that national staff face lower risks, studies have found that assumption to be faulty. Among other things, fewer security resources, including training and equipment, are made available to national staff than to expatriate staff. With remote management becoming increasingly popular as a way of continuing to work in dangerous areas without risking expatriate staff lives, there are serious ethical issues about transferring risk from international staff to local organizations.[20] Working through intermediaries may be safer for international staff, but it increases the danger to the staff of the intermediary organizations.

Growing security threats to humanitarian workers emanate in part from their relationship not only with Western donor governments, but also with governments involved in conflicts. For example, U.S. humanitarian NGOs providing assistance in Afghanistan with or without funding from the U.S. government often are perceived as supporting the U.S. military's role in the conflict. It is hard for any U.S.-based organization to be neutral—and perceived as neutral—in a conflict in which the United States is a principal military protagonist and sees civilian assistance as part of its military strategy.

Even when insurgent groups are very aware of the differences between NGOs, UN aid agencies, and military forces, they may target humanitarian operations simply because it is easier to attack a UN facility than a military one. Or they may deliberately want the shock value of violating international standards and norms by attacking unarmed aid providers; in that respect their motivations may be similar to those of terrorists who attack civilians. Or in countries like Afghanistan, Iraq, and Somalia, attacks on humanitarian workers may be intended to "undermine stability and authority, discourage the presence of humanitarian actors and send a violent message that aid agencies are seen as part of a Western agenda."[21] As Erik Abild of the Refugee Studies Centre at the University of Oxford explains in the context of Somalia, "the greatest concern for most agencies is that they are perceived to be a part of a western agenda and connected to the American led "war on terror."[22] But Abild goes on to say that the most disturbing part of his research was "not that attacks were the result of perceptions of partiality or ineffectiveness, but rather precisely because aid workers are effective." Aid delivery can confer legitimacy, and targeting of aid workers not only makes delivery of aid more risky but also undermines the government's authority by demonstrating its inability to protect aid workers.[23]

The bombing of UN headquarters in Baghdad on August 19, 2003, not only resulted in the deaths of twenty-one UN staff, including Sergio Vieira de Mello, the special representative of the secretary-general, but also led all UN agencies to withdraw their international staff from Iraq and to run their Iraq programs through "remote management." Although UN agencies have since increased their international staff presence in Baghdad, their movements remain highly restricted and they depend on the coalition forces for security. The issue of security of UN staff in Iraq illustrates the complex interaction between history, perceptions, and threats on the ground. While the UN is seen in many parts of the world as an idealistic, neutral organization, it has a different reputation in Iraq. The sanctions that the UN had imposed on Iraq for years were tremendously unpopular among Iraqis and resulted in widespread civilian casualties from restrictions on the import of food, medicine, fuel, agricultural inputs, and other products needed for the production of essential goods. The widespread corruption in the UN's Oil for Food program was well-known in Iraq, and many believed that UN officials were enriching themselves with Iraqi resources. Finally, the weapons inspections were perceived as humiliating for the country. Even in the best of circumstances, the United Nations would have faced an uphill battle in reestablishing its credibility among the Iraqi public, and the circumstances were far from good. Linking UN security to the coalition forces made it almost impossible for the UN to present itself as a neutral, impartial agency concerned only with the well-being of the population. When UN staff arrive in communities accompanied by U.S. or Multi-National Force–Iraq (MNF-I) forces, their neutrality is immediately compromised.

Choices that the UN has made in Somalia also have had an impact on the security of aid workers. As Abild explains, the UN chose to support the Transitional Federal Government (TFG) in Somalia during the 2006–08 Ethiopian intervention. While that was in line with the UN's standard support for the national government, it was interpreted in Somalia as favoring one side in the conflict. Both donors and the UN were on record as supporting the TFG, which created difficulties for humanitarian agencies, particularly in their efforts to reach populations in areas not under the control of the TFG—which amounted to at least 98 percent of the country. "For aid agencies to insist on impartiality and neutrality, and to operate in areas controlled by non-TFG actors, was seen [by the UN and donor countries] as undermining the state-building efforts of the UN and donors, and thereby in opposition to their political agenda. In this sense, to be neutral became political."[24] By allying itself with a government that controls a small minority of the territory, the UN is perceived as a party to the conflict—and hence as a target by insurgent groups.

For years, the security of humanitarian workers depended on their acceptance by warring parties as impartial, neutral, and independent actors who did not get involved in the politics of conflict. But the fact is that the United Nations is a political body that makes political decisions. Through its Department of Political Affairs (DPA) and Department of Peacekeeping Operations (DPKO), the UN tries to bring about an end to conflict by negotiating with warring parties, by applying sanctions to enforce Security Council decisions, and by putting peacekeepers in the field to enforce peace agreements. Those are not politically neutral activities. The UN's humanitarian agencies—such as UNHCR, UNRWA, UNICEF, and WFP—therefore face a difficult task in trying to provide assistance in accord with humanitarian principles of neutrality and impartiality. While their security on the ground depends on their being perceived as nonpolitical humanitarian actors, they are affected by actions taken by other UN bodies, including the Security Council and other departments within the secretariat. When UN agencies also try to protect people, their task becomes even more difficult.

Humanitarian actors face terrible dilemmas in making decisions about staff security. They need security to carry out their relief operations and to try to protect affected communities, but when they rely on military forces, they may create violent resentments that actually increase the threat to their safety. Yet traditional security measures often are inadequate. At the same time, security arrangements that are too risk-averse may unduly limit access to beneficiaries and thus limit humanitarian space.[25] Since the 2003 attack on UN headquarters in Iraq, the UN has developed much stricter security guidelines on staff travel and activity. Some have argued that the greatest impediment to UN access to affected communities now is its own internal security guidelines.

There also is a major dilemma in the fact that there is an inverse relationship between the safety of the operating environment for humanitarian workers and human need. In today's conflict situations, the greater the human need, the more dangerous it is for humanitarian workers. In fact, agencies usually are forced to withdraw or curtail their operations in areas where human suffering is the greatest. In Darfur, for example, the areas of greatest need are precisely the areas that humanitarians do not have access to and therefore cannot help. Abild reports that in 2008 the number of international aid workers in Somalia decreased by 50 percent, even as the estimated number of people in need of assistance went up by 77 percent.[26] Even when agencies do not withdraw their staff, a "bunker mentality" often limits their ability to reach affected populations. In Afghanistan, for example, travel outside of Kabul has been progressively restricted.[27]

How to Protect Staff?

How do organizations protect their own staff? As discussed in chapters 3 and 4, different organizations have different provisions on the use of armed escorts and private security companies. They also have different procedures for making decisions on security. While UN security operations are highly centralized, with decisions on staff travel to certain areas made by the UN Department of Safety and Security (DOSS) in New York, the International Committee of the Red Cross has decentralized its security operations. Decisions on security at ICRC are made at the national level, reflecting ICRC's reliance on acceptance by the community for most of its protection. There are three basic strategies to protect staff: acceptance by the local community, protection (for example, limiting travel, protecting compounds, and remote management), and deterrence (for example, using armed guards).[28]

Acceptance. The security policy of Red Cross/Red Crescent affiliates continues to be rooted in their humanitarian principles. The IFRC manual on staff security lays out seven pillars of security, beginning with "acceptance." Acceptance includes political acceptance of the activities of Red Cross/Red Crescent affiliates by the authorities as well as staff acceptance of cultural issues and operating methods. The second pillar of security, identification, is of central and particular importance to the Red Cross. Concretely, it is expressed in the requirement that that all staff wear their Red Cross/ Red Crescent badge while on duty; that staff vehicles and facilities be clearly identified with the logo; and that all staff movements to sensitive areas be announced in advance. The third pillar is information: collecting and sharing security information, analyzing security incidents, and cultivating good relations with the media. Security rules and regulations, which all staff are expected to know and to follow and which are regularly updated, are the fourth pillar. Personal behavior, the fifth pillar, includes a range of activities, from being aware of security problems and knowing local habits, dress codes, and the like to being careful not to provoke others by behavior seen as offensive. Communication is the sixth pillar, particularly the ability to communicate clearly and effectively by radio. Protection, the seventh and final pillar, includes selecting secure residences equipped with functioning communication systems and emergency items.[29]

Many international NGOs have similar strategies for providing security for their staff. Although the Red Cross/Red Crescent emblems are unique in their universality, traditionally other organizations also have relied on identification of their staff, facilities, vehicles, and other property as a way of asserting their humanitarian character. And, of course, logos are important for other reasons, such as increasing the visibility of agencies, which is useful in raising funds to support their work.

But in Iraq, Afghanistan, and Somalia—all places where humanitarians have been targeted—identification can increase the risk to humanitarian operations. Casey Barrs lays out a number of strategies that can be used by international organizations to continue their work while reducing the risk, including downgrading identity (stop logo branding, forgo identification, and obscure the agency's paper—and funding—trail); downsizing infrastructure; dispersing workers, supplies, and distribution sites; and delegating work to others.[30] Such strategies can allow humanitarian operations to continue, but they entail costs and questions. There is a fine line between being discreet and being dishonest. Conflicts often are characterized by an environment of suspicion in which even unfounded accusations that humanitarian agencies are spying or acting on behalf of political interests increase the risk that agency staff will be targeted for attack.

The need to protect the staff of humanitarian organizations is directly related to humanitarian efforts to protect populations at risk. Looking at humanitarian operations in Iraq at the height of the violence in 2006, Greg

Hansen found that "there is no substitute for presence. The low visibility of assistance and protection efforts in Iraq confounds misperceptions about humanitarian work and the lack of acceptance of humanitarian organizations." And as international staff withdrew, attacks on Iraqi staff increased in 2005 and 2006.[31]

Remote Management. Remote management has been used in different situations to continue service delivery when international agencies are no longer able to operate in an area because of security concerns. Over the years, in places as diverse as the Horn of Africa, Chechnya, and Myanmar, agencies have worked from a distance through what typically were ad hoc arrangements often known as cross-border operations. Today the term "remote management" refers to the practice of transferring responsibility for service delivery to local staff or local organizations while international staff provide oversight from afar. There are various models of carrying out remote operations, which vary in the degree of decisionmaking authority that implementing staff or partners have.

Carrying out operations remotely allows humanitarian work to continue and avoids the complete closure of programs. But there are costs. Some have argued that it simply transfers the risks from international to national staff. It also changes the nature of the relationship between the international agency and its beneficiaries: rather than having a direct personal relationship with beneficiaries, the international agency becomes more of a funding/management entity. And there are practical challenges, including less efficient service delivery, difficulties in ensuring accountability, and the risk of corruption.[32] Hansen found that the low-profile policies of international agencies in Iraq, including remote management, also affected Iraqi staff, noting that "working relationships are under increasing strain as low-profile approaches dictate that staff work from their homes, with less frequent face-to-face contact within and between organizations." He also found that the lack of international presence contributed to the lack of trust and perceptions of sectarian bias in decisions about allocation of resources and personnel management.[33]

But when the choice facing an agency is either to stop operations in an area where people are in need or to work through local intermediaries, most humanitarian agencies choose to continue operations in spite of the disadvantages of remote management.

Deterrence. The use of armed escorts to provide security to humanitarian agencies has long been controversial. Humanitarian agencies have resisted using such escorts, fearing that their neutrality would be compromised by their close association with military forces. In 2001, the Inter-Agency

Standing Committee developed nonbinding guidelines for the use of military or armed assets in humanitarian operations; the guidelines begin with the statement that "as a general rule, humanitarian convoys will not use armed or military escorts" and then lay out the criteria to be used to determine when exceptions might be necessary as a last resort.[34] Exceptions may be justified, the document notes, when the responsible political authorities are unable to provide the necessary security, when the level of human need is such that lack of assistance would cause unacceptable harm, when armed escorts can be provided in such a way that the security of humanitarian staff and beneficiaries is not compromised, and when the use of armed escorts does not threaten the long-term viability of operations.[35]

Sometimes host governments require military escorts to protect humanitarian workers, as the government of Pakistan did in September 2010 when it believed that there was a threat of violence against humanitarian agencies working with flood-affected communities in rural areas. In that case, some of the NGOs resisted the restrictions even though doing so meant that their staff were unable to operate in certain areas. For example, Rebecca Barber explained Oxfam's position as follows:

> In most cases, we are being told that this is for our own protection, and because the police are responsible for our security. Oxfam understands and appreciates the concern that the district police have for the security of international staff, and we value their support. However, Oxfam believes that travelling with police escorts compromises our impartiality and independence, which are two of the core humanitarian principles that guide all of our work. We also believe that the use of armed escorts, rather than enhancing our security, has the potential to undermine the safety and security of our staff and beneficiaries.[36]

In a wide-ranging survey of humanitarian organizations, Stoddard, Harmer, and DiDomenico found that while most of the major humanitarian organizations have contracted for security services, the use of armed escorts remains the exception and concentrated in a few countries—for example, Somalia.[37]

Perceptions

Humanitarian actors traditionally have relied on acceptance as a security strategy. Acceptance is a function of how parties to a conflict and the affected population *perceive* individual humanitarian organizations or the humanitarian community in general. Relations with military forces can influence their perceptions. "If humanitarian assistance is perceived, rightly or wrongly, as associated with military activities, being supportive of or as being partisan to one party to the conflict, humanitarian actors at best lose the acceptance necessary to operate safely, and at worst become deliberate targets of attacks."[38]

But there are other factors that influence the way that humanitarians see their work, the kinds of work that they do, and ultimately the way that they are perceived in the community. Donors, beneficiaries, and humanitarian organizations themselves expect humanitarian actors to do more than ever before—not just to provide immediate relief but to build local capacity, facilitate long-term development, and, increasingly, to protect people. In fact, the efforts by humanitarian agencies to protect people may be leading them into increasingly dangerous territory. Providing water, medical care, tents, and food do not suffice—there also is the expectation that humanitarian agencies will keep people safe and that the aid that they provide will enable the full realization of beneficiaries' human rights.

Many humanitarians have concluded that it is not enough to simply alleviate suffering without seeking to address the causes of suffering. A common anecdote repeated in various settings in the 1990s was the metaphor of relief workers picking bodies and injured people out of a river. "It's not enough to bandage them up," staff would say, "we have a responsibility to find out what's happening upriver and stop the bodies being thrown in the river." And yet addressing the causes of humanitarian emergencies is a challenge to humanitarian principles of neutrality and impartiality. Moreover, most of the international NGOs working in humanitarian assistance also work in long-term development programs, and many have programs to work on issues such as gender, the environment, children, health, and community empowerment.

Humanitarians increasingly see themselves as agents of change or transformation. In cases such as the Indian Ocean tsunami or the earthquake in Haiti, the drive to "build back better" is based on the premise that humanitarian assistance should go beyond just meeting immediate humanitarian needs—it also should create more just societies, more efficient governments, and stronger civil society organizations. As Andrew Natsios testified,

> [a]s the U.S. transitions from short-term humanitarian assistance towards the reconstruction of Haiti's shattered capital and economy, our aid must alter the power structure within the Haitian government and economy, to open the society up to genuine democratic principles and to a free market economy.[39]

Building democracy and capitalism are not objectives of most humanitarian actors, but many make the case that building the capacity of local organizations not only helps the relief effort but contributes to the flourishing of civil society, which in turn supports democratic processes.

Humanitarian actors frequently run into difficulty over gender issues. The Red Cross/NGO code of conduct, for example, includes provisions that dictate, on one hand, that aid is to be distributed on the basis of need alone and, on the other, that local culture and customs are to be supported. In societies that consider women's needs subordinate to those of men, distributing aid on the basis of need alone can be a highly political act. For example, most humanitarian agencies would find it difficult to provide schools for boys and not for girls, yet providing education to girls can be perceived as meddling with local culture. And efforts to protect women, including to protect them from domestic violence, can be even more controversial, especially when such efforts include human rights training for women.

A recent guide for humanitarian practitioners observed:

> It would seem that a "new humanitarianism" is emerging, one that more explicitly expands the humanitarian agenda to include governance, livelihood security, social protection, and other more development-like activities, focusing mostly on environments where risk remains continually high, state services continually low, and violence endemic—the so-called "fragile" or inappropriately-named transitional states.[40]

As humanitarians have broadened the definition of humanitarian work to include protection, they are perceived as more political actors. When that is coupled with the increasing trend toward making humanitarian work an instrument of political and military actors—as when NGOs or the UN are expected to support a given political agenda through humanitarian action—the question arises of whether the broader approach to humanitarian work is still humanitarian.

Can there be humanitarian action without impartiality, neutrality, and independence? In the Occupied Palestinian Territories, for example, is it possible for humanitarian actors to remain neutral when the occupying power limits access and delivery of humanitarian supplies? Can the actions of humanitarian actors who depend on Western powers for their funding be truly independent? The perception that humanitarian actors are not neutral, independent, or impartial threatens their security and limits their ability to act. This issue has been implicit in many of the critical studies on humanitarian action in recent years.[41]

The Gap between Humanitarian Assistance and Development

For more than twenty-five years, the gap between relief and development has been widely lamented. In theory, humanitarian agencies were intended to meet the immediate needs of people affected by conflict or natural disaster to enable them to survive; the agencies then would move out, presumably to tackle the next humanitarian crisis, while development agencies moved in. But that has never happened smoothly, in spite of wide recognition that a smooth transition between humanitarian and development assistance is in the best interests of the affected community, its government, and international stability.[42]

The relief-development gap is due in part to differences in the ways in which humanitarian and development actors work. The institutional cultures of all UN and NGO actors are unique, of course, but humanitarian organizations tend to stress rapid response, operational capacity, and flexibility. They tend not to work through local governments in implementing programs, and they often prefer to carry out operations themselves or through established partners rather than take the time to build the capacity of local partners. To overstate the case, the most important task for humanitarian agencies is to "get the job done": to make sure that people are fed, that water is available, that medical supplies are in the right place. In their view, if the government or local actors can assist with delivery, fine; if not, they should stand to the side while the international humanitarian community carries out the work. In fact, emergency operations have been criticized for actively disempowering local institutions, particularly local governments.[43]

There are limits to the sustainability of emergency programs, but emergency response, by definition, is expected to be temporary. Humanitarian actors often undertake programs that are intended to last beyond the emergency, but although "schools and clinics which are rebuilt with the logo of the European Commission Humanitarian Aid Office or USAID provide concrete benefits to the local population . . . they do little to build the credibility of national institutions in the eyes of the population in a manner which will sustain longer-term peace and recovery."[44] And building a school assumes that the government will be able to pay the recurring costs of teachers' salaries.

In contrast, development organizations work hand-in-hand with governments, and they emphasize the importance of process—the way that things are done. Building local capacity is essential to their development mandate. For development efforts to be sustainable, they must be rooted in the community and owned by the local population. The days are (hopefully) long gone when international development organizations arrived in a country to "do" development according to a predetermined plan. Humanitarian actors often see their development counterparts as slow, bogged down in bureaucratic procedures, and much too "cozy" with governments. Development actors tend to see emergency responders as cowboys or lone rangers who parachute in to provide assistance without considering community needs.

There also are differences in funding mechanisms. Humanitarian actors depend on the ability of the international community to mobilize funds relatively quickly through multilateral channels like the Consolidated Appeals Process (CAP) and the Central Emergency Response Fund (CERF). Most of the funds are used to support immediate relief rather than longer-term development initiatives. Development actors have different funding mechanisms, which are based on multiyear plans. It is clear that donors are more generous, at least in the initial phases of an emergency, in supporting life-saving measures than initiatives that are intended to transition into development. A review of the UN's primary mechanisms for mobilizing emergency assistance, OCHA's 2009 consolidated appeals and flash appeals—together amounting to $9.7 billion in revised requirements—reveals that overall, while 92 percent of the $3.3 billion requested for food was received, only 53 percent of the $416,000 in economic recovery and infrastructure funds requested was covered.[45] Furthermore, the requested amounts show the overwhelmingly greater emphasis placed by the UN and its funding partners on food assistance than on efforts intended to support the transition to development.

The term "early recovery" has emerged within the humanitarian community as the latest effort to address the "gap" between relief and development. Specifically, it refers to the transition in assistance from emergency response to longer-term development. It is entrusted to the cluster on early recovery led by the UN Development Program.

The early recovery cluster has devoted considerable energy to describing what early recovery is, defining it as a multidimensional process, guided by development principles, that seeks to build on humanitarian programs and to catalyze sustainable development opportunities. Early recovery aims to generate to the extent possible self-sustaining, nationally owned, resilient processes for postcrisis recovery, which encompass livelihoods, shelter, governance, the environment, and social issues, including the reintegration of displaced populations. It stabilizes human security and, where the opportunity exists, begins to address the underlying risks that contributed to the crisis.[46]

According to the early recovery cluster, the objectives of early recovery are to

—augment ongoing emergency assistance operations through measures that foster the self-reliance of the affected population and meet the most critical needs in order to rebuild livelihoods

—promote spontaneous recovery initiatives by the affected population and mitigate the rebuilding risk through self-help efforts, minimization of secondary risks, and so forth

—establish the foundations for long-term recovery through rebuilding/ reinforcing local governance institutions, building capacity, and clearly dividing roles and responsibilities among national actors.[47]

In fact, relief actors seldom leave immediately once a humanitarian crisis is over. For example, UNHCR often has a long-standing involvement with returning refugees and increasingly with returning IDPs. But humanitarian agencies do tend either to reduce the scale of their involvement or to change the focus of their activities, or both, once a political agreement has been reached. While they may have been responsible for feeding thousands of displaced people in camps, once the camps have been closed and a peace agreement signed, they generally do not see it as their responsibility to continue providing food to people back in their communities. And development actors rarely begin implementing programs as soon as a peace agreement is signed. Just as most IDPs adopt a "wait and see" attitude before deciding to return, so too development actors often wait until it is safe and until the war is really, truly, completely over before they begin development programs. Even so, it takes time before long-term plans can be developed. Thus, there often is a gap—between the time that humanitarian actors decide that their work is done and development actors determine that it is safe enough to implement large-scale programs.

While humanitarian and development actors are talking about early recovery, other actors refer to peace building, state building, and stabilization operations, which usually are taking place at the same time. In all of those efforts, there is a perceived need to show concrete signs of progress quickly in order to prevent a resurgence of conflict. Early recovery, it should be noted, is intended to apply to both conflicts and natural disasters while peace building, state building, and stabilization refer exclusively to postconflict situations. As Bailey and Pavanello illustrate, there is considerable confusion about how early recovery relates to those broader initiatives even as the focus in early recovery has shifted from linking relief and development to integrating aid and security.[48]

Meanwhile, the term "early recovery" has a different meaning in other sectors. A report commissioned by the United Kingdom's Department for International Development (DFID), for example, explicitly excluded humanitarian action, including protection of civilians, from its analysis of early recovery activities. The report goes on to say that "[e]arly recovery strategy must be cognizant of humanitarian action, and facilitate and share space with it, not compete with it—but humanitarian action is not the same thing as early recovery, and should not be conflated with it."[49]

The jury is still out on whether early recovery, as understood by the humanitarian community, will succeed in bridging the gap between relief and development. Given the decades-long discussion about the transition from relief to development, there is a certain cynicism about whether this new effort will yield concrete results. Moreover, most observers of the cluster system see early recovery and protection as the two weakest clusters, and there is concern that the focus on early recovery is simply "rebranding" existing activities, which will not add any notable value to them.[50] The most recent phase of the ongoing evaluation of the cluster system found systemic obstacles to the functioning of the early recovery and the protection clusters, including difficulties in defining their mandates, lack of expertise, and political issues, such as concerns by humanitarian agencies about UNDP's strong links to governments "that are actively involved in conflicts or to integrated missions and peacekeeping forces."[51]

Early recovery, as defined by the cluster, sees protection as an important component of its work under the general rubric of improving community security and social cohesion. But protection usually is depicted as access to justice, informal dispute resolution, and rule of law. UNDP's policy on early recovery states that "while longer-term reform of the security sector must normally await a peace settlement, planning for DDR [disarmament, demobilization, and reintegration] of ex-combatants must be initiated during early recovery in order to stabilize the situation, reduce insecurity and promote protection of civilians."[52] The early recovery clusters in countries affected by conflict have sought to incorporate protection into early recovery activities. In Uganda, for example, one of the seven programmatic categories identified by the early recovery cluster is "improving protection, human rights and rule of law," while in Darfur, an early recovery program focused on rule of law, including support for local lawyers to build up legal aid services and training and support for judges to help them recognize and address sexual and gender-based violence.[53] In Timor Leste, Louisa Medhurst noted that the early recovery cluster was started too late and the protection issues that it sought to address were being addressed largely by government or other bodies.[54]

Nation building, state building, peace building/reconciliation, stabilization, early recovery—all are terms currently used by different actors in dealing with the multiple challenges of postconflict situations. But they are not just terms. They are paradigms that determine the way that one looks at a particular issue and the solutions that one finds for a particular challenge. For example, military actors focusing on stabilization and reconstruction tend to see humanitarian assistance as a way of promoting security while early recovery puts the focus on the transition to sustainable development.

Accountability to Beneficiaries

One of the main trends in the humanitarian field over the last fifteen years or so has been the effort to increase agency accountability not only to donors for the funds that they provide, but also to the individuals and communities that actually receive humanitarian assistance. Donors have developed increasingly stringent requirements for reporting on the use of funds, and there are watchdog agencies that provide comparisons of the ways in which NGOs spend their funds. Accountability to beneficiaries has developed along a separate track. For instance, the code of conduct in disaster relief for the International Red Cross and NGOs states, "We hold ourselves accountable to both those we seek to assist and those from whom we accept resources" while another principle states that "ways shall be found to involve programme beneficiaries in the management of relief aid."[55]

Accountability to beneficiaries is not the same thing as consulting with beneficiaries in program design. "Whilst learning from 'beneficiaries' in order to enhance an organization's strategy for change is essential, this is different from being accountable to them. Accountability has to do with how one manages the unequal distribution of power in places when those that are meant to benefit from one's work have weak political and economic voice."[56] In other words, consulting with beneficiaries is good program planning, while accountability involves being responsible to the "consumers" of aid. Mechanisms for soliciting feedback on programs from beneficiaries have been difficult to implement.[57]

The drive for accountability to beneficiaries has been largely an NGO initiative. The principles of the Good Humanitarian Donorship initiative, for example, while reaffirming the importance of accountability, do not mention accountability to beneficiaries. Several donor governments, however, have taken up the issue, notably ECHO (the European Commission's humanitarian aid department), which now includes beneficiary accountability in its risk assessment guidelines to auditors, and DFID, which has incorporated accountability features in its funding guidelines.[58]

Over the past decade, accountability has become a major issue for NGOs, which have used a rights-based approach in their efforts to develop common standards. Leading those efforts has been the Sphere Project, which was launched in 1997 to improve the quality of assistance and to enhance the accountability of the humanitarian response through an explicit rights-based approach. Sphere's handbook, first published in 2000, includes its Humanitarian Charter, which is intended to be for all humanitarian actors, as well as minimum standards for humanitarian assistance and proposed universal standards in fields such as nutrition and water/sanitation. The 2004 edition incorporated the additional cross-cutting issues of gender, children, elderly, disabled, HIV/AIDS, and protection.[59]

The humanitarian charter developed by Sphere is an aspirational document: "This Charter expresses the shared belief of humanitarian agencies that all people affected by disaster and armed conflict have a right to receive assistance and protection to ensure the basic conditions for life with dignity."[60] It acknowledges that needs are met by communities themselves but reaffirms the primary responsibility of the state to "provide timely assistance to those affected, to ensure people's security, and to provide support for their recovery."

The charter and accompanying standards represented an effort to apply a rights-based approach to humanitarian assistance—a marked departure from the prevailing view at the time, which was that humanitarian assistance was all about responding to needs. Over the years, Sphere has become the gold standard, and it is used in many different countries and contexts—including those in which the Sphere standards are seen as aspirations rather than as minimum standards. In many cases, conditions make it impossible to attain those standards, especially insecurity, lack of access, and lack of sufficient resources. Sphere standards also go beyond providing a means of evaluating individual agency performance by "providing a basis for defining a common agenda and a set of criteria for gauging collective performance."[61]

But Sphere has not been without its critics.[62] As James Darcy, one of the original drafters, has said, "perhaps the greatest danger lies in creating the impression that the achievement of the conditions necessary for life with dignity is both the responsibility of agencies and lies within their power to bring about."[63] The 2004 evaluation found that "the Sphere Project is perceived to be an important and positive influence on the practice of contemporary humanitarian assistance" and that "the adoption of the rights-based approach has been a major influence on the thinking and the operations of many NGOs and other humanitarian agencies."[64] However, the evaluation also found that the "rights-based approach"—the cornerstone of Sphere's approach to humanitarian assistance—was not well understood.

Dufour and others question the rights-based approach: "It is one thing for a refugee to have the right to *non-refoulement*; it is another to have a right to adequate water supply."[65] They note that applying the Sphere standards does not guarantee that the activities carried out are also humanitarian, citing as an example the U.S. army's application of Sphere standards in Afghanistan. They note discrepancies in the way in which basic human rights are applied. "In Bosnia, for example, ensuring affected populations' dignity entailed providing affected populations with consumer goods they relied on in their daily lives, e.g. plastic diapers for babies and ladies' hygienic items—a luxury by Rwandan standards."[66] These discrepancies raise questions about the universality of basic rights. There also are questions about who is responsible for respecting the right to humanitarian assistance—national authorities, aid agencies, donor governments? Dufour and others cites a donor representative commenting on the Sphere evaluation: "Donors would go crazy if we told them shelter was a right. Can you imagine someone suing the U.S. State Department for human rights violations for not giving them adequate shelter?"[67] Sphere also can be used to legitimize the actions of nonhumanitarian actors. "An officer from the coalition in Afghanistan expressed his surprise at NGOs['] reactions against the engagement of the military in humanitarian operations: 'Why are they against us? We also use the Sphere standards.'"[68]

Discussions on the Sphere standards foreshadowed some of the current discussions on protection in raising questions about the relationship of a rights-based approach to humanitarian action. Following several years of discussion, in 2009 the Sphere board agreed to develop a chapter on protection to help agencies using the Sphere standards to understand how a general humanitarian approach can address protection needs. The draft chapter focuses on five aspects of protection: preventing unlawful discrimination among affected people; shielding people from physical harm or infringements of their dignity; ensuring that affected people have access to means of subsistence; allowing people to assert their rights; and ensuring that people can exercise their freedom of movement and choice of residence.[69] While Sphere standards in other sectors establish minimum standards, that is not the case with the protection chapter "because protection by definition depends on a contextual analysis of who is at risk, of what, from whom, and at what moment."[70]

ICRC's professional standards for protection work devote considerable attention to ensuring that affected communities are not put at risk when actors are engaged in protection. The standards stress the importance of the participation of at-risk populations in protection activities, in part because by doing so, they can better judge the performance of protection actors and increase accountability. However, the standards note that the imbalance of power between the communities and protection actors limits accountability. And communities have little recourse when the work of protection actors is "inadequate, inappropriate or ineffective."[71]

ALNAP, the Active Learning Network for Accountability and Performance, published a guide for humanitarian agencies that includes helpful practical advice for including a protection dimension throughout their work, from setting protection objectives to monitoring protection outcomes.[72] The guide notes that humanitarian assistance can be an entry point to protection, that protective assistance can save lives, that information serves a protection role, and that presence and accompaniment also are important in protecting the human rights of beneficiaries.[73]

The Humanitarian Accountability Partnership International (HAP-I) was established in 2003 to hold its members accountable for the work that they do—accountable to beneficiaries and accountable to each other.[74]

These rights-based networks and standards contribute to NGO involvement on the ground in areas where refugees' rights are being violated. For example, to respond to the violation of refugees' rights to education, the Inter-Agency Network for Education in Emergencies (INEE), made up of UN agencies and NGOs, was established. After extensive consultations with more than 2,250 individuals from around the world, INEE recently launched global minimum standards for education in emergencies, chronic crises, and early reconstruction.[75] Those standards provide a tool for NGOs working with refugees and IDPs and a standard for determining when basic human rights are not being met.

On the ground, NGOs have sometimes taken the lead in developing standards for their own operations. In Afghanistan, for example, NGOs often are confused with private contractors and for-profit organizations. "In the given situation of Afghanistan, where many people register and pretend to be an NGO, we needed to clarify our standards of operations," said Anja De Beer, executive coordinator of the Agency Coordinating Body for Afghan Relief (ACBAR), in explaining the development of a new code of conduct. That code of conduct, signed by ninety of the some 2,400 national and international registered NGOs that operate in different areas of the country, was developed in light of accusations of NGO misuse of funds.[76]

Accountability to beneficiaries is an idealistic endeavor rooted in the desire of many humanitarian agencies to move beyond the traditional power dynamic inherent in donor-recipient relationships to develop means of ensuring that their work fully respects the rights and dignity of those whom they assist. It is an effort to translate principles into practice. But it is not a risk-free activity, particularly when it comes to protection. In conflict situations, it is impossible for humanitarian agencies to make the kinds of promises to protect people that they can make to provide a minimum number of liters of water a day. While they may have difficulties in providing water because of conflict or political obstacles, providing water and providing protection entail different responsibilities. Humanitarian agencies should not be expected to explain why they were unable to prevent an attack on a village or the rape of a woman collecting firewood. It is not their responsibility. They certainly can prevent discrimination in the distribution of assistance, but ensuring recipients' freedom of movement and choice of residence often lies outside their area of competence. While they can take steps to mitigate armed attacks by providing shelter or treating the wounded, some actions are beyond their control.

The three humanitarian dilemmas discussed here—shrinking humanitarian space, confusion over the transition from humanitarian emergency to long-term development, and accountability to beneficiaries—all come together in the difficult period following a conflict. There has been an assumption that the processes are linear—that a conflict is followed by peace, that relief assistance is replaced by long-term development activities—but the reality is that they unfold unevenly over time and usually not in a clear linear pattern. Humanitarian assistance often is needed after a peace agreement has been signed. Even during conflicts, there often are opportunities to introduce community-based development initiatives.

The terms "stabilization," "stability operations," and "stabilization and reconstruction" are used most often by the military. Initially referring to the need to ensure security in the immediate postconflict period, when military forces are obviously needed, stabilization has come to encompass a range of activities to be carried out by the military and/or civilian operations. "Again and again, those who have fought insurgencies have learned that they cannot win without public support and that they cannot gain that support without improving and protecting local lives and livelihoods."[77] There is increasing awareness among military actors that successful stabilization and reconstruction involves the collaboration of a range of political and humanitarian actors and that there are areas in which civilian action must be dominant. "The single most important contribution that U.S. military personnel can make to humanitarian efforts is to ensure a reasonably secure environment that enables relief agencies to operate freely and access needy populations."[78]

While that poses logistical dilemmas for military actors, it often raises red flags for civilian humanitarian actors who believe that their security, access, and ability to work depend on being perceived as impartial humanitarian actors—which means keeping their distance from the military.[79] In other words, it is precisely in the postconflict or "early recovery" phase, when humanitarian agencies are trying to hand over the work to development actors, that humanitarian space is most at risk of being restricted by the blurring of lines between military and civilian actors.

So where does accountability to beneficiaries fit in this picture? It may well be that humanitarian agencies are working to establish this "new" line of accountability as an alternative to accountability to their donors, particularly to donors seeking to use them to support political and military objectives. An alternative explanation is offered by John Mitchell, who wrote that the new level of participatory rhetoric serves for some

> a dual purpose: not only does it sidestep the problem of demonstrating impact, but it also fits with the current geopolitical agenda and the tactics for winning the war on terror. The reality is that, despite the humanitarian principles of impartiality and proportionality, most aid remains tied to bigger political objectives. As this 'war' increasingly involves winning hearts and minds, so the importance of consultation, of understanding people's views and needs, increases. In this context, the language of participation contains within it both humanitarian ideals and military and political objectives.[80]

Accountability to beneficiaries also is linked with emerging concepts of community-based protection, defined by ActionAid's manual as "activities aimed at facilitating individuals and communities to achieve respect for their rights in safety and dignity."[81] While acknowledging that not all community-driven and –determined action is positive or protective, this approach "shifts the focus away from international humanitarian and development actors as the starting point of protection interventions, and towards supporting community and local partners in their own efforts."[82] And community-based protection also implicitly tries to deal with the gap between the relief and development activities of international actors by building the capacities of communities not only to protect themselves from immediate danger but also to strengthen community resilience for the long term as well.

7 | *Natural Disasters and Protection*

When a large-scale natural disaster occurs—such as the 2004 tsunami in South Asia or the 2010 earthquake in Haiti—the international humanitarian community springs into action. Search and rescue teams are deployed by governments, humanitarian agencies mobilize staff, communications systems are set up, and large quantities of relief goods are shipped off to help people in need. The priority is always the delivery of life-saving assistance, and until the last five or six years, that was assumed to be the sole criterion for evaluating the success of relief efforts. Since the 2004 tsunami, however, there has been growing concern with the protection of people affected by disasters and an awareness that, just as in the case in armed conflict, assistance may have negative effects on communities and on power relations between donors and recipients of aid. As Alex de Waal has written, "power inequities are typically accentuated in all stages of disaster, from prevention and insurance, through protection and evacuation at the height of crisis, to relief and rehabilitation."[1] Those who are providing assistance and protection have power and resources that are desperately needed by communities in the aftermath of a disaster.[2] Just as the international community has embraced the concept of protection in responding to people affected by conflicts, so too has it accepted the need to take protection into account in planning and delivering assistance and in assessing the humanitarian response to natural disasters. This chapter looks at the protection issues arising from natural disasters.

Defining Natural Disasters

Definitions of "natural disaster" focus either on the magnitude of the natural hazard or the response capacity of the affected community, both of which are important and related to protection issues. "Natural disaster" is defined in the Operational Guidelines on Human Rights and Natural Disasters, endorsed by the Inter-Agency Standing Committee in 2006, as "the consequences of events triggered by natural hazards that overwhelm local response capacity and seriously affect the social and economic development of a region."[3] The International Disaster Response Law Guidelines put forward by the International Federation of Red Cross and Red Crescent Societies (IFRC) define a disaster as

> a serious disruption of the functioning of society, which poses a significant, widespread threat to human life, health, property or the environment, whether arising from accident, nature or human activity, whether developing suddenly or as the result of long-term processes, but excluding armed conflict.[4]

There are difficulties in distinguishing between "natural" and "manmade" disasters, an observation that is commonly made in humanitarian circles. To avoid the problem, such events often are referred to simply as disasters or disasters triggered by natural hazards. Some would go so far as to argue that there are no "natural" disasters—that a "disaster" is the result of the failure of authorities to prevent negative effects of natural phenomena or their failure to respond adequately. Most humanitarian actors recognize that disasters result from both natural phenomena and human actions. For example, mudslides increase in Nepal as a result of both glacier runoff (a natural cause, although one that may be accelerated by global warming) and deforestation (a man-made cause). The devastating toll on Haiti of four hurricanes in 2008 was obviously the result of the storms themselves, but certainly they were exacerbated by long-term deforestation and poor government policies. In fact, in that year, deadly hurricanes hit both Haiti and Cuba, but while 700 people died in Haiti, only seven fatalities were reported in Cuba.[5]

Another burning definitional issue that often comes up in humanitarian circles is the relationship between sudden-onset and slow-onset disasters. While floods, hurricanes, and earthquakes occur with little advance warning, it may take months or years for droughts or environmental degradation to seriously affect the development of an area or to overwhelm local capacity. While the difference between the two makes intuitive sense, there is no consensus on the dividing line between sudden- and slow-onset disasters. For example, flooding (usually considered a sudden-onset disaster) sometimes occurs over a period of weeks while some droughts occur over a period of months. Humanitarian actors are always on the front line in responding to sudden-onset disasters, but local communities and development actors are usually the first to sound the alarm about slow-onset disasters. As discussed in chapter 9, the distinction between sudden- and slow-onset disasters is especially relevant to projections about the effects of climate change on displacement.

In the course of 2009, there were 335 natural disasters worldwide, which killed 10,655 people, affected more than 119 million others, and amounted to over $41.3 billion in economic damage.[6] And that was considered a relatively good year in comparison with some others. For example, in 2008, disasters took the lives of more than 235,000 people, affected 214 million, and resulted in economic losses of over $190 billion.[7]

As Margareta Wahlström pointed out in 2007, "over the past 30 years, disasters—storms, floods and droughts—have increased threefold according to the UN International Strategy for Disaster Reduction (ISDR)."[8] Some disasters are large, high-profile events, well covered by the media, that attract significant amounts of international assistance, but most are much smaller in scale and never make it to the front pages of international newspapers. The cumulative impact of smaller-scale disasters can be as devastating to a community as a large, one-time catastrophic event and yet generate far less response. Often the news coverage of a particular disaster is determined by what other news events are taking place at the same time. Thus, "when Hurricane Stan hit Guatemala roughly a month after Hurricane Katrina, it resulted in a similar number of fatalities but generated only a fraction of the media coverage and subsequent aid response."[9]

Despite the increasing frequency and severity of natural disasters, many humanitarian actors continue to see natural disasters and those displaced by them as marginal to the central thrust of humanitarian action: responding to those affected by conflict. The assumption has been that conflicts and natural disasters are fundamentally different and that response to natural disasters is basically a question of logistics while complex emergencies and conflicts always bring forth protection issues. There is, after all, a large body of international law—international humanitarian law—that applies exclusively in situations of conflict. Refugee law applies only to those persons displaced across national borders because of persecution and war—not to those fleeing drought or earthquakes. And certainly there are different causes and consequences in conflicts and disasters. But recent research indicates that often the impact of conflicts and disasters on communities is similar and that humanitarian response is especially complex when disasters strike communities already weakened by conflict.

Similarities between Conflict-Affected and Disaster-Affected Communities

Those affected by conflicts and disasters share many of the same character-istics. First, the human experiences of those affected by natural disasters and conflicts are very similar. For example, people displaced by both flooding and fighting often lose family members, endure separation of family members, lose their possessions, and experience trauma and depression. They have similar protection and assistance needs. They lose important documents, which limits their ability to access public services.[10] They lose property, and it may take years (if ever) before they receive compensation for their loss.

In both conflicts and natural disasters, vulnerable groups suffer more. For example, globally, for every adult male who drowns in a flood, three to four women die.[11] One study of a 1991 cyclone in Bangladesh noted that many women perished with their children at home because they had to wait for their husbands to return and make the decision to evacuate.[12] Sexual abuse and rape of women often is a tool of war, and gender-based violence—car-ried out within the family and community as well as by external groups such as gangs, military forces, and police—is unfortunately a common occurrence among women displaced by both natural disasters and conflict. Children displaced by both natural disasters and conflicts often are more susceptible to recruitment by armed forces and to trafficking. Vulnerable groups also frequently experience discrimination in the provision of assistance. In many camps where persons displaced by conflict live, food is—at least initially—more likely to go to healthy men than to children or persons with disabilities. And in New Orleans, the elderly, immigrants, and African American com-munities suffered disproportionately from the effects of Hurricane Katrina.[13]

Second, displacement is a common result of both disasters and conflicts, and most people displaced by either remain within their country's borders. They are internally displaced persons (IDPs), as defined in the UN Guiding Principles on Internal Displacement, and they have the full range of rights included therein. It is their national governments that are responsible for protecting and assisting them and facilitating durable solutions for their displacement. When the guiding principles were drafted in the mid-1990s, there was considerable discussion about whether or not to include those dis-placed by disasters. The decision to include them was based on the fact that those displaced by natural disasters also experience human rights violations. Even though people uprooted by natural disasters ultimately were included in the guiding principles, Roberta Cohen points out that governments often have gone to great lengths to avoid referring to them as IDPs. In Aceh, for example, the government labeled those uprooted by the tsunami as "homeless," and U.S. government officials described those displaced by Hurricane Katrina as "refugees," "evacuees," and finally "disaster victims."[14]

Third, poverty makes things worse for both victims of natural disasters and victims of conflict. Natural disasters in poorer countries have higher casualties than disasters of similar magnitude in wealthier countries. For example, on December 10, 1988, the Spitak earthquake, registering 6.9 on the Richter scale, hit Armenia, killing at least 100,000 people and leaving 500,000 to 700,000 homeless.[15] Shortly thereafter, the Loma Prieta earthquake occurred in San Francisco, California. Measuring 7.1 on the Richter scale, it killed 6 people and damaged 12,000 homes, leaving 3,000 homeless.[16] More recently, an earthquake in New Zealand destroyed 100,000 homes, but remarkably caused no human fatalities. The United Nations Development Program (UNDP) reports that while on average the fifty poorest countries are exposed to only 11 percent of the world's natural hazards each year, they suffer 53 percent of the deaths. In contrast, countries with high levels of human development, despite their exposure to 15 percent of all hazards, account for only 1.5 percent of the death toll.[17]

Within countries, it is almost always the poor and marginalized who are disproportionately affected by natural disasters. They tend to live in less safe environments and housing. Shoddily constructed slum dwellings are more vulnerable to earthquakes, landslides, and flooding than the homes where the rich are more likely to live. As witnessed in the January 2010 earthquake in Haiti, the neighborhoods in which the country's elite lived were less impacted by the tremors, and their homes were more likely to withstand the shocks than those in poorer neighborhoods, which tended to be poorly constructed on more marginal land, to be built more closely together, and to house more people.[18] Poverty, conflict, and natural disasters also are interconnected, as explored below.

There are other, less obvious similarities between those displaced by natural disasters and conflicts. In both cases, it is the responsibility of the state to protect and assist affected individuals and communities, but international actors usually respond when the state's capacity is limited. The international system of response to both natural disasters and conflict is fairly well developed, although in both cases there seems to be a greater initial response to high-profile crises that diminishes as situations become protracted. The weakest point in the international system for both natural disasters and conflicts is prevention or mitigation. In the case of natural disasters, early warning systems have been developed—although, of course, more could be done.[19]

But early warning systems alone are not enough. In the case of natural disasters, the international humanitarian community has come up with the Hyogo Plan of Action and the International Strategy for Disaster Risk Reduction,[20] which offer concrete suggestions for reducing the human impact of natural disasters; unfortunately, they are not yet priorities for most national governments or international donors. In the field of conflict prevention, many early warning initiatives are under way—by civil society, governments, and international organizations—but at times lack of political will and the pesky issue of sovereignty create insurmountable obstacles to acting on warnings, even when they are timely.[21] Human rights activists, for example, long warned that the political situation in Rwanda was explosive, just as humanitarian workers warned of an upcoming famine in Ethiopia in 1983—two years before it attracted major media attention. Early warning without early action does not prevent either conflicts or the devastating effects of natural hazards.

Research is scarce, but there appear to be some differences between conflict-induced and natural disaster–induced displacement, although in most cases, the differences are not absolute, but differences in degree. First, solutions may be different for those displaced by natural disasters and by conflicts. For all IDPs, the UN Guiding Principles on Internal Displacement spell out three solutions—return to the place of origin, integration into the place of displacement, and settlement in another part of the country—and stress that IDPs should have the right to choose the solution. But in some natural disasters, IDPs do not have the option of return—for example, those displaced by riverbank erosion in India or by the volcanic eruption on Montserrat, which rendered more than half of the Caribbean island uninhabitable. The issue of inability to return assumes greater importance in the context of climate change (discussed further in chapter 9). If predictions that sea levels will rise as a result of climate change are correct, the option of returning for those displaced is likely to be difficult or nonexistent. For IDPs displaced by conflict, return to the community of origin always remains an option—even though it may be politically difficult and may take a long time to realize.

A second possible difference is that generally those displaced by natural disasters are likely to return home more rapidly than those displaced by conflicts. One of the few studies to systematically compare duration of displacement by its cause found that 80 percent of those displaced by natural disasters in four South Asian countries had been displaced for one year or less, while

57 percent of those displaced by armed conflict and 66 percent of those displaced by development projects had been displaced for more than five years.[22] However, this difference also may be one of degree. Some Central Americans still are displaced from Hurricane Mitch in 1998, although there is no system for tracking and monitoring the extent to which they have found solutions. In both conflict- and natural disaster–induced displacement, sometimes governments simply decree that displacement has ended, as in Angola and Sierra Leone. The Inter-Agency Standing Committee has adopted the Framework for Durable Solutions, which maintains that the ending of displacement is a process during which the need for specialized assistance and protection diminishes; it involves both the process by which solutions are found and the conditions of return, integration, or resettlement.[23]

A third difference—or difference in degree—is that the number of people who cross national borders because of natural disasters seems to be much lower than the number of those displaced internally. In many cases, conflicts force people to leave not only their communities, but also their countries. Thus, it is common to have both refugees and IDPs from the same conflict—for example, Sudanese displaced in Darfur and Sudanese refugees in neighboring Chad or Iraqi IDPs and Iraqi refugees in neighboring countries.

Those who are forced to flee their countries solely because of natural disasters are not considered to be refugees under international law. In some cases in which people have crossed national borders because of natural disasters, such as those fleeing the Ethiopian famine in 1984–85, the humanitarian community has provided assistance as if they were indeed refugees. However, famines are at least as much the result of political actions as of natural causes.[24]

The argument is sometimes made that national authorities are more likely to accept international assistance for people displaced by natural disasters than for those displaced by conflicts because it is less "political." However, the recent case of Cyclone Nargis in Myanmar is evidence that acceptance of foreign assistance is far from certain or automatic. And three years ago, in the aftermath of Hurricane Katrina, the U.S. government was unwilling—or unable—to accept immediate offers of assistance.[25]

In conflict situations, multinational forces have been used in a number of cases, such as Bosnia, Afghanistan, and Iraq, to protect the delivery of humanitarian relief.[26] But, as discussed earlier, their presence often is controversial because many humanitarian actors feel that the involvement of military forces contradicts the humanitarian principles of neutrality and independence.[27] Military assets are generally more accepted in natural disasters because their engagement is seen as less "political" and their countries less tied to the causes of the disaster. There also seems to be an assumption that military responses to natural disasters are more motivated by humanitarian concerns and hence more "neutral" than in conflict situations.[28]

However, as Walter Kälin, the UN representative of the secretary-general on the human rights of IDPs, pointed out with respect to tsunami-affected countries:

> While it is often the case that the military is the national institution most equipped with the logistics, personnel and supplies to undertake initial rescue and humanitarian response to large disasters, ongoing military control of aid and of camps can also endanger beneficiaries, because it can heighten the IDPs' vulnerability to sexual exploitation and abuse as well as children's military recruitment, and dampen displaced persons' ability to control decisions affecting their lives. This risk is especially high in situations of internal armed conflict, where the proximity of the military can render the camps a military target for no-state armed groups.[29]

Military officials themselves often see clear connections between their overall military capacity and their support for disaster assistance, as evident in the following comments from U.S. Army Major Kelly Webster on returning from his deployment to Haiti:

> The similarities between COIN [counterinsurgency] and FDR [foreign disaster relief] operations are innumerable. The basic skills associated with successful counterinsurgency campaigns (addressing the needs of the people; coordinating simultaneous actions across multiple lines of effort; working by, with, and through diverse partners to win the trust and confidence of the population) proved readily transferable to disaster relief operations. . . . Faced with a humanitarian crisis of historic proportions, differences and longstanding misperceptions quickly faded into the background. Over time, several of the NGOs became the BCT's [Brigade Combat Team's] closest relief partners.[30]

The Relationship between Natural Disasters and Conflict

The relationship between disasters and conflict plays out in different ways. In some cases natural disasters occur in places where conflict has already disrupted the lives of people—for example, the Philippines, Iraq, Somalia,

Kenya, Colombia, and Haiti. Because the definition of "natural disaster" is linked to a society's response capacity, state and social structures that have been weakened by conflict are less likely to be able to respond to the effects of a natural hazard, making it more likely to result in a natural disaster. For example, in 2010 the extreme weakness of the Somali government (which controlled only a small area of the capital city) as a result of long-standing conflict left it unable to respond to either the drought or floods occurring in the country. If there were no conflict in Somalia, both the state and community institutions would be better able to cope with natural hazards, perhaps avoiding disasters all together.

Although the situations vary, the occurrence of a natural disaster in an area affected by ongoing conflict can lead to increased misery for people whose lives have already been disrupted. For example, in the Philippines, camps for people displaced by conflict in Mindanao were flooded in 2008, undermining their ability to cope.[31] A natural disaster can lead to further displacement, as when people displaced by conflict are forced to move yet again because of the disaster. In the case of the Mindanao floods, some of the conflict IDPs were forced to move again because of the flooding. Following the tsunami in Sri Lanka, some of those displaced by the conflict there were displaced again.

In addition, natural disasters occurring in conflict areas can increase the hardship on communities hosting the displaced. In Somalia, rural areas hard-hit by flooding in 2009 were already having difficulty growing sufficient food for their communities, and the arrival of Somalis displaced by the fighting in Mogadishu increased the strain. The majority of recent IDPs from Mogadishu went to the nearby Afgooye corridor—making it the "highest density of internally displaced persons in the world—over half a million IDPs along a stretch of 15 kilometers of road."[32]

Finally, natural disasters occurring in conflict areas often mean greater difficulties for relief agencies in accessing affected communities. That is the case particularly where governments are unwilling to extend access to humanitarian actors. For example, after the 1990 earthquake in Gilan province in Iran, which measured 7.7 on the Richter scale, killed 50,000 people and decimated entire villages, the government initially insisted that the country would handle the crisis on its own and turned away international assistance.[33] By the time that the government was willing to enlist assistance from abroad, a significant proportion of those affected reportedly had died otherwise preventable deaths.[34] A similar initial rejection of international aid by the government of Burma/Myanmar following Cyclone Nargis in May

2008 complicated the relief effort. In the aftermath of severe flooding in Pakistan in July-August 2010, the government facilitated humanitarian access to many of the affected areas but maintained security restrictions in the Federally Administered Tribal Areas (FATA) and Balochistan—areas where many thousands had already been displaced by conflict.

Conflicts exacerbate the impact of natural disasters by weakening state, community, and individual capacity to respond, but there are surprisingly few long-term empirical studies on the relationship between conflict and natural disasters. Nel and Righarts looked at data for 187 countries and other political entities for the period 1950 to 2000 and found that rapid-onset natural disasters significantly increased the risk of violent civil conflict both in the short and the medium term, specifically in low- and middle-income countries that have high inequality, mixed political regimes (neither fully autocratic nor democratic), and sluggish economic growth.[35] Similarly, Olson and Drury found that the more developed a country, the less likely a natural disaster is to have political consequences.[36]

Rakhi Bhavnani explains the detrimental effects of natural disasters, from physical to sociological:

> Sudden changes brought on by natural disasters exacerbate problems that people face on a daily basis, heightening conditions for conflict such as grievances, political opportunity, and mobilization. Disasters create grievances that lead to conflict by causing mass disruption, impacting individual behavior, community and political organizations, and the power relationships between individuals, groups, and the organizations that serve them. In the immediate aftermath of a disaster, a country's physical infrastructure is affected, often preventing the adequate distribution of food and medical supplies. Crops are destroyed, giving rise to food shortages, famines, and localized conflicts over resources. As a disaster destroys many key social and political institutions, it threatens political stability and creates a power vacuum and opportunity for warlords and criminal gangs to usurp power. . . . A natural disaster has the propensity to reshape society and along with it, its ability to manage risk, grievances, and political change.[37]

Using the EM-DAT International Disaster Database data on sudden- and slow-onset disasters from 1991–99 and various conflict databases and news reports, Bhavnani tested his hypothesis that natural disasters contribute to conflict and concluded that they do.[38] In other words, it seems that particularly for developing countries with weak governments, a natural disaster can cause political instability. Countries such as Guatemala (1976 earthquake) and Nicaragua (1976 earthquake) are a case in point because their respective governments fell largely due to popular discontent over the way that the disaster response was organized. Further afield, the inadequate response of the West Pakistan government to the 1970 typhoon in East Pakistan was a principal contributing factor in the ensuing war, which resulted in independence for East Pakistan and the establishment of Bangladesh the following year. More recently, Taiwan's prime minister, Liu Chao-shiuan, resigned in 2009 just one month after Typhoon Morakot, the most catastrophic storm to strike Taiwan in fifty years.[39] The typhoon wrought havoc on the island nation, killing at least 639 people, with another 58 missing, and resulting in $3 billion in damage.[40]

One of the most interesting comparisons of the relationship between conflict and natural disasters dealt with the effect of the 2004 Indian Ocean tsunami on the conflicts in Sri Lanka and Aceh, Indonesia. At the time that the tsunami struck, both countries were mired in protracted conflicts. In Aceh, the response to the tsunami seems to have contributed to the resolution of a long-simmering conflict between the government and the insurgent movement Gerakan Aceh Merdeka (GAM), known as the Free Aceh movement. In contrast, the response to the tsunami in Sri Lanka seems to have exacerbated tensions between the Tamil Tigers (the Liberation Tigers of Tamil Eelam, or LTTE) and the government of Sri Lanka.

What made the difference? Many factors contribute to both a conflict and its resolution. Several researchers have made the point that these two cases were at different stages of conflict and that the tsunami—and the response to the tsunami—had different impacts on the warring parties. Bauman and his colleagues argue that in the thirty-year Indonesia/Aceh conflict, both sides had come to realize that a military solution was unviable; they were looking for a political solution, but they lacked an exit strategy.[41] Both the government and the insurgents were seriously affected by the tsunami. The government lacked the capacity to rebuild Aceh without international support and was forced to allow international actors into the region—access that had previously been largely denied because of the conflict. The international presence provided a sense of security to the population, and, coupled with both strong international support and committed political leadership, peace negotiations were restarted. In August 2005, a memorandum of understanding was signed in which the Indonesian government recognized the right of Aceh to "special autonomy," a solution short of the secession that had been demanded earlier. The agreement ended the conflict, which had caused 15,000 deaths and displaced from 150,000 to 250,000 people.[42]

In comparison, when the tsunami struck Sri Lanka, the peace process was stalled, the LTTE held a strong position, and the tsunami itself affected the Tamil and Sinhalese communities differently. At the time, the majority of the 390,000 conflict-induced IDPs were Tamils living in the north and east parts of the country. But the majority—though by no means all—of those affected by the tsunami were Sinhalese living in the south. All together, some 457,000 Sri Lankans were displaced by the tsunami.[43] While there was discussion in Sri Lanka about Tamils and Sinhalese working together to respond to the victims of the tsunami, in fact, there were tensions from the beginning as both sides sought to use the occasion—and the relief—to strengthen their own positions.

The Sri Lankan government was worried that the LTTE would use the tsunami to gain international sympathy, recognition, and direct assistance and consequently blocked opportunities that they thought would benefit the LTTE. At the same time, the LTTE did not trust the government to distribute assistance fairly and sought direct access to aid.[44] There was a strong sense of grievance among the Tamil population that assistance was going primarily toward tsunami-affected people in the south, mostly Sinhalese, while those affected by the tsunami in the north and east, mostly Tamil, did not receive a proportionate share. And the conflict-displaced, mostly Tamils in the north and east, were receiving much less. Efforts to develop a joint response by Sinhalese and Tamils failed. The discrimination in treatment between conflict-induced and tsunami-affected IDPs in Sri Lanka contributed to the tensions. Tamils complained that the government failed to provide adequate assistance. Intercommunal recriminations reappeared. Hope and expectations plummeted, and the conflict reignited in late 2006, displacing still another 200,000 people. In 2009, the Sinhalese-dominated government defeated the LTTE in a brutal military offensive.

One of the lessons of the tsunami is an affirmation of Mary Anderson's classic argument that humanitarian assistance can either mitigate or accelerate conflicts.[45] Differences in assistance provided to those affected by conflict and to those affected by disasters can provoke resentment between communities, as evidenced in the post-tsunami relief efforts. The Worldwatch Institute's study of Aceh, Sri Lanka, and Kashmir led to the conclusion that compassion alone is unlikely to carry warring factions through the complexities of a peace process without political change that addresses the root causes of the conflict.[46]

State Responsibility and Natural Disasters

Governments are responsible for protecting the rights of their populations through all phases of natural disasters—from disaster preparedness through emergency response and long-term recovery and reconstruction.[47] As the report of the representative of the secretary-general for the human rights of IDPs makes clear,

> Governments of affected states may prefer, for a variety of reasons, to provide all necessary assistance themselves; and this is a legitimate exercise of national sovereignty and responsibility. However, when Governments refuse outside offers of humanitarian assistance, but at the same time are themselves unable or unwilling to provide adequate assistance to their own populations, they fail to discharge their responsibilities under international law as restated in Guiding Principle 25.[48]

This issue came to the fore in the response to Cyclone Nargis, which hit Burma/Myanmar in May 2008 and ended up killing 85,000 people (with another 54,000 missing and presumed dead), displacing hundreds of thousands, and affecting 2.5 million people. The call for intervention by French foreign minister Bernard Kouchner led to a lively debate about whether the responsibility to protect doctrine applies in natural disasters.[49] It also raised questions about whether there is a right to humanitarian assistance—an issue that has been hotly debated within the international legal community. Indeed, some argue that although there is no explicit provision in international law of such a right, the well-accepted rights to food, health care, and shelter infer a right to humanitarian assistance when the government lacks the capacity to protect such basic rights.[50]

National governments are not monolithic bodies. A major national disaster typically calls for response from a variety of national actors and agencies as well as an assortment of municipal and local authorities. As evident in the response to Hurricane Katrina, differences in mandates, resources, perceptions, and capacities of government agencies can complicate relief efforts. For example, Samir Elhawary and Gerardo Castillo cite research that reveals that while decentralization of political authority in El Salvador led to an increase in responsibilities for disaster preparedness and response at the municipal level, it did not increase municipalities' capacity to carry out their increased responsibilities.[51] Their research into the role of the state following the 2007 Peruvian earthquake found that local authorities had systems in place but lacked the capacity to respond effectively, leading the central government to create a parallel response system, which in turn undermined the local response effort. The researchers conclude that the arrangement "was essentially a political strategy on the part of the government, designed to bolster its political capital, appease some of its critics and potentially undermine some of its political opponents in the region."[52]

Often there are differences in the perceptions of a government, national NGOs, and the international community regarding both the nature of a disaster and the government's response:

> Different actors "see" disasters as different types of events and, because they perceive them as such, they prepare for, manage and record them in very different ways. State and state agencies "see" disasters in one way; the people directly affected "see" them in another (not least according to the nature and extent of their vulnerabilities); non-governmental organizations (NGOs) involved in providing needed services to communities "see" them in still other ways (depending on their ideological complexion); while scientists, technocrats and experts have their own variants of "seeing." The media, too, if it does not exactly "see" risk in a particular way certainly helps to shape public discourse about it.[53]

Natural Disasters and Protection

It was the 2004 tsunami that moved the issue of human rights and natural disaster response higher on the international agenda, in part because of the sheer magnitude of the disaster and the scale of the response. Unlike the response to most natural disasters, the response to the tsunami was well funded. With sufficient funding, relief agencies were able to develop ambitious programs and generally did not need to coordinate their efforts with others. At its worst, that led to competition between agencies for beneficiaries and projects that were discriminatory in impact, although usually not by design. While discrimination has likely been a feature in most disaster relief efforts, the sheer presence of hundreds of NGOs, bilateral aid agencies, and international organizations made the negative consequences of the relief effort more apparent to observers. As Mihir Bhatt, director of the All India Disaster Mitigation Institute (AIDMI), said, "The disaster came after the tsunami," referring to the competition among agencies and the discriminatory impact of their programs.[54] The fact that relief agencies generally were well funded also made it possible for them to devote more resources to monitoring and evaluation, highlighting not only inequitable patterns of assistance but a range of protection issues.[55]

The international disaster response community has long been aware of the need for assessment of vulnerabilities in developing relief programs. Increasingly those assessments look at the protection needs of specific groups because the most vulnerable groups in a population are the most invisible; if they are to be served, proactive outreach is required.

Protection Concerns of Specific Groups

Often there are security risks around temporary shelters for communities displaced by natural disasters. For example, after Hurricane Mitch in 1998 there were allegations of gang infiltration in urban shelters in Honduras that resulted in robberies, rapes, and even killings due to the lack of law and order.[56] In Haiti after the 2010 earthquake numerous cases of rape and sexual assault in IDP camps were reported by media and NGOs. Because of the paralysis of the police and the justice system, which also were heavily hit by the earthquake, and the general distrust of state institutions, most of the cases were unreported.[57] Girls in camps also were at risk of sexual exploitation. In several camps, women reported to Amnesty International that it was common for many girls to exchange sex for food or material goods.[58] After Hurricane Katrina, sexual violence was widespread in trailer camps set up to house those displaced by the storm. A 2006 survey conducted by the International Medical Corps in the trailer camps found alarmingly high rates of gender-based violence. The rate of rape was found to be 53.6 times higher than the highest baseline rate in the state. In the 274 days following the disaster, the rate of women experiencing beatings by their spouse was 3.2 percent—more than triple the U.S. annual rate."[59]

Gender inequities are evident in most responses to disasters. For example, the Sri Lankan government offered funding to families affected by the tsunami, but in Batticaloa, in the eastern coastal area, authorities recognized only male-headed households, so women whose husbands had died were not eligible to receive assistance. Sri Lankan and Acehnese women described many instances in which they received relief supplies in the form of goods but were not able to access recovery grants, which went only to men as heads of households. Without cash to start over, it would be difficult for them to rebuild their livelihoods.[60] In Thailand, families received twice as much aid from the government to bury their male relatives as their female ones.[61] The loss of livelihood also often pushes men to migrate from rural areas to towns in search of work, leaving their wives to feed their children.[62] Concerns about reproductive rights often are not addressed immediately following a disaster, although women still give birth when earthquakes occur, still need contraception while living in tents, and still need sanitary supplies.[63]

Child protection is always a concern in the chaos following a major disaster, but in the case of the 2010 Haitian earthquake, it was especially troubling. The large number of unaccompanied or separated children (1 million) in a country where there were almost 400,000 orphans before the earthquake is an indication of the scale of the problem, but it was even more difficult given the related issues of unregistered orphanages, pressures for international adoptions, and the *restavek* system.[64] Kälin reported discovering in several situations an increase in domestic violence against children, in child exploitation resulting from the lack of livelihoods for parents after disasters, and in child marriages.[65] Children also may face discrimination in the wake of a disaster, as in Bangladesh after the 2005 floods, when some—particularly very poor children, street children, unaccompanied children, and those from ethnic or religious minorities—were refused refuge in shelters.[66] In many instances, people displaced by a natural disaster are temporarily accommodated in schools. That often means that children in the host community, as well as the displaced children, are denied the opportunity to continue their education. Moreover, typically what is intended to be a short-term arrangement turns into a protracted arrangement during which access to education is denied. Post-earthquake Haiti was no exception. UN-OCHA reported that IDPs had to be evicted from several schools to enable the schools to be reopened.[67]

One of the lessons learned in the tsunami response is that assistance often can be discriminatory in impact even if it is not intended to be. Government policies can reinforce social divisions; sometimes it is intentional, sometimes it is not.[68] In the aftermath of the tsunami in Tamil Nadu, India, discrimination against Dalits in the provision of relief and removal of bodies and refusal to share emergency shelters with them were rampant.[69] After the 2001 Gujarat earthquake, almost every village had camps segregated by caste and religion. In the towns of Anjar and Bhachchau, Dalits and Muslims did not have the same access to adequate shelter, electricity, running water, and other supplies that was available to higher-caste Hindus.[70] During the monsoon floods in India in 2007, many Dalits lived in rickety homes in flood-prone areas outside main villages, leaving them especially exposed. Nonetheless, they often were last to get emergency relief, if they received it at all.

A survey by Dalit organizations of fifty-one villages on August 8–9, 2007, found, among other things, that 60 percent of the dead were Dalits, that none of the Dalit colonies (or *tolas*) attached to the main villages had been visited by government relief officials, and that Dalits' housing had suffered the worst damage because most was of poor quality and located in low-lying areas.[71] Earlier, in the Rajasthan floods in 2006, Dalits were asked to leave relief camps for fear of "polluting others."[72] Following the worst floods in Pakistan's history in 2010—dubbed the worst humanitarian crisis in the UN's history—there were some reports of Pakistani minorities being turned away from government-established camps and of discrimination in the provision of aid reportedly based on ethnicity, caste, or religion.[73]

Sometimes international agencies can unintentionally discriminate in relief assistance because they inadvertently hire local staff from a particular caste or class, which leads to inequitable assistance in practice. The need for English-speaking local staff or staff with particular skills may feed into that.

In Afghanistan, a Humanitarian Policy Group study found that "due to the (perceived) nature of Afghan society and cultural sensitivities, emergency programming in Maslakh drew heavily on the camp leadership and governance structures set up during the Taliban regime." According to the study, that influenced the conduct of needs assessments because camp leaders "were allowed to marginalize" certain groups "by excluding them from assessments in the first place." The study cites the example of Pashtun IDPs after the fall of the Taliban, who, due to their ethnic association with the Taliban, were reportedly victims of discrimination in accessing aid."[74]

Indigenous groups, because of their close ties to the land, often are especially affected by natural disasters. Moreover, they typically experience discrimination in assistance. When Romania suffered severe flooding in 2005 that ruined farmland and property and drove thousands from their homes—the Roma were doubly affected, facing not just floodwaters but also entrenched discriminatory attitudes. *The Sofia Echo,* one of Bulgaria's English-language newspapers, reported:

> Floods have also brought a considerable increase in infectious diseases to the city. . . . Health officials said that the rate of infection among Roma was higher, because of the minority's "disregard for personal hygiene." Such prejudiced remarks may negatively influence response activities, lead to an inadequate identification of problems, create additional trauma for survivors, and prejudice the distribution of resources in relief and recovery activities.[75]

Indigenous groups also are rarely prepared for the radical shift in their living situations that results from moving from a rural to an urban environment. In fact, it is difficult to distinguish internally displaced persons from indigenous pastoralist or nomadic communities even when they are forced to change their regular migration routes because of natural disasters.[76]

The World Health Organization (WHO) estimates that about 10 percent of the world's population lives with a disability.[77] Yet there are many accounts of disaster planning that does not take into account the particular needs of persons with disabilities, either in evacuation plans or in delivery of relief.[78] People with visual or hearing impairments are less likely to notice warning signals and evacuate quickly during disasters while those whose mobility is limited may find it difficult to move to safe locations and may require assistance in accessing relief shelters and using latrines.[79] In Haiti, for example, even before the earthquake struck, some 800,000 persons were living with disabilities, including 200,000 children. An estimated 194,000 to 250,000 people were injured in the earthquake, many of whom will suffer from long-term disabilities in addition to the accompanying social stigma, including the estimated 2,000 people with amputations due to earthquake injuries.[80]

Also in Haiti, there were reports that many of the needs of the elderly were not met during the early stages of disaster relief. Despite the privation facing children and younger women (many of whom were left as head of household and were more vulnerable to sexual and gender-based violence) in Haiti since the earthquake, it was the elderly who were at greatest risk by far in the weeks and months following the earthquake. "Older people have been overlooked in relief efforts because they are more frail, less mobile and less vocal in their demands for food and water," United Nations officials explained.[81] Often food aid is not suited for elderly people. Cynthia Powell, spokeswoman for HelpAge, an international group that provides aid to senior citizens throughout the world, noted that

> Haiti's elderly have had to make do with aid efforts primarily geared toward children and adults. Elders without teeth must try to eat hard protein biscuits distributed by United Nations relief workers or whole-grain cereals that their bodies no longer digest properly. In the rush to distribute help as quickly as possible, these details can sadly get lost.[82]

In addition, homes for the elderly in Haiti were converted into IDP camps after the earthquake without providing for the particular protection needs of their former inhabitants.[83]

Among those affected by the 2005 South Asia earthquake, mental health problems were more prevalent among people aged sixty and over, including "increased isolation, feelings of being a burden more than an asset, inter-generational conflict, and the feeling that their major losses will not be able to be restored in their lifetimes," according to the author of a psychosocial needs assessment conducted in September 2006.[84] On the other hand, the experience and skills of old persons often are untapped after disasters: "There is often also the assumption that the elderly are too old to work, which means they are excluded from schemes to help people recover their livelihoods after a disaster."[85]

One of the difficult issues in providing protection during disasters occurs when there is a need to evacuate people in the face of impending disaster, to relocate communities to reduce their exposure to natural hazards, or to prevent communities from returning to their homes because of the risks or effects of disasters. In most cases, people do not want to leave their homes, and they often do not believe government assessments of risk. Moreover, they fear losing their property and belongings if they are relocated. However, "a failure to assist persons who cannot leave zones where they face imminent dangers for life and limb caused by a disaster on their own may amount to a human rights violation if competent authorities knew or should have known the danger and would have had the capacity to act."[86]

The UN Guiding Principles on Internal Displacement specify that governments are responsible for preventing and avoiding arbitrary displacement, which in the case of natural disasters means that displacement is prohibited unless the safety and health of those affected requires their evacuation. When there is no alternative to displacement, all measures should be taken to minimize its adverse effects. When relocation is necessary other than at the emergency stage, the guiding principles spell out additional measures that should be taken. For example, the government must make a decision to relocate, in accord with law; provide full information to those to be displaced; obtain the free and informed consent of those to be displaced; involve those affected, particularly women, in planning the relocation; ensure that competent legal authorities enforce the law; and guarantee the right to an effective legal remedy when disputes arise. But forced evacuations can only be a matter of last resort.

In August 2005, the U.S. government issued a mandatory evacuation order for residents of New Orleans in light of the impending arrival of Hurricane Katrina. While about 80 percent of New Orleans residents heeded the evacuation order, those who did not have personal vehicles—who tended to be African American and Latino—were less likely to escape the city. Kromm and Sturgis argue that the impact of the government's evacuation plan, which relied on personal vehicles as the primary means of escape, was discriminatory.[87] Nor were adequate provisions made to issue warnings in languages other than English, although more than 1 million foreign-born individuals lived in areas affected by Katrina, or to arrange for the evacuation of prisoners and detainees.[88] A report by the Urban Institute found that there were no city or state plans for moving patients in the event of a disaster, although 1,749 patients occupied the eleven New Orleans–area hospitals surrounded by floodwaters.[89]

But in spite of the principles, in many cases people are forced to leave their communities without being informed, giving their consent, or having access to remedies. Experience also shows that people will return to their homes, even if they are in dangerous zones, if they are separated from their families or communities. They also will return if they cannot find jobs in the area to which they have been relocated. After Hurricane Mitch, many houses built in low-risk areas were largely abandoned because of the lack of livelihood opportunities. In Aceh, people migrated to tsunami-affected areas, because there were more possibilities for relief and resources.[90]

The fact that often those displaced by natural disasters have lost their legal documents, including titles to properties, and that many of those displaced did not have formal title to their property before the disaster make the issue of recovery of property, particularly housing and land, very difficult. In Aceh, many poorer members of coastal communities did not own their land before the tsunami but rented it from wealthier Acehnese or "squatted" on state land. In fact, three groups (renters, squatters, and the landless) formed the bulk of the 70,000-strong population housed in around 150 government barracks scattered across Aceh. The lack of a clear policy for the landless has led to a huge amount of uncertainty and delay, and it is the reason why many of the landless survivors were still homeless and without the prospect of a home two years after the disaster.[91]

In Haiti difficult negotiations between the government and property owners led to long delays in efforts to move IDPs living in camps at risk of flooding into temporary shelters, which meant that many of the victims were still living in unsafe camps at the onset of the rainy season.[92] Gender issues also come into play, particularly on questions of inheritance. When a husband was killed during the Kashmir earthquake in 2005, his land usually went to his eldest son, even if his wife survived and occupied and used it.[93] In the tsunami-affected countries, women often were afraid of losing land or property rights or of being unable to inherit property because of the loss of deeds and personal documents during the tsunami. In many places, such as Aceh, women traditionally have had serious difficulties in claiming ownership rights to land or property registered under their husbands' or fathers' names. "Many women in Aceh were found not to know they had guardianship rights of their children or the right to savings in bank accounts of their deceased husbands—this was discovered only through meetings with religious leaders, as both issues are traditionally covered only in Shari'a courts."[94]

There is growing recognition that livelihoods are the key to recovery, and yet over and over again, people whose livelihoods were destroyed in natural disasters find themselves unable to rebuild their lives. After the tsunami, for example, people who had earned their living by fishing were resettled to inland communities "and ended up destitute since no adequate livelihood alternatives were available in the resettlement areas."[95] In Honduras, although reconstruction and resettlement in the aftermath of Hurricane Mitch had been handled well, the lack of attention to livelihoods meant that people continued to be dependent on assistance for long periods of time.[96]

Although it is not a first-order priority, those affected by natural disasters often have difficulty exercising their political rights. In Burma the government proceeded with its nationwide referendum on a new constitution just eight days after Cyclone Nargis struck. Its only concession was to delay the vote in some cyclone-affected townships by two weeks despite the fact that, even two weeks later, well over 1 million affected Burmese still had not received any form of assistance.[97] Widespread destruction and displacement made it impossible for many cyclone victims to participate in the referendum.

After Hurricane Katrina in August 2005 and the displacement of over 1 million residents from New Orleans and the Gulf Coast, concerns were raised about the denial of voting rights to those displaced. When the city of New Orleans held its first major election after the storm in April 2006, an estimated 200,000 of a total of 299,000 registered voters were living outside the city. That meant that two-thirds of the voting population was displaced. Despite requests from civil rights advocates that satellite voting centers be established in cities in other states hosting large numbers of displaced residents, the requests were refused. Even contacting those displaced to provide information about absentee ballots was hampered by the lack of effective data collection.[98]

The Haiti earthquake wreaked havoc not only on the country's infrastructure but also on the governance of the country. The Haitian parliament was dissolved in mid-May, legislative elections were postponed, and both parliamentary and presidential elections were rescheduled for November 2010.[99] The earthquake took place at a time when the political situation already was volatile, during an election year marked by widespread protests and fierce competition between Haiti's more than one hundred political parties. Being able to register and vote was probably not the highest priority for either the affected communities or the relief community, but the fact that 15 to 20 percent of the population was displaced and many voting registries undoubtedly were destroyed means that restoring the political infrastructure of the country will be a long-term process. If the poor are more likely to be displaced and if the displaced are less likely to be able to register and vote, then questions will be raised about the legitimacy of elections.

Disaster Risk Reduction

It is the responsibility of governments to protect their populations from natural disasters, and central to that effort is action to reduce the risks of natural hazards. While governments cannot prevent cyclones or earthquakes, they can take measures to reduce the impact of such events on their people.

The internationally accepted 2005 Hyogo Framework on Disaster Risk Reduction sets out three strategic goals: to integrate disaster risk reduction into sustainable development policies and planning; to develop and strengthen institutions and mechanisms to build the capacity of communities to deal with hazards; and to systematically incorporate risk reduction approaches into emergency preparedness, response, and recovery programs.[100]

It is probably fair to say that no government has implemented adequate measures to reduce the risks of natural disasters although some governments, such as Japan's, have invested around 1 percent of their annual budgets since the 1950s to protect against disasters.[101] Some South Asian governments have made significant commitments to disaster risk reduction, including developing and implementing building standards and providing shelters in areas likely to be struck by typhoons and cyclones. Such efforts pay off. During the 2001 Bhuj earthquake in India, most government buildings that conformed to construction codes suffered only limited damage, while schools and hospitals that did not collapsed.[102] When Cyclone Sidr struck in November 2007, an estimated 3.2 million Bangladeshis were evacuated from the coastal areas and over 2 million already were in special shelters when the cyclone hit. About 4,000 Bangladeshis died—in contrast, around 140,000 died in 1991 and up to 500,000 died in 1970 in similar cyclones.[103]

It often is difficult for governments of developing countries to invest in DRR measures, especially when the likelihood of a particular disaster is small and the immediate needs of the population are high. Some donor governments, such as the United Kingdom's, have made a commitment to include around 10 percent of their development funding explicitly for DRR.[104] Reducing the risk of disasters is good development programming, and it does not have to be a separate initiative—in fact, it is more effective when incorporated into development plans and programs. And disasters are a development issue. According to Oxfam, between 2 and 6 percent of South Asia's GDP is lost every year to natural disasters.[105]

Many innovative techniques and programs have been developed to reduce the risk of disasters, many of which are low-cost and can be carried out by communities themselves.[106] But all of those initiatives take time and at least some funds, funds that usually are not available in marginalized communities. For example, ALNAP cites the case of a preparedness program in Bangladesh that shows that although vulnerable people may know how to take measures that can protect them from floods, they have little or no surplus income to invest in taking those measures.[107]

International Response to Human Rights Issues Emerging from Natural Disasters

While the laws of war have a long history, the development of norms and standards for responding to natural disasters has been much more recent. In 2002 the International Federation of the Red Cross and Red Crescent Societies initiated the International Disaster Response Law initiative, which culminated five years later in the adoption of Guidelines for the Domestic Facilitation and Regulation of International Disaster Relief and Initial Recovery Assistance in November 2007.[108] The guidelines seek to clarify the responsibilities of governments in dealing with international humanitarian organizations responding to natural disasters in their territory, but they remain as guidelines rather than a binding convention. Except for protection of humanitarian workers, the guidelines do not address protection issues.

On the protection side, the Operational Guidelines on Human Rights and Natural Disasters, adopted by the Inter-Agency Standing Committee in 2006 and revised in 2010, set out what humanitarian actors should do to implement a rights-based approach to humanitarian action in the context of natural disasters.[109] They are based on the conviction that human rights are the legal underpinning of all humanitarian work related to natural disasters.

The guidelines emphasize that persons affected by natural disasters should enjoy the same rights and freedoms under human rights law as others in their country and should not be discriminated against. They reassert the principle that states have the primary duty and responsibility to provide assistance to persons affected by natural disasters and to protect their human rights. They also state that all communities affected by the disaster should be entitled to easily accessible information concerning the nature of the disaster that they face and possible mitigation measures, early warning information, and information about ongoing humanitarian assistance.

The operational guidelines are based on the realization that while all human rights are important, priorities must be set in the aftermath of a disaster. The first priority is to protect life, personal security, and the physical integrity and dignity of affected populations, and the second priority is to provide the basic necessities of life, including adequate food, water, sanitation, shelter, clothing, and essential health services. Other economic, social, and cultural rights (education, housing, livelihoods) are the third priority, and civil and political rights (freedom of movement, assembly, electoral rights, and so forth) are the fourth priority.

The operational guidelines offer concrete guidance to those responding to natural disasters—whether governments, international organizations, or nongovernmental organizations. For example, in the immediate aftermath of a flood, governments usually are not able to provide educational facilities for children. That can (and must) come later, once the children are protected against violence and have access to the basic necessities of life. Similarly, the right to documentation is a crucial issue for many people affected by disasters, but affected communities have a more urgent need for sufficient food and water.

Some impressive efforts have been made to incorporate a rights-based approach to natural disaster response. For example, OHCHR and UNDP developed a checklist as a tool to help disaster responders ensure that their plans and programs are addressing the needs of the community as a whole as well as preventing groups that already are marginalized or vulnerable from being further disadvantaged.[110]

Even with the best intentions of all concerned, sometimes it is not possible to ensure that the rights of all those affected by an emergency are fully and immediately respected. For example, access to affected populations often is difficult, those responsible for responding to disasters may themselves be affected, groups that already are socially vulnerable are usually the most affected by disasters, and the logistical demands of delivering needed assistance items to the right place may be significant. Resources almost always are limited in the initial phase of disaster response. However, in preparing for disasters, governments and relief agencies are expected to carry out their planning in such a way as to ensure that human rights are respected. With the passage of time, it usually is more feasible for disaster response to incorporate an explicit focus on human rights.

Political Consequences of Natural Disasters

"In November 1755, an earthquake and tsunami struck Lisbon killing between a third and a fourth of the city's population. This event is primarily remembered for its effects on the culture, philosophy and science of Europe but also had major political consequences. The earthquake is cited as one of the factors that disrupted Portuguese colonial expansion. It is also said to have fueled resistance to the aristocracy, including an attempted assassination of the king."[111]

Natural disasters, and the government's response to them, normally have either positive or negative political consequences. The Chinese government generally was given high marks for rapid mobilization of the army to respond to the immediate needs of the victims of the May 2005 earthquake in Sichuan (dispatching troops within fourteen minutes of the earthquake, according to the government).[112] However, as the scale and pattern of destruction became clearer—the quake resulted in 87,000 deaths and left 5 million homeless—popular protests emerged, in particular over the devastating impact on schools compared with impact on the homes of high party officials. Among other measures, the Chinese government relaxed its one-child policy for those who had lost children in the earthquake.

Pelling and Dill offer seven examples of ways in which disasters can have political effects:

—Disasters often hit politically peripheral regions hardest, creating regional political tension.

—Disasters may be a product of development policies and can lead to scrutiny of dominant political and institutional systems.

—Existing inequalities can be exacerbated by post-disaster government manipulation.

—The way in which the state and other sectors act in response and recovery is largely predicated on the kind of political relationships that existed between them before the crisis.

—Regimes may interpret spontaneous collective actions by nongovernment sectors in the aftermath of a disaster as a threat and respond with repression.

—In the aftermath of disaster, political leaders may regain or even enhance their popular legitimacy.

—The repositioning of political actors in the aftermath of a disaster unfolds at multiple levels as various actors use disaster relief and recovery to extend their influence over development policies and program.[113]

Natural disasters not only have political consequences on the governments of the countries in which they occur, but also on the international system, as discussed below.

International Humanitarian Reform and Natural Disasters

As discussed in chapter 4, the international humanitarian reform initiated in 2005 by the UN, which was inspired by the initially poor humanitarian showing in the Darfur crisis in 2003, was intended to respond to the institutional gap in responsibility for internally displaced persons. The cluster system was intended to increase accountability and effective response by naming designated lead agencies to coordinate response in a given area. Interestingly, it is most difficult to find a UN agency willing and able to serve as lead agency for the protection cluster on natural disasters.

While UNHCR is the acknowledged lead agency for the protection cluster in cases of conflict, the agency initially was reluctant to take on responsibility for leading the protection cluster in natural disasters. Indeed, within the Global Protection Cluster Working Group, a subgroup was established on natural disasters under the leadership of the representative of the secretary-general for the human rights of internally displaced persons and later by the International Disaster Law Organization. Interestingly, neither organization is operational in the sense of having programs in the field.

But when it comes to the country level, because no agency is assigned to lead on protection, the process is a variation on the earlier collaborative approach used to assign responsibility for IDPs, which never functioned well. When a natural disaster occurs, the resident coordinator is supposed to consult with the three agencies with a mandated protection function—UNICEF, UNHCR, and OHCHR—to determine which will take the lead on protection. As Roberta Cohen points out, in most cases UNICEF has assumed the lead, but its protection role is limited.[114] It has received high marks in child protection, tracing families, and helping separated children and preventing their exploitation in disasters. But other vulnerable groups, such as the elderly, the disabled, ethnic and religious minorities, and those with HIV/AIDS, have not received as strong a focus. In the Mozambique floods, evaluators found that the plight of the elderly without families often was overlooked, as was that of women, although there were many initiatives that centered on children.[115]

Since the nature of this ad hoc arrangement was not very predictable, there were pressures on UNICEF and to a lesser extent UNHCR to take responsibility for ensuring that people affected by natural disasters are protected. UNICEF spent several years debating the possibility but decided in 2008 not to, fearing that its child protection role would become diluted with the broader responsibilities. However, it did agree to participate on an ad hoc basis in areas where it felt that it could assume the coordination role without weakening its child protection responsibilities.

OHCHR has a clear protection mandate, but as a largely nonoperational agency, it has limited capacity to respond. UNHCR often has become involved in on-the-ground response to natural disasters, but only in countries where it has a presence, as it did after the 2004 tsunami, the 2005 earthquake in Pakistan, and the 2010 Haitian earthquake. Recently, UNHCR has indicated a willingness to take a more active role in protection response to natural disasters, and it has been actively engaged in the discussions on climate change–induced displacement. António Guterres, the UN high commissioner for refugees, stated that

> [w]ith our deep experience of protecting people, extensive worldwide presence and improved integration of emergency preparedness, UNHCR can bring to the protection cluster for persons displaced by natural disaster the predictable leadership and proven results required. As with our leadership of the protection cluster for those displaced forcibly by conflict, I view such leadership in natural disasters as a logical extension of our responsibilities.[116]

In Haiti, OHCHR has been serving as cluster lead for protection (with UNICEF for child protection and UNFPA for gender-based violence), but it has come under criticism from other agencies for its poor response.[117] The reluctance of international agencies to engage with communities affected by natural disasters is not only manifest in the protection cluster. While UNHCR agreed to serve as cluster lead for camp coordination and camp management in conflict situations, it was difficult to find a lead to assume those tasks in natural disasters. In Haiti, for example, camp coordination and camp management falls to IOM for coordination, while the cluster on shelter is the responsibility of IFRC.

While there is a long history of humanitarian concern with protection in the midst or aftermath of conflict, attention to the protection needs of communities affected by natural disasters developed much more recently. In particular, humanitarian agencies have focused on ensuring that the relief that they provide does not discriminate (intentionally or unintentionally) and that it meets the needs of all affected groups. The way in which governments and international actors respond after disaster strikes can have serious political consequences. Indeed, there is growing recognition that more attention needs to be paid to the relationship between natural disasters and political conflict. Both tend to occur in countries with limited state capacity and limited economic resources. In both instances, the people most affected are likely to be among the poorest and most marginalized. With prospects of climate change increasing the severity and frequency of sudden-onset disasters, more attention needs to be paid to understanding their political consequences. And when the discussion broadens to include the impact of slow-onset disasters, such as drought, the story becomes even more complicated, as discussed in chapter 9.

8

Paying for Protection: Humanitarian Financing

When international actors get involved in protecting people whose lives are in danger, they need financial resources. Peacekeepers need troops and equipment, international NGOs need funds to purchase fuel-efficient stoves, and humanitarian agencies often need money to pay for their own security. Affected communities often are desperate for resources—funds to pay for their flight to a safer community, jobs to replace livelihoods lost by war or mudslides, or money to pay warlords to leave them alone. But the funds to support communities in their initial protective efforts come largely from their own resources or from relatives and friends who send remittances to them. Once communities have been displaced, they may be able to obtain assistance through government programs, international agencies, or local civil society organizations. As discussed, increasingly that assistance is intended to provide not only the basic necessities of life but also physical protection.

This chapter looks at patterns of financing protection, primarily by looking at international actors and, more specifically, at the relatively small club of traditional government donors. In terms of volume of assistance, they are not the largest donors—the dollar value of remittances, for example, dwarfs all flows of official development assistance—but they are the most important in terms of their impact on the international humanitarian system. It is the traditional donors—a handful of whom account for 95 percent of all humanitarian relief—who keep humanitarian ideals alive, who shape the programs and priorities of multilateral organizations, and who determine whether an individual displaced by flooding will be able to rebuild his or her home or whether a woman assaulted by an insurgent group gets care.

When you step back and look at the overall system of humanitarian financing, it is a strange system indeed. A handful of donor governments contribute large amounts of money, which is then spent by others—either intergovernmental agencies or NGOs. While there is some bilateral funding by donors, much more humanitarian funding is channeled through multi-lateral or nongovernment sources than is the case with development funds. International NGOs act as contractors/partners of both governments and UN agencies in implementing programs while insisting that they are inde-pendent agencies. INGOs in turn often contract with local NGOs/partners to carry out the work in the field. Compared with funding of development programs, humanitarian response is especially time-sensitive. When a large-scale emergency occurs, there is an immediate need for experienced relief workers—for sanitation engineers and logistics specialists—but it is expen-sive to keep such personnel on staff in between emergencies. Perhaps one of the reasons that the military is increasingly active in disaster response is its standby capacity. In any event, for civilian responders, scaling up costs money, and in the midst of an emergency, funds are needed immediately, despite the difficulty of sustaining capacity between large-scale emergencies. As one NGO representative commented, "What we need is a good disaster. We really scaled up after the tsunami, but now are going to have to let a lot of staff go unless there's another major disaster soon."[1]

The system is characterized by unpredictable and at times seemingly capricious funding. Whether emergency relief is provided often depends on what other disasters are happening at the same time, whether the emer-gency occurs in a country of strategic importance to a major donor, or even whether tourists from Western countries have been caught up in a conflict or natural disaster. While the basic principle of humanitarian action is that "assistance shall be given on the basis of need alone," in practice the dis-parities are striking. For example, "[i]n the tsunami, total funding was over $7,100 for every affected person, which contrasts starkly, for example, with funding of only $3 per head actually spent on someone affected by floods in Bangladesh in 2004."[2]

It is important to emphasize again that official development aid is just the tip of the iceberg in terms of the flow of funds from developed to developing countries.[3] As table 8-1 indicates, the $26.8 billion in official development assistance (both humanitarian and long-term development funds) provided by the United States is overshadowed by the funds transferred through pri-vate philanthropy and especially by remittances from migrants to their fami-lies back home. Globally, remittances were estimated to total $338 billion in 2008, up from $289 billion in 2007, with big increases reported in South Asia (36 percent), a much smaller increase in Latin America (2 percent), and

Table 8-1. *U.S. Total Net Economic Engagement with Developing Countries, 2008*

Outflows	Billions ($)	Percent
U.S. overseas development assistance	26.8	17
U.S. private philanthropy	37.3	23
Foundations	4.3	12
Corporations	7.7	21
Private and voluntary organizations	11.8	32
Volunteerism	3.6	10
Universities and colleges	1.7	5
Religious organizations	8.2	22
U.S. remittances	96.8	60
Total outflows	160.9	100
Inflows (unspecified U.S. private capital flows)	28.8	100
Net U.S. economic engagement	132.1	

Source: Center for Global Prosperity, *The Index of Global Philanthropy and Remittances 2010* (New York: Hudson Institute, 2010), p. 12.

slower rates in sub-Saharan Africa, Europe, and Central Asia. The largest recipients of remittances in 2008 were India, China, and Mexico.[4] Remittances play an especially important role in supporting communities affected by conflict or natural disasters. The Center for Global Prosperity provides several examples of how they work in disaster-prone countries:

In Ethiopia, remittance receiving households use their cash reserves during times of food shocks, while non-receivers are more likely to sell valuable assets. Households receiving remittances in Burkina Faso and Ghana are more likely to have concrete houses as opposed to mud ones and have a greater access to communications, both of which help households overcome harsh conditions. In general, remittance flows increase during and after natural disasters and other crises, indicating that they are an important financial backstop.[5]

In terms of official development aid, much more attention—and scrutiny—is paid to development assistance than to humanitarian aid. There are well-established (though rarely met) global targets that call on developed countries to spend 0.7 percent of GDP on development assistance. While development contributions and budgets are discussed by legislative bodies and development aid is seen as an important instrument of foreign policy, much less attention has been devoted to humanitarian aid. Many of the analyses and databases on development assistance simply exclude humanitarian financing. The assumption is that humanitarian work is urgent, needs-driven, and determined less by foreign policy than by the scale of a disaster. The aid needs to be transferred quickly—after all, emergency needs are, by definition, urgent and time-sensitive. While large-scale disasters such as the 2010 Haitian earthquake require massive amounts of money that may require special legislative approval, generally legislative bodies budget funds for humanitarian action to be used by departments of humanitarian response.

But patterns of humanitarian funding are changing, and more analysis and scrutiny of that funding is needed. As shown in table 8-2, the amount of humanitarian funding is increasing—both in absolute terms and relative to the amount of long-term development assistance. Governments and the United Nations alike are seeing humanitarian assistance as a tool to support political objectives such as conflict resolution, and they are trying to integrate humanitarian action into military missions or whole-of-government programs. The traditional assumption for decades has been that humanitarian assistance is provided during an emergency or in the immediate aftermath of a natural disaster and then long-term development actors come in to do the serious long-term work. But as discussed in chapter 6, that assumption no longer holds. Increasingly there is simultaneous provision of humanitarian and development aid and often financial support for peacekeeping as well.

While humanitarian aid is intended to be life-saving, in fact there are long discussions about what should be considered as humanitarian aid rather than development assistance. And often that is where protection—long associated with humanitarian endeavors—comes in. For example, advocates insist not only that education is a basic human right during emergencies but also that it protects children and young people and should be funded by humanitarian contributions. Some governments do support educational programs with humanitarian funding. Others argue that to include education in a humanitarian response is a distortion of the life-saving criterion that distinguishes humanitarian relief from development funding. There are differences even within governments. For example, in the United States, the Bureau for Population, Refugees, and Migration (BPRM) supports educational programs as part of its emergency response while the Office for Foreign Disaster Assistance (OFDA) does not.

It is difficult to separate financing of protection from general humanitarian assistance. Even for agencies that divide their work into protection

Table 8-2. *Humanitarian Funding and ODA, 2000–09*[a]

Year	Total official humanitarian assistance, DAC donors ($ billions)[b]	Total ODA, DAC donors ($ billions)[c]	Total ODA, Non-DAC donors[d]
2000	6.5	54.0	916 million
2001	6.3	52.7	929 million
2002	6.5	58.6	2.9 billion
2003	7.9	69.4	3.1 billion
2004	7.9	79.9	3.3 billion
2005	10.8	107.8	3.2 billion
2006	9.8	104.8	4.7 billion
2007	8.7	104.2	4.9 billion
2008	11.2	122.3	8.7 billion
2009	...	119.6	...

Source: Development Initiatives, Summary, Global Humanitarian Assistance Report 2009, November 2009 (www.globalhumanitarianassistance.org).

a. All figures in the billions are rounded to nearest hundred millionth.

b. DAC comprises twenty-three countries plus the European Commission. Figures exclude South Korea, which became the twenty-fourth member in January 2010. Development Initiatives, "Latest DAC Data Release Reveals Big Rise in Humanitarian Expenditure in 2008," December 18, 2009 (www.globalhumanitarianassistance.org/blog/latest-dac-data-release-reveals-big-rise-humanitarian-expenditure-2008).

c. Current prices. Data from OECD, Query Wizard for International Development Statistics (http://stats.oecd.org/qwids).

d. Current prices; rounded to nearest tenth. Data not available for 2009. Data from OECD, Query Wizard for International Development Statistics (http://stats.oecd.org/qwids/ [accessed June 2010]). Twenty non-DAC countries report their aid to the DAC, including South Korea, whose membership in the DAC became effective on January 1, 2010; for full list, see www.oecd.org.

and assistance, such as UNHCR, it is difficult to calculate how much of the funding is devoted to protection because those activities are mainstreamed into much of the agency's ongoing work. UNHCR's budget for its Division of International Protection Services (DIPS) is broken down between its headquarters office and its "global programmes" (see table 8-3). Global programs, in turn, are broken down into two tranches: "Operational activities" include education; global clusters (IDP programs); registration; resettlement projects; refugee women, children, and adolescents; environment; research, evaluation, and documentation; and communications. "Programme support activities" includes DIPS, among other departments. In 2009 the budget

Table 8-3. *UNHCR Budget 2009–11, Including Division of International Protection Services*

U.S. dollars

Budget	2009	2010	2011
Total UNHCR budget at headquarters	160,391,146	150,220,955	149,757,419
DIPS budget at headquarters			
Office of the Director	2,817,826	2,748,032	2,748,032
Specialized sections	8,086,031	7,363,735	7,363,735
Total DIPS budget at headquarters	10,903,857	10,111,767	10,111,767
Total UNHCR budget for global programs[a]	134,961,903	94,421,720	90,921,720
DIPS program support activities budget			
Resettlement field support	129,706	29,400	29,400
Global clusters (IDP programs—field support)	272,143	0	0
Total DIPS program support activities budget	401,849	29,400	29,400
Total budget for DIPS	11,305,706	10,141,167	10,141,167

Source: Adapted from UNHCR, *UNHCR Global Appeal 2010–11*, pp. 8–10 (www.unhcr.org/4b051f8a9.pdf)

a. Global programs budget includes operational activities and program support activities.

for DIPS at headquarters was nearly $11 million, or around 7 percent of the $160 million UNHCR budget at headquarters. The 2009 budget for DIPS program support activities under global programs was around $400,000 of a total global programs budget of nearly $135 million and comprised the following activities: "resettlement field support," and "global clusters (IDP programs–field support)."[6]

In addition, protection funding falls under "operational activities," under the rubric of "protection and voluntary repatriation," which was budgeted at $5.1 million for 2009, $2.6 million for 2010, and the same amount, $2.6 million, for 2011. However, it is difficult to assess any allocation to protection under the other operational activities, such as children and adolescents.

For agencies such as UNHCR, there often is a direct relationship between the agency's ability to protect refugees and its funding. Beth Elise Whitaker, for example, found that the security of Burundian refugees in Tanzania decreased when UNHCR was forced to cut assistance to the refugees. "As rations of food and nonfood items were cut, refugees became desperate to make up the shortfall and provide for their families. Often, they had little choice but to steal crops and goods from the fields and homes of local farmers." Relations between the host community and the refugees deteriorated and the government began pressing for the refugees to be repatriated.[7]

As for the ICRC, total ICRC protection expenditures for 2009 amounted to 183.4 million Swiss francs (CHF) ($190 million), CHF 567 million ($587 million) for assistance, and CHF 153 million ($158 million) for prevention expenditures, of a total expenditure of CHF 1.1 billion ($1.1 billion) in 2009.[8]

Donors' Support for Protection

As mentioned in chapter 3, Development Assistance Research Associates (DARA) uses a large number of indicators to assess donor performance in upholding the principles of the Good Humanitarian Donorship Initiative. Commitment to protection and international law is included in its scoring and ranking of twenty-three donors from the Organization for Economic Cooperation and Development–Development Assistance Committee (OECD-DAC). In fact, protection and international law is one of the five criteria—in addition to responding to needs; prevention, risk reduction, and recovery; working with humanitarian partners; and learning and accountability—that DARA uses to rank donors. DARA uses the OCHA and UNHCR definition of protection:

> A concept that encompasses all activities aimed at obtaining full respect for the rights of the individual in accordance with the letter and spirit of human rights, refugee and international humanitarian law. Protection involves creating an environment conducive to respect for human beings, preventing and/or alleviating the immediate effects of a specific pattern of abuse, and restoring dignified conditions of life through reparation, restitution and rehabilitation.[9]

Table 8-4 shows all of DARA's rankings for the top five and bottom five DAC countries, as well as the actual scores on pillar 4, protection and international law.[10] According to DARA's indicators, Sweden, Norway, and Denmark, which also are among the top five most generous donors on a per-citizen basis, are among the top five most committed to protection and respect for international law in their humanitarian funding. The United States is ranked abysmally low in pillar 4, outranking only Portugal. However, for the only subindicator listed for that pillar for both countries, "respect for human rights law," Portugal scored 7.07 and the United States scored 1.0 on the HRI ten-point scale.[11] Unfortunately, most governments do not indicate the percentage of their humanitarian contributions supporting protection activities.

Table 8-4. *DARA Rankings of OECD-DAC Countries—Humanitarian Response Index 2009: Best- and Worst-Ranked Countries for Protection and International Law (PIL)*[a]

Best- and worst-ranked countries	Overall PIL rank	Pillar 1: Responding to needs	Pillar 2: Prevention, risk reduction, and recovery	Pillar 3: Working with humanitarian partners	Pillar 4: Protection and international law (score out of 10)	Pillar 5: Learning and accountability	Generosity and burden sharing
Top 5							
Sweden	2	2	6	2	1 (8.3)	5	9
Norway	1	1	7	1	2 (8.1)	7	1
Denmark	4	6	2	3	3 (7.95)	1	6
European Commission	5	5	3	11	4 (7.39)	3	...
Australia	10	12	8	13	5 (7.11)	6	10
Bottom 5							
Portugal	23	23	21	21	23 (4.77)	23	22
United States	14	9	18	15	22 (5.19)	15	13
Italy	21	20	20	22	21 (5.38)	21	20
Japan	19	17	13	19	20 (5.52)	12	18
Greece	22	21	23	23	19 (5.89)	22	16

a. Out of twenty-three OECD-DAC countries. Taken from DARA *Humanitarian Response Index 2009* data online: "Overall Donor Ranking—Pillar 4: Promoting Principles and Standards" (www.daraint.org/node/128#), and DARA, *The Humanitarian Response Index 2009: Whose Crisis? Clarifying Donor's Priorities* (New York: Palgrave Macmillan, 2010). The print version refers to pillar 4 as "Protection and International Law."

Scale of Humanitarian Financing

There was a dramatic increase in humanitarian funding over the course of the 1990s—an increase due in large measure to the complex conflict situations that challenged the humanitarian community on political as well as humanitarian grounds. Between 1990 and 2000, official humanitarian aid more than doubled in real terms, from $2.1 billion to $5.9 billion, and it also increased as a proportion of total official development assistance (ODA), from 5.83 percent to 10.5 percent.[12] Beginning in 2000, the amount of humanitarian assistance increased—but this time largely as a result of large-scale natural disasters. Undoubtedly when the data are collected for 2010, a similar spike will be seen following the January 2010 earthquake in Haiti.

Americans, for example, donated $774 million within five weeks after the earthquake.[13] Table 8-2 lists overall estimates of humanitarian funding over the past decade.

While the number of actors carrying out humanitarian work on the ground has expanded dramatically, the club of traditional donors is a small one. "The US, Canada, Germany, Japan, the Netherlands, Norway, Sweden, Switzerland and the UK together account for 93% of official humanitarian aid. ECHO, a multilateral organization that also acts as a donor, was responsible for approximately 10% of official humanitarian aid in 2000."[14]

Governments are the main donors to UN agencies and multilateral organizations. Some UN agencies engage in private sector fundraising—UNHCR, UNICEF, UNRWA, and UNHCR all have national campaigns that function largely like local NGOs.[15] But UNICEF has been by far the most successful in generating private sector and NGO funding, which accounted for 28 percent of the agency's total income for 2009.[16]

The fact that most international humanitarian funds come from a small number of donors means that there is a tendency for UN agencies and international NGOs alike to respond to donor agendas in terms of "I can do that, too" in order to secure funding, leading in some cases to agencies becoming overextended and/or working in areas where they do not have sufficient expertise.[17] It also means that countries of strategic interest to the major donors usually are funded at much higher levels than countries of little specific concern to them. Thus in 2003, for example, Afghanistan and Iraq accounted for 30 percent of all humanitarian aid flows to identified recipient countries.[18]

There has been growing interest within donor governments in public service contracting, driven largely by concerns about the efficiency and effectiveness of state provision of public services. Before the 1990s, official humanitarian aid was managed by relatively small departments within government ministries. Procedures and bureaucracies were relatively light—at least in comparison with those of development assistance—in order to keep response flexible, which meant that partners had considerable autonomy and flexibility. But that has changed with the increase in the range of potential partners. There is no longer the assumption that the UN or ICRC are best able to assess needs and formulate appropriate responses, and donors are investing more in their own ability to analyze the humanitarian needs of a particular country. That means that donors can be more assertive in funding specific projects that correspond to those needs.[19] Donors also have become more demanding in terms of procedures, monitoring and evaluation, and outputs. Beginning in the 1990s, there has been an increase in the field presence of donors, especially from the United States, ECHO, and DFID, which provide closer oversight of humanitarian operations—in some cases "potentially reinforcing a culture whereby agencies are seen as the executing agencies of donors' set policy."[20]

In the United States, USAID and OFDA have lost ground within the U.S. government and vis-à-vis the Department of Defense.[21] The OECD/DAC peer review confirms that "the continued redirection of Official Development Assistance away from USAID . . . carries risks, both because it is the most experienced [U.S.] government provider of aid and because it contains much of its development expertise."[22]

Donors occasionally have tried to do more to coordinate their efforts—for example, in Timor-Leste, Albania, Afghanistan, and Somalia. But those were relatively modest efforts and unrelated to coordination initiatives on larger political objectives.[23] There are a few cases in which donors have worked together effectively to press governments to respect the rights of affected communities. For example, in Sri Lanka, donors threatened that they would not continue to fund camps for IDPs until the government began a serious return/resettlement effort.[24]

Before 2002, there was not much talk of the accountability of donor governments themselves—although they were increasingly demanding that NGOs and UN agencies increase their own accountability. That began to change in 2003, when donors commissioned a set of key studies known as the Humanitarian Financing Initiative. The study concluded that "[d]onors, as a group, achieve less than the sum of their parts; that is, donor behavior is a patchwork of policies and activities by individual governments that, taken together, do not create a coherent or effective system for financing humanitarian needs across the world." According to the study, effectiveness is compromised by donor earmarking, by short funding cycles, by unrequited pledges and late funding, and by tying contributions to a donor's own national NGOs and contractors. Humanitarian principles are not the main driver of donor behavior in financing humanitarian work; foreign and domestic politics take priority instead.

Financing of Protection in UN Appeals

A listing of 2009 Consolidated Appeals Process (CAP) and Flash appeals with the amount and percentage of coverage by sector is presented in table 8-5. Overall, 66 percent of appeals were funded, ranging from 36 percent of the appeal for Côte d'Ivoire to 85 percent for Zimbabwe. Overall, 40 percent of

Table 8-5. *Funding for UN Consolidated and Flash Appeals, 2009*

Appeal (2009 midyear review or revision)	UN appeal total[b]	Percent covered	Total humanitarian funding[c]	Percent covered									
				Protection	Education	Health	Food	Shelter & NFIs	Water and Sanitation	Agriculture	Coordination & Support Services	Mine Action	Economic Recovery
Sudan	2.11bn	67	1.55bn	42	41	48	89	67	51	53	68	77	41
DRC	946.3m	63	643m	12	19	23	83	22	19	57	62	…	9
Somalia	851.8m	61	579m	34	14	49	75	19	48	37	64	…	48
Occupied Palestinian Territories	804.5m	70	705.9m	25	64	53	71	50	58	47	121	57	77
Zimbabwe	719.4m	85	642m	40	1	60	40	…	85	59	63	…	2
Pakistan (2008–09)	680.1m	72	659m	54	29	53	90	65	72	16	81	…	3
Afghanistan	664.9m	70	611.6m	30	159	4	94	65	41	27	85	25	204
Iraq and region	650.2m	63	541.2m	64	45	58	73	51	39	0	76		78
Chad	400.6m	69	331.92m	40	15	28	93	…	42	14	75	23	…
Sri Lanka	270.1m	68	242.6m	82	30	36	100	62	43	11	46	121	6
Kenya	580.5m	70	450.4m	38	26	52	87	151	67	17	31	…	68
Uganda	247m	67	188.1m	30	0	14	86	0	27	68	77	0	…
Côte d'Ivoire	36.7m	36	14.5m	42	…	36	35	…	29	15	67	…	…
Central African Republic	100m	72	78.7m	57	565	51	93	133	81	68	82	…	0
Total	9.7bn	66	—	40	31	45	84	52	47	48	74	49	50

a. U.S. dollars, millions (m) and billions (bn). These categories are the main sectors, but they exclude other lines of funding such as logistics, "multisector," and "sector not specified," which may be present in a particular appeal. The protection sector in appeals is actually called "Protection/human rights/rule of law." The food sector is called "nutrition" in some appeals, and shelter may appear as "shelter and NFIs."

b. U.S. dollars, revised if applicable.

c. Includes contributions to the Consolidated Appeal and additional contributions outside of the Consolidated Appeal Process (bilateral, private, CERF, Red Cross, and so on), as of December 3, 2009.

the needs identified as protection were covered; the only sector with a lower percentage covered was education. The highest percentage of coverage was food, at 84 percent, followed by coordination mechanisms, at 74 percent. Interestingly, protection was funded at relatively high percentages in Sri Lanka (82 percent) and Iraq (64 percent) and at abysmally low percentages in Democratic Republic of the Congo (12 percent) and the occupied Palestinian territory (25 percent).

While most of the funds channeled to support humanitarian activities come from the governments that are members of the DAC, contributions from nontraditional countries and regions—China, India, South Korea, Central Europe, and the Gulf states—are increasing.[25] That is in part a consequence of the perception that aid and economic growth reinforce trade and security relationships. In some cases, such as the Gulf states, it is a concrete expression of solidarity with other Arabs, particularly in the occupied territories. In fact, the Gulf states provided over 90 percent of reported humanitarian assistance from non-DAC donors.[26]

Critiques of Donor Governments

Mary Anderson's Listening Project seeks to assess the humanitarian system on the basis of interviews with beneficiaries—who, although they are the targets of the humanitarian system, are rarely asked their opinion of the quality of assistance. She reports that beneficiaries raise four particular criticisms of donor behavior: they impose external agendas instead of listening to what people need; they are too concerned with the speed of response; they do not sustain a physical presence; and they fail to develop participatory and partnership arrangements. She quotes one interviewee, for example, as saying, "They arrive; they help us; they leave. And we never hear from them again. So, what did we do wrong?"[27]

Other criticisms of donor behavior refer to donors' difficulty in raising and allocating funds for both prevention of humanitarian crises and for rehabilitation and redevelopment. Rather, donors put a premium on rapid disbursement of emergency funds.[28] As one observer wrote, donors respond to starvation, but not to hunger or stunting.[29] Rarely is new money allocated to meet long-term needs. While the immediate response usually involves new money, longer-term programs usually are funded with money reprogrammed from other sources.[30] Thus, for example, following the announcement by the U.S. government of significant funds for Haitian earthquake relief, NGOs were told to cut the budgets of their U.S. government-funded projects to "pay for the assistance to Haiti."[31]

Table 8-6. *Disparity between Amount of Disaster Aid Pledged and Amount Delivered*

Crisis	Amount pledged ($)	Amount delivered ($)
Cambodian war rehabilitation	880 million by June 1992	460 million by 1995
Rwandan genocide	707 million in January 1995	<71 million by July 1995
Hurricane Mitch, Central America	9 billion in 1998	<4.5 billion by December 2004
Bam earthquake, Iran[a]	1 billion in January 2004	116 million by December 2004

Source: Peter Walker and others, "Smoke and Mirrors: Deficiencies in Disaster Funding," *British Medical Journal,* vol. 330 (2005), p. 248.

a. Data from Elizabeth Mansilla, Universidad Nacional Autónoma de México.

One particularly egregious complaint concerns the gap between the funds that are pledged and those that are delivered. At donors' conferences or through the media, donors take pride in announcing large pledges—particularly in cases of high-visibility emergencies. Yet with respect to the funds that they actually deliver, the reality is quite different, as demonstrated in table 8-6.

Private Funding

According to OCHA's financial tracking service, private contributions rose from 14 percent of total humanitarian assistance in 2001 to about 35 percent in 2005.[32] Development Initiatives reports that over half of the $4.9 billion spent by NGOs in 2007 came from the public or from other charitable sources such as corporations, while the remaining $2.3 billion was funded by multilaterals and DAC donors.[33] NGOs' contributions from their own funds are significant.

According to the *Index of Global Philanthropy 2010,* U.S. corporations contributed $7.7 billion to international development assistance in 2008—a $900 million increase over 2007 and a $2.2 billion increase over 2006. However, $7 billion of that amount was for pharmaceutical and medical donations. Given that figure, it is not surprising that the health care industry was the largest single giving sector in 2008, directing 27 percent of its giving abroad—in comparison, 13 percent of overall corporate contributions were directed abroad.[34] Corporations are more likely to contribute financially to natural disasters than to conflict-related emergencies, partly from a concern that the company's reputation could be harmed from involvement in political issues. Nor do corporations respond to slow-onset disasters, such as drought.

It is estimated that U.S. foundations donated around $4 billion in funds for international aid in 2006, up from $2.2 billion in 2005. According to the Foundation Center, 55 percent of international grants by foundations go to health projects, 21 percent go to development and emergency relief projects, and 8 percent go to environmental projects.[35] Most foundations do not fund ongoing operational work, although they may fund pilot projects intended to raise awareness of a particular situation or to demonstrate the utility of a particular approach. In terms of protection, foundations such as the John D. and Catherine T. MacArthur Foundation, the McKnight Foundation, the Ford Foundation, and the Mellon Foundation all provided substantial support to development of standards and norms related to protection of specific groups, particularly during the mid-1990s to the mid-2000s.

Multilateral Funding Instruments

The Consolidated Appeals Process is a major means by which UN agencies and NGOs respond to natural disasters and emergencies. It was established as a fundraising mechanism by the United Nations General Assembly in 1991 to connect host governments, aid agencies, and donors.[36] Since its inception, the CAP has developed into a central strategizing tool for the coordination and implementation of humanitarian assistance. But in spite of the development of tools and guidelines, there is little consistency and uniformity within the CAP—different countries produce different kinds of CAPs. Various country versions of the CAP have been criticized for lacking a substantive strategic plan, based on joint assessments and prioritized needs.[37] The amount of funding requested by aid organizations and provided by donors has tripled since the CAP's inception, increasing from the $2.1 billion raised in 1992[38] to $6.3 billion in 2009.[39] By looking through the proposed projects included in a consolidated appeal, donors can choose to fund particular projects or agencies or to contribute to a general fund.[40]

To encourage rapid response in emergency humanitarian situations, the General Assembly created the Central Emergency Revolving Fund (CERF) in 1991, with an annual loan component of up to $50 million to aid agencies. Even with this cash-flow mechanism, however, humanitarian organizations encountered problems in implementing swift and coordinated aid pro-grams: donor funding often was guided more by political considerations than need, leaving low-profile emergencies consistently underfunded.[41] In an effort to remedy such shortfalls, in 2005 the General Assembly trans-formed the Central Emergency Revolving Fund into the Central Emergency Response Fund by adding a grant element to the fund. The annual target for the grant facility is set at $450 million and relies on voluntary contributions, primarily from governments.[42]

The objectives of the Central Emergency Response Fund are to promote early action and response to reduce loss of life; enhance response to meet time-critical requirements; and strengthen core elements of humanitarian response in underfunded crises.[43] The CERF was intended to support life-saving activities, and in 2010 guidance was provided by OCHA on what is and is not considered life-saving. Life-saving activities are those

> actions that within a short time span remedy, mitigate or avert direct loss of life, physical and psychological harm or threats to a population or major portion thereof and/or protect their dignity. Also permissible are common humanitarian services that are necessary to enable life-saving activities and multi-agency assessments in the instance of sud-den onset disasters.[44]

Preparedness, prevention, disaster risk reduction, and early warning activities therefore are not considered life-saving and are not eligible for CERF support. The guidance note then breaks down humanitarian response by cluster and indicates the type of activities that can be considered life-saving. Under protection, the following activities are considered life-saving:

—deployment of emergency protection teams in disasters and emergencies

—profiling, registration, and documentation of affected populations

—identification and strengthening/setup of community-based protection mechanisms

—provision of life-saving information to the affected population

—establishment of support measures to ensure access to justice with a special focus on IDPs, women, and children.

Life-saving assistance for gender-based violence (GBV) includes

—strengthening and/or deploying GBV personnel

—identifying high-risk areas and factors driving GBV in emergencies and strengthening protection strategies, including safe access to fuel resources

—improving access of survivors of gender-based violence to secure and appropriate reporting, follow-up, and protection and to police.

Other activities considered life-saving and thus eligible for CERF funding include a range of activities under child protection, mine action (including mine risk education for displaced and/or returning populations), and support services, including provision of common security measures for safe delivery of humanitarian efforts.[45]

This review of funding mechanisms indicates that there is a gap between the humanitarian principles of impartiality, neutrality, and humanity on the one hand and the allocation of funds on the other. As noted previously, the discrepancies in response to communities affected by the 2010 Indian Ocean tsunami and those affected by other flooding are enormous. Other inequities also are apparent:

> For example, in the Darfur area, the NGO calculated that the amount spent on refugees totaled three times more per capita than that spent on IDPs. In Burundi, where OFDA spent $2.49 million on 116,000 IDPs, the per capita rate was $21 for an IDP whereas the per capita rate for a refugee was $127 since PRM spent $2.6 million on 20,618 refugees.[46]

The system for financing international humanitarian action is a complex one. Researchers attempting to follow the "money trail" find extensive data on the contributions of the large government donors but much less reliable information on the far larger amounts from remittances or private charitable organizations. It also is difficult to separate out financing of protection from other humanitarian activities. As humanitarian agencies incorporate protection work into their ongoing mainstream activities, that difficulty is bound to persist.

But given the increasing importance that humanitarian actors are placing on both protection and accountability, it is surprising that so few data exist on the basic question of how much money is being spent on protection activities—either by individual agencies or by the international system as a whole. Certainly one of the difficulties is that humanitarian agencies increasingly are mainstreaming protection work into their ongoing activities and thus are unable to separate out the specific funds spent on protection. But if humanitarian agencies are to be accountable for their work on protection, it would seem to be incumbent on them to indicate both the funds that they are spending on protection and the indicators that they use to determine whether the money is well spent. Does increasing funding for protection translate into more lives saved? Does a dollar spent on protection save more lives than a dollar spent on, say, child immunization? Is mainstreaming protection into all activities more effective or less effective than stand-alone protection programs? Is training staff to see their work in terms of protection more cost-effective than setting up a protection unit?

Of course, those questions are not just about funding; they also are about how humanitarian actors assess the impact of their protection work. And as we have seen throughout this book, the lack of precision in defining protection makes it hard to identify patterns of financing for protection and harder to assess performance.

9

Future Challenges for Humanitarian Actors

Predicting what will happen in the future is, of course, difficult for everyone, but perhaps especially so for humanitarian actors, who are used to responding to crises in the here and now. Humanitarian actors sometimes also worry that making predictions could have adverse consequences. Predicting genocide or widespread violence in a country could make it difficult to carry out humanitarian operations (or even to obtain visas, for that matter). And planning ahead for a specific emergency can either make an agency look foolish if a crisis does not materialize or create a self-fulfilling prophecy. For example, if a surge of refugees from a given country is expected and food and relief items are prudently prepositioned, people may leave their communities either because they think that the humanitarians are privy to information to which they are not or because they perceive an advantage to accessing the aid placed conveniently nearby. Contingency planning does take place, of course, particularly for natural disasters and for the possibility that conflicts will escalate. But most of the planning focuses on particular crises rather than long-term trends and their potential impact on the international system itself.

This chapter looks at three megatrends that are likely to shape the nature of humanitarian work in the future. Humanitarian actors have recognized all three as almost certain to occur, although attempts to address them have been rather piecemeal and tentative. Changes in the dynamics and means of conflict, urbanization, and climate change are three trends that already are apparent, but changes in each of them and particularly in their interrelated dynamics will be the main drivers of humanitarian engagement in the future. And all have implications for protection.

Changing Dynamics and Means of Conflict

Conflict in the future is likely to be protracted, to be fought by armed groups for personal gain, and to be to be fought in cities. Those trends have been developing over the past few decades, but the humanitarian system is still focused on emergency rather than long-term response and on state and non-state actors who have at least some knowledge of international humanitarian law. It has been only in the past few years that attention has been focused on the particular challenges of working in urban settings. At the same time, high-technology armaments will come into widespread use by advanced industrial states, with implications for international humanitarian law—and for protecting civilians.

Since World War II, most of the world's conflicts have been intrastate rather than interstate wars and most of the casualties have been civilian rather than military. Battle severity, measured as battle deaths, has significantly declined in the post–cold war period.[1] Wars today are fought by smaller armies, impact less territory, and cause fewer war deaths than conflicts of the cold war era, when superpowers provided large quantities of conventional arms to combatants in places like Angola, Ethiopia, and Afghanistan, leading to large-scale casualties.[2] The number of civilians killed in civil conflict today is significantly lower than during the cold war.[3] While the global trends are definitely positive, the fact remains that in all regions civil conflict and one-sided violence continue to kill, displace, and maim civilians.

Today's low-intensity conflicts are typically carried out by poorly trained rebel forces using small arms and light weapons. Avoiding large-scale military confrontations, their strategies include terrorizing, exploiting, and displacing civilian populations. Not all conflicts are low intensity, of course. Between 2004 and 2008, somewhere between 80,000 and 100,000 Iraqi civilians were killed in violence following the U.S. invasion.[4] The civilian death toll in conflicts includes not only those who are killed by weapons, but also those who die because of the increased mortality resulting from malnutrition, disease, and lack of access to health care. Thus in October 2010, ICRC reported that civilian casualties in Kandahar, Afghanistan, had doubled over the previous year, largely because people were finding it more difficult to access medical facilities.[5]

While the incidence of major armed conflict declined between 1999 and 2009,[6] organized campaigns of one-sided violence have increased. One-sided violence is defined as "the intentional use of armed force against civilians by a government or formally organized group that results in at least 25 deaths in a calendar year. One-sided violence is not armed conflict as such, as it directly and intentionally targets civilians who cannot defend themselves with arms."[7]

Moreover, a gamut of armed actors are engaging in conflict, including insurgent groups, paramilitary forces, terrorist networks, and fighters motivated primarily by greed. A range of paramilitary groups are recruited to do the dirty work of governments and economic interests. Often having links to illicit economies, such as drug trafficking or diamond smuggling, groups motivated by greed tend to be fairly autonomous and under the control of a strong man or warlord operating in a particular geographic area.[8] Dubbed "warriors" by Ralph Peters or "postmodern warriors" by Michael Ignatieff, such individuals have a great deal of experience in fighting but lack professional training and commitment to the ideals of international humanitarian law.[9] Many were recruited as children and have known no life but fighting with insurgent forces. These groups also attack humanitarian workers in all regions, and they have little compunction about attacking civilians; indeed terrorizing civilians and driving them off their land often is the objective of the violence.

Nonstate actors have engaged in criminal activities to finance their struggles for years. What is new today is the growth in the number of exclusively criminal gangs and the blurring of lines between street gangs and other nonstate actors. Most definitions of "gang" refer to a group of three or more individuals who engage in criminal activity and identify themselves with a common name or sign. Gangs are prevalent in developed countries such as the United States, in failed states such as Somalia, and in emerging countries such as Brazil. Once found principally in large cities, violent street gangs now affect public safety, community image, and quality of life in communities of all sizes in urban, suburban, and rural areas. No region of the United States is untouched by gangs. Gang prevalence in the United States was significantly elevated in 2008 compared with recorded lows in the early 2000s."[10]

Although research on international gangs is limited, it appears that they are primarily made up of young men living in urban areas and that they engage in illicit activities. It also appears that gang activity is growing, due in part to demographic and economic trends,[11] and that the lines between child soldiers and gangs are breaking down. In both cases, gangs and armed groups provide a sense of community and identity for their members. While child soldiers typically are forcibly recruited by armed groups, which use them to support military objectives that may include terrorizing local communities, gangs often are rooted in their communities and depend on community support to carry out their activities:[12]

Although these gangs may fight for one side, they are rarely fully under the control of the structures of war, so it is difficult to predict when they will follow the orders of the commanders who nominally preside over them. They are organized by and are primarily loyal to the members of their own group and very often operate with impunity and recklessness toward others in their society.[13]

While in some cases states are parties to the conflict and use force to suppress insurgent movements, as in Sri Lanka, in many other cases states lack the capacity to protect civilians from attack or exploitation by armed elements. According to Peter Singer, "The CIA today counts some fifty countries that have 'stateless zones,' where the local government has lost all effectiveness or simply given up."[14] And when conflicts are protracted, a particular dynamic of violence is created that is difficult to overcome, even when peace agreements are signed. The breakdown of social values and the loss of authority of the state and of civic institutions can lead to the emergence of gangs that take advantage of the resulting lawlessness to threaten, rob, rape, and kill civilians. As we have seen, conflict recurs after half of all cases where peace agreements have been reached.

All of that has implications for protection of civilians. Hugo Slim makes the case that protecting civilians is a long-term process of changing values and behavior.[15] There is no easy fix. The United Nations will continue to try to resolve conflicts through integrated missions and humanitarian agencies will find it increasingly difficult to insist that aid be distributed in accordance with principles of neutrality and impartiality.

Most humanitarian work in the future—as it is in the present—will be in protracted crises. While humanitarians do make contingency plans, much of the planning is geared primarily toward improving the efficiency of response in the immediate aftermath of a disaster rather than to long-term humanitarian response. Existing standby arrangements, for example, put experienced humanitarian workers and protection officers on the ground within a matter of hours or days, but they are not intended to support humanitarian operations for years.[16]

Protection needs change over time. The immediate threat to the security of people displaced by conflict may diminish because they are physically removed from the violence, but domestic violence may increase as a result of the frustration of living in limbo. Temporary shelters that were adequate in the immediate aftermath of an emergency degrade over time, as evidenced by the deplorable living conditions in collective shelters in the

Balkans. Access to livelihoods and work become more important over time, particularly when assistance diminishes. It becomes more difficult to maintain earlier levels of financial contributions for long-term "care and maintenance" operations. Land and property issues become central to determining solutions for those displaced by violence,[17] and disputes over those issues produce conflicts that make it difficult to protect people.

While displacement will continue to drive humanitarian emergencies, there are likely to be more IDPs and fewer refugees as governments continue to restrict the entry of people fleeing conflict. Both internal and international migration flows will become increasingly mixed as people flee because of conflicts, poverty, and natural disasters and because of the interactions among them. It will be more difficult to distinguish between people fleeing conflict and those seeking economic opportunities, particularly in urban areas, and there will be growing resistance to singling out the displaced as having a preferential claim to assistance or protection.

There has always been a difference between conflicts in which the United States has a major stake—currently Iraq and Afghanistan—and other conflicts, which may be quite localized. While some have seen Iraq and Afghanistan as the wars of the future, it is unlikely that the United States will engage in many more of such long-term costly ventures. Domestic pressures against foreign entanglements, the realization that terrorism is not linked to a particular geographic territory, and the difficulty in actually winning such a war as well as economic pressures mean that it is unlikely that there will be many wars of this kind in the future.[18]

However, in areas where the U.S. military is directly involved in conflict, stabilization measures will be the key to the conduct of the war—and they will present humanitarian actors with tough choices in working with the military. "If the U.S. and other Western governments prioritise narrow security objectives over basic human welfare, humanitarian actors will almost certainly seek to resist—albeit tempered in some cases by continuing financial reliance on the donor governments leading the stabilisation charge."[19] And yet if military forces become more active in addressing basic human welfare needs, humanitarian actors also become uncomfortable.

In high-profile cases in which U.S. military and political interests are engaged, traditional humanitarian actors face difficult choices in reconciling their humanitarian principles with political realities. Recognizing that their work cannot be neutral and impartial in such settings, NGOs can decide not to provide humanitarian assistance, leaving such operations to political and military forces. They can accept their roles as instruments of foreign and military policy while trying to do the best for the people that they can reach. Or they can carry out their work the best way that they can while continuing to try to shape government policy. However, UN agencies face a special set of pressures, in that usually they cannot choose not to provide assistance.[20] In conflicts in which the United States is not a protagonist, U.S.-based humanitarian actors have more flexibility and can carry out operations with less conflict with humanitarian principles because it is easier for them to maintain a degree of independence from the belligerent parties.

Finally, technological developments in military weapons systems will have far-reaching consequences for the future of warfare—and for civilians. Peter Singer's *Wired for War* details the increasing use of robotic technologies in warfare, explaining the dynamics that are driving their use and raising questions about their impact on future warfare, the military, and the laws of war. He argues that wars increasingly will be fought by unmanned drones and robots, controlled by computer technicians a safe distance away. The use of Predator drones with Hellfire missiles currently is an essential component of U.S. military strategy against al Qaeda in Pakistan. Moreover, as Singer explains, robots can be programmed to make decisions without later human involvement.

The jury is still out on whether such technologies will reduce future atrocities by taking some of the passion and personal angst out of warfare. A remote operator, Singer argues, "[i]sn't in the midst of combat and isn't watching their buddies die around them as their adrenaline spikes." But on the other hand, there is the "fear . . . that turning killing into merely the elimination of icons on a computer screen might make . . . killing easier and abuses and atrocities more likely."[21] A greater distance between those carrying out the fighting and the victims also makes it less likely that they will actually see the suffering, making it more difficult to act on the basis of the humanitarian principle of humanity.

Singer found that none of the robotics researchers ever referred to international humanitarian law or to ICRC, but such technological developments have serious implications for the laws of war, and the questions that they raise are profound. Is the person guiding the flight of drones from a base in the United States considered to be a legal combatant? If so, is he or she a valid target walking around the streets of Las Vegas? And who is accountable if something goes wrong, the person programming the device in the United States or the commander in the field?[22] And what about when robots themselves make the decisions?

Theoretically, some of the new weapons systems—for example, precision-guided munitions—can limit harm to civilians. "If a programmer knows that they might be prosecuted for war crimes if their software code is missing a line, then they are more likely to double-check that code one more time."[23] But Singer reminds us that mistakes and accidents also occur with unmanned systems.[24] While the United States has led the technological advances in this field, robotics are rapidly being acquired by other governments and by non-state actors. He even cites the case of recent U.S. college graduates concerned about international inaction in the face of the conflict in Darfur who set about raising money to hire mercenaries or use drones to stop the conflict. Although they eventually abandoned their plan, the case illustrates the fact that individual civilians can contemplate acquiring military assets to intervene directly in a conflict in ways that were not possible a decade ago.[25]

So, on one hand increasingly sophisticated technologies remove professionally trained soldiers or conventional soldiers trained in international humanitarian law from the battlefield while on the other, conflicts are being driven by armed groups that are far from professional and that terrorize populations using nothing more than small arms. The notion that there is a physical battlefield where troops on opposing sides fight each other is perhaps becoming obsolete, with implications for civilians and the humanitarian agencies trying to assist and protect them. Those developments are intensified by trends toward a more urban location for humanitarian work.

Urbanization

Humanitarian work increasingly will be carried out in urban areas, in part because of simple demographics. Half of the world's population—some 3.3 billion people—currently live in urban areas, and that figure is expected to rise to 5 billion by 2030. Eighty percent of these urban dwellers will live in the developing world. One billion people, one-third of the urban population, currently live in slums.[26] While the world's megacities are the most obvious manifestation of this trend, over half of the world's urban population lives in cities of fewer than 500,000 inhabitants, cities that are least-equipped to deal with the pressures of urbanization, the growth of urban violence, or natural disasters. Small towns generally attract less investment and donor interest than large cities and are less prepared to deal with crises when they occur. Most of the casualties in the 2005 Pakistan earthquake, Hurricane Mitch, and the Bam earthquake, for example, were in small towns.

Cities and towns are concentrations of people, resources, assets, services, opportunities—and crime. The probability of being a victim of violent crime is substantially higher in urban than in rural areas. "As a world average—two out of three inhabitants of cities are victimized by crime at least once over a five-year period.[27] Most crimes are committed by male adolescents, who also are the primary victims of such crimes. "Risk factors that influence youth becoming involved in [criminal activities] include family problems such as violence and poor parenting; poverty; inadequate housing and health conditions; poor schooling or lack of education; peer pressures; discrimination and lack of training and work opportunities."[28] The demographic "youth bulge" means that there are more young people in developing countries and economic opportunities have, thus far at least, not been able to keep up with the growing demand for jobs. The resulting pressure is manifest in increasing crime and violence.

Crime tends to occur in poor neighborhoods, and when crime increases, those with resources—middle-class and wealthier individuals—move farther away, further polarizing cities. The rise of urban youth gangs, the growth of organized crime, and the ubiquity of drugs and guns have created areas where police, government, and humanitarian agencies dare not enter. Mark Schneider and Damien Helly, of the International Crisis Group, described the situation in Cité-Soleil, the largest slum in Haiti and reportedly the worst slum in the Western hemisphere:

> insecurity—from those urban gangs, from political spoilers, and from drug traffickers—had stalled any real chance for major investments in the impoverished communities that lace through the capital. Too many kidnappings, too many assaults, and too many drive-by shootings had turned the capital into a no-go zone for all but the most adventurous development agencies.[29]

In May 2010, the Jamaican government's efforts to arrest a drug and arms dealer, Christopher "Dudus" Coke, erupted into a bloodbath when 1,000 police and soldiers assaulted a public housing complex in Kingston in which Coke reportedly was hiding. During the month it took for the government to arrest Coke, seventy-three people were killed, the government declared a national state of emergency, flights were cancelled, and tourism—a major industry in Jamaica—took a nosedive. Coke, it turns out, had a reputation in the community as a bit of a Robin Hood character, distributing food, building a medical center, and sending kids to school; consequently, the police faced opposition from the community as well as from Coke's military forces.[30]

The sheer scale of urban violence is staggering. Peter Singer notes that thousands of people are killed every year in the Brazilian *favelas* and that the government has given up trying to control them.[31] The lines between urban crime and armed conflict are becoming blurred. Military planners are aware that coming wars will be fought in cities. As Ralph Peters wrote some fifteen years ago, "The future of warfare lies in the streets, sewers, high-rise buildings, industrial parks, and the sprawl of houses, shacks and shelters that form the broken cities of our world. We will fight elsewhere, but not so often, rarely as reluctantly, and never so brutally."[32]

"For the armed forces, towns present a particular challenge because of the risks associated with street fighting and the opportunities for the enemy to hide, especially in the areas that it has liberated."[33] But for armed groups, towns have a particular attraction—a concentration of coveted wealth, symbols of power, communications, and transport hubs providing the opportunity to trade in goods. For town dwellers, the conduct of hostilities by warring parties in an urban setting intensifies the effects of conflict. Front lines move around the town. Civilian buildings provide shelter for combatants who move from one house to another. "Moreover, in a town affected by armed violence, the coexistence or even the cohabitation of civilians with armed groups is part of everyday life."[34] Or as Peters describes, "Noncombatants, without the least hostile intent, can overwhelm the [military] force, and there are multiple players beyond the purely military, from criminal gangs to the media, vigilante and paramilitary factions within militaries, and factions within those factions."[35] The question for international humanitarian law becomes "Where is the battlefield?"

Local governments, the frontline responders in humanitarian crises occurring in their areas, often are weak and lack both the funds and the capacity to respond to urban casualties.[36] Sometimes other groups are able to fill the gap. For example, the Israeli-Lebanon conflict in July 2006 claimed over 1,100 lives, injured thousands more, displaced hundreds of thousands, and severely damaged civilian infrastructure. Municipal authorities were ill equipped and slow to respond while Hezbollah was able to provide immediate financial support to communities and individuals affected by the war.

The displacement that occurs as a result of both armed conflict and natural disasters, coupled with large-scale economically motivated migration from rural to urban areas, creates an ever-changing urban environment. People move in and out of cities. "The vulnerability of these migrants not only places extra demands on urban services and resources but also increases the general susceptibility of urban areas to crises or disasters as well as the potential 'importation' of conflict and violence by the migrants."[37] Migrants or displaced communities also are vulnerable to violence when the social structures and networks that serve to warn them of risks are disrupted by the move to cities.

ICRC notes that community mechanisms for survival in cities differ from those in rural areas although they are not necessarily more difficult to employ. The simple assumption that people can at least produce food in rural communities overlooks the highly developed informal sector and black markets in cities. However, mutual support mechanisms in urban areas are probably less effective than in rural areas, "particularly for migrants, displaced persons or rootless refugees, although there is no empirical evidence to confirm that view. Moreover, vulnerable members of the population such as old people, who are taken care of by their community in a village, are often isolated in towns.[38]

Humanitarian agencies have long operated on an inherently "rural" model of response to communities affected by armed conflict, wherein refugees and displaced persons are concentrated in camps managed by international actors. Working in an urban environment is a completely different ball game. It is more difficult to distinguish between the urban poor and the displaced, between those affected by crime and those affected by urban conflict. Not only do many of the displaced not want to be identified, but the mobility in cities limits the ability of humanitarian agencies to contact them. Currently two-thirds of the world's 10.5 million refugees live in towns and cities, as do most of the world's internally displaced population.[39]

UNHCR is beginning to address the phenomenon of urban displacement. António Guterres, the UN High Commissioner for Refugees, explained, "Urbanization is an irreversible trend. More and more of the people we care for—refugees, returnees, the internally displaced and the stateless—will live in cities and towns and we need to adjust our policies accordingly."[40] The High-Level Dialogue on Urban Refugees and the development of UNHCR policies on both urban refugees and internally displaced persons in non-camp settings represent initial steps in that direction. Traditionally humanitarian actors have focused their efforts on refugees and IDPs—people displaced by conflicts—rather than on those who have not moved. But the fact that most refugees and IDPs currently live in urban areas challenges that paradigm. Those displaced by violence may not, in fact, be more vulnerable than the urban poor, and targeting them for assistance may create resentment and conflict with the local population.[41] The best way to assist these groups may be to support municipal governments' efforts to provide services to all urban residents.

It also is difficult for humanitarians to implement programs to provide health care, sanitation, water, and food in urban areas because of the complexity of the basic infrastructure and the high level of technical skill required to repair the damage caused by urban conflict. While humanitarian agencies often function as the sole authority in camp situations, urban settings include many more actors. ICRC has acknowledged the need to be realistic about its role in such situations:

> It is outside the scope of humanitarian agencies to re-establish the economic activity of a town so that it can become self-sufficient in terms of food. Assistance programmes would not suffice. Agricultural production in urban areas can only make a negligible contribution to the food needed to supply the entire urban population.[42]

The dividing line between urban and camp-based populations also is becoming more blurred. In Dadaab, Kenya, some 280,000 refugees currently live in three camps—more than three times the capacity of the camps. In effect, the camps have become highly congested cities. The fact that the displaced in Darfur live in camps that essentially function as urban areas has implications for long-term solutions for the IDPs and for the region as a whole. If peace and security are ever restored in Darfur, will the displaced—now accustomed to urban living and to the services that are possible in urban areas—be eager to return to their formerly rural lifestyles?

Certainly generational differences are apparent in areas of high urban displacement, such as Lebanon and Colombia. While parents may dream of returning to their rural communities, their children have grown up as urban residents and are unlikely to see the same attractions in isolated villages and rural areas.

Urban areas also are especially susceptible to damage from natural disasters, as evidenced most recently by the 2010 Haitian earthquake. As urban areas grow, poor neighborhoods spread into ever-more marginal land—such as riverbanks, ravines, and mountainsides—which means that when a mudslide, earthquake, or hurricane occurs, poor neighborhoods are disproportionately affected. The fact that a large percentage of the world's cities are located on coastlines renders them more susceptible to hurricanes and cyclones. And of course, the potential for epidemics is much higher in urban areas because of the concentration of population.

Climate Change

Humanitarian actors are beginning to grapple with the possible effects of climate change, with particular focus on the potential displacement of large numbers of people. Many observers, from scientists to staff of human rights organizations, have tried to predict the number of people who might be forced to leave their communities due to changes in the climate. For example, one organization predicted that one billion people will be displaced by climate change in the coming years.[43] The International Organization for Migration projects 200 million environmentally induced migrants by 2050, defining "environmentally induced migrants" as persons or groups of persons who, for compelling reasons of sudden or progressive changes in the environment that adversely affect their lives or living conditions, are obliged to leave their habitual homes or choose to do so, either temporarily or permanently, and who move either within their country or abroad.[44] This definition represents an advance over earlier references to climate change or environmental "refugees," which refugee advocates strenuously opposed.[45] UNHCR argued, for example, that the notion of "environmental refugee" has no basis in international law and rejected the suggestion made by some that the 1951 refugee convention be amended to include environmental causes: "UNHCR considers that any initiative to modify this definition would risk a renegotiation of the 1951 Refugee Convention, which, in the current environment, may result in a lowering of protection standards for refugees and even undermine the international refugee protection regime altogether."[46]

Climate change has, of course, been a part of the history of our planet since its creation. As a geographer recently reminded us:

> The passage across the Bering Straits [to] America 13,000 years ago was possible due to the low sea levels of the ice age, while the Medieval Climate Optimum which lasted between [the] 8th and 13th centuries AD seems to have stimulated the population of Polynesia by making navigation relatively easy thanks to regular winds and clear skies . . . also desertification of the Sahara and the Arabian peninsula has played an important part in the densification of population on the banks of the Nile and . . . consequently contributed to the birth of ancient Egyptian civilization.[47]

And it has long been accepted that changes in weather patterns can lead to migration, as witnessed more recently in the drought-produced migration from the American Dust Bowl in the 1930s and the migration of large numbers of people from the Sahel because of drought in the early 1970s.

However, since 1970, there has been growing scientific concern about global warming and climate change as a result of human action. According to the Fourth Assessment of the Intergovernmental Panel on Climate Change (IPCC), "[m]ost of the observed increase in the global average temperature since the mid-20th century is very likely due to the observed increase in anthropogenic greenhouse gas concentrations."[48] Those results are based on more than 29,000 observational data series from the seventy-five studies used by the IPCC in making the assessment and show significant changes in physical and biological systems, "more than 89% of which are consistent with the direction of change expected as a response to warming."[49]

And while climate change will clearly impact urban populations, the relationship also runs the other way. As Anna Tibaijuka, director of UN-HABITAT, says, "urbanization brings about irreversible changes in our production and consumption patterns. How we plan, manage and live in our expanding cities determines, to a large extent, the pace of global warming."[50] Urbanization is a force driving regional warming (heat islands), which can exacerbate drying trends.[51]

Most of those writing about climate change and displacement argue that climate change has effects on the environment that force people to leave their homes. While there is a consensus that climate change is real and that it produces environmental effects that can displace large numbers of people, different authors emphasize different environmental effects. Furthermore, predictions of how many people will be displaced over a particular time period vary tremendously. In fact, the predictions are all over the map, depending in part on assumptions that are made about which environmental changes are caused by climate change and in part on assumptions about how the international community will respond—or fail to respond. Perhaps typical of the connections that are drawn is the following assertion by Jeffrey Sachs:

> Climate changes affect crop productivity through changes in temperature, rainfall, river flows and pest abundance. Droughts and floods are becoming more frequent. Tropical diseases such as malaria are experiencing a wider range of transmission. Extreme weather events such as high-intensity hurricanes in the Caribbean and typhoons in the Pacific are becoming more likely. Changes in river flow already threaten hydroelectric power, biodiversity, and large-scale irrigation. Rising sea levels in the coming decades may inundate coastal communities and drastically worsen storm surges.[52]

These changes all affect migration and displacement. When crop productivity declines or droughts last longer than usual, rural agriculturalists often move to cities in search of jobs. Natural disasters often displace people; while much of the displacement is temporary, some natural disasters permanently change the landscape, preventing people from returning to their communities.

Walter Kälin, the representative of the secretary-general for the human rights of internally displaced persons, has identified at least five movement scenarios stemming from climate change:

—hydrometeorological disasters (for example, flooding, hurricanes, mudslides)

—"sinking" small island states

—environmental degradation and slow-onset disasters (for example, reduction of water availability, desertification, recurrent flooding, salinization of costal zones)

—zones designated by governments as being too high-risk and dangerous for human habitation

—armed conflict triggered by a decrease in essential resources (for example, water, food) owing to climate change.[53]

Each of the five scenarios has implications for both international law and humanitarian agencies. The scenarios are discussed below in order of the certainty of the evidence—thus it is certain that sudden-onset natural disasters are increasing as a result of climate change, but much less certain how slow-onset disasters will affect displacement.

Natural Disasters

It is widely recognized that climate change causes an increase in the number and severity of sudden-onset natural disasters, which in turn cause displacement. Hurricanes and floods, for example, occur suddenly, forcing people to leave their communities in order to escape the destruction. Most of those displaced by sudden-onset natural disasters who remain within the borders of their own country become internally displaced persons while those who cross international borders as a direct result of natural disasters are considered migrants.

Evidence from the Emergency Events Database (EM-DAT), maintained by the World Health Organization's Collaborating Centre for Research on the Epidemiology of Disasters (CRED), indicates fairly clearly that natural disasters are increasing and that within the category of natural disasters, hydrometeorological events are increasing faster. Hydrometeorological disasters include floods and wave surges; storms; droughts and related disasters (extreme temperatures and forest/scrub fires); and landslides and avalanches.[54]

While some of the reported increase in the frequency of natural disasters is undoubtedly the result of better data collection (particularly in comparison with collection in the earlier years of the twentieth century), there does seem to be evidence that the number and severity of hydrometeorological events are increasing. Some have argued, for example, that warmer water in the Atlantic is contributing to the ferocity of hurricanes in the Caribbean and North America; others have made similar arguments in the case of Pacific typhoons. The National Oceanic and Atmospheric Administration (NOAA) found that "those systems that do approach their upper-limit intensity are expected to be slightly stronger in the warmer climate due to the higher sea surface temperatures."[55] The evidence that the frequency and severity of natural disasters is increasing is solid. We do not yet know how many people are likely to be displaced by these events, but the number will likely rise.

Rising Sea Levels

Global warming will cause a rise in sea levels, creating another strong link between climate change and displacement. The most recent Intergovernmental Panel on Climate Change report projects temperatures to increase by between 1.8 degrees C and 4.0 degrees C, resulting in an increase in sea levels of between 0.2 and 0.6 meters by 2100, with a greater increase possible. According to a World Bank study, a one-meter increase in sea levels would displace 56 million people in eighty-four developing countries.[56] Further, if rising temperature trends continue, widespread deglaciation of the Greenland and West Antarctic ice sheets would occur over an extended period of time. The complete melting of the Greenland ice sheet would raise sea levels 7 meters; the melting of the West Antarctic sheet would raise levels another 5 meters, drastically impacting the earth's population centers.[57] Other groups raise even more alarming scenarios and projections. A recent report by the International Peace Academy, for example, argues that in the worst-case scenario, the breaking off of the west Antarctic and Greenland ice sheets would raise sea levels by 15 meters. If the more stable east Antarctic ice sheet melts, sea levels could rise by 60 meters.[58]

The countries most affected by rising sea levels are small island states, such as the Maldives and many Pacific islands, as well as countries with low-lying and heavily populated coastal areas, such as Vietnam and Bangladesh. A recent study by Sugata Hazra found that over the past thirty years, roughly

80 square kilometers of the Sundarban islands in India have disappeared, displacing more than 600 families and submerging two islands. The Sundarban islands are among the world's largest collection of river delta islands, with 4 million people living on them. While there is a natural process of islands shifting size and shape, the study concludes that there is little doubt that human-induced climate change has made them especially vulnerable.[59] The South Pacific island country of Tuvalu, which comprises nine small islands with a total area of 26 square kilometers, already has witnessed population movement as hundreds of families have moved onto the two main islands in response to changing environmental conditions. That internal migration has been compounded by rapid population growth, which further increases the stress on scarce resources and land.

Kiribati, with a population of 92,000, is acutely aware of the threats that it faces due to climate change. In 2005, Kiribati's president, Anote Tong, spoke at the UN General Assembly about the need for nations to seriously consider the option of relocation, acknowledging that the issue needs to be discussed now.[60] The possibility that island states could disappear as a result of rising sea levels has led some to think through what resettlement would mean in practice and how it should be timed. Ilan Kelman of the Center for International Climate and Environmental Research in Oslo, for example, suggests that resettlement schemes should be explored before the islands disappear and lays out several ways that resettlement might take place.[61]

While much of the attention has focused on the possibility of the disappearance of island states, these countries also face threats to livelihood and the basic necessities of life. Small island developing states are especially vulnerable in four areas: agriculture and fisheries, water resources, coastal zones, and the tourism sector.[62]

The evidence that climate change is leading to an increase in sudden-onset natural disasters and to rising sea levels is strong, and both are likely to have an impact on displacement. A recent study by the UN Office for the Coordination of Humanitarian Affairs (OCHA) and the Internal Displacement Monitoring Centre (IDMC) estimated that about 37 million people were displaced as a result of sudden-onset natural disasters in 2008.[63] Most of that displacement is assumed to be short-term and to take place within the borders of countries. If sea levels rise and measures are not taken to mitigate the effects of the rising coastlines, it is likely that people will be displaced, but the estimates of the specific numbers to be displaced depend in large measure on the assumptions that are made. The relationship between slow-onset disasters and migration is more complex.

Slow-Onset Disasters

Many have argued that by impacting traditional weather patterns, climate change will force people to leave their communities because they can no longer sustain themselves. The Intergovernmental Panel on Climate Change states that by 2020, 75 to 250 million people in Africa will be affected by water stress and rain-fed agriculture yields could be reduced by up to 50 percent.[64]

The forecasted impact of climate change on Asia is similarly drastic. The IPCC says that melting glaciers will result in increased flooding and rock avalanches in the Himalayas followed by decreased river flow over the next several decades. Further, freshwater availability in "Central, South, East and South-East Asia, particularly in large river basins, is projected to decrease which, along with population growth and increasing demand arising from higher standards of living, could adversely affect more than a billion people by the 2050s."[65] IPCC goes on to warn of the impact of such changes on disease: "endemic morbidity and mortality due to diarrhoeal disease associated with floods and droughts are expected to rise in East, South, and South-East Asia due to projected changes in the hydrological cycle . . . increases in coastal water temperature would exacerbate the abundance and/or toxicity of cholera in South Asia."[66]

While there is little doubt that changing weather patterns and slow-onset disasters affect livelihoods, their relationship to displacement is more complex than appreciated by those who argue that "environmental refugees are people who can no longer gain a secure livelihood in their homelands because of drought, soil erosion, desertification, deforestation and other environmental problems, together with associated problems of population pressures and profound poverty."[67]

We know that the number of people affected by drought is much higher than the number affected by hydrometeorological events. For example, during the period between 1979 and 2008, 718 million people were affected by storms, while 1.6 billion were affected by droughts.[68] But we simply do not know the impact of drought on migration. There is some evidence, for example, that rather than encouraging migration, poor rainfall and bad harvests limit the ability of households to move long distances. And the relationship between food production and environmental factors may not be a straightforward case of people being unable to grow crops because of inadequate rainfall. In fact, "food insecurity or famine may be intentionally manipulated by power-holders, and this in turn may result in migration due to changed or disrupted livelihoods and/or displacement."[69]

There also are conceptual difficulties. For example, some use the term "slow-onset disaster" to refer to the impact of climate change on livelihoods. Strauss argues that migration resulting from gradual change is likely to be far greater than the displacement resulting from individual catastrophic events. She also argues that long-term environmental changes are more likely to cause permanent migration than sudden catastrophes.[70] But the term "slow-onset" cries out for further clarification. How slow is slow? Does the disaster occur over months or years? Decades? Centuries? How does the term relate to concepts such as increasing poverty or environmental degradation or social marginalization and exclusion? How permanent is "permanent migration"?

Traditionally, people who left their communities because they were poor or in order to search for other livelihoods were considered migrants. Those who remain within the borders of their country are internal migrants; those who travel to other countries are international migrants. Weather clearly plays a role in contributing to poverty, but certainly it is not the only factor. The interconnections between poverty and the environment require much more analysis. Generalizations about the relationship between environmental degradation and population movement mask a great deal of the complexity that characterizes migration decisionmaking. Moreover, it is extremely difficult to isolate the specific contribution of environmental change in many forms of population movements.[71] McDowell and Morell argue that many situations commonly considered to be environmental displacement should more accurately be considered as displacement resulting from development.[72]

It is well-known that poor people are disproportionately affected by natural disasters. Twenty years ago, the World Commission on Environment and Development argued that "poverty is a major cause and effect of global environmental problems. It is therefore futile to attempt to deal with environmental problems without a broader perspective that encompasses the factors underlying world poverty and international equality."[73] According to the IPCC, poverty is the factor that can most negatively affect a society's vulnerability to climate change.[74] However, most of those writing about climate change and displacement do not systematically consider the impact of poverty on displacement or the interrelationship between poverty and environmental changes or the relationship between population growth, environmental pressures, and displacement.

If a causal connection between environmental change and displacement is to be demonstrated, then studies should show—as global environmental migration expert Richard Black argues—that migration increases when environmental degradation gets worse. Unfortunately, such studies simply do not exist.[75] The European Union's studies on the relationship between environmental factors and climate change, the most ambitious to date, concluded that climate change is contributing to increased pressure to migrate but also that "climate change is not the only potential environmental trigger for migration—the environmental problems faced by migrants, potential migrants and non-migrants in the case study areas are manifold."[76]

Government Restrictions on Land Use

It may be, as Kälin argues, that people are displaced because their governments have designated their communities of origin as being too high-risk and dangerous for human habitation. That occurred in both India and Sri Lanka following the 2004 tsunami when the governments declared exclusion zones to prevent people from returning to communities close to the coastline. The extent to which governments are able to provide support for communities will determine whether these groups have additional unmet needs. In spite of somewhat arbitrary and inconsistent changes in its policy of excluding settlements within 100 meters of the coast, the Sri Lankan government ensured that beneficiaries could remain on or near their original homes in private shelters, an alternative that the communities preferred to relocation to more distant areas or to collective centers.[77]

There are no international standards or guidelines for governments to use in prohibiting people from living in certain areas because of climate change. Guidelines developed by the World Bank provide direction for resettlement of populations when development projects such as dams are undertaken and include provisions against arbitrary displacement,[78] but the question of when evacuations (in the case of sudden-onset disasters) or relocations (for long-term effects of climate change) should occur remains largely unaddressed in international law.

Climate Change, Displacement, and Conflict

UN Secretary-General Ban Ki-moon drew attention to the relationship between conflict and climate change in a June 2007 editorial: "Amid the diverse social and political causes, the Darfur conflict began as an ecological crisis, arising at least in part from climate change."[79] Some estimates say that rainfall in the region has decreased nearly 40 percent over the past fifty years, forcing ethnically Arab nomadic herders and sedentary black farmers into conflict over arable land and access to wells.[80] Secretary-General Ban went on to warn that "violence in Somalia grows from a similarly volatile mix of food and water insecurity. So do the troubles in Ivory Coast and Burkina Faso."[81]

But most academic researchers shy away from blaming conflicts exclusively on the environment, instead attributing the causes of conflict to a more complex interplay of factors. A major study carried out for the World Bank concluded that much of the literature exaggerates the impact of environmental factors in causing or exacerbating conflict.[82] Similarly, UCLA professor William Clark concluded that "conflicts arising from environmental change are much less likely than conflicts generated by religious, ethnic and other rivalries." And yet, Clark notes:

> Environmental stress is likely to be linked to conflict indirectly but significantly. Its impacts will come directly from declining resources and conflicts over those resources and from the tensions created by populations that are displaced or who move seeking improved life chances in other regions. However, most of the conflicts will embed environmentally induced conflict under the guise of religious, ethnic or civil conflict.[83]

Conflict over scarce resources and the impact of displacement/migration on receiving communities usually are depicted as the main drivers of climate change–induced conflict. UNHCR staff members Aidan A Cronin, Dinesh Shrestha, and Paul Spiegel report that "of the 47 nations regarded as being either water stressed or water scarce in 2007, 25 are regarded as facing a high risk of armed conflict or political instability as a consequence of climate change."[84] Reuveny conducted a study of thirty-eight cases of environmentally induced migration in the second half of the twentieth century and found that half of the cases displayed no sign of violence or conflict while the other half resulted in some kind of violence, even if it was often unorganized or attributable to nonmigration forces.[85]

It is interesting that military forces in the United States and Europe see climate change as a "threat multiplier" that "exacerbates existing trends, tensions and instability," with the European Commission making the case that climate change "threatens to overburden states and regions which are fragile and conflict prone."[86]

Legal Status of Those Displaced by Climate Change

Several factors affect the legal status of those displaced by the consequences of climate change. It is likely that most of those displaced by environmental events will remain within their country's borders[87] and the prevailing international normative standards will apply to them: they are internally displaced persons to whom the UN Guiding Principles on Internal Displacement apply. Those who cross an international border because of conflict fall under the international refugee regime and should receive protection and assistance accordingly. But there is a gap for those who leave their countries because their livelihoods have disappeared as a result of changing weather patterns or because of the consequences of a sudden-onset natural disaster.

One of the still-unresolved issues in the field is the question of how voluntary the population movements are. Are people forced to leave or do they choose to leave? The Environmental Change and Forced Migration Scenarios (EACH-FOR) project of the European Commission distinguishes between "environmental migrants" and "environmental displacees." The distinction rests on whether migration is voluntary or forced: environmental migrants are "those who choose to move voluntarily from their usual place of residence primarily due to environmental concerns or reasons"; environmental displacees are "those who are forced to leave their usual place of residence, because their lives, livelihoods and welfare have been placed at serious risk as a result of adverse environmental processes and events."[88] But such distinctions are difficult to draw in practice.

Discussions become more complicated still when the question arises of people who "pre-empt the worst" by leaving before environmental degradation results in the devastation of their livelihoods and communities.[89] If there is a consensus that those who are displaced because of climate change are entitled to international support, who will decide whether persons left their countries voluntarily or because they were forced to do so? And what criteria will be used? In practice, it is likely that rather than there being a voluntary-forced dichotomy, there are degrees of voluntariness stretched along a continuum that depend on people's tolerance for risk and a personal set of criteria that they use in making decisions to leave their communities/countries.

Finally, most discussions of climate change–induced displacement seem to assume that displacement is permanent. Clearly if an island-country sinks below the ocean as a result of climate change, there are no possibilities for return. But if rainfall decreases for a season or two (or ten) as has been the case throughout human history, who is to determine that that represents a different magnitude of change than the "normal" environmental factors that have propelled economic migration throughout the ages? Moreover, those who remain behind, who may represent the most resilient in their communities—or the most vulnerable—may have particular needs for protection and assistance.[90]

Mitigation and Adaptation

Many of those writing about the impact of climate change on displacement do not assume that either mitigation or adaptation measures will be taken or will be effective. But certainly some countries—from Tuvalu to Bangladesh—are implementing measures that are intended to prevent displacement and to mitigate the impact of disasters on their populations. For example, Bangladesh moved 3 million people out of harm's way as Cyclone Sidr approached, saving thousands of lives in the process. In that case, temporarily displacing people was a mitigation effort that saved lives.[91] Similarly, the Bangladeshi government has made significant progress in protecting its population from the regular cyclones that affect the country by constructing cyclone shelters.[92] There is significant evidence that the risks of natural disasters can be diminished with planning, foresight, and commitment of resources.[93] What is not so certain, however, is whether national governments and the international system will have the political will to make the necessary investments in such measures.

Implications for the Humanitarian Community

The humanitarian community is at the forefront of immediate response to sudden-onset natural disasters, but as discussed, it is not well situated to respond to long-term needs stemming from slow-onset disasters. If in fact millions of people are displaced, either internally or across national borders, as a result of environmental changes stemming from climate change, then development actors will have to be engaged to support both adaptation/mitigation measures and long-term support for displaced communities to regain livelihoods, acquire shelter, and prevent outbreaks of disease. As Biermann and Boas argue, the protection of migrants is "essentially a development issue that requires large-scale, long-term planned resettlement programs for groups of affected people mostly within their country."[94]

And yet, as mentioned, relations between humanitarian and development actors have been problematic, and it is hard to see how those differences can be overcome to meet the needs of future large-scale displaced populations. The way that a disaster response is organized may be related to how long term displacement is. If communities of origin are rebuilt quickly, humanitarian actors have a role to play and people can return to their communities.[95] But few regions of the world are prepared to manage human mobility related to slow-onset disasters.[96]

Climate change thus simultaneously represents a "threat multiplier" in terms of its impacts on human vulnerability and a "demand multiplier" in its likely impacts on humanitarian needs and increases the consequent pressures on the international humanitarian system. It also is a "scale and complexity multiplier" in terms of its impacts on migration, including forced migration.[97]

Drawing the Connections

This chapter looks at three megatrends that are likely to affect humanitarian work in the future: conflicts that are both more protracted and carried out by a complex array of actors; urbanization; and climate change. It is perhaps the intersection of the three that is most frightening. States that lack the capacity to deal with conflicts also are the least likely to mobilize an effective response to natural disasters—or as the Inter-Agency Standing Group put it, "The inter-relationship between the two [conflicts and natural disasters] will become more overt as natural events trigger political turmoil, which in turn will lead to violent conflict and more natural, technological and systems failures."[98]

In addition, natural disasters of the future will have a disproportionate impact on cities. "Already, around two-thirds of the world's mega-cities with populations greater than five million fall at least partly in low-lying flood-prone areas; possibly a fifth of the urban populations of the poorest countries live in hazard-prone environments."[99] If climate change does result in decreasing agricultural output, increasing numbers of poor rural migrants will make their way to already overburdened cities, increasing the pressure and the potential for urban conflict even more. It is known that poor communities are likely to live on marginal land and be more vulnerable to natural disasters; with further increases in urban populations in developing countries, prospects for sea-level rises affecting coastal cities, and urban violence at an all-time high, that could become the virtual doomsday scenario. And the cities likely to be affected are those with the least capacity and fewest resources to develop adequate contingency planning and adapt to the increasing incidence of disasters.[100]

These three megatrends all have implications for both protection and future humanitarian work. Protection in the sense of keeping people physically safe is challenged by the proliferation of different types of nonstate actors. Humanitarian agencies have experience in responding to victims of insurgencies and counterinsurgency campaigns in which people are displaced from rural areas or small villages. They have much less experience in responding to situations in which the main protagonists are criminal gangs and in which people are displaced in urban areas, where it is harder to identify people in need of protection and more difficult to devise suitable strategies for protecting them. Traditionally, refugees have been housed in camps managed by UNHCR and supported by a range of NGOs. Protection of the camps from physical attack has taken different forms over the years, but generally it has been provided, to varying degrees, by the police and military forces of the host country. Protection of camps from outside attack and from violence within the camps has always been uneven. Few would argue that refugee camps have been safe spaces for most of their inhabitants. But at least humanitarian actors knew what should be done and who was responsible when camps were not protected. When people are displaced in urban areas, protection becomes more difficult, particularly when the threats come from criminal gangs living in the same urban areas and particularly when police forces lack the capacity or will to confront the gangs. And with the multiplicity of actors, it is more difficult to determine who is responsible when people are not protected.

Protecting people from the effects of natural disasters also is more difficult in urban areas, as discussed in chapter 7. But it is the intersection between violence and natural disasters where the most difficult protection challenges are likely to emerge. Haitians living in Cité Soleil were affected by the earthquake, but humanitarian access to the victims was limited not just by the mounds of rubble but also by the insecurity resulting from violent groups living in the community. Even before the earthquake, much of Cité Soleil had been a "no-go" area for humanitarian actors. After the earthquake, it became even more difficult: criminals escaping during the earthquake took refuge in Cité Soleil, gangs had more ready access to resources in the form of relief supplies, and armed groups could operate with even more impunity due to the weakened security and judicial systems.

If, as predicted, more people move to cities as a result of slow-onset disasters resulting from climate change, such as drought, pressures on urban resources will increase. If, as is likely, the economies of such cities are unable to provide jobs for desperate people, it is likely that criminal gangs will continue to grow. Humanitarian agencies have developed strategies for protection that rely on presence, assistance, and advocacy, but all of those are challenged in urban areas. It can be more difficult for humanitarian staff to be present with those at risk when they are dispersed throughout a city and when humanitarian workers are targeted by gangs eager to loot their relief items. Assistance programs are more difficult to mount in urban areas when the most vulnerable are living among the community. In fact, singling out the displaced for assistance may create further resentments and conflict; the protection needs of the displaced may not be very different from those of members of the communities in which they live. It may be, for example, that woman-headed households are more vulnerable and in need of protection whether they are displaced or not.

Implementing assistance programs for conflict-affected or for displaced groups may put these groups at risk. Advocacy traditionally has been used by humanitarian actors in several ways: by calling on governments and nonstate actors to respect international standards with regard to protecting civilians, by calling for UN peacekeeping missions to protect civilians, by negotiating access with armed actors, and by speaking out when access is denied or when civilians are threatened. All of those efforts are more difficult to carry out when the main protection threats come from large numbers of small, urban, armed groups or gangs. As discussed in chapter 5, UN peacekeeping missions have been weakest in their community policing function—a function that is especially needed in urban areas. Denouncing urban violence in Cité Soleil is unlikely, on its own, to result in increased protection of civilians living there.

While it is the responsibility of national governments to protect their citizens, protecting people in urban areas is fundamentally a task of the municipal police force. Security sector reform and establishment of rule of law generally are not traditional focuses of humanitarian actors; they fall within the purview of development actors. Yet if protection of civilians is to mean anything in urban areas, development actors must do much more in this area, and humanitarian agencies will be challenged to develop new ways of working with development actors.

10

Concluding Observations and Recommendations

Protection as a concept emerged from international humanitarian law, refugee law, and human rights law, three traditions that developed to respond to specific needs at particular historical moments. International humanitarian law emerged in the nineteenth century, originally to protect soldiers who were no longer active participants in combat. Refugee law developed to meet the crisis of the large-scale movement of people, particularly Russians, across European borders in the 1920s. The breakthrough in the development of international human rights law occurred in the immediate aftermath of World War II, and the development of IHL was shaped by cold war politics. The world has changed considerably since the development of these normative instruments, yet they remain the foundation of efforts to protect people from different threats across the globe. Implementing international humanitarian law during conflict has always been difficult, and implementation during today's conflicts, which are characterized by the proliferation of nonstate actors, is no exception.

What seems to have changed today is the perception that humanitarian actors are independent, neutral, and impartial actors and that their work should therefore be respected. That perception has changed, particularly in parts of the Islamic world, where much of today's humanitarian work is focused. Even as humanitarian actors increasingly try to incorporate protection into their work, their access to vulnerable civilians is becoming more problematic and they themselves are no longer protected by their status as humanitarian actors. While there is a long history of governments and nonstate actors violating IHL by attacking civilians, what is new is that increasingly they are targeting humanitarian actors. As fewer people cross international borders in search of safety and as governments have become more sophisticated in their efforts to restrict entry of asylum seekers, refugee law applies to a decreasing percentage of the world's displaced. Much of the successful implementation of human rights law has focused on specific groups—for example, children, women, and persons with disabilities—but simply adding these groups together does not provide a holistic view of protection of civilians. Nor does the adoption of international normative standards and national legislation automatically translate into a safer world for civilians.

For the most part, displacement has driven the discussion on protection. Refugee law developed in the aftermath of the breakup of the Russian empire, and growing recognition of the particular needs and rights of internally displaced persons emerged during the post–cold war period. But efforts to address the particular needs of IDPs challenged notions of sovereignty in ways that the development of the international refugee regime did not. International efforts to protect IDPs—whether displaced by ethnic cleansing in Bosnia or a decade later by complex conflicts in Darfur—meant that the global community had to confront the messy issue of sovereignty, and to do so it had to develop new concepts, such as protection of civilians and the responsibility to protect doctrine. While important normative developments, neither of those concepts has yet been translated into action to promote the physical security of people on the ground. Displacement by natural disasters has (thus far) been largely internal and short term, but questions are likely to arise about the international community's responsibility to protect those displaced by the environmental consequences of climate change.

The decade of the 1990s began with a surge of optimism for the United Nations. The collapse of the Soviet Union created hopes that the global body would be able to respond quickly and effectively to prevent crises. Those hopes were dashed by the conflicts in Somalia, Rwanda, and Bosnia, where the international community was unable to prevent violence, genocide, and ethnic cleansing. Wrenching ethical questions challenged humanitarian workers on the ground. Paying for protection of humanitarian workers in Somalia meant more money for warlords to buy arms, which further fueled the conflict. Humanitarians could protect Bosnians by evacuating them from their communities, but in doing so, they were contributing to ethnic cleansing. Assisting refugees in camps in what was then Zaire meant protecting the perpetrators of genocide. The present concern with protection is an effort to respond to the crises of the 1990s.

Humanitarians have felt helpless in situations in which civilians are targeted, relief has become a useful commodity to fuel war, and major protagonists are driven by greed rather than ideology. Unable to tackle the root causes of violence and unable to physically protect victims of attacks, they have turned to doing what they can to incorporate protection into their humanitarian programs. They have been encouraged in doing so by donor governments that also have felt frustrated at the inability of the international community to bring an end to conflicts. The United Nations, as discussed, has initiated many reform processes to increase its effectiveness and coherence, but it has not yet found a formula that enables timely interventions to prevent widespread violence. The major actors have therefore turned to increasing humanitarian assistance and to supporting the protection initiatives of humanitarians to compensate for their inability to take action that would diminish threats to civilians. That is not a new phenomenon. It was certainly a characteristic of the early years of the Bosnian conflict, for example, but it is becoming more widespread in the absence of clear positions for addressing conflicts such as Darfur, the Democratic Republic of the Congo, and other complex emergencies.

More—and more diverse—actors are seeking to protect people in humanitarian crises. Among those involved in global governance, in the military, and in the humanitarian world, protection has become a mantra. While humanitarians increasingly try to incorporate protection into their assistance programs, military forces in at least a few high-profile areas are trying to incorporate assistance programs into their military strategies. However, humanitarians do not do a very good job of protecting civilians from violence and the military does not do a very good job of assisting people.

Humanitarian actors are trying to have it both ways—to claim the moral high ground by asserting their humanitarian principles and to get involved in the almost-always political undertaking of protecting people. Many, perhaps most, of the efforts of humanitarian actors to incorporate protection into their humanitarian work are excellent initiatives. However, although they are sound programming decisions, they are not, with a few exceptions, really increasing people's physical security. It is good from both a rights perspective and from a pragmatic project management perspective to consult with beneficiaries, to ensure that programs do not discriminate against particular groups, and to ensure the sustainability of programs. But that is not protection—at least not as ordinary people understand the term, as Marc du Bois of Médecins Sans Frontières (Doctors without Borders) has pointed out so eloquently.[1] The development of more professional standards for humanitarian work generally and for protection specifically is a positive development. Even when humanitarian actors have different definitions of protection and approach protection work in different ways, it is encouraging that there is a consensus on certain basic principles.

While the mid-1990s was a time of soul searching regarding the difficult ethical issues involved in deciding what protection means in the midst of armed conflict, the mid-2000s were characterized by the entry of natural disasters on the protection agenda. That meant that the international community had to grapple both with new forms of conflict and with new needs and protection issues arising from natural hazards—a trend that is likely to accelerate with climate change.

Unfortunately, some of the current efforts to focus more on protection have become mired in bureaucratic jargon and procedures in which matrices and working groups have become the focus of the effort rather than the well-being of people on the ground. For example, many good people are working hard to make the UN's protection clusters work and there seems to be a consensus that coordination is better. But are people safer because of the work of the protection cluster? Are protection clusters even engaging those who are fundamentally responsible for protecting people on the ground? Should they?

Protection is about preventing people from getting hurt. But humanitarian assistance was intended to respond to people who already have been hurt, and it functions best when that is what it does. In human rights terms, protection is about responding to violations of human rights, while relief is about alleviating the consequences of those violations. People are protected when the threat of violence against them is reduced and/or when their capacity to respond is strengthened. With a few exceptions, humanitarians are not very good at reducing threats or strengthening capacity, though they are really good at providing assistance.

The International Committee of the Red Cross is an exceptional humanitarian actor in that it does engage parties in a conflict to try to prevent attacks as well as provide assistance to affected communities. It also is exceptional in the degree to which it tries to remain neutral and impartial in the most difficult of circumstances. But there are limits to its ability to protect people in situations of mass one-sided violence. During the Rwandan genocide, ICRC was the only international humanitarian actor that stayed in the country. The incredibly brave staff managed to save some lives, but they were powerless to stop the genocide. Even if ICRC had had 10,000 staff in Rwanda, it is unlikely that ICRC could have stopped the widespread killing.

The reality is that humanitarian action can rarely protect civilians from people determined to hurt them. However, humanitarians can reduce the exposure of civilians to violence, can build the capacity of communities to resist aggression, and can sound the alarm when civilians are threatened.

Definitions and Paradigms

A protection paradigm for humanitarians needs to be grounded in humility and the realization that humanitarians cannot and should not be expected to physically protect people. In order to protect civilians, much more intensive engagement is needed with national authorities and nonstate actors by mediators and by regional and international institutions. With the exception of ICRC, humanitarian agencies are not well positioned to carry out that work. Rather, diplomatic pressure, technical assistance to governments, and the full range of activities outlined in the preparatory work for the International Commission on Intervention and State Sovereignty (ICISS) are needed.

That was the thinking behind much of the work done on responsibility to protect (R2P), although the concept has been tarnished by the emphasis on coercive military intervention as a response strategy. Although the use of the presence of unarmed international field missions to protect civilians has not received nearly the level of attention as R2P or the protection of civilians in Security Council discussions, the Centre for Humanitarian Dialogue makes the case that it has an important role to play. In studying the impact of international missions, such as UNAMET in East Timor, the Sri Lanka Monitoring Mission, and OHCHR's Human Rights Mission for Rwanda, the study concludes that field presence has the capacity to enhance the protection of civilians. That presence, they argue, is "not a passive presence for its own sake"; it requires key strategies of sustained diplomacy, visibility, encouragement and empowerment, convening and bridging, and public advocacy.[2] Those strategies merit further discussion and implementation in diverse situations.

We have to be much more precise about what protection means. The lack of a clear definition of a concept that has become so central to so many organizations is striking. Peacekeepers operating with a mandate to protect civilians have different understandings of protection, and child protection advocates have a much more focused approach to protection than most humanitarian actors. The humanitarian agencies that participate in the global protection cluster working group still engage in lengthy discussions about what protection means.[3]

The dominant definition of protection used by humanitarian actors was developed by ICRC in 1999 and subsequently endorsed by the Inter-Agency

Standing Committee. This definition provides an important rights-based frame for protection. This is a maximalist definition:

> The concept of protection encompasses: all activities aimed at ensuring full respect for the rights of the individual in accordance with the letter and the spirit of the relevant bodies of law, i.e. human rights law, international humanitarian law, and refugee law.[4]

The advantages of such a broad definition are many. It encompasses a broad array of rights. It is easier to get consensus on "all" activities and "full respect for the rights of the individual" than to deal with the always-contentious issue of prioritizing rights. This definition has already been accepted by the broadest array of humanitarian actors. It is a definition especially well-suited for humanitarians, who usually cannot physically protect people at risk of attack but can certainly ensure that at least some of the rights of the individual are upheld. The definition merges nicely with the concepts of human security and economic, social, and cultural rights and thus has a broader appeal than an exclusive focus on physical safety. It parallels developments in the human rights world, which has moved away from focusing exclusively on civil liberties to embracing the full range of economic, social, and cultural rights. Protecting people means more than ensuring their physical safety—it is no longer appropriate to conclude that rights have been upheld when people are physically secure but starving. Another advantage of sticking with the maximalist definition is that a great deal of conceptual work and many activities already have been done on the basis of this definition.

But there also are disadvantages to such an expansive definition of protection. First, it stretches the concept of protection so far that it incorporates almost all humanitarian and development work and risks becoming meaningless. It includes many measures that are simply good programming, such as consulting with beneficiaries and conducting comprehensive needs assessments. Relying on this broad definition also lets governments off the hook, including governments of countries affected by conflict, donor governments (which cannot stop attacks in Darfur, for example, but can contribute large sums of money to "do protection" in the field), and governments of the global South, which have an excuse not to forcefully support efforts to stop a conflict because, after all, humanitarian agencies are engaged in protection on the ground. The vast array of humanitarian activities now labeled as protection contributes to an illusion that the international community is making great progress in protecting people. Sadly, it also creates expectations within affected communities that humanitarians simply cannot meet.

Most humanitarian agencies working on protection issues have adopted the ICRC/IASC definition in one form or another. Reach Out, a refugee protection training initiative developed by NGOs, states that

> [r]efugee protection is all about ensuring that the rights of refugees are respected, secured and fulfilled. This goes well beyond urgent life-sustaining services including food, water and sanitation, health care and shelter. Protection is about making economic, social, cultural, civil and political rights real. Until they are provided effective national protection, refugees are threatened and may be unable to assert their rights for themselves.[5]

Child protection agencies, as noted in chapter 4, traditionally have focused on a narrower conception of protection that includes protection from violence, exploitation, abuse, and neglect. Beyond the child protection agencies, a few actors have moved to limit the definition of protection to focus on physical safety or security. Oxfam defines civilian protection as "efforts that improve the safety of civilians exposed to widespread threats of violence, coercion or deliberate deprivation."[6] The European Commission's Humanitarian Organization (ECHO) states that "protection activities are understood as non-structural activities aimed at reducing the risk for and mitigating the impact on individuals or groups of human-generated violence, coercion, deprivation and abuse in the context of humanitarian crises resulting from both man-made or natural disasters."[7]

What are the pros and cons of a narrower definition of protection? A definition focused on physical security—a minimalist definition—allows more focus and more accountability and directs attention toward those with the power to stop violence rather than toward humanitarian organizations, which work primarily with those affected by human rights violations. Operating under a narrower conception of protection, humanitarian agencies would seek to ensure that their programs—whether assistance or advocacy—do not endanger the physical safety of civilians. For example, by ensuring equitable and nondiscriminatory distribution of assistance, they would avoid contributing to conflicts within a community. In other words, their protection efforts would be based on the principle of "do no harm" and would support communities' efforts to protect themselves. Moreover, organizations could still incorporate a rights-based approach to programming while using a narrower definition of protection.

Conceptually, there are disadvantages to using a narrower definition. People can be physically secure and still experience serious violations of their human rights (for example, they may lack of access to medical care or their freedom of movement may be restricted). A focus on physical safety does not address the issue of dignity—a concept recognized as essential to humanitarian work that is incorporated in the broader definition of protection. A narrow definition also may be perceived as a retreat from the holistic approach to human rights that many humanitarian actors have incorporated into their work. Human rights activists strongly resist efforts to prioritize rights, insisting on the equal importance of them all. A narrower focus also directs attention away from humanitarian agencies and toward political actors, military forces, and police. There also is a danger that, after many years of efforts to mainstream protection into all assistance work, defining protection more narrowly would reinstate the former divisions between protection and assistance.

One way of addressing at least some of the definitional concerns would be to maintain the broad framework of the ICRC/IASC definition with its strong roots in human rights law but to recognize that, on the operational level, different orders and types of activities are needed and should be carried out by different actors. Humanitarian agencies cannot and should not be expected to do it all. Table 10-1 shows a typology of activities falling under the broad rubric of protection that was derived in part from the successful acceptance and use of the Operational Guidelines on Human Rights and Natural Disasters.[8] The guidelines recognize the holistic nature of all human rights but make the case that, as a practical matter, priorities must be set in the immediate aftermath of a natural disaster. When people are trapped under the rubble of an earthquake, they first need to be rescued, then they need life-saving assistance, and then they need education, voting rights, and so forth. While in conflict situations the threats to the physical security of people often are ongoing (and more complicated to address than pulling people out of collapsed buildings), there are parallels, in that the priority is placed on the protection of life, that can be useful in a broader formulation of protection.

Recommendations

While protection must remain a central focus of humanitarian effort, it must be based on the understanding that humanitarian agencies cannot protect people from physical violence. What humanitarian actors can do is to build up the ability of individuals and communities to withstand pressures; prevent assistance programs from contributing to conflict or making things worse for civilians; draw attention to unmet protection needs; warn

Table 10-1. *Typology of Protection Activities*

Order of protection	Examples of violations	Parties responsible for stopping violations	Tools
1: *Physical security or physical protection* Protecting the life and integrity of a person; ensuring personal safety and security	Physical violence, including attacks, killing, rape, and mutilation; forced displacement; ethnic cleansing; illegal deportation	*National actors* Threatened communities (by escaping, hiding, putting up resistance, making payoffs, and so forth); national governments, including police/military forces *International actors* Peacekeeping operations; ICRC (by negotiating to prevent attacks); UNHCR (by taking actions to prevent *refoulement*); unarmed civilian missions; humanitarians (by maintaining a presence, providing medical care, supporting community preparedness measures, and not exacerbating the conflict); human rights groups and media (by documenting violations)	Responsibility to protect; protection of civilians in mandates of peacekeeping operations; diplomacy; sanctions; legal protection; rule of law; unarmed field missions (International community needs to acknowledge that humanitarians usually cannot provide physical protection.)
2: *Humanitarian protection* Providing adequate access to basic requirements of life (food, water, medical care, shelter, and so forth); must be nondiscriminatory to prevent conflicts	Denial of access of humanitarians to communities; attacks on humanitarian workers; deliberate destruction of livelihoods; discrimination in providing assistance	*National actors* National governments and NSAs (by providing assistance directly and allowing access by humanitarian actors to affected populations) *International actors* Humanitarian agencies (by ensuring that appropriate assistance reaches people in need, adapting aid to reduce risk/empower communities); donor governments (by making funds available); media (by disseminating information on violations)	Humanitarian diplomacy for access to people affected; humanitarian funding; good humanitarian programs that incorporate the principle of "do no harm"
3: *Human rights* Protecting individuals' full enjoyment of all rights	Denial of education, livelihood, freedom of movement, political rights, cultural rights, compensation for property lost, dignity of the person, justice	*National actors* National governments; national human rights institutions; national and local civil society organizations *International actors* Humanitarian, development, and human rights organizations; justice mechanisms; media	Rights-based approach to development and assistance; human rights and election monitoring

individuals and communities of impending threats; and keep people alive while political actors find solutions to conflicts or until people affected by natural disasters are enabled to resume their lives.

It is important to distinguish between physical protection (or physical safety or security) and humanitarian protection, which is defined here as access to life-saving assistance but not to broader economic, social, and cultural rights. The protection of human rights is a broader concept, embodying the full range of human rights. Conceptually, of course, drawing the distinctions is problematic. For example, in order for civilians to be protected in conflict or postconflict situations, full respect for both the rule of law and women's and minorities' rights is needed. Efforts to promote human rights can contribute to a context that supports protection of civilians. But such longer-term efforts should not be seen as a substitute for meeting the immediate on-the-ground needs for physical protection of people living in dangerous situations.

Different actors have different roles to play in the various orders of protection. For those nonhumanitarian international actors working to provide physical protection of civilians—whether peacekeeping operations, military forces, or unarmed civilian monitoring or accompaniment missions—clear definitions and mandates are needed. Much more work is needed to understand the roles of national and local governments in protecting civilians at risk in their countries and in recognizing the ways that communities protect themselves. For example, recognition is needed of the role of remittances and other informal financial transfers in providing humanitarian protection to people at risk. A collection of good practices of community strategies of self-protection and an assessment of ways of minimizing community risk would be helpful.

Given the likelihood that natural disasters will increase in the future, much more attention is needed on the question of protection, both from the effects of natural hazards and from dangers that arise after a disaster occurs. Research is needed on the role of urban planners and municipal authorities in preparing for sudden-onset natural disasters; on the conceptual definition of slow-onset natural disasters; and on alternative ways of addressing the gap in international legal protection for those forced to leave their countries because of climate change–induced environmental factors. Guidelines should be developed to assist governments considering evacuation or relocation of populations from areas likely to be affected by natural disasters or climate change.

As national military and police forces have the resources needed to physically protect people and are likely to remain major humanitarian actors in the event of natural disasters and in at least some conflict situations, further dialogue is needed between them and humanitarian actors involved in such tasks. While useful civil-military guidelines have been developed, serious "cultural" differences remain between the groups that affect collaboration when emergencies do arise. Opportunities should be sought to provide for dialogue and training and for people from the different communities to get to know one another without the pressure of trying to sort out mandates and chains of command in the heat of an emergency. In the United States, Inter-Action and the U.S. Institute of Peace already have developed good relations with U.S. military personnel, but the regular meetings could be expanded and opportunities sought for participation in training opportunities offered by both groups. For example, while there have been efforts to "embed" humanitarian workers in military or mixed units, such as the provincial reconstruction teams (PRTs), it might be interesting to find ways of exposing military personnel to civilian relief operations as a way of enabling the military to better understand the unique institutional culture of these agencies.

While many humanitarians feel that the military is encroaching on "their" territory and is making their work more difficult by blurring the lines between military and civilian efforts, the fact is that the military is a major actor in humanitarian response in many countries and needs to be recognized as such. In discussing divisions of responsibility between the two groups, it could well be useful to focus on the different orders of protection outlined above; if the military is recognized as having the primary role in physical protection of civilians and humanitarian actors are recognized as having primacy in humanitarian protection, many of the current difficulties might be mitigated. Some of the confusion and resentment that exist today stems from the all-encompassing nature of the current definition of protection.

The unique role of ICRC needs to be recognized and respected by both humanitarian actors and broader political interests. It is in the interest of all parties to have an independent, neutral, and impartial actor that has access to all sides of a conflict. While every effort should be made to include ICRC in relevant coordination and information-sharing mechanisms, ICRC should continue to keep its distance from integrated missions, peacekeeping operations, national and global clusters, and other initiatives that might be perceived as compromising ICRC's neutrality. Other actors should not see ICRC's distance as representing anything other than a desire to protect its unique mandate and role in humanitarian operations.

International humanitarian law changes slowly, but given the pace of technological change taking place with robotic armaments, ICRC should convene a group of experts from the military research and international law communities to begin to identify the gaps in international humanitarian law resulting from the widespread use of those technologies. If the normal time frames for changing IHL prevail, any laws developed are likely to be obsolete by the time they are completed. Of course, ICRC and other international organizations should continue to promote adherence to international humanitarian law, refugee law, and human rights law. Respect for international normative standards is essential in creating an environment in which physical security, humanitarian protection, and human rights are upheld.

Protection of civilians has entered UN discourse, as outlined in chapter 6, but there are still ambiguities about what it means on both the conceptual and operational levels. OCHA can take number of steps to clarify what protection of civilians means for humanitarian action, specifically whether protection of civilians refers to physical protection, humanitarian protection, or protection of all human rights. OCHA should develop a very short summary statement of what it means to protect civilians that can be broadly used (and understood) by a range of communities and individuals in different contexts. OCHA then should collect the best practices in using humanitarian support for protection of civilians and, building on the workshops that it has previously organized, facilitate discussions with humanitarian actors on the ground on what protection of civilians means in practice.

UN peacekeeping operations should represent the first line of defense in protecting civilians in areas where they are deployed. But conceptual and practical confusion over what protection of civilians means in peacekeeping mandates is a serious limitation to protection in practice. The Department of Peacekeeping Operations (DPKO) should immediately and urgently develop doctrine to support the protection of civilians mandates already incorporated into most of its peacekeeping missions. The doctrine should be used not only in authorizing or renewing peacekeeping mandates, but also in reviewing the way in which existing peacekeeping operations function. Consistency should be sought on such issues as the "caveats" in protection of civilians mandates and training provided to both police and military units. Donor and troop-contributing governments and research institutes should provide support to DPKO's efforts to develop conceptual clarity regarding the mandates and their implementation.

UNHCR's expertise lies in refugee protection. Its willingness to assume new responsibilities with respect to protection of both conflict- and disaster-induced IDPs is a positive development in that it is seeking to fill an urgent gap in protection of vulnerable people. Some are concerned that assuming those responsibilities will weaken its ability to fulfill its core mandate of refugee protection, but a greater danger is that it will continue to see the new groups—IDPs and disaster-affected communities—simply as add-ons to its central work with refugees. Given the fact that there are at least four times more IDPs than refugees, that could become a case of the tail wagging the dog.

Working with IDPs and working with refugees usually require different approaches and skill sets, including different relationships with governments, different legal standards, and different solutions for IDPs. Working with IDPs presents greater difficulties with access and staff security and often a greater need for closer relations with military actors. Working with IDPs means that UNHCR will be expected to work in the context of integrated missions and will need to develop closer and probably different relationships with the Department of Political Affairs (DPA) and DPKO. Changing institutional cultures is difficult, but for UNHCR to meet the challenges of future displacement, it should reposition itself as primarily a displacement agency rather than a refugee agency. UNHCR should not change its name or mandate. Instead, it should see its primary role as providing humanitarian protection to IDPs and supporting efforts led by others to physically protect displaced populations. That change would require internal discussions of the implications of such a change and discussions with a range of other actors in order to move in that direction. Again, there is a role for donor governments, the nongovernmental community, and research institutions in supporting such a move.

Regarding the concept of responsibility to protect, the backlash against the concept has been so great that either the UN should make an all-out push to overcome the resistance (for example, by using the term anytime that diplomatic or other initiatives are taken to prevent widespread human rights abuses) or should quietly opt for a "strategic pause" until the political climate improves in the future. If the UN feels that the concept should be pursued now, emphasis should be placed on the role of national governments in exercising their sovereignty in a responsible fashion. As spelled out in chapter 6, that could include collecting good examples of the practice of sovereign responsibility in difficult situations and providing technical expertise with respect to development and implementation of national laws and policies. The only way that R2P can fulfill its intended purpose is to focus on prevention, to support what national governments can and should do to prevent widespread atrocities, and to back away from discussions of nonconsensual military intervention.

Regarding humanitarian reform, the most recent independent evaluation has clearly spelled out the issues that need to be addressed: more emphasis on securing and supporting strong humanitarian leadership and insisting that the cluster system include strong local or national participation. The evaluation also emphasized that the two weakest clusters are protection and early recovery.⁹ Clarifying the definition of protection as suggested above would help the protection cluster to be more effective in its efforts to coordinate protection work. Obviously, if actors have a different understanding of what they are trying to do in protecting people, then it is more difficult to coordinate their actions. And if the emphasis is on protecting people on the ground, much more emphasis needs to be placed on supporting humanitarian actors in national and local contexts.

The difficulties experienced in the early recovery cluster are symptomatic of the "silos" in which the international development and humanitarian bureaucracies operate. The difficulty in bridging the humanitarian relief–development gap, which has been recognized since the mid-1980s, has been discussed so often and has generated so many recommendations that many in the humanitarian community have little hope that the gap will ever be closed. Yet given the increasingly protracted nature of conflicts, the fact that recovery after natural disasters typically takes decades, and the likelihood that natural disasters are going to increase as a result of climate change, perhaps it is time to consider radical solutions. For example, perhaps donors should make their contributions to both development and humanitarian agencies contingent on genuine cooperation between the two. Donor governments also should examine ways of addressing the gap between relief and development operations in their own aid bureaucracies. If staff of humanitarian and development organizations are to move out of their silos, agency leadership needs to make that a priority and to build it into their performance review systems. Perhaps the leaders of UNHCR and UNDP, to use only two examples, should as a matter of routine visit each other's operations in the field and should agree to co-locate their offices in the field whenever possible. In order to move beyond the very different institutional cultures of humanitarian and development work, perhaps increasing staff secondments and exchanges between the organizations would be helpful. The early recovery cluster could facilitate workshops for staff of both humanitarian and development organizations to reflect together on ways of working in protracted emergency situations. Given the long history of discussions of the gap between relief and development, much more commitment, creativity, and "out-of-the-box" thinking are needed. Early recovery is a life-or-death issue in many parts of the world, and conventional approaches simply have not worked very well.

Research is needed on the relationship between early recovery, stabilization, and peacebuilding, highlighting the similarities and differences between these approaches. There is finally recognition that the immediate postconflict period (or transition, as it is sometimes called) is crucial—not just for peace and stability in the country or for the affected population, but for international order generally. Clarity on the conceptual level would be helpful, but efforts are also needed to increase collaboration between people from different organizational backgrounds, including the military, who are working to prevent postconflict societies from slipping back into conflict.

Regional organizations typically have been on the margins of international debates on humanitarian issues. Yet the experience of the Association of Southeast Asian Nations (ASEAN) in responding to Cyclone Nargis in Myanmar in 2008 and the leadership role played by the African Union in supporting peace operations on the continent as well as in developing the first binding treaty on internal displacement are indications of the role that they could play in humanitarian response in the future. Regional organizations should be more systematically brought into humanitarian discussions, particularly on questions of protection.

Donor governments have an especially important role to play in the question of protection of civilians. Not only do they provide the bulk of the financial resources to support humanitarian action, but their governments are major political actors and, in at least some cases, have decisionmaking roles as members of the UN Security Council. They should individually—and collectively through the Good Humanitarian Donorship Initiative—assess their understandings of protection, the costs and limitations of expecting humanitarian agencies to provide physical protection of civilians in dangerous situations, and the ways in which their governments are supporting physical protection, humanitarian protection, and protection of human rights.

NGOs should review their current policies and practices on protection in order to ensure that they are clear in their understanding of protection and that they are not promising more than they can deliver or being used as a cover for the lack of effective political action. There should be honest and self-critical reflection within organizations on whether it is possible for NGOs to provide physical protection to communities of concern and about the tensions between humanitarian principles and a protection-driven focus.

In addition to providing humanitarian assistance, a particular and perhaps unique contribution that NGOs can make is to build the capacity of communities to protect themselves. They can help strengthen community networks, leadership, and organizational capacity, enabling local civil society organizations to provide essential services within their communities. Casey Barrs has gone a step further to suggest that humanitarian actors can provide advisers to work with communities to prepare strategies that can physically protect them from armed groups, such as evacuation plans and alternative livelihood strategies. International NGOs need to work more closely with national and local NGOs in seeking more effective ways to support community-driven protection strategies.

In early July 2010, John Holmes, under secretary-general for humanitarian affairs and emergency relief coordinator, gave his last report to the UN Security Council. He said that in the decade since the council had first focused on the protection of civilians, there had been significant developments in the normative framework. "Nevertheless," he concluded. "I fear all too little has changed for the better on the ground in recent years." And that, too, is the conclusion of this study. In spite of the growing focus on protection within the humanitarian community, people are still in danger of losing their lives. In spite of a plethora of international standards, supranational criminal standards, guidelines, manuals, and training on sexual and gender-based violence, gender-based violence is still used against civilians as a weapon of war. Strong humanitarian agencies such as the UN Relief and Works Agency for Palestine Refugees in the Near East (UNRWA) could not protect Palestinian civilians in Gaza from Israeli attack in December 2008 and January 2009. Strong pressure from donors could not force the Sri Lankan government to evacuate civilians in its final offensive against the insurgents in 2009.

Humanitarian agencies have a vital role to play in protecting people affected by conflict and disasters, but they need to recognize that humanitarian protection is not the same as physical security. The international community needs to hold political leaders and leaders of armed groups accountable for protecting their own people; it should not expect humanitarian actors to take on that role. Recognizing the limits of humanitarian action may be a necessary first step toward measures that would ensure the physical protection of civilians.

Notes

Introduction

1. Ann Scott Tyson, "Gates Warns of Militarized Policy," *Washington Post*, July 16, 2008 (www.washingtonpost.com/wp-dyn/content/article/2008/07/15/AR200807 1502777.html). See testimony from Admiral Michael G. Mullen, chairman, Joint Chiefs of Staff: *House Armed Services Committee hearing on Security and Stability in Afghanistan and Iraq: Developments in U.S. Strategy and Operations and the Way Ahead*, 110th Cong., 2nd sess., September 10, 2008, and testimony from Robert M. Gates, secretary of defense, *Senate Armed Services Committee hearing on Current Situation in Iraq and Afghanistan*, 110th Cong., 2nd sess., September 23, 2008. Both are available at www.dod.gov/dodgc/olc/tstmny.html. See also General Stanley A. McChrystal, "Commander's Initial Assessment," August 30, 2009 (http://media.washingtonpost. com/wp-srv/politics/documents/Assessment_Redacted_092109.pdf).

2. General Petraeus's COIN guidance also states: "We cannot kill or capture our way to victory"; see *COMISAF's Counterinsurgency Guidance*, August 1, 2010, International Security Assistance Force/North Atlantic Treaty Organization, available at www.isaf.nato.int. For General McChrystal's COIN guidance, see *ISAF Commander's Counterinsurgency Guidance*, International Security Assistance Force/North Atlantic Treaty Organization, August 26, 2009 (www.nato.int/isaf/docu/official_texts/counter insurgency_guidance.pdf).

3. See Sadako Ogata, *Turbulent Decade: Confronting the Refugee Crises of the 1990s* (New York: W.W. Norton), p. 25.

4. International Commission on Intervention and State Sovereignty, *The Responsibility to Protect: Research, Bibliography, Background* (Ottawa: International Development Research Centre, December 2001), p. 178.

5. UN General Assembly, Resolution 60/1, 2005, World Summit Outcome, A/RES/60/1, October 24, 2005, paras. 138–39. For further information on the 2005 World Summit, see: www.un.org/summit2005.

6. Mary B. Anderson, *Do No Harm: How Aid Can Support Peace—Or War* (Boulder, Colo.: Lynne Rienner, 1999), pp. 11–12.

Chapter One

1. Oxford English Dictionary Online, draft revision, September 2010 (www. oed.com).

2. At the same time, states have used expulsion of dissidents, revocation of citizenship, and forced transfers of people as state-building techniques (for example, the deportation from their homes in Georgia to Central Asia of over 100,000 Meskhetian Turks in the 1940s by Joseph Stalin and Saddam Hussein's forced "Arabization" of Iraqi Kurdistan). In those cases, it seems that the state put the interests of state building above the need of protecting its citizens.

3. However, as shown in chapter 5, there are different and incomplete understandings of what that mandate means on the ground.

4. United Nations, "The Universal Declaration of Human Rights," December 10, 1948 (www.un.org/en/documents/udhr).

5. Sandra J. Maclean, David R. Black, and Timothy M. Shaw, "Introduction: A Decade of Human Security: What Prospects for Global Governance and New Multilateralisms?" in *A Decade of Human Security: Global Governance and New Multilateralisms* (Hampshire, United Kingdom: Ashgate, 2006), p. 4.

6. S. Neil MacFarlane and Yuen Foong Khong, *Human Security and the UN: A Critical History* (Indiana University Press, 2006).

7. Ann Scott Tyson, "Gates Warns of Militarized Policy: Defense Secretary Stresses Civilian Aspects of U.S. Engagement," *Washington Post,* July 16, 2008 (washington post.com/wp-dyn/content/article/2008/07/15/AR2008071502777.html).

8. As of May 31, 2010, excluding a political mission, the United Nations Assistance Mission in Afghanistan. Department of Peacekeeping Operations, "UN Peacekeeping Operations Background Note" (www.un.org/en/peacekeeping/bnote.htm).

9. See for example, Hugh Brody, *The Other Side of Eden: Hunters, Farmers, and the Shaping of the World* (New York: North Point Press, 2002), p. 40.

10. The four other pillars are *shahadah* (profession of faith); *salat* (prayer); *sawm* (fasting); and *hajj* (pilgrimage). In the case of *zakat* (meaning "purification" and "growth"), 2.5 percent of a person's wealth is given each lunar year, not to exceed a specific amount; only those who are able to give are required to do so.

11. Craig Calhoun, "The Imperative to Reduce Suffering," in Michael Barnett and Thomas G. Weiss, *Humanitarianism in Question: Politics, Power, Ethics* (Cornell University Press, 2008), pp. 73–97.

12. MacFarlane and Khong, *Human Security and the UN: A Critical History*, p. 2.

13. Benjamin G. Cloyd, *Haunted by Atrocity: Civil War Prisons in American Memory* (Louisiana State University Press, 2010), p. 62.

14. David P. Forsythe, *The Humanitarians* (Cambridge University Press, 2005), p. 15.

15. See Caroline Moorehead, *Dunant's Dream: War, Switzerland, and the History of the Red Cross* (London: HarperCollins, 1998) for a comprehensive and fascinating story of the Red Cross. Note that although Dunant was awarded the Nobel Peace Prize in 1901, he died a few years later, a pauper and a source of considerable controversy.

16. Over time, national societies have taken an expanded role in conflict-related activities, such as assisting wounded and sick soldiers and prisoners of war. That development has sometimes been controversial. See, for example, Christophe Lanord, "The Legal Status of National Red Cross and Red Crescent Societies," *International Review of the Red Cross,* December 31, 2000, pp. 1053–77 (www.icrc.org/Web/eng/siteeng0.nsf/html/57JQT9).

17. Francis Haller, "Famine in Russia: The Hidden Horrors of 1921" (www.icrc.org/web/eng/siteeng0.nsf/html/5RFHJY).

18. The Ottoman Empire, although it had acceded to the Geneva Convention of 1864, first used the red crescent on its ambulances during its war with Russia, 1876–78. The red crescent and the red lion and sun, used by what was then Persia, were recognized in 1929; Iran adopted the red crescent instead in 1980.The two symbols were recognized by the Geneva Conventions of 1949. The red crystal was formally sanctioned with the adoption of the third additional protocol to the 1949 Geneva Conventions in 2005. For more information, see the ICRC website (www.icrc.org).

19. Forsythe, *The Humanitarians*, 2005, p. 174.

20. Ibid., p. 35.

21. Please see Moorehead, *Dunant's Dream: War, Switzerland, and the History of the Red Cross,* for fascinating insights into Dunant's vision and the history of the movement.

22. The principle of unity stipulates that there can be only one Red Cross or Red Crescent Society in any country and that the national society must be open to all and carry out humanitarian work throughout its territory. The principle of voluntary participation stipulates that participation in the Red Cross/Red Crescent movement is voluntary and not prompted by the desire for personal gain. The principle of universality stresses that the Red Cross movement is a worldwide one in which all national societies have equal status and responsibilities.

23. "The Seven Fundamental Principles" (www.redcross.int/EN/fundprincips/namibiaseven.asp).

24. ICRC, "The Code of Conduct: Principles of Conduct for the International Red Cross and Red Crescent Movement and NGOs in Disaster Response Programmes" (www.ifrc.org/publicat/conduct/code.asp).

25. James Turner Johnson, "Maintaining the Protection of Non-Combatants," *Journal of Peace Research*, vol. 37, no. 4 (Special Issue on Ethics of War and Peace) (July 2000), pp. 421–48, citation on p. 427.

26. Ibid., p. 428.

27. Ibid., p. 429.

28. Hugo Grotius, *On the Law of War and Peace* (New York: Kessinger Publishing, 2004).

29. The Convention for the Amelioration of the Condition of the Wounded in Armies in the Field (Geneva, August 22, 1864) was replaced by the Geneva Conventions of 1906, 1929, and 1949 on the same subject. The convention of 1864 remained in force until 1966, when the last state party to it that had not yet acceded to a later convention (Republic of Korea) acceded to the conventions of 1949. The Convention for the Amelioration of the Condition of the Wounded and Sick in Armies in the Field (Geneva, July 6, 1906) was replaced by the Geneva Convention of 1929, but it remained in force until 1970, when the last state party to it that had not yet adhered to one of the later conventions (Costa Rica) acceded to the conventions of 1949. See further at www.icrc.org.

30. Citations from articles 55 and 56, respectively; Hague Convention of 1907.

31. See Anthony Dworkin, "The Geneva Conventions at Sixty," August 10, 2009 (www.crimesofwar.org).

32. ICRC, "The Geneva Conventions of 1949," September 2009 (www.icrc.org).

33. For further information, see the ICRC website (www.icrc.org/eng/ihl).

34. ICRC, "The Geneva Conventions at Sixty: Learning from the Past to Better Face the Future," August 2009 (www.icrc.org/web/eng/siteeng0.nsf/htmlall/geneva-convention-60-news-060809?).

35. See, for example, Calhoun, "The Imperative to Reduce Suffering," p. 91.

36. See Dworkin, "The Geneva Conventions at Sixty," 2009, p 3.

37. Although in pursuing their assistance functions, humanitarian agencies sometimes negotiate with governments and armed actors to allow relief to go through, as they did in Operation Lifeline Sudan and UNICEF's "days of tranquility" to permit vaccination of children.

38. The relationship between its prevention, protection, and assistance activities has been a source of considerable discussion within ICRC.

39. ICRC, *Strengthening Protection in War: A Search for Professional Standards,* 2001.

40. Ibid., pp. 21–22.

41. For example, Sphere Project, *Humanitarian Charter and Minimum Standards in Disaster Response,* 2004 (revision to be completed in 2011); ICRC, *Professional Standards for Protection Work Carried Out by Humanitarian and Human Rights Actors in Armed Conflict and Other Situations of Violence,* 2009; Inter-Agency Standing Committee, *Women, Girls, Boys, and Men: Different Needs, Equal Opportunities. Gender Handbook in Humanitarian Action,* 2006; UNHCR, *Operational Protection in Camps and Settlements: A Reference Guide of Good Practices in the Protection of Refugees and Other Persons of Concern,* 2006; Global Protection Cluster Working Group, *Handbook for the Protection of the Internally Displaced Persons* (March 2010).

42. Interview with author, ICRC, Geneva, 2010.

43. ICRC, "Professional Standards for Protection Work Carried Out by Humanitarian and Human Rights Actors in Armed Conflict and Other Situations of Violence."

44. There are many excellent surveys of refugee protection. See for example, Guy Goodwin-Gill and Jane McAdam, *The Refugee in International Law* (Oxford

University Press, 2007); Erika Feller, Volker Türk, and Frances Nicholson, *Refugee Protection in International Law: UNHCR's Global Consultations on International Protection* (Cambridge University Press, 2003); Niklaus Steiner, Mark Gibney, and Gil Loescher, *Problems of Protection: The UNHCR, Refugees, and Human Rights* (New York: Routledge, 2003).

45. See Burton F. Beers, "Protection of American Citizens Abroad," in *Encyclopedia of American Foreign Policy: Studies of the Principal Movements and Ideas*, vol. 3, edited by Alexander DeConde (New York: Charles Scribner's Sons, 1978), pp. 827–35, for a fascinating discussion of the various ways in which the U.S. government has sought to protect its citizens abroad over time.

46. See, for example, Kelly Kate Pease and David P. Forsythe, "Human Rights, Humanitarian Intervention, and World Politics," *Human Rights Quarterly*, vol. 15, no. 2 (1993), pp. 290–314, citation from p. 298.

47. Ibid., p. 298.

48. Gil Loescher, *Beyond Charity: International Cooperation and the Global Refugee Crisis* (Oxford University Press, 1993), p. 35. Loescher cites John Hope Simpson, *The Refugee Problem* (Oxford University Press, 1939) and Michael Marrus, *The Unwanted: European Refugees in the Twentieth Century* (Oxford University Press, 1992).

49. Loescher, *Beyond Charity*, p. 33. Also see Guy S. Goodwin-Gill, "The Politics of Refugee Protection," *Refugee Survey Quarterly*, vol. 27, no. 1 (2008), pp. 8–23.

50. Gooodwin-Gill, "The Politics of Refugee Protection," p. 12.

51. Loescher, *Beyond Charity*, p. 37.

52. Marrus, *The Unwanted*, especially pp. 135–38.

53. Gooodwin-Gill, "The Politics of Refugee Protection," p. 39.

54. Ibid., p. 41.

55. Cited by Loescher, *Beyond Charity*, p. 44.

56. Ibid., p. 46.

57. Marrus, *The Unwanted*.

58. Loescher, *Beyond Charity*, p. 50.

59. Ibid., p. 51.

60. For the full text, see UNHCR, "Convention and Protocol Relating to the Status of Refugees" (www.unhcr.org).

61. 1967 Protocol Relating to the Status of Refugees. For the full text, see UNHCR, "Convention and Protocol Relating to the Status of Refugees"(www.unhcr.org).

62. Ivor C. Jackson, "Some International Protection Issues Arising during the 1970s and 1980s with Particular Reference to the Role of the UNHCR Executive Committee," *Refugee Survey Quarterly*, vol. 27, no. 1 (2008), pp. 30–39.

63. See David Forsythe, "UNHCR's Mandate: The Politics of Being Non-Political," New Issues in Refugee Research, no. 33 (UNHCR, 2001) (www.unhcr.org).

64. UNHCR Statute, paragraph 8. The statute is annexed to UNGA Resolution 428 (V), December 1949.

65. Goodwin-Gill, "The Politics of Refugee Protection," 2008, p. 22.

66. Gil Loescher and James Milner, *Protracted Refugee Situations: Domestic and International Security Implications*, Adelphi paper 375 (2005), p. 24.

67. Rüdiger Schöch, "Afghan Refugees in Pakistan during the 1980s: Cold War Politics and Registration Practice," UNHCR New Issues in Refugee Research, research paper 157, June 2008 (www.unhcr.org).

68. Elizabeth Ferris, *Beyond Borders* (Geneva: World Council of Churches, 1993).

69. See Ninette Kelley, "International Refugee Protection: Challenges and Opportunities," *International Journal of Refugee Law* 19, no. 3 (2007), pp. 401–39.

70. Gil Loescher, *The UNHCR and World Politics: A Perilous Path* (Oxford University Press, 2001).

71. Sadako Ogata, *The Turbulent Decade: Confronting the Refugee Crises of the 1990s* (New York: W.W. Norton, 2005).

72. Loescher, *The UNHCR and World Politics*, p. 363.

73. Feller, Türk, and Nicholson, *Refugee Protection in International Law: UNHCR's Global Consultations on International Protection*.

74. Ogata, *The Turbulent Decade*.

75. International Council of Voluntary Agencies (ICVA), "NGO Statement on Agenda Item 4(i)—International Protection Note on International Protection," Standing Committee of the [UNHCR] Executive Committee of the High Commissioner's Programme, 27th meeting, June 24–26, 2003 (www.icva.ch). See other annual statements by NGOs at UNHCR's Executive and Standing Committee meetings (www.icva.ch).

76. Interestingly, Loescher recounts an initiative in the early 1990s when UNHCR, under Sadako Ogata, made a power play to become a super-agency addressing all humanitarian issues—an initiative that failed when UN Secretary-General Kofi Annan named a new under secretary-general position and changed the Department of Humanitarian Affairs to the Office for the Coordination of Humanitarian Affairs. Loescher, *The UNHCR and World Politics*, pp. 291–92.

77. Goodwin-Gil, "The Politics of Refugee Protection," p. 23.

78. Figure includes 4.6 million newly displaced by conflict in 2008. For figures on those displaced by conflict as of December 2009, see Internal Displacement Monitoring Center (IDMC), *Internal Displacement: Global Overview of Trends and Developments in 2009* (Geneva: Norwegian Refugee Council, May 2010), p. 8. For more on the natural disasters figure, which includes more than 20 million displaced by climate-related sudden-onset disasters, see IDMC/UN OCHA, *Monitoring Disaster Displacement in the Context of Climate Change*, September 2009, p. 9. Both publications are available at www.internal-displacement.org.

79. UNHCR, *2009 Global Trends: Refugees, Asylum-Seekers, Returnees, Internally Displaced and Stateless Persons*, June 15, 2010, p. 1 (www.unhcr.org/pages).

80. For a history of the way in which IDPs became an issue of international concern, see Thomas G. Weiss and David A. Korn, *Internal Displacement: Conceptualization and Its Consequences* (New York: Routledge, 2006).

81. Roberta Cohen and Francis M. Deng, *Masses in Flight* (Brookings, 1998), citation from p. 3.

82. Cecile Dubernet, *The International Containment of Displaced Persons* (Aldershot, United Kingdom: Ashgate Publishing, 2001).

83. Cohen and Deng, *Masses in Flight*, p. 4.

84. Jean-Philippe Lavoyer, "Refugees and Internally Displaced Persons: International Humanitarian Law and the Role of the ICRC," *International Review of the ICRC* 305 (1995), pp. 162–80 (www.icrc.org).

85. United Nations, "Guiding Principles on Internal Displacement," 1998 (www.brookings.edu/idp).

86. See Catherine Rey-Schyrr, "Le CICR et l'assistance aux réfugiés arabes palestiniens (1948–1950) [The ICRC and Assistance to Palestinian Arab Refugees (1948–1950)]," *Revue internationale de la Croix-Rouge* [International Review of the Red Cross] 843 (September 2001), p. 739–61 (www.icrc.org).

87. UNGA Resolution 212 (III), November 19, 1948.

88. See Lex Takkenberg, "UNRWA and the Palestinian Refugees after Sixty Years: Some Reflections." *Refugee Survey Quarterly*, vol. 28, nos. 2 and 3 (2009), pp. 253–59.

89. Ibid., pp. 253–54.

90. Article 7C of the UNHCR Statute provides that "the competence of the High Commissioner . . . shall not extend to a person . . . [w]ho continues to receive from other organs or agencies of the United Nations protection or assistance." The statute is annexed to UNGA Resolution 428 (V), December 1949. Cited by Lex Takkenberg, "The Protection of Palestine Refugees in Territories Occupied by Israel," *International Journal of Refugee Law*, vol. 3, no. 3 (1991), p. 418.

91. Takkenberg, "The Protection of Palestine Refugees in Territories Occupied by Israel," p. 418.

92. See Lex Takkenberg, *The Status of Palestinian Refugees under International Law* (Oxford University Press, 1998), p. 66.

93. UNGA Resolution 302 (IV), December 8, 1949, cited in Harish Parvathani, "Addressing the 'Protection Gap': UNRWA, UNHCR, and the Palestine Refugees," UNRWA Policy Analysis Unit, January 2004, p. 6. See further Lance Bartholomeusz, "The Mandate of UNRWA at Sixty," *Refugee Survey Quarterly*, vol. 28, nos. 2 and 3 (2009).

94. Loescher, *The UNHCR and World Politics*, p. 56.

95. Ernst Friedhelm, "Problems of UNRWA School Education and Vocational Training," *Journal of Refugee Studies*, vol. 2, no. 1 (1989), p.92.

96. UN Security Council, *Report Submitted to the Security Council by the Secretary-General in Accordance with Security Council Resolution 605 (1987)*, UN Doc. S/19443, January 21, 1989, para. 39.

97. Angela Williams, "UNRWA and the Occupied Territories," *Journal of Refugee Studies*, vol. 2, no. 1, (1989), pp. 156–62.

98. For an authoritative exposition of the agency's mandate in this regard, see Bartholomeusz, "The Mandate of UNRWA at Sixty," section 3.3.3 (www.unrwa.org).

99. Takkenberg, *The Status of Palestinian Refugees under International Law*, p. 280.

100. Ibid.

101. See for example, Takkenberg, *The Status of Palestinian Refugees under International Law*, p. 301, and UNRWA, *UNRWA Emergency Appeal 2008*, p. 24 (www.unrwa.org). There have been other very important expansions of UNRWA's protection role. In terms of staffing, in 2007 the UN General Assembly decided that the UNRWA post of senior policy protection adviser should be funded from the regular budget of the UN, which institutionalizes protection within UNRWA's operations. See Bartholomeusz, "The Mandate of UNRWA at Sixty,"section 3.3.3. See also UNRWA, *Medium-Term Strategy: 2010–2015*, in particular the fourth Human Development Goal: "Enjoy Human rights to the fullest extent possible."

102. ICRC, *Middle East and North Africa: ICRC Annual Report 2009*, May 2010, pp. 365–69 (www.icrc.org).

103. Harish Parvathani, "Addressing the 'Protection Gap': UNRWA, UNHCR, and the Palestine Refugees," Analysis Unit, January 2004, p. 3 (on file with the author).

104. See Human Rights Watch, *Rain of Fire: Israel's Unlawful Use of White Phosphorus in Gaza*, March 25, 2009 (www.hrw.org). See also James Hider and Sheera Frankel, "Israel Admits Using White Phosphorous in Attacks on Gaza," *The Times*, January 24, 2009 (www.timesonline.co.uk).

105. See Amnesty International, *Israel/Gaza: Operation "Cast Lead": Twenty-Two Days of Death and Destruction*, July 2009 (www.amnesty.org). The number of children was quoted in UN General Assembly, *Report of the United Nations Fact Finding Mission on the Gaza Conflict*, September 2009 [Goldstone Report](www2.ohchr.org).

106. Al-Haq, *'Operation Cast Lead': A Statistical Analysis*, August 2009 (www.alhaq.org).

107. UNRWA, "Attacks against the UN in Gaza Must Be Investigated," January 25, 2009 (www.unrwa.org); Human Rights Watch, *Rain of Fire*, p. 3. It is important to note that the provision of shelter in UNRWA installations was just one part of the agency's protection response during the operation. For example, UNRWA distributed food and relief items to the affected population and provided first aid to the wounded. Throughout the conflict, UNRWA also consistently and publicly called for restraint and for respect of the civilian population. Since then UNRWA has continued to provide support to almost 50,000 refugee families whose homes were destroyed or damaged, and the agency has continued to provide psychological support and counseling to those traumatized by the conflict. UNRWA also has continued to call for accountability for violations of international law.

108. See, for example, Secretary-General Board of Inquiry, May 15, 2009, A/63/855-S/2009/250, and UN General Assembly, *Report of the Commissioner-General of the United Nations: Relief and Works Agency for Palestine Refugees in the Near East, 1 January–31 December 2009*, A/65/13 (SUPP), December 31, 2009, paras. 38–39. See also Chris Gunness, "Letter to the Editor of *Yedioth* from UNRWA Spokesperson Rejecting False Allegations," January 8, 2010 (www.unrwa.org). The *Yedioth* is Israel's largest circulating newspaper.

109. UNRWA, "Attacks against the UN in Gaza Must Be Investigated."

110. UN General Assembly, *Report of the United Nations Fact Finding Mission on the Gaza Conflict*, paras. 75 and 1335 (www2.ohchr.org).

111. Ibid., paras. 108 and 1691.

112. Ibid., para. 1969(c).

113. See Nicholas Morris, "What Protection Means for UNRWA in Concept and Practice," March 2008 (www.unrwa.org).

Chapter Two

1. James Frederick Green, *The United Nations and Human Rights* (Brookings, 1956), p. 6.

2. Egon Schwelb, *Human Rights and the International Community: The Roots and Growth of the Universal Declaration of Human Rights*, 1948–1963 (Chicago: Quadrangle Books, 1964), p. 15.

3. Ibid. Also see J. Rehman, *The Weaknesses in the International Protection of Minority Rights* (The Hague: Kluwer Law International, 2000).

4. Schwelb, *Human Rights and the International Community*, pp. 15–16.

5. Green, *The United Nations and Human Rights*, p. 9.

6. For more on minorities, see Schwelb, *Human Rights and the International Community*, pp. 20–22.

7. Green, *The United Nations and Human Rights*, pp. 15–16. Also see Susan Waltz, "Universalizing Human Rights: The Role of Small States in the Construction of the Universal Declaration of Human Rights," *Human Rights Quarterly* 23 (2001), p. 48.

8. See for example, Green, *The United Nations and Human Rights*, pp. 4–5.

9. Paul Gordon Lauren, "'To Preserve and Build on Its Achievements and to Redress Its Shortcomings': The Journey from the Commission on Human Rights to the Human Rights Council," *Human Rights Quarterly* 29 (2007): 37–345.

10. Because of that tension, some of the advocates for a commission had argued for its membership to be composed of independent individual experts rather than representatives of governments, but that went too far for some states. It was finally decided that the commission would be made up of eighteen representatives of governments, acting on instructions from their capitals (a number that grew over the years to fifty-three).

11. Lauren, "'To Preserve and Build on Its Achievements and to Redress Its Shortcomings,'" p. 320.

12. Lauren, "'To Preserve and Build on Its Achievements and to Redress Its Shortcomings'"; Yvonne Terlingen, "The Human Rights Council: A New Era in UN Human Rights Work?" *Ethics and International Affairs* 21, no. 2 (2007), 167–78; Sibylle Scheipers, "Civilization vs. Toleration: The New UN Human Rights Council and the Normative Foundations of the International Order," *Journal of International Relations and Development* 10 (2007), 219–42.

13. United Nations, *A More Secure World: Our Shared Responsibility. Report of the Secretary-General's High-Level Panel on Threats, Challenges, and Change*, A/50/566, 2004, pp. 74–75, 91 (www.un.org/secureworld/).

14. Ibid., p. 74, para. 283.

15. "Annan Says Rights Body Harming UN," *BBC*, April 7, 2005 (http://news bbc.co.uk/1/hi/world/europe/4419333.stm). Also see Terlingen, "The Human Rights Council."

16. Secretary-General of the United Nations, *In Larger Freedom: Towards Security, Development, and Human Rights for All*, pp. 45–46, 61 (www.un.org/largerfreedom/).

17. UN General Assembly, A/RES/60/1, October 24, 2005, p. 33.

18. In the 170-4 vote to establish the council, only the United States, Israel, the Marshall Islands, and Palau voted against the resolution, with Iran, Venezuela, and Belarus abstaining. UN General Assembly, A/RES/60/251, April 3, 2006.

19. For more information, see FIDH Delegation to the UN, *The Universal Periodic Review Handbook*, 2009 (www.fidh.org).

20. See Office of the High Commissioner for Human Rights, "Special Procedures of the Human Rights Council" (www.ohchr.org).

21. For further information on OHCHR's activities, see www.ohchr.org.

22. For an effort to evaluate the effectiveness of NHRIs, see International Council on Human Rights Policy, *National Human Rights Institutions: Impact Assessment Indicators*, draft report for consultation (Geneva: ICHRP, 2005).

23. Report of the Secretary-General, September 9, 2002 (A/57/387).

24. United Nations, *Convention on the Prevention and Punishment of the Crime of Genocide*, Article 2 (http://untreaty.un.org).

25. Willliam Schabas, "The Genocide Convention at Fifty," USIP Special Report (Washington: USIP, 1999), p. 4.

26. Ibid., p. 6.

27. CBC News in Depth, "Sudan: The Genocide Convention," September 18, 2006 (www.cbc.ca/news/background/sudan/genocide-convention.html).

28. However, data are an issue: UNHCR obtained data for and was able to report on only 6.57 million stateless people in fifty-eight countries as of 2009. Still, that is a significant jump from the data UNHCR was able to provide in 2005, on only 1.45 million stateless people in thirty-three countries.

29. However, "the Final Act of the Convention calls upon states to 'consider sympathetically' the possibility of according *de facto* stateless persons the treatment which the Convention offers to *de jure* stateless people. (The Final Act makes reference to persons having renounced protection of their state for reasons considered valid. At the time this was equated with *de facto* statelessness.)," cited in Brad K. Blitz, *Statelessness, Protection, and Equality* (Refugee Studies Centre, University of Oxford, September 2009), p. 7. Other categories of stateless persons exist, such as "noncitizens" and "formerly deported persons," which some states and UNHCR use in designating stateless persons. Furthermore, "scholars have suggested that the term 'stateless' may be expanded to included internally displaced persons (IDPs) who are in conflict with the state and therefore unable to avail themselves of basic services or protection," cited in Blitz. Blitz cites scholars J. Boyden and J. Hart, "The Statelessness of the World's Children," *Children and Society* 21, no. 4 (2007), pp. 237–48.

30. Blitz, *Statelessness, Protection, and Equality,* table 1, p. 16. Also see Katherine Southwick and M. Lynch, *Nationality Rights for All: A Progress Report and Global Survey on Statelessness* (Washington: Refugees International, March 2009).

31. UNHCR, Division of International Protection, *UNHCR Action to Address Statelessness: A Strategy Note,* March 2010, p. 14.

32. UNGA Resolutions A/RES49/169, December 23, 1994, and A/RES/50/152, December 21, 1995.

33. For example, Executive Committee Conclusion No. 106 of 2006 on the "Identification, Prevention and Reduction of Statelessness and Protection of Stateless Persons."

34. UNHCR, "Progress Report on Statelessness 2009," EC/60/SC/CRP, May 10, 2009 (www.unhcr.org/4a48da519.html). The other three pillars include the refugee program, reintegration, and internally displaced persons (www.unhcr.org/cgi-bin/texis/vtx/search?page=search&docid=47d803c12&query=4%20pillars%20budget).

35. As of February 28, 2010. For a full list, see UNHCR (March 2010), Annex II, pp. 27–30.

36. For example, the Convention on the Political Rights of Women (1952), Convention on the Nationality of Married Women (1957) , Convention on Recovery Abroad of Maintenance (1956), and Convention on the Consent to Marriage (1962).

37. The United Nations Special Rapporteur on Violence against Women, Its Causes and Consequences, *Fifteen Years of the United Nations Special Rapporteur on Violence against Women, Its Causes and Consequences (1994–2009): A Critical Review* (www2.ohchr.org/english/issues/women/rapporteur/docs/15YearReviewofVAWMandate.pdf).

38. United Nations Security Council, Resolution 1325 (2000), S/RES/1325 (2000), October 31, 2000 (www.un.org).

39. IRIN, "Liberia: Rape in Liberia Still Goes Unpunished," December 4, 2006 (www.irinnews.org).

40. Lars Bolzman, "The Advent of Child Rights on the International Scene and the Role of the Save the Children International Union 1920–1945," *Refugee Survey Quarterly,* vol. 27, no. 4, 2009, pp. 26–36. For the text of the declaration, see www.un-documents.net/gdrc1924.htm.

41. Parliament of Canada, *Who's in Charge Here? Effective Implementation of Canada's International Obligations with Respect to the Rights of Children: Interim Report, Standing Senate Committee on Human Rights,* November 2005 (www.parl.gc.ca/).

42. Bolzman, "The Advent of Child Rights on the International Scene," p. 34. For the text of the 1948 declaration, see www.crin.org/resources/infoDetail.asp?ID=1309.

43. For the text of the 1959 declaration, see www.unicef.org/lac/spbarbados/Legal/global/General/declaration_child1959.pdf.

44. Convention on the Rights of the Child, Preamble (www.unicef.org/crc/).

45. UN Treaty Collection, *Multilateral Treaties Deposited with the Secretary-General,* Chapter IV (http://treaties.un.org/Pages/ParticipationStatus.aspx). See also Amnesty International, "Children's Rights—Convention on the Rights of the Child: Frequently Asked Questions (www.amnestyusa.org/children/crn_faq.html).

46. Convention on the Rights of the Child, Article 3(1).

47. United Nations General Assembly, A/RES/54/263, Annex I and II, May 25, 2002.

48. See UNICEF, "Convention on the Rights of the Child" (www.unicef.org/crc/index_30210.html).

49. UNICEF, "UNICEF's Mission Statement" (www.unicef.org/about/who/index_mission.html).

50. UNICEF, *Annual Report 2009*, pp. 38–39 (www.unicef.org/publications).

51. UNICEF, "Child Protection Information Sheet," 2006.

52. "A Preface by Graça Machel," in *Child Soldiers Global Report 2004* (Coalition to Stop the Use of Child Soldiers), pp. 9–10 (www.child-soldiers.org).

53. See Special Representative of the Secretary-General on Children in Armed Conflict (SRSGCAC), "The Machel Reports" (www.un.org/children/conflict/english/machelreports.html). See also a profile on Machel at http://people.brandeis.edu/~dwilliam/profiles/machel.htm.

54. Icelandic Human Rights Centre, "Elderly Persons" (www.humanrights.is/the-human-rights-project/humanrightscasesandmaterials/humanrightsconceptsideasandfora/Undirflokkur/elderlypersons/).

55. See, for example, the African Charter on Human and Peoples' Rights, the San Salvador Protocol, the Charter of Fundamental Rights of the European Union (2000), and the Revised European Social Charter. In 1982 the World Assembly on Aging adopted the Vienna International Plan of Action on Aging, which was endorsed in UN General Assembly Resolution 37/51. In 1991, in pursuance of the plan of action, the General Assembly adopted the UN Principles for Older Persons (Resolution 46/91), encouraging states to adopt certain principles relating to the status of the elderly, including the independence, participation, care, self-fulfillment, and dignity of elderly persons. A year later, the General Assembly adopted a Proclamation on Aging, and in 2002, the Second World Assembly on Aging adopted a Second International Plan of Action on Aging, which has as its objective the full realization of all human rights and fundamental freedoms of all older persons and the elimination of all forms of violence and discrimination against older persons.

56. Figures are according to Migrants Rights International, which notes that estimates exclude those with irregular status and who are undocumented (www.migrantwatch.org).

57. For example, a group of UN experts on migrants, racism, minorities, indigenous people, education, and cultural rights spoke out against the stringent immigration law (SB 1070) passed in April 2010 in the state of Arizona in the United States, saying that it could violate international human rights treaties to which the United States is a party. The statement cited the ICRMW and CERD. OHCHR, "Arizona: UN Experts Warn against 'a Disturbing Legal Pattern Hostile to Ethnic Minorities and Immigrants,'" May 10, 2010 (www.ohchr.org); Reuters, "U.N. Experts Join Criticism of Arizona Immigration Law," May 11, 2010 (www.reuters.com/article/idUSTRE64A42Z20100511).

58. For the full text of these instruments, see OHCHR, "International Law"(www2.ohchr.org).

59. See OHCHR, "Special Rapporteur on the Human Rights of Migrants" (www2. ohchr.org/english/issues/migration/rapporteur/index.htm).

60. Larry Minear, "Partnerships in the Protection of Refugees and Other People at Risk: Emerging Issues and Work in Progress," UNHCR New Issues in Refugee Research, Working Paper 13, July 1999, p. 4.

61. Jane McAdam, "The Refugee Convention as a Rights Blueprint for Persons in Need of International Protection," UNHCR New Issues in Refugee Research, Research paper no. 125, July 2006, p. 8.

62. Ibid., pp. 6–7.

63. See, for example, UNHCR's note on international protection, September 13, 2001, UN Doc A/AC.96/951, p. 4. See also UNHCR, "UNHCR and Human Rights," 1997 (www.unhcr.org/refworld/docid/3ae6b332c.html).

64. James Hathaway, "Reconceiving Refugee Law as Human Rights Protection, *Journal of Refugee Studies* 1991, p. 4; Brian Gorlick, "Human Rights and Refugees: Enhancing Protection through International Human Rights Law," UNHCR, New Issues in Refugee Research, Working Paper 30, October 2000.

Chapter Three

1. Inter-Agency Standing Committee (IASC), "Protection of Internally Displaced Persons," policy paper, December 1999, p. 7.

2. Casey A. Barrs, "Preparedness Support: Helping Brace Beneficiaries, Local Staff, and Partners for Violence," paper presented at the 2009 Conference on Protection, Refugee Studies Centre, 2009, p. 1 (www.rsc.ox.ac.uk); subsequently published in May 2010 under the auspices of the Cuny Center (www.cunycenter.org) .

3. UN Security Council, *Report of the Secretary-General to the Security Council on the Protection of Civilians in Armed Conflict*, S/2001/331, March 30, 2001, p. 18.

4. Sorcha O'Callaghan and Sara Pantuliano, "Protection Action: Incorporating Civilian Protection into Humanitarian Response," Humanitarian Policy Group Report 26 (London: Overseas Development Institute, December 2007), p. 9.

5. Sphere Humanitarian Charter 2010, section 2 (1), draft (www.sphereproject.org).

6. Barrs, "Preparedness Support," 2009, pp. 3–5.

7. Ibid., p. 13.

8. Ibid., p. 14.

9. Susanne Schmeidl, Alexander D. Mundt, and Nick Miszak, *Beyond the Blanket: Towards More Effective Protection for Internally Displaced Persons in Southern Afghanistan* (Washington: Brookings-Bern Project on Internal Displacement, May 2010), p. 67.

10. Alessandro Monsutti, "The Hazaras of Afghanistan: Coping through Emigration and Remittances," in *Forum: War, Money, and Survival* (Geneva: ICRC, 2000), pp. 72–73; Patricia Weiss-Fagen and Micah Bump, *Remittances in Conflict and Crises: How Remittances Sustain Livelihoods in War, Crises, and Transitions to Peace*, policy paper (New York: International Peace Academy, February 2006).

11. See *Internal Displacement and the Construction of Peace: Summary Report* (Washington: Brookings-Bern Project on Internal Displacement, February 2009) (www.brookings.edu/idp). Also, author's interview with Gimena Sánchez, Washington Office for Latin America, May 2010.

12. Schmeidl, Mundt, and Miszak, *Beyond the Blanket*, pp. 68–70.

13. Barrs, "Preparedness Support," 2009, p. 30. Also see Casey Barrs, *How Civilians Survive: A Preliminary Inventory,* Cuny Center, September 2010.

14. For Humanitarian Accountability Partnership, see www.hapinternational.org, and for more information on the Steering Committee, see the Inter-Agency Standing Committee website (www.humanitarianinfo.org/iasc).

15. *Moving beyond Rhetoric: Consultation and Participation with Populations Displaced by Conflict or Natural Disasters* (Washington: Brookings-Bern Project on Internal Displacement, October 2008).

16. See ABColombia, *Climate of Fear: Colombian Human Rights Defenders under Threat,* October 2009. See also Amnesty International, Center for International Policy, Human Rights Watch, "Call for Action against Escalating Threats and Attacks in Colombia," May 24, 2010 (www.reliefweb.int).

17. Geraldine Chatelard and Humam Misconi, "Regional Perspectives on Iraqi Displacement: A Research Report and Discussion Paper," in *Resolving Iraqi Displacement: Humanitarian and Development Perspectives, 18–19 November 2009, Doha, Qatar* (Washington: Brookings-Bern Project on Internal Displacement, April 2010), pp. 9–26 (www.brookings.edu/idp).

18. Mark Cutts, "Surviving in Refugee Camps," in *Forum: War, Money, and Survival* (Geneva: ICRC, 2000), pp. 62–68.

19. UN General Assembly, Resolution 46/182 (paragraphs 3–5), December 9, 1991.

20. A. Sat Obiyan, "A Critical Examination of the State versus Non-Governmental Organizations (NGOs) in the Policy Sphere in the Global South: Will the State Die as the NGOs Thrive in Sub-Saharan Africa and Asia?" *African and Asian Studies,* vol. 4, no. 3 (2005), pp. 301–325, idea from p. 319.

21. Ashraf Ghani and Clare Lockart, *Fixing Failed States: A Framework for Rebuilding a Fractured World* (New York: Oxford University Press, May 2008), p. 21.

22. Department for International Development (DFID), *Why We Need to Work More Effectively with Fragile States,* January 2005.

23. Robert Zoellick, "Fragile States: Securing Development," presentation at the International Institute for Strategic Studies, Geneva, September 2008, p. 4 (www.iiss.org).

24. Ibid., p. 4.

25. *New York Times,* "Aid Groups Say Sri Lanka Curtails Access to Refugees," May 22, 2009 (www.nytimes.com).

26. Mark Bradbury and Michael Kleinman, *Winning Hearts and Minds? Examining the Relationship between Aid and Security in Kenya* (Medford, Mass.: Feinstein International Center, Tufts University, April 2010), p. 70 (http://fic.tufts.edu/).

27. Paul Harvey, *Towards Good Humanitarian Government*, Humanitarian Policy Group Brief 37 (London: Overseas Development Institute, September 2009), p. 1.

28. Victoria Bannon and David Fisher, "Legal Lessons in Disaster Relief from the Tsunami, the Pakistan Earthquake, and Hurricane Katrina," *Insight* (newsletter of the American Society for International Law), vol. 10, no. 6 (March 2006).

29. Ivo Daalder and Paul Stares, "Saving Burma's People: The UN's Responsibility to Protect," *New York Times*, May 13, 2008. See also International Coalition for the Responsibility to Protect, "The Crisis in Burma" (www.responsibilitytoprotect.org).

30. Ann C. Richard, *Role Reversal: Offers of Help from Other Countries in Response to Hurricane Katrina* (Washington: Center for Transatlantic Relations, 2006).

31. Zoellick, "Fragile States: Securing Development," p. 8.

32. ICRC, "Professional Standards for Protection Work Carried Out by Humanitarian and Human Rights Actors in Armed Conflict and Other Situations of Violence," 2009, p. 31 (ww.icrc.org). See also ICRC, "Movement Policy on Internal Displacement," in *International Review of the Red Cross*, vol. 91, no. 875 (September 2009), p. 599 and p. 607.

33. Harvey, *Towards Good Humanitarian Government*, September 2009, p. 4.

34. Madeline Kristoff and Liz Panarelli, "Haiti: A Republic of NGOs?" Peace Brief (Washington: United States Institute of Peace, April 2010) (www.usip.org).

35. Inter-Agency Standing Committee, *Handbook for the Protection of Internally Displaced Persons*, June 2010 (www.unhcr.org/refworld/idps.html).

36. Draft circulated for comment by February 26, 2010, and available to members at www.icva.ch/doc00001880.html. Draft also available at http://oneresponse.info/Disasters/Haiti.

37. NGO Humanitarian Reform Project, *The Participation of NGOs in Cluster Co-Leadership at Country Level: A Review of Experience*, February 2010 (www.icva.ch).

38. Brookings-Bern Project on Internal Displacement, *Protecting the Displaced in Colombia: The Role of Municipal Authorities: A Summary Report* (Washington: Brookings-Bern Project on Internal Displacement, July 2009) (www.brookings.edu/idp).

39. Elizabeth Ferris, "In El Salvador, a Firsthand Look at Human Rights and Natural Disaster Response," Foreign Policy Trip Reports 12, Brookings, May 6, 2010 (www.brookings.edu/idp).

40. Didier Bigo, "Protection: Security, Territory, and Population," in *The Politics of Protection: Situations of Insecurity and Political Agency,* edited by Jef Huysmans, Andrew Dobson, and Raia Prokhovnik (New York: Routledge, 2006), pp. 85–86.

41. See Office for the Coordinator of Humanitarian Affairs, *Humanitarian Negotiations with Armed Groups* (http://ochaonline.un.org/).

42. ICRC, *Interpretive Guidance on Direct Participation in Hostilities* (www.icrc.org). Geneva Call, an NGO that aims to stop the use of land mines by nonstate actors, defines NSAs as "any armed actor operating outside State control that uses force to

achieve its political/quasi-political objective. Such actors include armed groups, rebel groups, liberation movements and de facto governments" (www.genevacall.org).

43. Lam Akol, "Operation Lifeline Sudan: War, Peace, and Relief in Southern Sudan," in *Choosing to Engage: Armed Groups and Peace Processes,* edited by Robert Ricigliano (London: Conciliation Resources, 2005) (www.c-r.org).

44. Hugo Slim, *Killing Civilians: Methods, Madness, and Morality in War* (Columbia University Press, 2008).

45. See Larry Minear and Hazel Smith, *Humanitarian Diplomacy: Practitioners and Their Craft* (Brookings, 2007).

46. Mary B. Anderson, *Do No Harm: How Aid Can Support Peace—or War* (Boulder: Lynne Rienner, February 1999), p. 39.

47. For an exploration of some of the complexities of nepotism and corruption, see Sarah Bailey, *Need and Greed: Corruption Risks, Perceptions, and Prevention in Humanitarian Assistance,* Humanitarian Policy Brief 32 (London: Overseas Development Institute, September 2008) (www.odi.org.uk).

48. Paul Harvey and others, *The State of the Humanitarian System: Assessing Performance and Progress: A Pilot Study* (London: Active Learning Network for Accountability and Performance and Overseas Development Institute, January 2010), p. 9.

49. Ian Smillie and Larry Minear, *The Charity of Nations: Humanitarian Action in a Calculating World* (Bloomfield, Conn.: Kumarian Press, 2004), p. 10; Martin Binder, "Humanitarian Crises and the International Politics of Selectivity," *Human Rights Review,* vol. 10 (2009), pp. 327–48.

50. Binder, "Humanitarian Crises and the International Politics of Selectivity."

51. Thomas G. Weiss and David A. Korn, *Internal Displacement: Conceptualization and Its Consequences* (London: Routledge, 2006), p. 24. See also Roberta Cohen and Francis M. Deng, *Masses in Flight: The Global Crisis of Internal Displacement* (Brookings, 1998), p. 10; and Roberta Cohen and Francis M. Deng, "Exodus within Borders: The Uprooted Who Never Left Home," *Foreign Affairs,* vol. 77, no. 4 (July–August 1998), p. 15.

52. Interview with author, December 2009.

53. Harvey and others, *The State of the Humanitarian System,* p. 9.

54. Cited in Smillie and Minear, *The Charity of Nations,* p. 146.

55. Ibid., p. 173.

56. "Ethics in International Relations Today," speech by U.S. Secretary of State Dean Acheson at Amherst College on December 9, 1964, cited in Eric A. Belgrad, "The Politics of Humanitarian Aid," in *The Politics of International Humanitarian Aid Operations,* edited by Eric A. Belgrad and Nitza Nachmias, pp. 3–19 (Westport, Conn.: Praeger, 1997), quote from p. 8.

57. C. A. Drury, R. A. Olson, and D. A. Van Belle, "The Politics of Humanitarian Aid: U.S. Foreign Disaster Assistance, 1964–1995," *Journal of Politics,* vol. 67, no. 2 (2005), p. 454.

58. Smillie and Minear, *The Charity of Nations,* p. 139.

59. See, for example, *One Year Later: Humanitarian Relief Sustains Change in Muslim Public Opinion: Results from a New Poll in Indonesia*, Terror Free Tomorrow (www.terrorfreetomorrow.org); Associated Press, "U.S. Hopes to Win Hearts and Minds in Pakistan," October 10, 2005 (www.msnbc.msn.com/id/9651378/); Reuters, "In Pakistan, Money Alone Can't Buy U.S. Love," March 26, 2010 (www.reuters.com/article/idUSTRE62P0PZ20100326).

60. Smillie and Minear, *The Charity of Nations*, p. 136

61. See USAID's website (www.usaid.gov). See also OFDA's "Protection Sector Updates: June 2010" (www.reliefweb.int).

62. Roberta Cohen and Dawn Calabia, "Improving the U.S. Response to Internal Displacement: Recommendations to the Obama Administration and the Congress" (Washington: Brookings-Bern Project on Internal Displacement, June 2010), p. 13; USAID, *USAID Assistance to Internally Displaced Persons Policy*, PD-ACA-558, October 2004.

63. Côte d'Ivoire, Democratic Republic of the Congo, Haiti, Indonesia, Iraq, Liberia, Pakistan, Somalia, Sudan, Tajikistan, and Zimbabwe. USAID/OFDA, Protection Sector Update—June 8, 2010 (www.reliefweb.int).

64. DFID, *Better Results for Poor People: Annual Report and Resource Accounts, 2008–09*, vol. 2, July 2009, p. 154 (www.dfid.gov.uk).

65. See DFID, *Better Results for Poor People*, vol. 1, July 2009 (www.dfid.gov.uk).

66. DFID, *Eliminating World Poverty: Making Globalisation Work for the Poor*, White Paper on International Development, presented to Parliament by the Secretary of State for International Development by Command of Her Majesty, December 2000, p. 33 (www.dfid.gov.uk).

67. Government of Sweden, *The Government's Humanitarian Aid Policy*, Comm. 2004/05:52, December 16, 2004, p. 6 (www.sweden.gov.se).

68. See information on START on DFAIT website (www.international.gc.ca).

69. DFAIT, "Legal and Physical Protection of Civilians," and DFAIT, "Children and Armed Conflict" (www.international.gc.ca).

70. Research conducted by the New York University Robert F. Wagner Graduate School of Public Service, as reported in Thomas Lum and others, "China's Foreign Aid Activities in Africa, Latin America, and Southeast Asia," Congressional Research Service, February 25, 2009 (www.fas.org).

71. Adele Harmer and Ellen Martin, *Diversity in Donorship: Field Lessons*, HPG Report 30 (London: Overseas Development Institute, March 2010) (www.odi.org.uk).

72. Lum and others, "China's Foreign Aid Activities in Africa, Latin America, and Southeast Asia."

73. DARA, *The Humanitarian Response Index 2009* (New York: Palgrave Macmillan, 2010).

74. Stephen Hansch, "Humanitarian Assistance Expands in Scale and Scope," in *Security by Other Means: Foreign Assistance, Global Poverty, and American Leadership*, edited by Lael Brainard (Washington: Center for Strategic and International Studies and Brookings Institution, 2007), pp. 121–60.

75. Refugees International, *U.S. Civil-Military Imbalance for Global Engagement: Lessons from the Operational Level in Africa*, July 2008, p. 1.

76. *NATO Handbook* (Brussels: NATO, 2001), pp. 128–129 (www.nato.int). See also CNN, "NATO Struggling to Keep Refugee Camps Sanitary," April 7, 1999 (www.cnn.com).

77. Christopher Spearin, "Private Security Companies and Humanitarians: A Corporate Solution to Securing Humanitarian Spaces?" *International Peacekeeping*, vol. 8, no. 1 (Spring 2001), pp. 20–43; quote on p. 374.

78. Sheila Herrling and Steve Radelet, "U.S. Foreign Assistance for the Twenty-First Century," Center for Global Development (www.cgdev.org).

79. Spearin, "Private Security Companies and Humanitarians," p. 374.

80. Steering Committee for Humanitarian Response, *Position Paper on Humanitarian-Military Relations*, January 2010, section 2.3 (www.reliefweb.int).

81. Reuben E. Brigety II, "Humanity as a Weapon of War," Center for American Progress, Sustainable Security Series, June 2008, p. 13.

82. Ibid., p. 6.

83. Department of the Army, *Civil Affairs Operations*, FM 3-05.40 (FM 41-10), September 2006, para. 3-23, p. 6

84. Bradbury and Kleinman, *Winning Hearts and Minds?* pp. 17–18.

85. *U.S. Army/Marine Corps Counterinsurgency Field Manual*, No. 3-24, December 2006, p. 40, para. 1–159 (www.usgcoin.org).

86. Ibid., p. 161, paras. 7 to 21.

87. Ibid., p. 192, paras. A-46 to A-47.

88. Cited by Paul D. Williams, *Enhancing Civilian Protection in Peace Operations: Insights from Africa*, research paper for the Africa Center for Strategic Studies (Washington: National Defense University Press, September 2010).

89. Ibid.

90. Victoria K. Holt, "The Military and Civilian Protection: Developing Roles and Capacities," *HPG Research Briefing* 2006, p. 1. See also Victoria Wheeler and Adele Harmer, *Resetting the Rules of Engagement: Trends and Issues in Military–Humanitarian Relations*, HPG Report 21, March 2006. Guidelines have been developed, including IASC, *Civil-Military Guidelines and Reference for Complex Emergencies*, March 2008; UN Department of Peacekeeping Operations (DPKO), *Civil-Military Coordination Policy*, September 2002; IASC, *Use of Military or Armed Escorts for Humanitarian Convoys: Discussion Paper and Non-Binding Guidelines*, September 2001; and UNHCR, *A UNHCR Handbook for the Military on Humanitarian Operations*, January 1995 (www.unhcr.org/refworld/civilians.html).

91. George F. Will, "The Military Tries Nation-Building in Afghanistan," *Washington Post*, May 9, 2010, (www.washingtonpost.com/wp-dyn/content/article/2010/05/07/AR2010050704311.html).

92. Hans Binnendijk and Patrick M. Cronin, *Civilian Surge: Key to Complex Operation* (National Defense University, December 2008), p. v (www.dtic.mil).

93. "Remarks by Secretary Gates at the 2008 Tribute Dinner," July 17, 2008 (www.usglc.org). Also see Robert M. Gates, "A Balanced Strategy: Reprogramming the Pentagon for a New Age," *Foreign Affairs*, (January–February 2009), pp. 29–40.

94. Interview with author, February 2010.

95. Binnendijk and Cronin, *Civilian Surge: Key to Complex Operations*, p. vi.

96. Ibid., p. vi.

97. Christopher Holshek, "Looking beyond the 'Latest and Greatest,'" in *The Pulse of Humanitarian Assistance*, edited by Kevin M. Cahill (New York: Fordham University Press and the Center for International Humanitarian Cooperation, 2007), p. 115.

98. Spearin, "Private Security Companies and Humanitarians," 2001, p. 375.

99. "Remarks by Secretary Gates at the 2008 Tribute Dinner," July 17, 2008 (www.usglc.org).

100. Charles F. MacCormack, "Coordination and Collaboration: An NGO View," in *The Pulse of Humantiarian Assistance*, edited by Cahill, p. 251.

101. Holshek, "Looking beyond the 'Latest and Greatest,'" in *The Pulse of Humantiarian Assistance*, edited by Cahill, p. 109.

102. See Bradbury and Kleinman, *Winning Hearts and Minds?* Also see Andrew Wilder, "Losing Hearts and Minds in Afghanistan," *Viewpoints: Afghanistan, 1979–2009: In the Grip of Conflict* (Washington: Middle East Institute, 2009) (www.mei.edu).

103. Larry Minear, *The U.S. Citizen-Soldier and the Global War on Terror: The National Guard Experience*, Feinstein International Center, Tufts University, September 2007; cited in Antonio Donini and others, *Humanitarian Agenda 2015: The State of the Humanitarian Enterprise*, Tufts University, March 2008, p. 16 (http://fic.tufts.edu).

104. Robert Egnell, "Between Reluctance and Necessity: The Utility of Military Force I Humanitarian and Development Operations," *Small Wars and Insurgencies*, vol. 19, no. 3 (2008), pp. 397–422.

105. For more on AFRICOM, see U.S. Government Accountability Office, *Defense Management: Actions Needed to Address Stakeholder Concerns, Improve Interagency Collaboration, and Determine Full Costs Associated with the U.S. Africa Command*, Report to the Subcommittee on National Security and Foreign Affairs, Committee on Oversight and Government Reform, House of Representatives, February 2009.

106. Dana Hedgpath and Sarah Cohen, "Money as a Weapon," *Washington Post*, August 11, 2008 (www.washingtonpost.com).

107. See, for example, Robert M. Perito, "The U.S. Experience with Provincial Reconstruction Teams in Iraq and Afghanistan," testimony before the House Armed Services Committee, Subcommittee on Oversight and Investigations, 110 Cong., October 17, 2007 (http://armedserrvices.house.gov); also see Joseph Christoff, *Provincial Reconstruction Teams in Afghanistan and Iraq*, October 1, 2008, U.S. Government Accountability Office (www.gao.gov).

108. Steering Committee for Humanitarian Response, *Position Paper on Humanitarian-Military Relations*, section 2.3.

109. See, for example, the Inter-Agency Standing Committee's "Guidelines on the Use of Military and Civil Defence Assets to Support United Nations Humanitarian Activities in Complex Emergencies" (March 2003, revised January 2006); "The ICRC and Civil-Military Relations in Armed Conflict" (2001); "Guidelines on the Use of Military and Civil Defence Assets in Disaster Relief: The 'Oslo Guidelines'" (May 1994, revised November 2006); InterAction's guidelines for U.S. NGOs: "Guidelines for InterAction Staff Relations with Military Forces Engaged in, or Training for, Peacekeeping and Disaster Response"; Steering Committee for Humanitarian Response, *Position Paper on Humanitarian-Military Relations*.

110. Steering Committee for Humanitarian Response, *Position Paper on Humanitarian-Military Relations*, section 2.4.

111. "Joint Statement by the Council and the Representatives of the Governments of the Member States meeting within the Council, the European Parliament, and the European Commission: The European Consensus on Humanitarian Aid," *Official Journal of the European Union*, January 30, 2008 (2008/C 25/01), p.1, para. 3.

112. Daniel Byman and others, *Strengthening the Partnership: Improving Military Co-ordination with Relief Agencies and Allies in Humanitarian Operations* (Santa Monica, Calif.: RAND, 2000), p. 84.

113. Several European aid agencies have joined together to conduct research under the Local to Global Protection Project. The first report on self-protection strategies in southeast Burma will be followed by case studies on Southern Sudan and Zimbabwe. See Ashley South with Malin Perhult and Nils Carstensen, "Self-Protection and Survival in Southeast Burma," *Humanitarian Exchange Magazine* 46 (March 2010). See also Ashley South, Malin Perhult, and Nils Carstensen, "Conflict and Survival: Self-Protection in Southeast Burma," Asia Programme Paper ASP PP 2010/04, Chatham House/Royal Institute of International Affairs, September 2010 (www.ashleysouth.co.uk).

114. South, Perhult, and Carstensen, "Self-Protection and Survival in Southeast Burma."

Chapter Four

1. Mark Dalton and others, *Study Four: Changes in Humanitarian Financing: Implications for the United Nations*, October 11, 2003, pp. iii, 24.

2. See UNFPA website (www.unfpa.org).

3. This was a problem with OCHA's predecessor, DHA, as well. See Gil Loescher, "The United Nations High Commissioner for Refugees in the Post–Cold War Era," in *The Politics of International Humanitarian Aid Operations*, edited by Eric A. Belgrad and Nitza Nachmias (Westport, Conn.: Greenwood Publishing Group, 1997), quote from p. 164.

4. Leon Gordenker, "By Way of Conclusion," in *The Politics of International Humanitarian Aid Operations*, edited by Belgrad and Nachmias, quote from p. 195.

5. SCHR, *Position Paper on Humanitarian-Military Relations*, January 2010, section 2.6, pp. 7-8.

6. On joint assessments, see James Darcy and Charles-Antoine Hofmann, *According to Need? Needs Assessment and Decision-Making in the Humanitarian Sector*, HPG Report 15, September 2003 (www.odi.org.uk).

7. See *Protection of Internally Displaced Persons*, Policy Paper Series 2 (2000), and *Strengthening Protection in War: A Search for Professional Standards* (ICRC, 2001).

8. ICRC, *Strengthening Protection in War*, p. 19.

9. Integrated Regional Information Networks (IRIN), "The Dangers of Promising to Protect," May 24, 2010 (www.irinnews.org).

10. UNHCR, *An Introduction to International Protection*, Teaching Module, no. 1, Geneva, 2005.

11. OCHA, *Guidance to Integrating Protection into Multi-Sectoral Assistance Response*, OCHA, May 18, 2009, draft (http://ochaonline.un.org).

12. Cited by Roberta Cohen and Francis M. Deng, *Masses in Flight: The Global Crisis of Internal Displacement* (Brookings, 1998), p. 187.

13. Ibid., p. x.

14. See for example, Brookings-Bern Project on Internal Displacement, *Reporting Crises: How the Media, Relief Agencies, and the Government Determine Humanitarian Response—Synthesis Report*, May 24, 2007, p. 4 (www.brookings.edu/events/2007/0524_idp_media.aspx). Also see Abby Stoddard, *Humanitarian Alert: NGO Information and Its Impact on U.S. Foreign Policy* (Bloomfield, Conn.: Kumarian Press, 2006).

15. Elizabeth Ferris, "The Role of Nongovernmental Organizations in the International Refugee Regime," in *Problems of Protection: The UNHCR, Refugees, and Human Rights*, edited by Niklaus Steiner, Mark Gibney, and Gil Loescher (New York/London: Routledge Press, 2003), pp. 117–40.

16. Rano Faroohar, "Where the Money Is?" *Newsweek*, September 5, 2005.

17. Ian Smillie and Larry Minear, *The Charity of Nations: Humanitarian Action in a Calculating World* (Bloomfield, Conn.: Kumarian Press, 2004), p. 184.

18. Wafula Okumu, "Humanitarian International NGOs and African Conflicts," *International Peacekeeping*, vol. 10, no. 1 (Spring 2003), pp. 120–37, quote from p. 127.

19. Cohen and Deng, *Masses in Flight*, pp. 207–08.

20. Jonathan Goodhand, *Aiding Peace: The Role of NGOs in Armed Conflict* (Boulder: Lynne Rienner, 2006), p. 173.

21. Mohammed Kidr, "Foreign NGOs Have Their Own Agenda," *Yemen Times*, October 5, 2006.

22. Joseph Mudingu, "How Genuine Are NGOs?" *New Times* (Rwanda), August 7, 2006 (www.globalpolicy.org).

23. Gil Loescher, "Refugees as Grounds for International Action," in *Refugees and Forced Displacement: International Security, Human Vulnerability, and the State*, edited by Edward Newman and Joanne van Selm (United Nations University Press, 2004), pp. 31–49.

24. Elizabeth Ferris, "The Potential Impact of the Indictment of Bashir on Darfur's Humanitarian Situation," September 26, 2008 (www.brookings.edu/idp).

25. Office of the United Nations High Commissioner for Human Rights, "Frequently Asked Questions on a Human Rights–Based Approach to Development Cooperation" (New York: United Nations, 2006), p. 15. This publication also contains an extensive bibliography of resources on rights-based approaches.

26. See for example, "Facts and Issues: A Rights-Based Approach to Development," in *Women's Rights and Economic Change*, no. 1, August 2003.

27. *Protecting Refugees: A Field Guide for NGOs* (Geneva: UNHCR, 2000).

28. A. Sat Obiyan, "A Critical Examination of the State versus Non-Governmental Organizations (NGOs) in the Policy Sphere in the Global South: Will the State Die as the NGOs Thrive in Sub-Saharan Africa and Asia?" *African and Asian Studies,* vol. 4, no. 3 (2005), pp. 301–25, cited on p. 307.

29. Interview with the author, October 2009.

30. Interview with the author, July 13, 2007.

31. Obiyan, "A Critical Examination of the State versus Non-Governmental Organizations (NGOs) in the Policy Sphere in the Global South," p. 311.

32. World Bank, *The World Bank Participation Sourcebook*, Appendix II: Working Paper Summaries: "Participation and Intermediary NGOs."

33. Cited by Cohen and Deng, *Masses in Flight*, 2008, p. 187.

34. Gita Steiner-Khamsi, "Too Far from Home? 'Modulitis' and NGOs' Role in Transferring Prepackaged Reform," *Current Issues in Comparative Education*, vol. 1, no. 1 (2002), p. 36.

35. Hazel Lang and Anita Knudsen, *Protracted Conflict: Protection Challenges for Humanitarian Agencies*, Briefing Paper, Australian Research Council, 2008, p. 10.

36. Nick Cater, "African NGOs Urge More Aid through Local Agencies," *Reuters AlertNet*, December 21, 2004.

37. Ibid.

38. Deng and Cohen, *Masses in Flight*, p. 205.

39. Lang and Knudsen, *Protracted Conflict*, 2008, p. 14.

40. Sorcha O'Callaghan and Sara Pantuliano, *Protective Action: Incorporating Civilian Protection into Humanitarian Response*, HPG Report 26, December 2007, pp. 21–37 (www.odi.org.uk).

41. Susan F. Martin and Elizabeth Moller, "NGOs and Practical Protection in Humanitarian Crises" (www.odihpn.org/report.asp?id=2493). Also see Diane Paul, *Protection in Practice: Field Level Strategies for Protecting Civilians from Deliberate Harm*, Network Paper 30 (London: Humanitarian Practice Network, 1999).

42. William Mclean, "Foreign NGOs Map New Route to African Legitimacy," Reuters, October 9, 2005.

43. See, for example, Lang and Knudsen, *Protracted Conflict*, pp. 13–14.

44. Brookings-Bern Project on Internal Displacement, "Not Time-Bound: National NGOs and Protection of Internally Displaced Persons," 2009.

45. Karin von Hippel, "Aid Effectiveness: Improving Relations with Islamic Charities," in *Understanding Islamic Charities*, edited by Jon B. Alterman and Karin von Hippel (Washington: Center for Strategic and International Studies, 2007) (http://csis.org/publication/understanding-islamic-charities).

46. Ibid.

47. See www.icva.ch.

48. Available at www.ifrc.org.

49. Cohen and Deng, *Masses in Flight*, 1998, p. 198.

50. See, for example, the Protection in Practice studies carried out between 2006 and 2008 by the Humanitarian Policy Group of the Overseas Development Institute (www.odi.org.uk); also see IASC, *Growing the Sheltering Tree: Protecting Rights through Humanitarian Action* (Geneva, 2002).

51. Greg Hansen, "Iraqis Defend Humanitarianism," *Iraq's Displacement Crisis: The Search for Solutions*, special issue of *Forced Migration Review* (June 2007), pp. 31–34.

52. O'Callaghan and Pantuliano, *Protective Action*. Also see "The 'Protection Crisis': A Review of Field-Based Strategies for Humanitarian Protection in Darfur," HPG Discussion paper, ODI, December 2006, p. 17.

53. See, for example, Interaction's Protection Working Group, *Making Protection a Priority*, 2004, p. 4 (www.interaction.org); and O'Callaghan and Pantuliano, *Protective Action*. Also see "The 'Protection Crisis,'" p. 17.

54. IRIN, "The Dangers of Promising to Protect," May 24, 2010.

55. Robbie Thomson, "Protection: A Good Idea Gone Too Far?" *Talk Back* (ICVA), vol. 8, no. 1, December 2006 (www.icva.ch).

56. Marc DuBois, "Protection: Fig Leaves and Other Delusions," *Humanitarian Exchange* 46 (March 2010), p. 2.

57. Ibid., pp. 3–4.

58. Rony Brauman, "When Suffering Makes a Good Story," in *Populations in Danger: A Médecins Sans Frontières Report*, edited by François Jean and Médecins Sans Frontières (London: John Libbey, 1992), p. 156.

59. Brookings-Bern Project on Internal Displacement, *Reporting Crises: How the Media, Relief Agencies, and the Government Determine Humanitarian Response*, p. 4.

60. Brauman, "When Suffering Makes a Good Story," 1992, p. 155.

61. Michael Ignatieff, "The Stories We Tell Television and Humanitarian Aid," *Social Contract*, vol. 10, no. 1 (Fall 1999), p. 6.

62. John C. Hammock and Joel R. Charny, "Emergency Response as Morality Play: The Media, the Relief Agencies, and the Need for Capacity-Building," in *From Massacres to Genocide: The Media, Public Policy and Humanitarian Crises*, edited by Robert I. Rotberg and Thomas G. Weiss (Cambridge, Mass.: World Peace Foundation, 1996), p. 116–19.

63. Peter Shiras, "Big Problems, Small Print: A Guide to the Complexity of Humanitarian Emergencies and the Media," in *From Massacres to Genocide*, edited by Rotberg and Weiss, p. 97.

64. Ibid., p. 109.

65. Steven Livingston, "Suffering in Silence: Media Coverage of War and Famine in the Sudan," in *From Massacres to Genocide,* edited by Rotberg and Weiss, p. 78.

66. Journalist participant, Brookings-Bern Project on Internal Displacement, *Reporting Crises: How the Media, Relief Agencies, and the Government Determine Humanitarian Response,* p. 4.

67. Ibid., p. 7.

68. Brookings-Bern Project on Internal Displacement, "Bloggers, Buzz, and Sound Bites: Innovative Media Approaches to Humanitarian Response," Washington, November 27, 2007 (www.brookings.edu/idp).

69. See, for example, Bev Godwin, "Government and Social Media," U.S. General Services Administration, March 2008 (www.usa.gov).

70. With thanks to Christopher Slagh for his background work on this issue.

71. Thomas Frank, "Social Media Play Part in Haiti's Recovery Efforts," *USA Today,* February 1, 2010 (www.usatoday.com/tech).

72. Google, "Google Crisis Response" (www.google.com/relief/haitiearthquake).

73. American Red Cross, "Haiti Update: Top-Line Facts" (http://newsroom.red cross.org).

74. James Poniewozik, "The Year of Charitainment," *Time,* December 19, 2005 (www.time.com/time/printout/0,8816,1142281,00.html). For more on celebrity involvement, see Darrell M. West, *Angelina, Mia, and Bono: Celebrities and International Development* (Brookings, 2007); Andrew Cooper, *Celebrity Diplomacy* (Boulder, Colo.: Paradigm Publishers, 2007).

75. Alex de Waal, "The Humanitarian Carnival: A Celebrity Vogue," *World Affairs* (Fall 2008).

76. Voilà, "T-Mobile, AT&T, and Sprint Donate for Earthquake Relief Effort" (www.voilacommunity.com).

77. For further information, see www.unglobalcompact.org.

78. Stephen Hopgood, "Saying 'No' to Wal-Mart?" in *Humanitarianism in Question: Politics, Power, Ethics,* edited by Michael Barnett and Thomas G. Weiss (Cornell University Press, 2008), p. 38.

79. Ibid., p. 120.

80. Christopher Spearin, "Private Security Companies and Humanitarians: A Corporate Solution to Securing Humanitarian Spaces?" *International Peacekeeping,* vol. 8, no. 1 (Spring 2001), pp. 20–43; quotation from p. 27.

81. Ibid., p. 27.

82. Tim Cross, "The Humanitarian Community and the Private Sector," in *The Pulse of Humanitarian Assistance,* edited by Kevin M. Cahill (New York: Fordham University Press and the Center for International Humanitarian Cooperation, 2007), p. 92.

83. Moshe Schwartz, *The Department of Defense's Use of Private Security Contractors in Iraq and Afghanistan: Background, Analysis, and Options for Congress,* Congressional Research Service, June 22, 2010, p. 4; August Cole, "Afghanistan Contractors

Outnumber Troops," *Wall Street Journal,* August 22, 2009 (http://online.wsj.com); Kevin Whitelaw, "Use of Private Security Grows in Iraq, Afghanistan," National Public Radio, October 1, 2009 (www.npr.org).

84. Congressional Research Service, *Private Security Contractors: Possible Legislative Approaches,* Report MM70119, cited by Schwartz, *The Department of Defense's Use of Private Security Contractors in Iraq and Afghanistan,* p. 5.

85. Schwartz, *The Department of Defense's Use of Private Security Contractors* , p. 5.

86. Afghanistan estimates include those not licensed; Schwartz, *The Department of Defense's Use of Private Security Contractors,* pp. 3–4, cites David Zucchino, "Private Security Forces Unnerve Afghans," *Chicago Tribune,* August 17, 2009. For Iraq estimates, Schwartz, p. 3, notes that the data are as of June 1, 2010, based on information provided by Lawrence Peter, director of the Private Security Company Association of Iraq, June 16, 2010.

87. Christopher Spearin, "Private, Armed, and Humanitarian? States, NGOs, International Private Security Companies, and Shifting Humanitarianism," *Security Dialogue,* vol. 39 (2008), pp. 363–82. Also see Peter Singer, *Corporate Warriors: The Rise of the Privatized Military Industry* (Cornell University Press, 2003).

88. Spearin, "Private, Armed, and Humanitarian?" p. 369.

89. DFID, *Operating in Insecure Environments,* September 2008 (www.nao.org.uk/publications).

90. Spearin, "Private, Armed and Humanitarian?" p. 369.

91. Abby Stoddard, Adele Harmer, and Victoria DiDomenico, *The Use of Private Security Providers and Services in Humanitarian Operations,* Humanitarian Policy Group Report 27 (London: Overseas Development Institute, October 2008), p.1.

92. Ibid., p. 2.

93. Alexander Van Taulleken, "No Justice without Power: The Case for Humanitarian Intervention," in *The Pulse of Humanitarian Assistance,* edited by Cahill, p. 73.

94. Simon Bagshaw and Diane Paul, "The Protection Survey," an advance version of a study prepared for the Internal Displacement Unit and the Brookings-SAIS Project on Internal Displacement and submitted to the Senior Inter-Agency Network on Internal Displacement and the Inter-Agency Standing Committee, October 2003; Diane Paul and Simon Bagshaw, *Protect or Neglect? Toward a More Effective United Nations Approach to the Protection of Internally Displaced Persons,* Brookings-SAIS Project on Internal Displacement and OCHA/Affairs/Inter-Agency Internal Displacement Division, November 2004 (www.brookings.edu/idp); Norwegian Refugee Council, *The Future of the Collaborative Response to Internal Displacement: NRC Position Paper,* August 2005 (www.internal-displacement.org). See also IASC, Protection of Internally Displaced Persons: Inter-Agency Standing Committee Policy Paper, December 6, 1999 (www.icva.ch/); IASC, *IDP Policy Package: Implementing the Collaborative Response to Situations of Internal Displacement: Guidance for UN Humanitarian and/or Resident Coordinators and Country Teams,* 2004 (www.icva.ch/).

95. See IASC, *IDP Policy Package.*

96. ICVA, "The Humanitarian Coordinator System: Issues for Discussion," informal paper prepared by the ICVA secretariat, September 2005 (www.icva.ch); IASC, "Strengthening the Humanitarian Coordinator's System: What Is Our Goal and How Do We Get There?" April 24, 2006 (www.humanitarianreform.org).

97. ICVA, "IOM, Darfur, and the Meaning of Undermining (MoU)" *Talk Back*, vol. 6–1, October 4, 2004 (www.icva.ch).

98. OCHA, *Humanitarian Response Review*, 2005 (www.reliefweb.int).

99. Ibid., p. 9.

100. Tim Morris, "UNHCR, IDPs, and Clusters," *Forced Migration Review* 25 (2006): 54–56 (www.fmreview.org).

101. Sue Graves and others, *Lost in Translation: Managing Coordination and Leadership Reform in the Humanitarian System,* Humanitarian Policy Brief 27 (London: Overseas Development Institute, July 2007), p. 5.

102. IASC, "Operational Guidance for Cluster Lead Agencies on Working with National Authorities," draft, January 2009; IASC, "Draft Operational Guidance for Cluster Lead Agencies on Working with National Authorities," 76th IASC Working Group, New York, April 7–9, 2010, available for members only at (www.icva.ch).

103. See for example, IASC, "Protection of Internally Displaced Persons." Inter-Agency Standing Committee Policy Paper, December 2009.

104. "Protection Mainstreaming: Concept Paper for the Protection Cluster Working Group," 2009, pp. 4–5.

105. Protection Cluster Working Group Matrix, summary page, March 31, 2010.

106. See "IASC Operational Guidance on the Concept of 'Provider of Last Resort'" (www.humanitarian reform.org).

107. Terms of Reference for Generic Sector/Cluster Leads at Country Level (www. humanitarianreform.org).

108. Graves and others, *Lost in Translation*, p. 3.

109. Abby Stoddard and others, *Cluster Approach Evaluation—Final,* November 2007 (www.humanitarianoutcomes.org).

110. *Synthesis Report: Review of the Engagement of NGOs with the Humanitarian Reform Process,* 2009 (www.icva.ch/ngosandhumanitarianreform.html), p. 4.

111. Summary of presentation by Jock Baker, "Session 1: Clusters and Accountability," in *Report on Meeting: Accountability to Affected Populations within the Clusters: Where We Are and What Next,* NGOs and Humanitarian Reform Project, March 17, 2010, p. 2 (www.hapinternational.org/).

112. IASC, "Strengthening the Humanitarian Coordinator's System: What Is Our Goal and How Do We Get There?" IASC Principals Meeting, Geneva, April 24, 2006.

113. *Synthesis Report.*

114. OCHA, "Humanitarian Response Review," August 2005 (www.reliefweb.int).

115. See www.globalhumanitarianplatorm.org for more information.

116. Available at www.icva.ch.

117. *Synthesis Report*, p. 5.

118. ICRC, *Strengthening Protection in War: A Search for Professional Standards,* 2001.

Chapter Five

1. There were other crises in the 1990s to be sure, notably the displacement of Kurds and the establishment of a safe area in Northern Iraq in 1991, the rise of the Taliban in Afghanistan, and conflict in Zaire/Democratic Republic of the Congo, but the three mentioned here were especially important in terms of the international humanitarian system.

2. Jeffrey Clark, *Famine in Somalia and the International Response: Collective Failure*, U.S. Committee for Refugees Issue Paper, November 1992. For further information on the background of the Somali conflict, see also Africa Watch, *A Government at War with Its Own People: Testimonies about the Killings and the Conflict in the North*, 1990. See also J. Hirsch and R. Oakley, *Somalia and Operation Restore Hope: Reflections on Peacemaking and Peacekeeping* (Washington: U.S. Institute of Peace Press, 1995). Also J. G. Sommer, *Hope Restored? Humanitarian Aid in Somalia, 1990–1994* (Washington: Refugee Policy Group, 1994).

3. Clark, *Famine in Somalia*, p. 13.

4. See Taylor B. Seybolt, *Humanitarian Military Intervention: The Conditions for Success and Failure* (SIPRI/Oxford University Press, 2007).

5. Ibid.

6. On a positive note, in spring 2010, the Bosnian government adopted a strategy on internal displacement that may make it easier for IDPs to find durable solutions.

7. John Borton and others, *Evaluating International Humanitarian Action* (New York: Zed Books, 1996).

8. Seybolt, *Humanitarian Military Intervention*, p. 77.

9. See William A. Schabas, *The UN International Criminal Tribunals: The Former Yugoslavia, Rwanda, and Sierra Leone* (Cambridge University Press, August 2006). See also Antonio Cassese, *The Oxford Companion to International Criminal Justice* (Oxford University Press, 2009). Specifically on the ICC, see Bruce Broomhall, *International Justice and the International Criminal Court: Between Sovereignty and the Rule of Law* (Oxford University Press, 2003).

10. Interview with author, January 2010.

11. William J. Durch, *UN Peace Operations and the Brahimi Report* (Washington: Stimson Center, October 2001), p. 2. For more on the shortcomings of UN peace-keeping operations, see David M. Malone and Ramesh Thakur, "UN Peacekeeping: Lessons Learned?" *Global Governance*, vol. 7, no. 1 (2001), pp. 11–17.

12. UN, *Report of the Panel on United Nations Peace Operations*, A/55/305 – S/2000/809 [Brahimi Report], August 2000 (www.un.org/peace/reports/peace_operations). Also see German Institute for International and Security Affairs, "The Brahimi Report: Overcoming the North–South Divide," 6th International Workshop, Berlin, June 29–30, 2001; Thierry Tardy, "The Brahimi Report: Four Years On," Workshop, Geneva Centre for Security Policy, June 20–21, 2004; William J. Durch and others, *The Brahimi Report and the Future of Peace Operations* (Washington: Henry L. Stimson Center, December 2003).

13. Ibid., p. xi.

14. Ibid., para. 63, p. 11.

15. UN Security Council Resolution 1327 (www.un.org/Docs/sc/).

16. Durch and others, *The Brahimi Report and the Future of UN Peace Operations.*

17. UN, *Report of the Panel on United Nations Peace Operations*, p. ix.

18. Humanitarian Policy Network, "The Brahimi Report—Politicising Humanitarianism," *Humanitarian Exchange Magazine*, no. 18 (March 2001), p. 39.

19. UN General Assembly, *Renewing the United Nations: A Programme for Reform,* Report of the Secretary-General, A/15/950, 14 July 1997.

20. Ibid., paras. 116–117.

21. Kathleen M. Jennings and Anja T. Kaspersen, "Introduction: Integration Revisited," in *International Peacekeeping*, vol. 15, no. 4 (2008), p. 445.

22. UN, *Note from the Secretary-General: Guidance on Integrated Missions*, January 17, 2006, p. 2 (www.reliefweb.int).

23. Espen Barthe Eide and others, *Report on Integrated Missions: Practical Perspectives and Recommendations*, Independent Study for the Expanded UN Executive Committee on Humanitarian Affairs Core Group, May 2005. See particularly Adele Harmer, "Integrated Missions: A Threat to Humanitarian Security?" *International Peacekeeping*, vol. 15, no. 4 (2008), pp. 528–39; in the same issue, see also "Introduction: Integration Revisited" and "Conclusion: Integration Going Forward," both by Kathleen M. Jennings and Anja T. Kaspersen, pp. 443–52 and pp. 582–87; Cedric de Coning, *Coherence and Coordination in United Nations Peacebuilding and Integrated Missions—A Norwegian Perspective, Security in Practice*, no. 5, 2007.

24. Eide and others, *Report on Integrated Missions*, pp. 14–15.

25. Ibid., p. 12.

26. Ibid., p. 13.

27. Ibid., p. 34. UN, *Note from the Secretary–General: Guidance on Integrated Missions*, p. 3.

28. Eide and others, *Report on Integrated Missions*, p. 37.

29. Ibid., p. 14.

30. Funmi Olonisakin, "'Military Humanitarianism' in Liberia," in Larry Minear and Hazel Smith, *Humanitarian Diplomacy: Practitioners and Their Craft* (Tokyo: United Nations University Press, 2007), p. 270.

31. Ibid.

32. Cited by Eide and others, *Report on Integrated Missions*, p. 29.

33. UN, *Note from the Secretary-General: Guidance on Integrated Missions*, p.1.

34. Harmer, "Integrated Missions: A Threat to Humanitarian Security?" p. 537.

35. Jacques Forster, "An ICRC Perspective on Integrated Missions," speech delivered at Conference on Integrated Missions, Oslo, May 30–31, 2005 (www.icrc.org/web/eng/siteeng0.nsf/html/6DCGRN).

36. See Kenneth M. Manusama, "Current Legal Developments: The High-Level Panel Report on Threats, Challenges, and Change and the Future Role of the United Nations Security Council," *Leiden Journal of International Law*, vol. 18, no. 03

(2005), pp. 605–20; Shepard Forman, "High-Level Panel on Threats, Challenges, and Change: Recommendation to Establish a Peacebuilding Commission," roundtable on "Building a New Role for the United Nations: The Responsibility to Protect," Fundación para las Relaciones Internacionales y el Diálogo Exterior, Madrid, Spain, June 3, 2005; Marco Odello, "Commentary on the United Nations' High-Level Panel on Threats, Challenges, and Change," *Journal of Conflict and Security Law*, vol. 10, no. 2 (2005), pp. 231–62; One World Trust, "An Analysis of the Report on the Secretary-General's High-Level Panel on Threats, Challenges, and Change," April 2005.

37. UN, *A More Secure World: Our Shared Responsibility. Report of the Secretary-General's High-Level Panel on Threats, Challenges, and Change*, A/59/565 (New York: United Nations, December 2004), p. 2 (www.un.org/secureworld/report2.pdf).

38. Ibid., paras. 231–38, pp. 62–63.

39. See United Nations, *Delivering as One: Report of the Secretary-General's High-Level Panel on UN System-wide Coherence in the Areas of Development, Humanitarian Assistance, and the Environment*, A/61/583 (New York: 2007) (www.un.org/events/panel); Soledad Aguilar and Elisa Morgera, "'Delivering as One' for the Environment: Reflection on the Report of the UN Panel on System-wide Coherence," *Environmental Policy and Law*, vol. 37, no. 4 (2007), pp. 271–80; Bonnie Kettel, "Challenging on the Margin: Gender Equality and the UN Reform Process," *Third World Quarterly*, vol. 28, no. 5 (2007), pp. 871–86; Brett D. Schaefer, "Time for a New United Nations Peacekeeping Organization," February 13, 2007 (www.heritage.org); Jonas Von Freiesleben, "System–Wide Coherence," in *Managing Change at the United Nations*, edited by Estelle Perry (New York: Center for UN Reform, 2008), pp. 37–54.

40. UNDP, "Delivering as One Pilots" (www.undg.org/index.cfm?P=163).

41. UN, "The Deputy Secretary-General Remarks on the Independent Evaluation of the 'Delivering as One' Pilot Countries," New York, March 10, 2010 (www.un.org/ga/president/64/issues/swcdsg100310.pdf).

42. See UN Department of Public Information, "Independent Evaluation of 'Delivering as One' to Generate New Insights, Says Deputy Secretary-General as High-Level Tripartite Conference Concludes," DSG/SM/511, June 16, 2010 (www.un.org/News/Press/docs/2010/dsgsm511.doc.htm).

43. "Delivering as One: Lessons Learned and Way Forward," remarks of UNDP Chair, Helen Clark, on the occasion of the High–Level Tripartite Conference on "Delivering as One: Lessons Learned and Way Forward," June 14, 2010, Hanoi, Viet Nam (www.undp.org/about/helen–clark.shtml).

44. Paul Collier, *The Bottom Billion: Why the Poorest Countries Are Failing and What Can Be Done about It* (Oxford University Press, April 2007), p. 27.

45. Alex J. Bellamy, *A Responsibility to Protect: The Global Effort to End Mass Atrocities* (Cambridge, United Kingdom: Polity Press, 2009), pp. 185–94.

46. ActionAid, CAFOD, Care International, *Consolidating the Peace? Views from Sierra Leone and Burundi on the UN Peacebuilding Commission* (London: ActionAid/CAFOD/CARE, 2007).

47. Pablo de Grieff, "Theorizing Transitional Justice," in *Transitional Justice,*

edited by Melissa Williams and Rosemary Nagy, in *Nomos* L (Yearbook of the American Society for Political and Legal Philosophy) (forthcoming).

48. ICC (www.icc–cpi.int/Menus/ICC/Situations+and+Cases/). See also ICRC, *International Criminal Tribunals, International Review of the Red Cross*, vol. 88, no. 861 (March 2006).

49. Beth K. Dougherty, "Right–Sizing International Criminal Justice: The Hybrid Experiment at the Special Court for Sierra Leone," *International Affairs*, vol. 80, no. 2 (2004), p. 312.

50. For basic information on a comparison of the three hybrid panels, see www. icclr.law.ubc.ca/Site%20Map/ICC/ExperiencesfromInternationalSpecialCourts.pdf.

51. Phillip Rapoza, "Judging East Timor," *International Judicial Monitor*, vol. 3, no. 2 (2008) (www.judicialmonitor.org).

52. UN News Centre, "Timor-Leste, not UN, Indicts Indonesian General for War Crimes," February 26, 2003 (www.globalsecurity.org); David Cohen, *Indifference and Accountability: The United Nations and the Politics of International Justice in East Timor*, East-West Center Special Reports 9 (June 2006), pp. 91–104 (www.eastwest center.org); Megan Hirst and Howard Varney, *Justice Abandoned? An Assessment of the Serious Crimes Process in East Timor* (New York: International Center for Transitional Justice, June 2005), pp. 10–11 (www.ictj.org).

53. IRIN, "Sierra Leone: 'Forced Marriage' Conviction a First," February 26, 2009 (www.irinnews.org); Human Rights Watch, "Landmark Convictions for Use of Child Soldiers," June 20, 2007 (www.hrw.org).

54. U.S. Department of State, "The U.S. Provides $4.5 Million to Fund Special Court for Sierra Leone Trial of Charles Taylor," Media Note, Office of the Spokesman, Washington, November 23, 2010 (www.state.gov).

55. Richard H. Cooper and Juliette Voïnov Kohler, "Moving from Military Intervention to Judicial Enforcement: The Case for an International Marshals Service," in *Responsibility to Protect: The Global Moral Compact for the 21st Century*, edited by Richard H. Cooper and Juliette Voïnov Kohler (New York: Palgrave Macmillan, 2008), p. 249–52.

56. Rule of Law Sub-Working Group, Protection Cluster Working Group, "Concept Paper—Early Responses on Access to Justice for Displaced Communities Interagency Participatory Assessment Tool," Geneva, July 1, 2009.

57. UNDP, "Programming for Justice: Access to All: A Practitioner's Guide to a Human Rights–Based Approach to Justice," 2005, p. 5. Also see UNDP–BCPR, *Strengthening the Rule of Law in Conflict and Post-Conflict Situations, a Global UNDP Programme for Justice and Security, 2008–2011*.

58. United Nations Department of Peacekeeping Operations, *United Nations Peacekeeping Operations: Principles and Guidelines* [Capstone Doctrine], 2008. See Victoria K. Holt, Glyn Taylor, and Max Kelley, *Protecting Civilians in the Context of UN Peacekeeping Operations: Successes, Setbacks and Remaining Challenges*, independent study jointly commissioned by the Department of Peacekeeping Operations and the Office for the Coordination of Humanitarian Affairs, November 2009 (www.unprh.unlb.org), p. 95.

59. Security Council Report, *Cross-Cutting Report No. 2: Protection of Civilians*, October 14, 2008, p. 6 (www.securitycouncilreport.org/site/c.glKWLeMTIsG/b.4664099/k.1776/CrossCutting_Report_No_2brProtection_of_Civiliansbr14_October_2008.htm), hereafter referred to as *Cross-Cutting Report No. 2*.

60. UN General Assembly/UN Security Council, *The Causes of Conflict and the Promotion of Durable Peace and Sustainable Development in Africa: Report of the Secretary-General, S/1998/318 – A/52/871*, April 13, 1998 (www.un.org/ecosocdev/geninfo/afrec/sgreport/main.htm).

61. *Cross-Cutting Report No. 2*, p. 6.

62. See also OCHA, "Institutional History of Protection of Civilians" (http://ochaonline.un.org).

63. *Cross-Cutting Report No. 2*, p. 7.

64. Egeland presented his ten-point action plan at the semi-annual briefing to the Security Council on the protection of civilians in armed conflict. See United Nations Security Council, S/PV.4877, December 9, 2003 (www.securitycouncilreport.org).

65. *Cross-Cutting Report No. 2*, p. 8.

66. Holt, Taylor, and Kelley, *Protecting Civilians in the Context of UN Peacekeeping Operations*, pp. 59–60.

67. *Cross-Cutting Report No. 2*, p. 26.

68. Ibid., p. 10.

69. Security Council Report, *Cross-Cutting Report No. 4: Protection of Civilians in Armed Conflict*, October 30, 2009, p. 4 (www.securitycouncilreport.org/site/c.glKWLeMTIsG/b.5556213/k.BED2/CrossCutting_Report_No_4brProtection_of_Civilians_in_Armed_Conflictbr30_October_2009.htm), hereafter referred to as *Cross-Cutting Report No. 4*.

70. UN Department of Public Information, "In Presidential Statement, Security Council Reaffirms Commitment to Protection of Civilians in Armed Conflict, Adopts Updated Aide Memoire on Issue," UN Security Council, SC/10089, 6427th Meeting, November 22, 2010 (www.un.org).

71. *Cross-Cutting Report No. 2*, p. 28.

72. *Cross-Cutting Report No. 4*, p. 19.

73. Ibid., p. 20.

74. See the provisional record of the meeting: UN Security Council, November 11, 2009, S/PV.6216 (www.securitycouncilreport.org).

75. *Cross-Cutting Report No. 4*, p. 18.

76. *Cross-Cutting Report No. 2*, p. 9.

77. Ibid., p. 22.

78. Funmi Olonisakin, *Peacekeeping in Sierra Leone: The Story of UNAMSIL* (Boulder, Colo.: Lynne Rienner, 2007). See also United Nations, Eighth Report of the Secretary-General on the United Nations Mission to Sierra Leone (2000), para. 60.

79. For example, see Erin A. Weir, *Greater Expectations: UN Peacekeeping and Civilian Protection* (Washington: Refugees International, July 2009).

80. Victoria K. Holt, "The Military and Civilian Protection: Developing Roles and Capacities," Humanitarian Policy Group Research Briefing (London: Overseas Development Initiative, 2006), p. 1.

81. For example, in a May 2008 conference on women targeted or affected by armed conflict, participants noted that missions are increasingly mandated to protect civilians, yet "this may not consistently be interpreted to encompass sexual violence"; *Cross-Cutting Report No. 2.*

82. Victoria K. Holt and Joshua G. Smith, *Halting Widespread or Systematic Attacks on Civilians: Military Strategies and Operational Concepts,* report from an International Experts Workshop, Accra, Ghana, February 14–16, 2007 (Washington: Henry L. Stimson Center, Spring 2008).

83. *Cross-Cutting Report No. 2,* p. 23.

84. Ibid., p. 24.

85. Holt and Smith, *Halting Widespread or Systematic Attacks on Civilians,* p. 27.

86. Ibid., p. 28.

87. Ibid., p 29.

88. *Cross-Cutting Report No. 2,* pp. 24–25.

89. Ibid., pp 36–37.

90. UN Security Council, Resolution 1894, S/RES/1894 (2009), November 11, 2009, para. 22.

91. Holt, Taylor, and Kelley, *Protecting Civilians in the Context of UN Peacekeeping Operations.*

92. Ibid., p. 57.

93. Ibid., see p. 170.

94. Ibid., see pp. 148–49.

95. Ibid., see p. 72.

96. Holt, Taylor, and Kelley, *Protecting Civilians in the Context of UN Peacekeeping Operations,* p. 192.

97. *Cross-Cutting Report No. 2,* p. 27.

98. Interview by author with a representative of a humanitarian organization, New York, February 2, 2010.

99. See for example, Anneke Van Woudenburg, "MONUC: A Case for Peacekeeping Reform," testimony before the U.S. House Committee on International Relations, Subcommittee on Africa, Global Human Rights, and International Operations, March 1, 2004 (www.hrw.org).

100. See, for example, Human Rights Watch, "Eastern DR Congo: Surge in Army Atrocities," November 2, 2009 (www.hrw.org).

101. Holt, Taylor, and Kelley, *Protecting Civilians in the Context of UN Peacekeeping Operations,* p. 315.

102. Interview with author, January 2010.

103. From OCHA, "Institutional History of Protection of Civilians."

104. Interview with Pierre Gentile, ICRC, March 2010.

105. ICRC, *Enhancing Protection for Civilians in Armed Conflict and Other Situations of Violence* (Geneva: 2008), p. 9.

106. Ibid.

107. Interview with ICRC staff by author, March 2010.

108. ICRC, *Professional Standards for Protection Work Carried Out by Humanitarian and Human Rights Actors in Armed Conflict and Other Situations of Violence* (Geneva, 2009) (www.icrc.org).

109. Holt, Taylor, and Kelley, *Protecting Civilians in the Context of UN Peacekeeping Operations*, p. 36.

110. Interview with author, NGO representative, February 2010.

111. Oxfam (GB) on behalf of Oxfam International, *Beyond the Headlines: An Agenda for Action to Protect Civilians in Neglected Conflicts* (London: 2003).

112. Oxfam, *Beyond the Headlines*, p. 6.

113. Ibid., p. 3.

114. *Protection of Civilians in Armed Conflict: Strategy of the Federal Department of Foreign Affairs (FDFA), 2009–2012* (Bern, Switzerland: 2009) (www.eda.admin.ch/eda/en/home/doc/publi/ppese.html#ContentPar_0013).

115. Ibid., p. 18.

116. U.K. Foreign and Commonwealth Office, *U.K. Government Strategy on the Protection of Civilians in Armed Conflict*, March 2010 (www.fco.gov.uk/en/about–us/publications–and–documents/publications1).

117. Ibid., p. 3.

118. The phrase "humanitarian intervention" was actually used as early as 1840, in reference to interventions to stop atrocities in Greece in 1827 and in Syria in 1860. Bernard Kouchner popularized the expression *droit d'ingérence* or the "right to intervene," launching the concept with legal scholar Mario Bettati at a conference in 1967. But the term *ingérence* connotes "interference" more than "intervention" in French, and it was met with hostility in the global South. Gareth Evans, *The Responsibility to Protect: Ending Mass Atrocity Crimes Once and for All* (Brookings, 2008), p. 32.

119. UN General Assembly, Resolution 2131, A/6014, December 21, 1965.

120. Javier Pérez de Cuéllar, *Report of the Secretary-General on the Work of the Organization*, UN Doc. A/46/1, September 13, 1991, p. 5.

121. Kelly Kate Pease and David P. Forsythe, "Human Rights, Humanitarian Intervention, and World Politics," *Human Rights Quarterly*, vol. 15, no. 2 (1993), p. 307.

122. Evans, *The Responsibility to Protect: Ending Mass Atrocity Crimes Once and for All*, p. 36.

123. Francis M. Deng and others, *Sovereignty as Responsibility: Conflict Management in Africa* (Brookings, 1996), pp. 27–33. Also see Francis M. Deng, *Protecting the Dispossessed* (Brookings, 1993), pp. 14–20.

124. Cited in Lee Feinstein and Erica DeBruin, "Beyond Worlds: U.S. Policy and the Responsibility to Protect," in *Responsibility to Protect*, edited by Cooper and Kohler, p. 182.

125. Kofi Annan, *We the Peoples: The Role of the United Nations in the 21st Century* (New York: United Nations, April 2000).

126. Co-chairs were Gareth Evans (Australia) and Mohamed Sahnoun (Algeria, diplomat and veteran UN Africa adviser). The members included Fidel V. Ramos (Philippines, former president); Cyril Ramaphosa (South Africa, ANC head); Eduardo Stein (Guatemala, foreign minister); Ramesh Thakur (India, scholar); Lee Hamilton (United States); Klaus Naumann (Germany, NATO general); Michael Ignatieff and Gisele Cote–Harper (Canada, human rights and conflict experts); Vladimir Lukin (Russian diplomat, parliamentarian); and Cornelio Sommaruga (former president, ICRC).

127. Gareth Evans, "The International Responsibility to Protect: The Tasks Ahead," address to Africa's Responsibility to Protect, Center for Conflict Resolution, Cape Town, April 23, 2007 (www.crisisgroup.org/home/indexcmf?id=4801&1=1), p. 3.

128. International Commission on Intervention and State Sovereignty (ICISS), *The Responsibility to Protect* (Ottawa: International Development Research Centre, December 2001).

129. Ibid.

130. Alex J. Bellamy, *A Responsibility to Protect: The Global Effort to End Mass Atrocities*, 2009.

131. Ibid., pp. 68–69. See also Feinstein and DeBruin, "Beyond Worlds," in *Responsibility to Protect*, edited by Cooper and Kohler, p. 183.

132. The OAU, established in 1963, was replaced by the AU in July 2002. Article 4(h) of the African Union Constitutive Act stipulates: "The right of the Union to intervene in a Member State pursuant to a decision of the Assembly in respect of grave circumstances, namely: war crimes, genocide and crimes against humanity" (www.africa–union.org).

133. Bellamy, *A Responsibility to Protect*, pp. 53–59.

134. See the World Summit Outcome Document: UN General Assembly, *Resolution 60/1, 2005 World Summit Outcome*, A/RES/60/1, 24 October 2005 (www.un.org).

135. Strauss Ekkehard, *The Emperor's New Clothes? The United Nations and the Implementation of the Responsibility to Protect* (Nomos, 2009), pp. 15–16, cited in Naomi Kikoler, "Responsibility to Protect," keynote paper delivered at an international conference, "Protecting People in Conflict and Crisis: Responding to the Challenges of a Changing World," sponsored by the Humanitarian Policy Group and Oxford University's Refugee Studies Centre, Oxford, United Kingdom, September 2009, p. 6 (www.rsc.ox.ac.uk/PDFs/keynotepaperkikoler.pdf).

136. Kikoler, "Responsibility to Protect," p. 6. "Serious harm" is from ICISS, *The Responsibility to Protect*.

137. Evans, "The International Responsibility to Protect: The Tasks Ahead," p. 6.

138. William Pace and others, "Realizing the Responsibility to Protect in Emerging and Acute Crises: A Civil Society Proposal for the United Nations," in *Responsibility to Protect*, edited by Cooper and Kohler, p. 233.

139. UN, "Statement by Edward Luck, Special Adviser to the UN Secretary-General at the Thematic Dialogue of the General Assembly on the Responsibility to Protect," July 23, 2009 (www.eyeontheun.org).

140. See Kikoler, "Responsibility to Protect," for details on criticisms of R2P during the debate as well as areas of consensus. UN General Assembly, *Resolution 63/308, The Responsibility to Protect,* A/RES/63/3087, October 2009. Paragraphs 138 and 139 of the World Summit Outcome Document pertain to limiting R2P's scope to four of the most serious human rights violations (genocide, war crimes, ethnic cleansing, and crimes against humanity) instead of adopting ICISS's criterion of "serious harm." See also World Summit Outcome Document: UN General Assembly, *Resolution 60/1, 2005 World Summit Outcome,* A/RES/60/1, October 24, 2005.

141. UN General Assembly, *Implementing the Responsibility to Protect: Report of the UN Secretary-General,* A/63/677, January 12, 2009. Citation is from p. 9.

142. Stanley Foundation, *Implementing the Responsibility to Protect,* January 15–17, 2010, pp. 3–4.

143. See International Coalition for the Responsibility to Protect, "The Crisis in Burma" (www.responsibilitytoprotect.org/index.php/crises/crisis–in–burma).

144. Cited in International Coalition for the Responsibility to Protect, "The Crisis in Burma." See also Ivo Daalder and Paul Stares, "Saving Burma's People: The UN's Responsibility to Protect," *New York Times,* May 13, 2008.

145. See International Coalition for the Responsibility to Protect, "The Crisis in Burma." See also Roberta Cohen, "Reconciling R2P with IDP Protection," *Global Responsibility to Protect,* vol. 2 (March 2010) pp. 15–37.

146. Gareth Evans, "The Responsibility to Protect in Environmental Emergencies," presentation to the American Society of International Law, 103rd Annual Meeting, Washington, D.C., March 26, 2009 (www.gevans.org/speeches.html).

147. Ibid., p. 4.

148. Roberta Cohen, "The Burma Cyclone and the Responsibility to Protect," Congressional Briefing on Security for a New Century, July 21, 2008 (www.brookings.edu/idp).

149. Cohen, "Reconciling R2P with IDP Protection," pp. 21–22; Roberta Cohen, "The Responsibility to Protect: The Human Rights and Humanitarian Dimensions," presented at the Panel on the Responsibility to Protect and Human Rights, Harvard Human Rights Journal Annual Symposium, February 20, 2009 (www.brookings.edu/idp).

150. Elisabeth Lindenmayer and Josie Lianna Kaye, "A Choice for Peace? The Story of 41 Days of Mediation in Kenya," International Peace Institute, August 2009, p. 4, cited in Kikoler, "Responsibility to Protect," 2009, p. 8.

151. See *The Economist,* "An Idea Whose Time Has Come and Gone?" July 23, 2009.

152. Kikoler, "Responsibility to Protect," pp. 7–8.

153. Adele Simmons and April Donnellian, "Reaching across Borders: Philanthropy's Role in the Prevention of Atrocity Crimes," in *R2P: The Global Moral Compact for the 21st Century,* edited by Cooper and Kohler, pp. 170–171.

154. Samantha Power, "Foreword," in *R2P: The Global Moral Compact for the 21st Century*, edited by Cooper and Kohler, pp. ix–xi.

155. Kenneth Roth, "Was the Iraq War a Humanitarian Intervention? And What Are Our Responsibilities Today?" pp. 103–113, in *Responsibility to Protect*, edited by Cooper and Kohler, p. 110.

156. See Eye on the UN for statements by Luck and other observers (www.eye ontheun.org).

157. One of the few exceptions is the 2009 Security Council resolution on Protection of Civilians, which reaffirms R2P.

Chapter Six

1. H. Eugene Douglas, "The Problem of Refugees in a Strategic Perspective," *Strategic Review* (Fall 1982), p. 20.

2. Erik Abild, *Creating Humanitarian Space: A Case Study of Somalia*, New Issues in Refugee Research, Research Paper 184 (UNHCR, December 2009).

3. Cited by Johanna Grombach Wagner, "An IHL/ICRC Perspective on Humanitarian Space," *Humanitarian Exchange Magazine* 32 (December 2005) (www.odihpn.org).

4. Inter-Agency Standing Committee, *Background Document: Preserving Humanitarian Space, Protection, and Security*, 2008, p. 1(www.unhcr.org).

5. Vicky Tennant and others, *Safeguarding Humanitarian Space: A Review of Key Challenges for UNHCR*, PDES/2010/01, February 2010 (www.reliefweb.int).

6. Ibid., p. 6.

7. Inter-Agency Standing Committee, *Background Document*, pp. 3–4. Also see Adele Harmer and Joanna Macrae, *Humanitarian Action and the Global War on Terror: A Review of Trends and Issues*, Humanitarian Policy Group Report (London: Overseas Development Institute, July 2003), p. 9.

8. Tennant and others, *Safeguarding Humanitarian Space*, p. 24.

9. NGO interview with author, January 2010.

10. Dorothea Hilhorst and Maliana Serrano, "The Humanitarian Arena in Angola: Whose Space?" paper presented at the World Conference of Humanitarian Studies, Groningen, Netherlands, February 5, 2009.

11. UN Doc. A/Res/49/59 (1994).

12. UN Information Service, "Optional Protocol Corrects Flaw in Convention on Safety of United Nations, Associated Personnel, Secretary-General Tells General Assembly Meeting," SG/SM/10256, GA/10431, December 9, 2005 (www.unis. unvienna.org/unis/pressrels/2005/sgsm10256.html).

13. UN, *Guiding Principles on Internal Displacement*, 1998, Principle 25 (www. brookings.edu/idp).

14. *Report of the Secretary-General on Protection for Humanitarian Assistance to Refugees and Others in Conflict Situations*, S/1998/883, September 22, 1998.

15. UN Security Council, Resolution 1502, August 2003, S/RES/1502 (2003) (www.un.org/Docs/sc).

16. UN Security Council, Resolution 1674, April 2006, S/RES/1674 (2006).

17. Abby Stoddard, Adele Harmer, and Victoria DiDomenico, "Providing Aid in Insecure Environments: Trends in Policy and Operations" (London: Overseas Development Institute), 2006. Also see Abby Stoddard, Adele Harmer, and Victoria DiDomenico, "Providing Aid in Insecure Environments: 2009 Update," Humanitarian Policy Group Policy Brief 34 (London: Overseas Development Institute, April 2009).

18. Sarah Bailey, "Aid Workers under Fire," Overseas Development Institute Blog, October 30, 2009 (http://blogs.odi.org.uk).

19. Lara Hammond, "The Power of Holding Humanitarianism Hostage and the Myth of Protective Principles," in *Humanitarianism in Question: Politics, Power, Ethics,* edited by Michael Barnett and Thomas G. Weiss (Cornell University Press, 2008), p. 175.

20. Katherine Haver, "Duty of Care? Local Staff and Aid Worker Security," *Forced Migration Review,* no. 28 (July 2007), pp. 10–11.

21. Bailey, "Aid Workers under Fire," October 2009, p. 1.

22. Abild, *Creating Humanitarian Space,* p. 19.

23. Ibid., p. 19.

24. Abild, *Creating Humanitarian Space,* p. 1.

25. Tennant and others, *Safeguarding Humanitarian Space,* p. 16. Also see Peter J. Hoffman and Thomas G. Weiss, *Sword and Salve: Confronting New Wars and Humanitarian Crises* (Lanham, Md.: Rowman and Littlefield Publishers, 2006), p. 171.

26. Abild, *Creating Humanitarian Space,* p. 1.

27. Interview, UN staff, December 2009.

28. Abild, *Creating Humanitarian Space,* p. 17.

29. International Federation of Red Cross and Red Crescent Societies, *Relief EU Field Manual,* September 2008, pp. 246–48.

30. See Casey Barrs, *Preparedness Support: Helping Brace Beneficiaries, Local Staff, and Partners for Violence,* May 2010, p. 4.

31. Greg Hansen, "Coming to Terms with the Humanitarian Imperative in Iraq," Humanitarian Agenda 2015 Briefing Paper, January 2007, p. 10.

32. Haver, "Duty of Care?" p. 10.

33. Hansen, "Coming to Terms with the Humanitarian Imperative in Iraq," pp. 11–12.

34. IASC, *Use of Military or Armed Escorts for Humanitarian Convoys: Discussion Paper and Non-Binding Guidelines,* September 2001 (www.humanitarianinfo.org/iasc).

35. Ibid.

36. IRIN, "Pakistan: Securing Aid Delivery," September 21, 2010 (www.reliefweb.int).

37. Abby Stoddard, Adele Harmer, and Victoria DiDomenico, "Private Security Providers and Services in Humanitarian Operations," *Humanitarian Policy Group Report 28* (London: Overseas Development Institute, September 2008).

38. Steering Committee for Humanitarian Response (SCHR), *SCHR Position on Humanitarian-Military Relations*, January 2010, section 3.

39. Testimony of Andrew S. Natsios, "After the Earthquake: Empowering Haiti to Rebuild Better," Senate Foreign Relations Committee Hearing on Haiti, May 19, 2010.

40. Feinstein International Center, *Humanitarian Horizons: A Practitioners' Guide to the Future*, Tufts University, January 2010, p. 26 (fic.tufts.edu).

41. See: David Rieff, *A Bed for the Night: Humanitarianism in Crisis* (New York: Simon and Schuster, 2002); Fiona Terry, *Condemned to Repeat? The Paradox of Humanitarian Action* (Cornell University Press, 2002); Hoffman and Weiss, *Sword and Salve*; Ian Smillie and Larry Minear, *The Charity of Nations: Humanitarian Action in a Calculating World* (Bloomfield, Conn.: Kumarian Press, 2004).

42. See, for example, Robert Gorman, *Refugee Aid and Development: Theory and Practice* (New York: Greenwood Press, 1993); Jeff Crisp, "Mind the Gap! UNHCR, Humanitarian Assistance, and the Development Process," *New Issues in Refugee Research*, Working Paper 43 (Geneva: UNHCR, May 2001); Alexander Betts, "International Cooperation and the Targeting of Development Assistance for Refugee Solutions: Lessons from the 1980s," *New Issues in Refugee Research*, Working Paper 107 (Geneva: UNHCR, September 2004).

43. See, for example, Monica Kathina Juma and Astri Suhrke, *Eroding Local Capacity: International Humanitarian Action in Africa* (Uppsala, Sweden: Nordic African Institute, 2002); Joseph Hanlon, *Mozambique: Who Calls the Shots?* (Indiana University Press, 1991).

44. Sarah Cliffe and Charles Petrie, "Opening Space for Long-Term Development in Fragile Environments," in *The Humanitarian Response Index 2007*, edited by Silvia Hidalgo and Augusto Lopez-Claros (Madrid: Dara, 2007), p. 57.

45. As of September 2010; see OCHA's Financial Tracking Service data (http://fts.unocha.org/pageloader.aspx?page=emerg-globalOverview&Year=2009). CAPs (consolidated appeals) represent the combined requests of UN agencies (and other international organizations, like the Red Cross and the International Organization for Migration) for support. They take time to put together, while flash appeals are the initial emergency request for immediate support, issued while the agencies are carrying out the assessments needed to produce a CAP

46. Humanitarian Reform, "Early Recovery" (www.humanitarianreform.org).

47. Ibid.

48. Sarah Bailey and Sara Pavanello, "Untangling Early Recovery," Humanitarian Policy Group Policy Brief 38 (London: Overseas Development Institute, October 2009), pp. 1–2.

49. NYU Center for International Cooperation, *Recovering from War: Gaps in Early Action,* New York, July 1, 2008, p. 15 (www.cic.nyu.edu). The report recommends a six-pillar approach for development of an early recovery system, based on DPKO, Department of Political Affairs (DPA), OCHA, UNDP's Bureau for Crisis Prevention and Recovery (BCPR), the World Bank, and UNHCHR.

50. Bailey and Pavanello, "Untangling Early Recovery," p. 4.

51. Groupe Urgence Réhabilitation Développement and Global Public Policy Institute, *Cluster Approach Evaluation 2, Synthesis Report,* April 2010, pp. 76–77.

52. UNDP Bureau for Crisis Prevention and Recovery, *UNDP Policy on Early Recovery,* February 2008.

53. UNDP Cluster Working Group on Early Recovery, in cooperation with the UNDG-ECHA Working Group on Transition, *Guidance Note on Early Recovery,* April 2008, p. 25 (http://irp.onlinesolutionsltd.net/outfile.php?id=53&href=http://irp.onlinesolutionsltd.net/assets/tools_guidelines/guidane%20note%20on%20early%20recovery.pdf).

54. Louisa Medhurst, "Protection and Early recovery in Timor-Leste," *Humanitarian Exchange Magazine* 46 (March 2010) (www.odihpn.org).

55. See www.ifrc.org.

56. Keystone, *Survey Results: Downward Accountability to "Beneficiaries": NGO and Donor Perspectives,* June 2006, p. 1 (www.hapinternational.org/pool/files/downward-accountability-to-beneficiaries-keystone-study.pdf).

57. See, for example, Brookings-University of Bern Project on Internal Displacement, *Moving beyond Rhetoric: Consultation and Participation with Populations Displaced by Conflict or Natural Disasters* (Brookings, October 2008).

58. IRIN, "Global: Beneficiary Feedback: 'Thanks but No Thanks?'" June 9, 2008 (www.irinnews.org).

59. For further information on Sphere, including the handbook (www.sphereproject.org).

60. *Sphere Humanitarian Charter 2010,* draft January 2010 (www.sphereproject.org).

61. James Darcy, "Locating Responsibility: The Sphere Humanitarian Charter and Its Rationale," *Disasters,* vol. 28, no. 2 (June 2004), p. 120.

62. See for example Charlotte Dufour and others, "Rights, Standards, and Quality in a Complex Humanitarian Space: Is Sphere the Right Tool?" *Disasters,* vol. 28, no. 2, pp. 124–41.

63. Darcy, "Locating Responsibility," p. 114.

64. Marci Van Dyke and Ronald Waldman, *The Sphere Project Evaluation Report,* January 2004, p. 5 (www.sphereproject.org/about/ext_eva/sphere_eval_fin.pdf).

65. Dufour and others, "Rights, Standards and Quality in a Complex Humanitarian Space," p. 128.

66. Ibid., p. 131.

67. Ibid.

68. Cited by Dufour and others, p. 139.

69. Sphere Project, Sphere Protection Chapter, draft, 2010, p. 1 (www.sphereproject.org/component/option,com_docman/task,doc_details/Itemid,203/gid,365/lang,english).

70. Ibid.

71. ICRC, *Professional Standards for Protection Work* (Geneva: ICRC), p. 23 (www. icrc.org).

72. ALNAP, *Protection: An ALNAP Guide for Humanitarian Agencies* (London: Overseas Development Institute, 2005).

73. Ibid. See especially section 7, pp. 79–98.

74. HAP-I includes in its members both INGOs and NNGOs—such as the Norwegian Refugee Council, Office Africain pour le Développement et la Coopération (OFADEC), COAST Trust, and CARE International.

75. See Minimum Standards for Education in Emergencies, Chronic Crises, and Early Reconstruction, p. 17 (www.ineesite.org).

76. IRIN, "Afghanistan: New Code of Conduct to Regulate NGOs," May 31, 2005 (www.irinnews.org).

77. Nora Bensahel and others, *Improving Capacity for Stabilization and Reconstruction Operations* (Santa Monica, Calif.: Rand National Defense Research Institute, 2009), p. 2.

78. Ibid., p. 32.

79. The U.S. Institute of Peace, "Reconstruction and Stabilization Operations: The Challenge before Us," conference conclusions of March 22 and 23, 2005 (www. crs.state.gov).

80. John Mitchell, "Accountability to the Beneficiaries of Humanitarian Aid: Old Messages, New Messengers," *Humanitarian Exchange Magazine*, no. 38 (June 2007) (www.odihpn.org).

81. ActionAid, *Safety with Dignity*, cited by Kate Berry and Sherryl Reddy, *Safety with Dignity: Integrating Community-Based Protection into Humanitarian Programming*, Humanitarian Practice Network Paper 68 (London: Overseas Development Institute, March 2010). The manual is available at www.actionaid.org.au.

82. Ibid.

Chapter Seven

1. Alexander de Waal, "Foreword," *Capitalizing on Catastrophe: Neoliberal Strategies in Disaster Reconstruction*, edited by Nandini Guenwardena and Mark Schuller (New York: Altamira Press, 2008), p. ix.

2. The inequity in power is sometimes reflected in the profits made in the reconstruction industry after a disaster. Naomi Klein refers to this as "disaster capitalism," which she defines as "orchestrated raids on the public sphere in the wake of catastrophic events, combined with the treatment of disasters as exciting market opportunities," in *The Shock Doctrine: The Rise of Disaster Capitalism*, 1st ed. (New York: Metropolitan Books, 2007), p. 6.

3. Inter-Agency Standing Committee, *Protecting Persons Affected by Natural Disasters: IASC Operational Guidelines on Human Rights and Natural Disasters* (Washington: Brookings-Bern Project on Internal Displacement, June 2006).

4. International Federation of Red Cross and Red Crescent Societies (IFRC), *Introduction to the Guidelines for the Domestic Facilitation and Regulation of International Disaster Relief and Initial Recovery Assistance* (Geneva), p. 11.

5. EM-DAT: The OFDA/CRED International Disaster Database, Université Catholique de Louvain, Brussels, Belgium (www.emdat.be). In 2008, hurricanes Fay, Gustav, Hanna, and Ike killed 698 people in Haiti in August and September, while Hurricane Ike killed seven people in Cuba.

6. Femke Vos and others, "Annual Disaster Statistical Review 2009: The Numbers and Trends," Centre for Research on the Epidemiology of Disasters, World Health Organization, Université Catholique de Louvain, p. 1. (http://cred.be).

7. Vos and others, "Annual Disaster Statistical Review 2008," p. 1.

8. Margareta Wahlström, "The Humanitarian Impact of Climate Change," *UN Chronicle Online Edition* (www.un.org/Pubs/chronicle/2007).

9. IFRC, *World Disasters Report*, 2006, p. 168.

10. Walter Kälin, for example, found that 70 percent of the tsunami-affected population in one country had lost their documentation. See *Protection of Internally Displaced Persons in Situations of Natural Disasters: A Working Visit to Asia by the Representative of the Secretary-General on the Human Rights of Internally Displaced Persons, Walter Kälin, 27 February–5 March 2005* (Washington: Brookings-Bern Project on Internal Displacement, April 2005), p. 20.

11. Lorena Aguilar, "Acknowledging the Linkages: Gender and Climate Change," presentation at the World Bank, Workshop on Social Dimensions of Climate Change, March 2008 (www.worldbank.org). Also see Lin Chew and Kavita N. Ramdas, *Caught in the Storm: The Impact of Natural Disasters on Women* (San Francisco: Global Fund for Women), December 2005.

12. World Health Organization, *Gender and Health in Disasters*, July 2002, p. 2.

13. Chris Kromm and Sue Sturgis, *Hurricane Katrina and the Guiding Principles on Internal Displacement* (Durham, N.C.: Institute for Southern Studies, January 2008).

14. Roberta Cohen, "An Institutional Gap for Disaster IDPs," *Forced Migration Review*, no. 32 (April 2009), p. 58.

15. See Pierre Verluise and Levon Chorbajian, *Armenia in Crisis: The 1988 Earthquake* (Wayne State University Press, 1995), pp. 31–34.

16. California Division of Mines and Geology Special Publication 104 and USGS PP 1551-A (http://seismo.berkeley.edu), cited in Philip W. Stoffer, *The San Andreas Fault in the San Francisco Bay Area, California: A Geology Fieldtrip Guidebook to Selected Stops on Public Lands*, U.S. Geological Survey, Open-File Report 2005-1127, 2005, p. 6 (http://pubs.er.usgs.gov).

17. UNDP, "Reducing Disaster Risk: A Challenge for Development," pp. 3 and 10.

18. Juan Carlos Chavez, "In Wealthy Enclave of Pétionville, Another Picture," *Miami Herald*, January 22, 2010; "The Earthquake Recovery Process in Haiti," statement by Walter Kälin, UN Human Rights Commission, Special Session on Haiti, January 27, 2010.

19. See, for example, the IASC/World Food Program, "Humanitarian Early Warning Service" (www.hewsweb.org). Also see Jochen Zschau and Andreas N. Küppers, *Early Warning Systems for Natural Disaster Risk Reduction* (Berlin: Springer-Verlag, 2003).

20. See UN International Strategy for Disaster Reduction (www.unisdr.org) for related materials.

21. See, for example, International Crisis Group's listing of early warning mechanisms (www.crisisgroup.org).

22. Calcutta Research Group, *Voices of the Internally Displaced in South Asia* (Kolkata: CRG, 2006), p. 121.

23. Brookings-Bern Project on Internal Displacement, *IASC Framework on Durable Solutions for Internally Displaced Persons* (Washington: Brookings-Bern Project on Internal Displacement, March 2010).

24. See the classic work by Amartya Sen, *Poverty and Famines: An Essay on Entitlement and Deprivation* (Oxford University Press, 1983).

25. See Anne Richard, *Role Reversal: Offers of Help from Other Countries in Response to Hurricane Katrina* (Washington: Center for Transatlantic Relations, 2006).

26. Richard F. Grimmett, "Instances of Use of United States Armed Forces Abroad: 1798–2006," CRS Report for Congress, updated January 8, 2007; Tim Morris, "Civil-Military Relations in Afghanistan," *Forced Migration Review*, no. 13 (June 2002), pp. 14–15; Taylor B. Seybolt, *Humanitarian Military Intervention: The Conditions for Success and Failure* (Oxford University Press, 2007).

27. See, for example, the guidelines developed by InterAction and the U.S. Institute for Peace on civil-military relations in humanitarian operations (www.usip.org).

28. See, for example, Sharon Wiharta and others, *The Effectiveness of Foreign Military Assets in Natural Disaster Response* (Stockholm: Stockholm International Peace Research Institute, 2008).

29. Walter Kälin, "Displacement Caused by the Effects of Climate Change: Who Will Be Affected and What Are the Gaps in the Normative Frameworks for Their Protection?" background paper submitted by the Representative of the Secretary-General on the Human Rights of Internally Displaced Persons, Oslo, Norway, October 2008, p. 17.

30. Kelly L. Webster, "Lessons from a Military Humanitarian in Port-au-Prince, Haiti," *Small Wars Journal*, March 28, 2010, p. 2.

31. International Committee of the Red Cross, "Philippines: Heavy Floods Aggravate Plight of Civilians Displaced by Conflict," September 24, 2008, cited in IDMC, "Philippines: An Estimated 8 Million People Affected by Natural Disasters in 2008" (www.internal-displacement.org).

32. UN Human Rights Council, *Report of the Representative of the Secretary-General on the Human Rights of Internally Displaced Persons, Walter Kälin*, A/HRC/13/21/Add.2, January 21, 2010.

33. *The Economist*, "When the World Shook," June 30, 1990, p. 45, cited in Rohan J. Hardcastle and Adrian T. L. Chua, "Humanitarian Assistance: Towards a Right of

Access to Victims of Natural Disasters," *International Review of the Red Cross,* no. 325 (December 1998), p.589.

34. See Hardcastle and Chua, "Humanitarian Assistance: Towards a Right of Access to Victims of Natural Disasters."

35. Philip Nel and Marjolein Righarts, "National Disasters and the Risk of Violent Civil Conflict," *International Studies Quarterly,* vol. 52, no. 1 (March 2008), p. 159.

36. R. S. Olson and A. C. Drury, "Un-Therapeutic Communities: A Cross-National Analysis of Post-Disaster Political Unrest," *International Journal of Mass Emergencies and Disasters,* vol. 15 (1997), p. 8.

37. Rakhi Bhavnani, "Natural Disaster Conflicts," Harvard University, February 2006, p. 4 (www.disasterdiplomacy.org/bhavnanisummary.pdf).

38. Ibid., p. 38.

39. See for example, Annie Huang, "Taiwan's Prime Minister Resigns over Response to Deadly Typhoon," Associated Press, September 8, 2009.

40. As of September 2009, according to National Disasters Prevention and Protection Commission; figures cited in See Hoe I. Ling and others, *Reconnaissance Report on Typhoon Morakot* (Columbia University, September 2009), p. 3 (www.geerassociation.org). U.S. press reports put the estimate of deaths at 670; see Huang, "Taiwan's Prime Minister Resigns over Response to Deadly Typhoon."

41. Peter Bauman, Mengistu Ayalew, and Gazala Paul, "Natural Disaster: War and Peace. A Comparative Analysis of the Impact of the Tsunami and Tsunami Interventions on the Conflicts in Sri Lanka and Indonesia/Aceh," unpublished manuscript. Also see P. LeBillon and A. Waizenegger, "Peace in the Wake of Disaster? Secessionist Conflicts and the 2004 Indian Ocean Tsunami," *Transactions of the Institute of British Geographers,* vol. 32, no. 3 (2007), pp. 411–27; and M. Renner and Z. Chafe, "Turning Disaster into Peacemaking Opportunities," in *the State of the World* (New York: Worldwatch Institute, 2006).

42. See also Peter Feith, "The Aceh Peace Process: Nothing Less than Success," U.S. Institute of Peace Briefing Paper, March 2007 (www.usip.org).

43. Internal Displacement Monitoring Centre (IDMC), *Sri Lanka: Escalation of Conflict Leaves Tens of Thousands of IDPs without Protection and Assistance,* p. 37 (www.internal-displacement.org).

44. Susanna M. Hoffman and Anthony Oliver-Smith, *Culture and Catastrophe: The Anthropology of Disaster* (Santa Fe, N.M.: School of American Research Press, 2002).

45. Mary Anderson, *Do No Harm: How Aid Can Support Peace—or War* (Boulder, Colo.: Lynne Rienner, 1999). Also see www.disasterdiplomacy.org for a discussion of the ways in which natural disasters create opportunities for diplomatic initiatives.

46. Michael Renner and Zoe Chafe, *Beyond Disasters: Creating Opportunities for Peace,* Worldwatch Report (Washington: Worldwatch Institute, 2007), pp. 5–6.

47. UN Human Rights Council, *Report of the Representative of the Secretary-General on the Human Rights of Internally Displaced Persons, Walter Kälin—*

Addendum—Protection of Internally Displaced Persons in Situations of Natural Disasters, A/HRC/10/13/Add.1, March 5, 2009.

48. Ibid., p. 15.

49. See, for example, Ivo Daalder and Paul Stares, "Saving Burma's People: The UN's Responsibility to Protect," *New York Times,* May 13, 2008 (www.nytimes.com).

50. David Fischer, "The Right to Humanitarian Assistance," in Walter Kälin and others, *Incorporating the Guiding Principles on Internal Displacement into Domestic Law: Issues and Challenges,* Studies in Transnational Legal Policy 41 (Washington: American Society of International Law and Brookings Institution, January 2010), pp. 47–128.

51. Samir Elhawary and Gerardo Castillo, *The Role of the Affected State: A Case Study on the Peruvian Earthquake Response,* Humanitarian Policy Group Working Paper (London: Overseas Development Institute, April 2008) (www.odi.org.uk).

52. Ibid., p. 3.

53. Greg Bankoff and Dorothea Hilhorst, "The Politics of Risk in the Philippines: Comparing State and NGO Perceptions of Disaster Management," *Disasters,* vol. 33, no. 4, 2009, p. 687.

54. Presentation at joint workshop on natural disasters and human rights sponsored by the Brookings-Bern Project on Internal Displacement and AIDMI, Chennai, India, April 2009. For a summary of proceedings, see Brookings-Bern Project on Internal Displacement, *Protecting and Promoting Rights in Natural Disasters in South Asia: Prevention and Response, Chennai, India, 9–10 April 2009—Summary Report* (Washington: Brookings-Bern Project on Internal Displacement, July 1, 2009) (www.brookings.edu/idp).

55. See, for example, Harry Masyrafah and Jock M.J.A. McKean, *Post-Tsunami Aid Effectiveness in Aceh: Proliferation and Coordination in Reconstruction,* Brookings Wolfensohn Center for Development, Working Paper 6, November 2008, p. 24. Also see East-West Center, University of California Berkeley, "After the Tsunami: Human Rights of Vulnerable Populations," October 2005. Also see Tsunami Evaluation Coalition, *Joint Evaluation of the International Response to the Indian Ocean Tsunami: Synthesis Report,* July 2006.

56. UN Human Rights Council, *Report of the Representative of the Secretary-General on the Human Rights of Internally Displaced Persons, Walter Kälin—Addendum—Protection of Internally Displaced Persons in Situations of Natural Disasters,* p. 17.

57. Nina Lakhani, "Rape on the Rise in Haiti's Camps," *The Independent,* February 7, 2010 (www.independent.co.uk). Also see Amnesty International, *Sexual Violence in Haitian Camps of the Displaced, beyond the Number,* March 22, 2010 (www.amnesty.org).

58. Amnesty International, *Haiti after the Earthquake: Initial Mission Findings,* March 2010, p. 12 .

59. IFRC, *World Disasters Report 2007: Focus on Discrimination* (London: Eurospan, 2007) (www.ifrc.org), p. 123.

60. UNIFEM, *UNIFEM Responds to the Tsunami Tragedy, Protection, and Rights* (www.unifem.org).

61. Lin Chew and Kavita N. Ramdas, *Caught in the Storm: The Impact of Natural Disasters on Women*, December 2005, p. 3.

62. Krishna Bandyopadhyay, Soma Ghosh, and Nilanjan Dutta, *Eroded Lives* (Kolkata, India: Mahanirban Calcutta Research Group, December 2006) (www.mcrg.ac.in).

63. See Brookings-Bern Project on Internal Displacement, *Summary Report: Protecting and Promoting Rights in Natural Disasters in South Asia: Prevention and Response*, July 2009, p. 20 (www.brookings.edu/idp).

64. See UNICEF, *Rebuilding Childhood in Haiti: Child Protection after the Earthquake*, February 17, 2010 (www.unicef.org). Also see OHCHR, "Separated Haitian Children Risk Being Sold, Trafficked, or Kept in Slave-Like Conditions—UN Human Rights Experts," February 2, 2010 (www.ohchr.org). *Restavek* is a term from the French *rester avec* ("to stay with") used to describe children who are given away by their parents to serve as unpaid domestic servants. According to UNICEF, an estimated 250,000 children in Haiti are *restaveks*. *Restaveks* often are exposed to abuse, including sexual violence, and today the practice is considered by many to be tantamount to child slavery. Originally, decades back, the practice was undertaken to give poor children from rural areas a better life: the children would serve rich families that would in turn provide them with education, food, and care. See, for example, Jim Loney, "Haiti 'Restavek' Tradition Called Child Slavery," Reuters, February 18, 2010 (http://www.reuters.com).

65. UN Human Rights Council, *Report of the Representative of the Secretary-General on the Human Rights of Internally Displaced Persons, Walter Kälin—Addendum—Protection of Internally Displaced Persons in Situations of Natural Disasters*, p. 17.

66. Save the Children UK, "Watermarks: Child Protection during Floods in Bangladesh" (Dhaka, Bangladesh: Save the Children UK, August 2006) (www.savethechildren.org.uk).

67. UN OCHA, *Haiti Earthquake*, Situation Report 34, April 16, 2010, pp. 3 and 7 (http://oneresponse.info/Disasters/Haiti).

68. Action Aid International, *Tsunami Response: A Human Rights Assessment*, January 2006 (www.actionaid.org.uk).

69. Timothy Gill, *Making Things Worse: How Caste Blindness in Indian Post-Tsunami Disaster Recovery Has Exacerbated Vulnerability and Exclusion* (Utrecht: Dalit Network Netherlands, February 2007) (http://www2.ohchr.org/english/bodies/cerd/docs/ngos/tsunami_report.pdf); Human Rights Watch, *After the Deluge: India's Reconstruction Following the 2004 Tsunami*, May 2005 (www.hrw.org).

70. Human Rights Watch, *Caste Discrimination: A Global Concern*, a report by Human Rights Watch for the United Nations World Conference against Racism, Racial Discrimination, Xenophobia, and Related Intolerance, Durban, South Africa, vol. 13, no. 3(G), August 2001 (www.hrw.org).

71. Rachel Baird, *The Impact of Climate Change on Minorities and Indigenous Peoples,* Minority Rights Group International, April 2008 (www2.ohchr.org).

72. S. Gatade, "Past as Living Present: Calamity and Discrimination," September 24, 2006 (www.countercurrents.org).

73. See, for example, "Discrimination in Aid," *Dawn* editorial, September 1, 2010 (www.dawn.com); IRIN, "Pakistan: Minorities Test Aid Impartiality," September 8, 2010 (www.irinnews.org).

74. Kevin Savage and others, *Corruption Perceptions and Risks in Humanitarian Assistance: An Afghanistan Case Study,* Humanitarian Policy Group Working Paper (London: Overseas Development Institute, July 2007), p. 9 (www.odi.org.uk).

75. Cited in International Federation of Red Cross and Red Crescent Societies, *World Disasters Report 2007: Focus on Discrimination,* 2007, p. 39 (www.ifrc.org)

76. UN Human Rights Council, *Report of the Representative of the Secretary-General on the Human Rights of Internally Displaced Persons, Walter Kälin—Addendum—Protection of Internally Displaced Persons in Situations of Natural Disasters,* p. 21.

77. WHO, *Action Plan 2006–2011,* p. 1 (www.who.int).

78. UN Human Rights Council, *Report of the Representative of the Secretary-General on the Human Rights of Internally Displaced Persons, Walter Kälin—Addendum—Protection of Internally Displaced Persons in Situations of Natural Disasters,* pp. 20–21.

79. Handicap International, *How to Include Disability Issues in Disaster Management: Following Floods 2004 in Bangladesh,* September 2005, p. 7 (www.handicap-international.de).

80. Women's Refugee Commission, *Persons with Disabilities and the Humanitarian Response in Haiti,* January 2010 (www.womensrefugeecommission.org).

81. Ian Urbina, "Earthquake's Burdens Weigh Heavily on Haiti's Elderly," *New York Times,* March 12, 2010 (www.nytimes.com).

82. Laura Figueroa, "Haiti's Elderly Earthquake Victims Struggle to Survive with Little Help," Haitian-Truth.Org (www.haitian-truth.org).

83. William Booth, "Old and Poor in Haiti Suffer Mightily after the Quake," *Washington Post,* March 13, 2010 (www.washingtonpost.com).

84. IFRC, *World Disasters Report 2007: Focus on Discrimination.*

85. Ibid., p 25.

86. UN Human Rights Council, *Report of the Representative of the Secretary-General on the Human Rights of Internally Displaced Persons, Walter Kälin—Addendum—Protection of Internally Displaced Persons in Situations of Natural Disasters,* p. 16.

87. Chris Kromm and Sue Sturgis, *Hurricane Katrina and the Guiding Principles on Internal Displacement,* January 2008, p. 13.

88. Ibid., p. 18.

89. Bradford H. Gray and Kathy Hebert, *After Katrina, Hospitals in Hurricane Katrina: Challenges Facing Custodial Institutions in a Disaster* (Washington: Urban Institute, July 2006), p. 2.

90. Eye on Aceh and Aid Watch, *A People's Agenda? Post-Tsunami Aid in Aceh,* February 2006 (www.acheh-eye.org),

91. Oxfam UK, *The Tsunami Two Years On: Land Rights in Aceh*, 30 November 2006 (www.oxfam.org.uk).

92. Katherine Baldwin, "Haiti Must Move Faster to Protect Quake-Displaced from Storms–Aid Agencies," *Reuters Alertnet*, 2 June 2010 (www.reliefweb.int).

93. IFRC, *World Disasters Report 2007: Focus on Discrimination*, note 5, p. 144.

94. UNIFEM, *UNIFEM Responds to the Tsunami Tragedy: One Year Later: A Report Card*, p. 3 (www.unifem.org).

95. UN Human Rights Council, March 5, 2009, A/HRC/10/13/Add.1, p. 18.

96. Ibid., p. 18.

97. Human Rights Watch, *"I Want to Help My Own People": State Control and Civil Society in Burma after Cyclone Nargis*, April 28, 2010 (www.hrw.org).

98. Kromm and Sturgis, *Hurricane Katrina and the Guiding Principles on Internal Displacement*, January 2008, p. 26.

99. International Crisis Group, *Haiti: Stabilisation and Reconstruction after the Quake*, Latin America/Caribbean Report 32, March 31, 2010, p. 1.

100. International Strategy for Disaster Reduction (ISDR), *Hyogo Framework for Action 2005–2015: ISDR International Strategy for Disaster Reduction—Building the Resilience of Nations and Communities to Disaster*, January 2005 (www.unisdr.org).

101. World Conference on Disaster Reduction, January 18–22, 2005, Kobe, Hyogo, Japan (www.unisdr.org), cited in Oxfam, *Rethinking Disasters: Why Death and Destruction Is Not Nature's Fault but Human Failure*, 2008 (www.oxfam. org.uk).

102. Vatsa Krishna, "Reducing Earthquake Loss: Towards a National Perspective," *Economic and Political Weekly*, April 20, 2002, cited in Oxfam, *Rethinking Disasters: Why Death and Destruction Is Not Nature's Fault but Human Failure*.

103. Oxfam, *Rethinking Disasters*, p. ii.

104. DFID, *Reducing the Risk of Disasters—Helping to Achieve Sustainable Poverty Reduction in a Vulnerable World*, DFID Policy Paper, March 2006 (www.dfid.gov.uk).

105. Oxfam, *Rethinking Disasters*, p. i.

106. United Nations International Strategy for Disaster Reduction Secretariat (UNISDR), *Linking Disaster Risk Reduction and Poverty Reduction, Good Practices and Lessons Learned*, 2008 (www.unisdr.org).

107. Cited by ALNAP, *Flood Disasters: Learning from Previous Relief and Recovery Operations*, January 2008, p. 3

108. IFRC, *Guidelines for the Domestic Facilitation and Regulation of International Disaster Relief and Initial Recovery*, 2007 (30IC/07/R4 annex) (www.ifrc.org).

109. Inter-Agency Standing Committee (IASC), *Protecting Persons Affected by Natural Disasters: IASC Operational Guidelines on Human Rights and Natural Disasters*, 2006; IASC, *Operational Guidelines on the Protection of Persons Affected by Natural Disasters*, 2010.

110. UNDP Pacific Centre and OHCHR Regional Office for the Pacific, *Checklist for Integrating Human Rights in Natural Disaster Management in the Pacific*, Suva, Fiji, 2007.

111. Nel and Righarts, "Natural Disasters and the Risk of Violent Civil Conflict," p. 27.

112. Bryan Hoyer, "Lessons from the Sichuan Earthquake," *Humanitarian Exchange Magazine* [Overseas Development Institute], no. 43 (June 2009).

113. M. Pelling and K. Dill, "'Natural' Disasters as Catalysts of Political Action," ISP/NSC Briefing Paper 06/01 (London: Chatham House, 2006), pp. 2–5.

114. Cohen, "An Institutional Gap for Disaster IDPs," p. 58.

115. Ibid., p. 59.

116. High Commissioner's Opening Statement to 60th Session of Excom, Palais des Nations, Geneva, September 28, 2009, p. 5.

117. Refugees International, *Haiti: From the Ground Up*, Field Report, March 2010 (sww.refugeesinternational.org).

Chapter Eight

1. Interview with author, 2007.

2. John Telford and John Cosgrave, *Joint Evaluation of the International Response to the Indian Ocean Tsunami: Synthesis Report* (London: Tsunami Evaluation Coalition, July 2006), p. 21. See also John Cosgrove, "Humanitarian Funding and Needs Assessment," in *The Human Response Index 2008: Donor Accountability in Humanitarian Action*, Development Assistance Research Associates (New York: Palgrave Macmillan, September 2008), p. 83.

3. For example, Donini writes, "Life-saving activities which do not conform to the western humanitarian canon such as *zakat*, remittances from Diasporas or contributions from communities, religious foundations and other sources in the south do not qualify for international statistics of ODA and do not make it into the humanitarian assistance hit-parade." Antonio Donini, "The Far Side: The Meta-Functions of Humanitarianism in a Globalized World," 2008, p. 6 (www.humansecuritygateway.com). Revised and republished under same title in *Disasters*, vol. 34, supplement 2 (April 2010), pp. S220—S237.

4. Center for Global Prosperity, *The Index of Global Philanthropy and Remittances 2010* (New York: Hudson Institute, 2010), p. 60.

5. Ibid., p. 63.

6. UNHCR, "Operational Support and Management," *UNHCR Global Appeal 2010–11*, pp. 8–10 (www.unhcr.org).

7. Beth Elise Whitaker, "Fnding the International Refugee Regime: Implications for Protection," *Global Governance*, vol. 14, no. 2 (2008), pp. 241–58, quotation from p. 250.

8. ICRC, *ICRC Annual Report 2009*, p. 444 (www.icrc.org). All figures are rounded.

9. UNHCR, *Master Glossary of Terms, Rev. 1*, Status Determination and Protection Information Section–Division of International Protection Services, June 2006

(www.unhcr.org/refworld/docid/42ce7d444.html). Cited in DARA, *Humanitarian Response Index 2009*, p. 245.

10. See DARA, *Humanitarian Response Index 2009*, pp. 210–233.

11. Ibid., pp. 228 and 233.

12. Macrae and others, *Uncertain Power: The Changing Role of Official Donors in Humanitarian Action*, 2002, p. 15.

13. Center for Global Prosperity, *The Index of Global Philanthropy and Remittances 2010*.

14. Macrae and others, *Uncertain Power*, p. 3.

15. Laura Altinger and Virginia Tortella, *The Private Financing of Humanitarian Action, 1995–2005*, Humanitarian Policy Group (London: Overseas Development Institute, June 2007), p. 21.

16. UNICEF, *Annual Report 2009*, June 2010, p. 39 (www.unicef.org/publications/index_53754.html).

17. Mark Dalton and others, *Study Four: Changes in Humanitarian Financing: Implications for the United Nations*, October 11, 2003, pp. 9–10.

18. Cosgrove, "Humanitarian Funding and Needs Assessment," p. 75.

19. Macrae and others, *Uncertain Power*.

20. Ibid., p. 6.

21. Larry Minear, "The United States as a Humanitarian Actor," in *The Human Response Index 2008*, p. 60.

22. Ibid., p. 55.

23. Macrae and others, *Uncertain Power*, p. 7.

24. Roberta Cohen and Dawn Calabia, *Improving the U.S. Response to Internal Displacement: Recommendations to the Obama Administration and the Congress* (Washington: Brookings-Bern Project on Internal Displacement, June 2010), p. 49.

25. In Adele Harmer and Lin Cotterrell, "Diversity in Donorship: The Changing Landscape of Official Humanitarian Aid," HPG Research Briefing 20 (London: Overseas Development Institute, September 2005), the authors note that it is difficult to study the financial flows of nontraditional donors as official aid is not consistently defined and there are no comprehensive data sources. However, they estimate that between 1999 and 2004, non-DAC contributions constituted between 1 percent and 12 percent of total global humanitarian assistance.

26. Ibid.

27. Mary B. Anderson, "The Giving-Receiving Relationship: Inherently Unequal?" in *The Human Response Index 2008*, quote from p. 105.

28. Walker and others, 2005, p. 249.

29. Ian Smillie and Larry Minear, *The Charity of Nations: Humanitarian Action in a Calculating World* (Bloomfield, Conn.: Kumarian Press, 2004), p. 132.

30. Peter Walker and others, "Smoke and Mirrors: Deficiencies in Disaster Funding," *British Medical Journal*, vol. 330 (2005), pp. 247–50, p. 247.

31. Interview with NGO, January 2010.

32. Andrea Binder and Jan Martin Witte, *Business Engagement in Humanitarian Relief: Key Trends and Policy Implications*, HPG background paper, June 2007, p. 5. The high percentage in 2005 was undoubtedly influenced by support for victims of the 2004 Indian Ocean tsunami.

33. Development Initiatives, *Global Humanitarian Assistance Report 2009*, July 1, 2009, p. 54.

34. Center for Global Prosperity, *The Index of Global Philanthropy and Remittances 2010*, p. 24.

35. Center for Global Prosperity, *Index of Global Philanthropy 2007* (Washington: Hudson Institute, 2007), p. 18.

36. World Food Program, "Review of Resource Mobilisation for World Food Programme Operations under the Consolidated Appeals Process," p. 1.

37. Dalton and others, *Study Four: Changes in Humanitarian Financing*, p. 17.

38. OCHA, "OCHA on Message: Consolidated Appeals Process," June 2010, p. 2.

39. OCHA, *Humanitarian Appeal 2010*, November 2009, p. 50. This is not to say that the increase in funding of CAPs was incremental. For example, there was a jump in the amount of money raised around 2002–03 and in 2005; the latter increase was due largely to the funding for Sudan's appeal, even excluding the 2005 Tsunami Flash Appeal.

40. Ibid., p. 2.

41. UN General Assembly, *Enhancing the Functioning and Utilization of the Central Emergency Revolving Fund: Note by the Secretary-General* (A/57/613), November 2002, p. 2.

42. Martin Barber and others, *Central Emergency Response Fund Two Year Evaluation*, July 2008, p. 1 (http://ochaonline.un.org).

43. OCHA, "Central Emergency Response Fund—Life-Saving Criteria," January 2010 (http://cerf.un.org).

44. Ibid., p. 3.

45. Ibid., pp. 9–10.

46. Cited by Cohen and Calabia, *Improving the U.S. Response to Internal Displacement*, pp. 43–44, on the basis of 2009 and 2010 interviews with NGO representatives, using 2006 figures.

Chapter Nine

1. Erik Melander, Magnus Öberg, and Jonathan Hall, "Are 'New Wars' More Atrocious? Battle Severity, Civilians Killed, and Forced Migration before and after the End of the Cold War," *European Journal of International Relations*, vol. 15, no. 3 (2009), pp. 505–36.

2. Human Security Report Project, "Shrinking Costs of War," Part II, in *Human Security Report 2009/2010: The Causes of Peace and the Shrinking Costs of War.*

December 2010 pre-publication version available at www.hsrgroup.org; forthcoming in print from Oxford University Press, 2011.

3. Bethany Lacina, Nils Petter Gleditsch, and Bruce Russett, "The Declining Risk of Death in Battle," *International Studies Quarterly,* vol. 50, no. 3 (2006), pp. 673–80.

4. The number of Iraqi civilian casualties has been a controversial matter, with different estimates given by the Iraqi government, the U.S. military, and the British organization, Iraq Body Count. See Lara Jakes, "U.S. Military Says 77,000 Iraqis Killed over 5 Years," Associated Press, October 14, 2010 (http://news.yahoo.com/s/ap/20101014/ap_on_re_mi_ea/ml_iraq_death_toll).

5. ICRC, "Afghanistan: War Casualties Soar in Kandahar Hospital," October 12, 2010 (www.icrc.org).

6. However, there were increases in 2005 and 2008. See the Uppsala Conflict Data Program data in the Stockholm International Peace Research Institute (SIPRI) yearbooks: Appendix 2A, "Patterns of Major Armed Conflicts, 1999–2008," in *SIPRI Yearbook 2009: Armaments, Disarmament, and International Security* (Oxford University Press, June 2009); Appendix 2A, "Patterns of Major Armed Conflicts, 2000–2010," in *SIPRI Yearbook 2010: Armaments, Disarmament, and International Security* (Oxford University Press, July 2010) (www.sipri.org).

7. See for example, Ekaterina Stepanova, "Trends in Armed Conflicts: One-Sided Violence against Civilians," in *SIPRI Yearbook 2009: Armaments, Disarmament, and International Security* (www.sipri.org).

8. See, for example, Vanda Felbab–Brown, "Peacekeepers among Poppies: Afghanistan, Illicit Economies, and Intervention," *International Peacekeeping,* vol. 16, no, 1 (February 2009), pp. 100–14.

9. Cited by Peter Singer, *Wired for War: The Robotics Revolution and Conflict in the 21st Century* (New York: Penguin Books, 2009), pp. 280–81.

10. National Alliance of Gang Investigators Associations in partnership with the Federal Bureau of Investigation, *2005 National Gang Threat Assessment* (www.ncjrs.gov), 2006.

11. Herbert C. Covey, *Street Gangs throughout the World* (Springfield, Ill.: Charles C. Thomas Publications, 2010).

12. However, that seems to pertain less to transnational criminal networks, such as drug trafficking networks, than to local gangs.

13. Mary Anderson, *Do No Harm: How Aid Can Support Peace or War* (Boulder, Colo.: Lynne Rienner), 1999, p. 12.

14. Singer, *Wired for War,* p. 286.

15. Hugo Slim, *Killing Civilians: Method, Madness, and Morality in War* (Columbia University Press, 2008).

16. For example, the UN's Inter-Agency Protection Capacity (PROCAP) program (http://ochaonline.un.org).

17. See Brookings-Bern Project on Internal Displacement, "Expert Seminar on Protracted IDP Situations," June 2007 (www.brookings.edu/idp).

18. See, for example, Sarah Collinson and others, *States of Fragility: Stabilisation and Its Implications for Humanitarian Action,* Humanitarian Policy Group Working Paper (London: Overseas Development Initiative, May 2001).

19. Ibid.

20. Sadako Ogata, former UN high commissioner for refugees, suspended the agency's operations in Bosnia in 1993 when she felt that the agency could no longer uphold humanitarian principles, but that did not last more than a few days before political pressures forced the agency to resume.

21. Singer, *Wired for War,* 2009, pp. 394–95.

22. Ibid., pp 386–87.

23. Ibid., p. 411.

24. Ibid., p. 398.

25. Ibid., pp. 261–62.

26. Inter-Agency Standing Committee, *Meeting Humanitarian Challenges in Urban Areas (MHCUA): Draft Assessment,* October 2, 2009, p. 2 (www.humanitarian info.org/iasc)

27. UN–HABITAT, *State of the World's Cities 2004–05: Globalization and Urban Culture,* p. 134 (www.unhabitat.org).

28. Ibid., p. 135. Also see IRIN, "Global: Urban Conflict—Fighting for Resources in the Slums," October 12, 2007 (www.irinnews.org).

29. Mark Schneider and Damien Helly, "Let's Offer Hope to Cité Soleil," *Miami Herald,* March 12, 2007 (www.crisisgroup.org).

30. See, for example, Shekhar Riat, "Kingston, Jamaica, Violence 2010: Death Toll," Apex News Network, May 31, 2010 (http://apexnewsnetwork.com).

31. Singer, *Wired for War,* p. 288.

32. Ralph Peters, "Our Soldiers, Their Cities," *Parameters* (Spring 1996), pp. 43–50, quotation from p. 43. See also "Our Soldiers, Their Cities," pp. 70–83 in Ralph Peters, *Fighting for the Future: Will America Triumph?* (Mechanicsburg, Pa.: Stackpole Books, 2001).

33. Marion Harrof–Tavel, "Armed Violence and Humanitarian Action in Urban Areas," ICRC, July 29, 2009 (www.icrc.org).

34. Ibid.

35. Peters, "Our Soldiers, Their Cities," *Parameters,* p. 44.

36. UN–HABITAT, *State of the World's Cities 2006/07: The Millennium Development Goals and Urban Sustainability: 30 Years of Shaping the Habitat Agenda,* 2006 (www.unhabitat.org).

37. Inter-Agency Standing Committee, *Meeting Humanitarian Challenges in Urban Areas (MHCUA).*

38. Harrof–Tavel, "Armed Violence and Humanitarian Action in Urban Areas."

39. "World Red Cross and Red Crescent Day 2010: Urbanization," ICRC, 2009 (www.icrc.org).

40. António Guterres, "Protection Challenges for Persons of Concern in Urban Settings," *Forced Migration Review* 34 (February 2010), pp. 8–9 (www.fmreview.org).

41. For a description of the particular needs and vulnerabilities of urban IDPs, see Karen Jacobsen and IDMC, *Internal Displacement to Urban Areas: The Tufts–IDMC Profiling Study, Case 1, Khartoum, Sudan.* September 2008; Case 2, Abidjan, Côte d'Ivoire; and Case 3: Santa Marta, Colombia (www.internal-displacement.org). See also Eveliina Lyytinen, *A Tale of Three Cities: Internal Displacement, Urbanization, and Humanitarian Action in Abidjan, Khartoum, and Mogadishu,* Research Paper 173, UNHCR, May 2009 (www.unhcr.org).

42. Harrof–Tavel, "Armed Violence and Humanitarian Action in Urban Areas."

43. Christian Aid, *Human Tide: The Real Migration Crisis,* May 2007, p. 5 (www. christianaid.org.uk).

44. IOM, "Discussion Note: Migration and the Environment," MC/INF/288, November 1, 2007, p. 1 (www.iom.int).

45. While the term was used in the 1970s by the Worldwatch Institute, it was first used publicly in 1985 by Essam El–Hinnawi, *Environmental Refugees* (Nairobi: UNEP). It also is frequently associated with Jodi Jacobson's *Environmental Refugees: A Yardstick of Habitability,* World Watch Paper 86, 1988. For critiques of the use of the term "refugees," see, for example, Richard Black, "Environmental Refugees: Myth or Reality?" *New Issues in Refugee Research, UNHCR,* Working Paper 34, March 2001. Also see Stephen Castles, "Environmental Changes and Forced Migration: Making Sense of the Debate," New Issues in Refugee Research, UNHCR, Working Paper 70, October 2002.

46. UNHCR, *Climate Change, Natural Disasters, and Human Displacement: A UNHCR Perspective,* October 23, 2009 (www.unhcr.org).

47. Etienne Piguet, "Climate Change and Forced Migration," UNHCR New Issues in Refugee Research, Working Paper 153, January 2008, p. 2 (www.unhcr.org).

48. Intergovernmental Panel on Climate Change, *Climate Change 2007: Synthesis Report: Contribution of Working Groups I, II, and III to the Fourth Assessment Report of the Intergovernmental Panel on Climate Change,* 2007, p. 9 (www.ipcc.ch).

49. Ibid., p. 9.

50. UN–HABITAT, *Cities and Climate Change,* February 8, 2010 (www.unhabitat. org).

51. Koko Warner and others, *In Search of Shelter: Mapping the Effects of Climate Change on Human Migration and Displacement,* May 2009, p. 2 (www.ciesin. columbia.edu).

52. Jeffrey Sachs, "The Climate Adaptation Challenge," address to the Global Humanitarian Forum, Geneva, October 11, 2007, p. 1 (www.ghf–geneva.org).

53. Walter Kälin, "The Climate Change–Displacement Nexus," presentation at the Panel on Disaster Risk Reduction and Preparedness: Addressing the Humanitarian Consequences of Natural Disasters, ECOSOC Humanitarian Affairs Segment, July 16, 2008 (www.brookings.edu/idp). Note that the order of the scenarios has been changed from the original.

54. International Strategy for Disaster Reduction, "Disaster Statistics 1991–2005" (www.unisdr.org).

55. National Oceanic and Atmospheric Administration (NOAA), "Global Warming and Hurricanes: Geophysical Fluid Dynamics Laboratory," Office of Oceanic and Atmospheric Research (OAR) (www.oar.noaa.gov).

56. World Bank, "Climate Changes and Impact on Coastal Countries," February 12, 2007 (http://econ.worldbank.org).

57. Intergovernmental Panel on Climate Change, *Climate Change 2007: Synthesis Report,* p. 17.

58. Nils Peter Gleditsch and others, "Climate Change and Conflict: The Migration Link," International Peace Academy, *Coping with Crisis Working Paper Series* (New York: International Peace Academy, May 2007), pp. 8–9 (www.prio.no).

59. Somini Sengupta, "Living on the Edge: Indians Watch Their Islands Wash Away," *International Herald Tribune,* April 10, 2007 (www.iht.com).

60. Maryanne Loughry and Jane McAdam, "Kiribati: Relocation and Adaptation," *Forced Migration Review* 31 (October 2008), pp. 51–52 (www.fmreview.org).

61. Ilan Kelman, "Island Evacuation," *Forced Migration Review* 31 (October 2008), pp. 20–21 (www.fmreview.org).

62. See Malte Humpert, "Paradise Lost: Climate Vulnerability of Small Island Developing States and the Potential Humanitarian Impacts," paper prepared for Georgetown University's INAF 698: Introduction to Humanitarian Crises, 2010.

63. UN Office for the Coordination of Humanitarian Affairs and the Internal Displacement Monitoring Centre, *Monitoring Disaster Displacement in the Context of Climate Change,* September 2009 (www.internal–displacement.org).

64. IPCC, *Summary for Policymakers: Contribution of Working Group II to the Fourth Assessment Report of the Intergovernmental Panel on Climate Change,* April 6, 2007, p. 13 (www.ipcc.ch).

65. Ibid.

66. Ibid.

67. Norman Myers, "Environmental Refugees: An Emergent Security Issue," Paper presented at the Thirteenth Economic Forum, Prague, May 2005. He makes many of the same arguments in "Environmental Refugees: A Growing Phenomenon of the 21st Century," *Philosophical Transactions of the Royal Society of London B* (2002) 357, pp. 609–13.

68. Frank Laczko, "Migration, the Environment and Climate Change: Assessing the Evidence" (Washington: German Marshall Fund of the United States, June 2010), p. 3 (www.gmfus.org).

69. Sarah Collinson, *Developing Adequate Humanitarian Responses* (Washington: German Marshall Fund of the United States, June 2010), p. 3 (www.gmfus.org).

70. Anke Strauss, "High-Level Segment of the Fifteenth Session of the Commission on Sustainable Development," speech delivered in New York, May 9, 2007 (www.iom.int).

71. Steve Lonergan, "The Role of Environmental Degradation in Population Displacement," *Environmental Change and Security Project Report,* no. 4 (Spring 1998),

pp. 11–12 (www.wilsoncenter.org/topics/pubs/ACF1493.pdf). Note the contrast with Norman Myers, who states, "But those people who migrate because they suffer outright poverty are frequently driven also by root factors of environmental destitution. It is their environmental plight as much as any other factor that makes them economically impoverished." Myers, "Environmental Refugees: An Emergent Security Issue," p. 2.

72. Christopher McDowell and Gareth Morrell, *Non-Conflict Displacement: A Thematic Literature and Organizational Review* (Geneva: Internal Displacement Monitoring Centre, August 10, 2007).

73. World Commission on Environment and Development, *Our Common Future* (Oxford University Press, 1987), p. 13.

74. As cited by Gleditsch and others, "Climate Change and Conflict: The Migration Link," p. 3.

75. Black, "Environmental Refugees: Myth or Reality?" p. 6.

76. Environmental Change and Forced Migration Scenarios (EACH-FOR), *Specific Targeted Project Scientific Support to Policies–SSP, D.3.4. Synthesis Report*, 2009, p. 4.

77. Jim Kennedy and others, "Post-Tsunami Transitional Settlement and Shelter: Field Experience from Aceh and Sri Lanka," *Humanitarian Exchange Magazine* 37 (March 2007) (www.odihpn.org).

78. UN, *Guiding Principles on Internal Displacement*, section II (www.brookings.edu/idp).

79. Ban Ki-moon, "A Climate Culprit in Darfur," *Washington Post*, June 16, 2007, p. A15.

80. Scott Baldauf, "Climate Change Escalates Darfur Crisis," *Christian Science Monitor*, July 27, 2007 (www.csmonitor.com). See also Scott Edwards, "Social Breakdown in Darfur," *Forced Migration Review* 31 (October 2008), pp. 23–24.

81. Ban Ki-moon, "A Climate Culprit in Darfur."

82. Clionadh Raleigh and others, "Assessing the Impact of Climate Change on Migration and Conflict," paper prepared for the Social Dimensions of Climate Change Workshop, World Bank, 2008.

83. William A. V. Clark, "Social and Political Contexts of Conflict," *Forced Migration Review* 31 (October 2008), pp. 22–23 (www.fmreview.org).

84. Aidan A. Cronin and others, "Water: New Challenges," *Forced Migration Review* 31 (October 2008), pp. 26–27 (www.fmreview.org). The article notes, "The views expressed are those of the authors and do not necessarily reflect the views of UNHCR or the UN."

85. Cited by Andrea Warnecke and others, "Climate Change, Migration, and Conflict: Receiving Communities under Pressure?" German Marshall Fund of the United States, June 2010 (www.gmfus.org).

86. See Paul J. Smith, "Climate Change, Mass Migration, and the Military Response," *Orbis*, vol. 51, no. 4 (Fall 2007); European Council, "Climate Change and International Security," paper from the High Representative and the European Commission to the European Council, March 14, 2008, p. 2 (www.consilium.europa.eu).

87. With the exception, of course, of those inhabitants of small island states who find that their islands disappear as a result of rising sea levels.

88. Olivia Dun and others, "Environmentally Displaced Persons: Working Definitions for the EACH–FOR Project," October 11, 2007, p. 2 (www.each–for.eu).

89. IOM, *International Dialogue on Migration No. 10: Expert Seminar: Migration and the Environment*, 2008 (www.iom.int).

90. Roger Zetter, "Legal and Normative Frameworks," *Forced Migration Review* 31 (October 2008), pp. 62–63 (www.fmreview.org).

91. Jenty Kirsch-Wood and others, "What Humanitarians Need to Do," *Forced Migration Review* 31 (October 2008), pp. 40–43 (www.fmreview.org).

92. See, for example, Margareta Wahlström, "Before the Next Disaster Strikes: The Humanitarian Impact of Climate Change," June 2007.

93. See, for example, the many resources available at www.unisdr.org.

94. Frank Biermann and Ingrid Boas, "Protecting Climate Refugees: The Case for a Global Protocol," *Environment* (November-December 2008), p. 2.

95. Koko Warner, "Assessing Institutional and Governance Needs Related to Environmental Change and Human Migration," German Marshall Fund of the United States, June 2010, p. 3 (www.gmfus.org).

96. Ibid., p. 5.

97. Collinson, "Developing Adequate Humanitarian Responses," pp. 1–2.

98. Humanitarian Futures Programme, *Integrated Action Plan: Final Report*, March 31, 2008, p. 16.

99. Cited by Collinson, "Developing Adequate Humantiarian Responses," p. 3.

100. Roger Zetter and George Deikun, "Meeting Humanitarian Challenges in Urban Areas," *Forced Migration Review* 34 (February 2010), pp. 5–7 (www.fmreview.org).

Chapter Ten

1. Marc du Bois, "Protection: Fig-Leaves and Other Delusions," *Humanitarian Exchange*, no. 46 (March 2010), pp. 2–4 (www.odihpn.org).

2. Centre for Humanitarian Dialogue, *Proactive Presence: Field Strategies for Civilian Protection: Summary*, Henri Dunant Centre for Humanitarian Dialogue, 2006, p. 38. Also see the full manual, at www.hdcentre.org.

3. See the IASC cluster phase 2 evaluation: Julia Steets and others, *Cluster Approach Evaluation 2 Synthesis Report*, April 2010 (www.humanitarianreform.org). For more information on the global protection cluster working group, see http://oneresponse.info/GlobalClusters/Protection/Pages/default.aspx.

4. See "Progress Report to the IASC Principals," December 2005 (www.humanitarianreform.org/Protection). See also IASC, "Protection of Internally Displaced Persons," Inter-Agency Standing Committee Policy Paper Series 2 (2000), p. 2. See further ICRC, *Strengthening Protection in War: A Search for Professional Standards* (May 2001).

5. From "You Are Part of It! Protecting Refugees," Reach Out brochure (www. icva.ch).

6. Nicki Bennett, "International Peacekeeping Missions and Civilian Protection Mandates: Oxfam's Experiences in Sudan, Democratic Republic of Congo, Chad, and Somalia," conference paper, September 2009, pg 1 (http://www.rsc.ox.ac.uk/ PDFs/sessionVgroup2nickibennett.pdf).

7. ECHO, "Humanitarian Protection: DG ECHO's Funding Guidelines," ECHO 0/1/ML D(2009), April 21, 2009, p. 3 (http://ec.europa.eu/echo).

8. IASC, *Protecting Persons Affected by Natural Disasters: IASC Operational Guidelines on Human Rights and Natural Disasters* (Washington: Brookings-Bern Project on Internal Displacement, 2006); revised version forthcoming pending adoption by IASC, planned for late 2010.

9. Steets and others, *Cluster Approach Evaluation 2 Synthesis Report*, pp. 76–78.

Index

Commissioner for Refugees work with, 28, 30, 32–33; in urban areas, 253–55; as victims of natural disaster, 203–4

International Commission on Intervention and State Sovereignty, 164, 165, 274

International Committee of the Red Cross: aid to Palestinian refugees, 33, 35–37; capacity to protect, 273; concept of protection in, 16–18, 157–58; coordination of aid efforts, 119, 124; origins, 8–10; protection spending, 234; recommendations for, 280–81; Red Cross/Red Crescent societies and, 10; response to Somalia crisis of 1990s, 127; role of, 2, 6, 14, 16, 49, 72, 92; in Rwanda, 130; standards for protection work, 196–97; strategies for protecting staff, 184

International Convention on the Elimination of All Forms of Racial Discrimination, 45

International Convention on the Protection of the Rights of All Migrant Workers and Members of Their Families, 58

International Council of Voluntary Organizations, 106

International Covenant on Civil and Political Rights, 44, 45, 56

International Covenant on Economic, Social, and Cultural Rights, 45, 56

International Criminal Court, *xiii*, 4, 15, 38, 81, 132, 143, 145–46, 177, 178; as protection, *xiii*, 17

International criminal prosecutions: ad hoc tribunals for, 143–44; costs, 144; for crimes of genocide, 49–52; evolution in modern era, 4, 15, 132, 142–46, 156; hybrid tribunals for, 144–45; implications for humanitarian assistance, 145–46; models for, 142; perceived involvement of humanitarian workers in, 178; of sexual and gender-based violence, 55; transitional justice measures, 143

International Disaster Law Organization, 225

International Federation of Red Cross and Red Crescent Societies, 9–11, 92, 184–85, 201, 222–23

International humanitarian law: anti-terrorist actions and, 15; application to internal conflicts, 14; community self-protection and, 62; criticism of, 15; historical and conceptual evolution, 2, 6, 8–16, 270; institutional oversight, 2, 6, 9–10, 16, 156; instruments of, 12–14; interconnection with other rights regimes, 59–61; obligations of nonstate actors, 72–73; in occupied territory, 35; principles of, 11; protections for internally displaced persons in, 31; protections for noncombatants, 14, 38–39; purpose, 12, 15–16, 59; recognition and understanding of, 15; recommendations for, 280–81; violations of, 15

International human rights law: conceptual basis, 43; derogation of treaty obligations, 44; geopolitical interests in evolution of, 44–45, 60; historical and conceptual evolution, 2–3, 6, 40–44, 270; institutional oversight, 6, 42–43, 45, 91–92; instruments, 43, 44; interconnection with other rights regimes, 59–61; national human rights institutions and, 48–49; natural disaster response and, 222–24; prevention and prosecution of genocide, 49–52; protections for children, 55–57; protections for elderly persons, 57–58; protections for internally displaced persons in, 31; protections for migrant workers, 58–59; protections for specific groups, 49, 50*t*; protections for stateless persons, 52–54; protections for women, 54–55; scope of, 43, 59; United Nations commissions and conventions on, 42–43, 44–48; Universal Declaration of Human Rights, 44; universal periodic review, 47